THE WILL

The phenomenon of action in which the mind moves the body has puzzled philosophers over the centuries. In this new edition of a classic work of analytical philosophy, Brian O'Shaughnessy investigates bodily action and attempts to resolve some of the main problems. His expanded and updated discussion examines the scope of the will and the conditions in which it makes contact with the body, and investigates the epistemology of the body. He sheds light upon the strangely intimate relation of awareness in which we stand to our own bodies, doing so partly through appeal to the concept of the body-image. The result is a new and strengthened emphasis on the vitally important function of the bodily will as a transparently intelligible bridge between mind and body, and the proposal of a dual aspect theory of the will.

BRIAN O'SHAUGHNESSY teaches philosophy at King's College London. He is the author of *Consciousness and the World* (2000) and many articles on the philosophy of mind.

THE WILL

A dual aspect theory
II

BRIAN O'SHAUGHNESSY

King's College London

CAMBRIDGE
UNIVERSITY PRESS

CAMBRIDGE UNIVERSITY PRESS
Cambridge, New York, Melbourne, Madrid, Cape Town, Singapore, São Paulo, Delhi

Cambridge University Press
The Edinburgh Building, Cambridge CB2 8RU, UK

Published in the United States of America by Cambridge University Press, New York

www.cambridge.org
Information on this title: www.cambridge.org/9780521619530

© Brian O'Shaughnessy 2008

First edition first published 1980
Second edition first published 2008

Printed in the United Kingdom at the University Press, Cambridge

A catalogue record for this publication is available from the British Library

ISBN   978-0-521-85367-5 hardback
ISBN   978-0-521-61953-0 paperback

For my father
William O'Shaughnessy

Contents to volume II

CONTENTS TO VOLUME I

CONTENTS TO VOLUME II

Acknowledgements

ACKNOWLEDGEMENTS FOR THE FIRST EDITION

I wish to record my indebtedness to a large number of colleagues and students, whose comments on many of the views expressed in this work have greatly helped me. Most especially to Miss S. Botros, Mr G. Cohen, Mr B. Klug, Miss S. Lumley-Smith, Professor N. Malcolm, Professor P. Winch, Professor R. Wollheim. And I would like particularly to thank my wife and family for their encouragement and support during the writing of the book. My thanks to *The Philosophical Review* for permission to reprint sections of 'The Limits of the Will' (1956). My thanks also to *The Journal of Philosophy* for permission to reprint sections of 'Observation and the Will' (1963), and of 'Trying (as the Mental "Pineal Gland")' (1973).

ACKNOWLEDGEMENTS FOR THE SECOND EDITION

I would like especially to thank Professor Naomi Eilan for encouraging me to write several sections of the work. In addition, to thank the participants in a seminar held at UCLA in 1986, and especially the comments of Mr Charles Crittenden, Mr Lawrence Fike, and Mr Warren Quinn. Finally, I would like once again to record my indebtedness to my wife for her encouragement and support.

Glossary

The following expressions occur in the text with the senses given below:

action: I here follow standard contemporary philosophical usage. Examples: murder, rape, theft. Non-examples: sleeping, knowing, ageing.

activity: I follow standard usage in reserving this term for the active process whose continuation goes to constitute action-events of their type. Examples: the processes of murdering, or of listening. Non-examples: murder, hearing.

basic action: I follow standard contemporary philosophical usage, so that the basic act is the act of immediately moving one's limbs. Examples: familiar cases of moving one's limbs. Non-examples: opening the door, moving one limb by the means of moving another limb, contracting one's biceps by moving that arm.

bodily action: a bodily action is either a basic action, or a constitutive action or instrumental action which occurred because a basic action or bodily trying occurred that was causally responsible for the t-kind event required for that T-type of action. Examples: twiddling one's thumbs, opening the front door by turning the latch key, contracting one's biceps by moving one's arm. Non-examples: listening, making one's mouth water by thinking of juicy steaks.

constitutive action: the stipulated sense I give to this expression is as follows. It is the act of bringing about events within the motor-mechanism of limb-moving by the immediate means of either moving or trying to move that limb. Examples: contracting one's biceps by moving one's arm, contracting one's biceps by trying to move one's imprisoned arm. Non-example: contracting one's biceps by means of an electrical stimulus.

xiii

event: this is the standard use observed by contemporary authors. Examples: skids, deaths, battles, murders. Non-example: the continuing solidity of a rock.

instrumental action: I follow standard usage. An act rates as instrumental of type T if an act of type T occurred because some act or trying caused the t-kind event required for T-type acts. Examples: opening a door by kicking, causing goose pimples by thinking of poetry, generating sweat by trying to move an imprisoned arm.

phenomenon: I use this as a generic term to cover both events and processes. Examples: earthquakes, thefts, dissolvings, meltings.

process: I think I follow standard usage here. I take it to be a phenomenal continuity, such that when that continuity has come to an end a single countable event has occurred that is the same in type. Example: the skidding (process) went on continuously for two seconds, so that a two-second-long skid (event) occurred. Non-example: the continuing solidity of a rock.

willed: the usage I follow is such that an event is willed if it is the event that is the first or immediate object of the active event that occurs when we act, and therefore also of the generating act-desire. Therefore neither the events brought about in instrumental actions nor the events produced in constitutive actions are willed, whether desired or not. Example: the arm movements of swimmers. Non-examples: the muscle changes in swimmers, the movement of a swimmer through the water, the noise I intentionally produce by knocking on a door. I shall use the letter 'ϕ' throughout the entire text to single out such an event.

willing of: the usage I follow is such that when an event ϕ is willed, then the act which was the act of ϕ-making, and effect of the act-desire directed towards ϕ occurrence, is 'a willing of ϕ'. Example: the basic act of arm raising is a willing of arm rise. I shall use the letter 'Φ' throughout the entire text to single out such a bodily action.

Note: I use the following terms interchangeably throughout the text: 'action'/'act', and also 'try'/'strive'.

PART III

Dual aspect theory

Introduction

Part I began with the question: Are there any *a priori* limits to what can be willed? Such a question springs naturally to mind as one starts to philosophise about the will. This is because the very first stages of a philosophical inquiry into the the will inevitably begin with the adoption of a radically interiorist volitionist and even quasi-magical theory of action. Then this somewhat dualistic doctrine in turn suggests that, rather as we might someday come to see the presently invisible and indeed in principle see almost anything, so the will might break free of its skin cage and in principle work its effects far and wide and without limit. Now this line of thought, while not of course committed to the philosophies of that era, has about it overtones of the early romantic movement – a time when the spirit was thought of as but loosely chained to its fleshly home – and quite easily keeps company with an idealist philosophy of Nature. And so one might suppose that all that prevents one's will from ranging without limit across nature at large is, first the ultimate contingencies of a metaphysics which simply and unaccountably affirms that *this* may be willed and *that* may not be willed; and second the sheer finitude of one's will's *power* – which one might nonetheless *strive* to make felt far and wide – in the manner of a spirit or even a Deity! As if the project of becoming God were merely impossible of fulfilment! This first and most extreme theory of the will conceives of it as a quasi-occult psychological force that suffers from no other constraints than the arbitrary decrees of metaphysical fate and its own apparent finitude.

Then the question that I posed concerning the possibility of *a priori*-given limits is anti-romantic and sceptical-realist in spirit. For it seeks to rein in the will's aspirations within the bounds of intelligibility. Not, I think, out of negativity of spirit, but in the interests of realism. Thus, it has no desire to clip its wings, yet seeks nonetheless to bring it down to the earth to which it belongs. Then to grasp that certain criteria must be satisfied if a phenomenon is to count as willed, and to see in addition that

these somewhat complex requirements are not what a quasi-magical volitionist theory would lead one to expect, and thereby come to understand
that they might outlaw *a priori* the very possibility of willing certain phenomena, is to advance the philosophy of action from its first libertarian
or untrammelled and interiorist stage to the next sceptical and as it were
disconsolate moment. It was with this in mind that I advanced reasons for
supposing that belief, and indeed action itself along with striving or trying,
all of logical necessity lay beyond the scope of the will. Then if the 'paradise'
of a potentially limitless power was hardly that of a fool, it must nonetheless have been entirely without substance. A disappointment, it may be, to
some. But hardly a surprise. As every life viewed from the inside appears
as a succession of defeats, at least if La Rochefoucauld is to be believed, so
the movement of thought appears as a series of false terms of reference, if
Philosophy is to be taken as any guide.

   These constraints were all upon the efficacy of 'mental willings': that
is, upon the attempt to will psychological phenomena (like belief and
striving). But what of 'bodily willings'? May we likewise hope to discover
limits of logical inflexibility to the range of efficacy of the bodily will?
Here a second question comes to light along with the original question
of *a priori*-given limits. Namely, that of the supposed *interiority* of this
phenomenon: the alleged absolute ontological elevation or 'superiority'
of the bodily will over the body and matter that it 'commands'. For the
analytic determination of the limits of bodily willing reveals facts which
strongly suggest that the body may leave its stamp overtly *within the very
mind itself*! (In short, sceptical-realism, so to say, carries the war over into
the enemy's camp.) In demonstrating the inherent absurdity of the limitless
aspirations of the quasi-magical volitionist will, it advances considerations
through which we may divine that, in bearing the unmistakable marks of
its earthly connections, the bodily will cannot in any case be quite out
of the ontological 'top drawer'. The conception of the will as a spiritual
force which, from an incomparably higher plateau of being, exercises a
potentially limitless sway over the domain of mere matter, proves to be
doubly suspect.

   The aim of the above sceptical-analytic stage of my inquiry was to provide
such an analysis of the constituent elements of the phenomenon and concept
of bodily action as would admit our assembling an example of willing
in which the will manages to strike out beyond the body and into the
environment at large – realistically: to accomplish this feat despite the
existence of limiting factors. One important limiting factor that emerged
was, that a regularly acting bodily mechanism has to be the avenue through

which the antecedents of physical action give rise to a willed event. This limits the domain of the willable enormously. But it is also of ontological import. For in tying the bodily will so tightly to the body, it provides reason for supposing that we are dealing with a more primitive psychological phenomenon than traditional radically interiorist volitionism has assumed: a phenomenon at the level of (say) sensations or hunger or thirst, all of which are in comparable manner closely dependent upon the body. Then this would be to reject traditional doctines of volitionism, which by and large model the volition upon the thought or the giving of internal commands. And it would be to tie the mind, absolutely overtly and from the inside, to the body and its matter. It would be to demonstrate a kind of 'iron in the soul'.

Such a view found corroboration in the conclusions of Part II. Thus, I attempted in Part II to explain the necessary presence of 'feel' in bodily action. It emerged that its role was entirely epistemological: that it was there to give to the will, in the peculiarly immediate manner that is needed for bodily action, both the bodily target-zone in which it is to strike and the goal-event willingly effected therein. Now such a givenness is without parallel. For it is at once intuitional *and* immediate *and* almost invariably attentively recessive *and* such that both the target-zone and goal-event are given without mediation by concepts. Whereas the thought gets its object through the aid of the concept, and visual perception gets its object intuitionally and through the imposition of concepts, through what does the stray impulse to tap a left foot find the left foot to set it tapping if and when the mind is deeply absorbed in other matters? It finds it without the mediation of concepts. There exists no 'feeling *as* . . .' analogue of the 'seeing as . . .' or 'hearing as . . .' of the other modes of perceptual awareness. The givenness of the limb is simply generated by the inhering of a set of 'feels' in a mind that is endowed with a determinate long-term image of body and hence of self *qua* material object. It happens without the assistance of more developed mental phenomena. Then this fact likewise suggests that bodily willing must be a much more primitive phenomenon than (say) thought or sight. That is, than volitionism in its customary form would suppose.

Part II continued the enterprise of providing a criterial analysis of bodily action. Thus, as a result of the explanation of the role of 'feel', the analysis proceeded to encompass the requirement that the very first target point of application of the bodily will should find veridical representation both in the short- and long-term body-image. Accordingly, a form of physical self-consciousness, the primitive and inarticulate seeming to oneself to be physically finite and of determinate character, emerged as a necessary element of bodily action. (For all action is the production of change in oneself – as it were a mode of restlessness.) Then Part III continues this analysis. For I will shortly enrich it with an additional psychological element: more, with *the* psychological element, viz. bodily willing itself. Now this may come as a surprise; for the discussion in Parts I and II, in diverting us from traditional volitionism, might seem to have rendered any such psychological item otiose. After all, the inner life of bodily action might seem to be exhaustively catalogued once we duly note the special cognitive relations in which we stand to any intentionally willed bodily phenomenon ϕ, together with the 'immediate presence' of a target limb and of willed ϕ therein. Once the central role of the intention is recognised – and it is the intention origin that explains the special cognitive relations to intentionally willed ϕ, which was after all the feature Wittgenstein had in mind when he remarked in his usual cryptic and insightful (and, here, sceptical-negative) way that 'voluntary movement is marked by the absence of surprise'[1] – one might well suppose it bad metaphysics to postulate another psychological entity after the intention: an hypostatisation of the special properties of the intention.

Let me express this in different terms. In attempting to cut loose from the suffocatingly interiorist and obscurantist world of quasi-magical volitionism, one moves naturally towards a neo-behaviourist position on this matter. Not to the extent of denying interior phenomena as such, but in grudgingly tending to 'cut down on them', and in this particular case in a compensatory tendency to 'play up' the conditionals linking the antecedents of bodily action with bodily events (thereby as it seems to me short-circuiting the phenomenon of willing out of the picture). Thus, in assembling the criteria of and the constraints upon bodily willings, one notices first of all the aforementioned special cogitive relation to intentionally willed phenomena, and secondly an all-important physical factor, viz. the activation of a bodily mechanism. Now such mechanisms are physical states that are ultimately detected through our demonstrating that they make it true that a whole battery of conditionals has application to the agent of a bodily action: for example, decides-he-at-instant-t-to-at-that-instant-halt-bodily-movment-$\phi \supset$ halts ϕ (etc.). These conditionals relate present intention-onset events with events in certain select bodily extremities. In fact, they are the ultimate court of appeal in determining the will-status of putatively willed bodily events. For the inner life can offer no decisive guarantee

---

[1] *Philosophical Investigations*, Oxford: Basil Blackwell, 1953, §628.

concerning *any* bodily event that it has been willed: absolutely *no* interior event can accomplish this feat; so that one may well imagine that this is the last that one is going to hear about 'distinctive interior willing events'! The meaning-conferring item, the intention, together with the conditionals, incarnate so to say in the bodily mechanism, look to be all that one needs to ensure of an event that it has been willed – whereupon 'it is willed' would prove to have been a rather fanciful and myth-laden way of characterising the situation. And there is one other seemingly decisive reason why one might suppose so. Namely, if I know of some ϕ that it was generated by a decision's suitably activating a bodily act-mechanism for such an event, then it is *entailed* of ϕ that it was willed! But if the force of this inference is logical, how can we have need of a distinctive willing event? Indeed, what conceptual room is there for such an item? Is not this precisely the time to reach for Occam's Razor? Ought we not at this point ruthlessly to cut away the intellectual foliage?

But to dispense with such an item would be to do without the Prince Hamlet of the narrative! Those who endorse such a position are I believe those – and they may easily be physicalists – with a commitment to a too sharp dichotomising of mind and body. Being understandably dubious of an 'act of the will' that matches the traditional specifications laid down by volitionists, they proceed to throw the baby out with that particular bath water! Eschewing the volition of the 'volitionists', there is a tendency to transfer the role which it plays in act-situations onto that relatively sophisticated meaning-conferring internal entity, the intention – thinking thereby to do justice to the internal situation prevailing in physical action. And so the *sui generis* psychological event of willing tends to find itself banished from the scene. According to this line of thinking, the *only* internal event that is distinctive to action is, the intention state's mutating to the point of having an indexically given here-and-this-instant object. Nothing more.

To my mind, this is wildly improbable. Consonant with the ontology of events that we owe to the efforts of Donald Davidson and others, I opt for a categorical psychological event characterisation of bodily action: not in place of one cast in terms of conditionals, but together with and in advance of. And so I shall in Part III be concerned to argue for the existence of acts-of-the-will: to demonstrate their presence in voluntary actions of all kinds; and in general to establish the precise nature of their relation to bodily action. Later in Part III I shall advance considerations which consolidate earlier suggestions that bodily actions may be ontologically less elevated than traditional volitionism supposes. This leads me into an examination of the ontological status of bodily action, which in turn necessitates my clarifying the ontological situation in the mind generally. In short, I hope by such means to salvage a drastically re-modelled volitionism, and at the same time to present a case against the traditional doctrine. Accordingly, I shall be arguing for the thesis that, vital as the intention is to bodily action, the volition is even more centre stage. And that act-desire is on a footing with the intention. Willing *and* act-desire *and* intention are each essential to the occurrence of a bodily action. Then this must be seen as a continuation of the process, begun in Part I, of assembling a detailed conceptual picture of bodily action. What is novel at this stage of the procedure is that we have inserted *acts of the will* into the picture. For what sort of a picture could it be if it omitted the most central element of all? – rather as if a portrait were to leave out the subject's face!

But before I consider this question in chapter 12, I shall first in chapter 9 examine the relation between physical action and perception. Here we encounter phenomena which strongly suggest a very general theory of the bodily will: what one might call a *dual aspect* theory. For we shall see that, from the point of view of observation, physical action is almost as near to us as our very thoughts, that it refuses to distance itself and appear on the horizon as a mere autonomous thing 'out there'. Such closeness to the mind suggests that the inner life of physical action should be treated with great seriousness, even to the point of admitting the act into the psychological realm, and although the act appears in Physical Nature! This 'transparence' to the observational standpoint, this 'systematic elusiveness' as of 'I' itself, has in my opinion a psychological source. It lies in the fact that the act relates immediately expressively to an internal item that is tightly integrated into the holistically bound contents of the mind, viz. the intention. This bond in turn integrates the act into that internally consistent network – even as the act manages ontologically to slip through the net. Herein lies the essentially ambiguous status of physical action that is the source of its especial interest and importance. For physical action is the exception that proves a certain rule. While it is paradoxically enough its close and indeed primitive kinship with perception, rather than the significant unlikenesses of these phenomena, that prevents it from appearing as just another object of observation to its agent, I do not believe the kinship to be such as or so total that we should ontologically construe the physical act as on a par with its immediate antecedents. And yet it is indicative of something. At the very least of causal proximity. But, I think, of more.

CHAPTER 9

Observation and the will

The problem I am concerned with in this chapter is that of the observation of one's own actions. Taking observation to be, not just perception, but perception that is a way of knowing, it seems clear that our fundamental relation to our own actions is non-observational. Then my primary concern here is to bring to light the full significance of this fact.

I. MY ACTIONS ARE SET IN MY WORLD

(a) Physical action is like one world intervening in another world

The astonishing thing about action is that it is possible at all. Thus, if a man is making a chair, you will find a physical causal explanation of the movement of each piece of wood from its initial to its final setting; everything that happens is in accordance with physical law; but you will look throughout this world for ever in vain for an analogous physical explanation of their coming together in the form that they did, a form that mirrors human need and the human body itself. (Try it.) There is no physicalistic connection between gloves and hands or between the waxen beings of Madame Tussaud and their human originals – unlike, say, the relation that holds between a man and his shadow. And yet the chair is a material object in physical space. So action seems like a leak from another realm or world into this world, a leak or intervention – an intervention such as God would effect were He able to effect change in the world without transgressing the Laws of Nature. It is true that this is not the unusual conception of a miracle. But suppose there existed an apparently endless arm roaming the universe, which we called God's Arm, the most distant reaches of which were situated near the farthest known galaxies; suppose all of its parts seemed to move in accordance with the laws of physics, but suppose nonetheless that any long-range prediction proved impossible – except occasionally through prophecy and doctrine. Were this example to make any sense, and for physical reasons it may well not, some might wish to describe this as an example of one universe intruding into another. By action we irreducibly alter the state of the universe: a form or pattern appears that was not there before, the existence of which does not seem to follow in any way from the physical state of the universe beforehand. This is *creation*. We are ultimate sources of change in the environment in the way a river or hurricane is not. A chair or table is a kind of gift to the universe as a whole, as if from another God, certainly from another creator. In action we alter the *status quo*. If I am drawing a line, it is not in the final analysis the product of a physical force: it is originating from me: not from my body considered as physical object – for example, as emitter of sweat or light waves – but from my body as vehicle of another realm: that of (my) reason and purpose. We stand within and without physical nature.

(b) I cannot observe my own actions because they belong to my world

What do I mean by saying that my present actions are of *my world*? I mean that, along with thoughts and desires and intentions, these intelligibly linked items stand to me and to me alone in the bedrock relation of being known as such for what they are and of depending upon me for their very being: they depend somewhat in the way the elements of 'The World of Science' depend upon Science as groundwork. All items of my world present their face to me, and their face is their entire being[1] – in all cases but one. Physical action faces Janus-wise in two directions, and it is just this dual character that constitutes the lifeline for this world of mine, rescuing it from oblivion. So certainly I mean that I do not stand to my actions in the relation of observer, just as I do not adopt an observational standpoint to tell that I am amused, uncomfortable, anxious, and so forth. The greatest distance at which I can be placed from some of these phenomena is one merely of *distraction*: I cannot ever be in a condition of ignorance for want of observation. Equally, my own actions are, in some cases, capable of being placed at a distance of distraction, but this too is a distance of awareness and not of observation. Thus, when I notice a purposive act from which I have been momentarily distracted – say, car-driving as I am conversing – I do so non-observationally and immediately. I return to myself.

So, at the risk of uttering a tautology, I shall say that what at any moment I am doing is, from my point of view, not a part of *the world* (which we all inhabit) but of *my world* (wherein are set those linked items which unburden

---

[1] For what more is there to a mental-image than seeming as it seems?

their heart exclusively to me). If I am making something, then what I am producing is continuously 'shed' as what I *have done* and becomes simply a part of the world: the pyramids that took decades to construct are as much a part of the landscape as mountains. But what at any moment I am *doing* is for me at the juncture of my world and the world: at that point 'inner' meets 'outer', whereupon 'inner' becomes objectified and is 'shed' into the world as a thing.

Suppose you are engaged in an action like drawing a line or writing a letter, and suppose that you begin to wonder why it is that you cannot relate as observer to that action. (After all, it is visible to oneself and others, and you can relate observationally to the deeds of another!) Then it seems to me natural to offer the following reply. It is the essential function of observation to apprise us of the world that we all of us inhabit, whereas this that I am doing is still of my world. This is not yet a part of nature, of the *status quo*, of what is, but is on the brink – on the brink of becoming so.

I shall now attempt to typify or characterise the phenomena of action and of perception. We could say that, were observation to be withdrawn from the world and directed onto my actions, involuted away from the world onto my world, were I *per impossibile* to relate to my actions in the observational mode, then this would succeed in removing that relation between the world and my world upon which rests the identity of both my world and my actions. For it is essential to actions that they can refer beyond themselves, and to set them down as constituents of the world would be to erase that relation and rob them of their very *raison d'être*. My actions would lose their sense, and my world would lose its identity. So I would lose the world too.

I shall classify the actions of others as of the world. For there is no comparable difficulty posed by the idea of relating observationally to the deeds of another. Such observation merely requires that we perceive the active part of the agent, together with the field or object of action, and there is no question of removing through the act of observation a relation between the agent and environment which founds the identity of his actions.

2. THE INTERDEPENDENCE OF PHYSICAL ACTION AND PERCEPTION

I turn now to a discussion of certain primitive formative situations, in order to bring out the interdependence which is I believe essential to the very existence of physical action and perception. I stress that such a claim of interdependence is a typification of these phenomena, and that seeming counter-examples occur at more developed stages of being.

(a) The ascription of visual powers rests upon behavioural foundations

The concepts of physical action and perception mutually require each other. While we can situate within some organisms the source of their own movements without ascribing to them the power either to act or to perceive – as in the case of amoebas which merely 'move along' and 'assimilate' food – we ascribe the power to act only to what has the power to perceive, and vice versa. Think how we identify these phenomena. We would not say of a shellfish that it could see simply because it changed colour when pointed towards nearby red things: after all, light has causal power. But it is different with animal perception, for here in general we need also to be able to speak of physical action. And the reverse is true of physical action, which can be identified only in the context of presumed perception. Thus, the primitive behaviours of pursuit and flight relate active movement with perception: we say that a crab or octopus *advances a limb because it sees* something moving or that a fish *flees because it saw* something large and unfamiliar. Conversely, we say of these creatures that they *must have seen something*, and we do so because of *how they act*. Their actions are because of their perceptions, and their perceptions are revealed in their actions.

These basic situations reveal at the level of formation the interdependence of physical action and perception. I will now continue this enterprise of typification by considering the formative situations in the case of human beings, and hope to demonstrate the same interdependence. Since most cases of tactile perception involve physical action, I will turn to the other great reality-constitutor, viz. the sense of sight. I will spend some time indicating how rudimentary its beginnings might be, for reasons which will shortly become evident.

(b) The visual experience of the infant

(1) Consider a possibly merely hypothetical minimal visual situation: a newly born endowed with a completely unused visual sense: a visual '*tabula rasa*' as one might say. How would we describe his visual field? As a two-dimensional blur of lights and colours? No – that is an adult's literary image striving to describe the nature of presumed infant experience through the agency of special adult experiences. Rather, I think we would say first of all that the infant *can see*, and mean that his eyes and nervous system are normal

and functioning. And as evidence we might adduce either cerebral data or
else the fact that he reacts to bright lights. In addition, I think we would
say – because of causal considerations *and* those responses – that when
awake his visual field must be inhabited by a continuity of visual sensations
(without necessarily implying that they engage his attention). And that
exhausts 'the short list'. If a newly born is endowed with a functioning
sense of sight, this much at least of a visual nature he can and more or less
must have. He need have no more.

But we may be inclined to make a stronger claim, viz. that *he is seeing*.
Indeed, we may argue that he *must be seeing* because his eyes are open. After
all, it is obvious that the light is bothering him, so surely he is seeing, and
it might be claimed that we would not say this if his eyes were shut. But
would we not? What if a bright torch were trained upon his eyes when
they were closed? Is it not clear, watching him screw up his eyes, that we
have as much right to say 'He is seeing' here as when he reacts similarly
with open eyes? So surely all we could legitimately mean by 'He is seeing
because his eyes are open', is, that because his eyes are open he must have the
right visual sensations produced by the environment in his visual field. But
visual perception is more than having the right visual sensations. In short,
we are not entitled to assume that the opening of infant eyes ensures infant
seeing. That his eyes are open is nowhere near so special a consideration
in the early days of infant experience as it becomes later on. We think
of it as opening up the door to seeing, as if the naked eyes presented us
with the spectacle of *seeing itself* upon the very surface of the eyes. In this
way we tend to go beyond the rudimentary claim that 'He can see', and
the constant temptation is to have recourse to the word 'seeing' in lieu of
the unavailable activity word 'looking', and say that 'at this moment he
is seeing' or 'he is seeing all the time'. But we must resist the temptation.
In the absence of physical action of the requisite kind, we would not be
entitled to posit within him the attentive events which constitute seeing.
We more or less have to content ourselves with the assertion, concerning
this possibly merely hypothetical infant, that *he can see*: the sense of that
rudimentary claim being, that it attributes no more than visual health, and
in those who are awake the inherence of a steadily on-going visual field of
visual sensations.

The precise sense of this claim is clarified by the fact that we would not
as yet be in a position to single out anything as *what he is seeing*. For in
the absence of motor-visual co-ordination and the evidence it provides, we
are in no posititon to identify objects of vision. While we would have to
acknowledge the inherence in him of visual sensations, and the fact that

a very bright light must cause disturbing visual sensations which he must notice, we have I think to accept that in principle he might for the most part fail to notice his visual sensations – and for that matter the light causing them. And the same holds *a fortiori* of visible physical objects. Thus, we cannot say that he must see the sky simply because his eyes are directed towards it. If instruments were to tell us that his eyes are focussed an inch or two ahead of him and we were to deduce that 'he sees two of everything', we could as yet legitimately mean no more than that the environment is generating double sensation-images of itself in his visual field: we cannot infer that he could now go on to see 'one of anything' (or everything). It follows that there can be no such thing as our describing 'what we would see if we were in his shoes for an instant'. Therefore literary renderings like 'a fog', 'a confused mass of lights', 'a bewildering chaos', should be resisted.

(2) We can learn from the above how little a thing is the 'pure' sense of sight, how little we ascribe in the absence of physical action – physical action which is, in turn, little more than a mass of movements like those of a tree in the breeze in the absence of these apparently so attenuated senses. As intuitions without concepts are blind, and concepts without intuitions are empty, so sensations without actions are incomprehensible and actions without sensations are meaningless. While the 'pure' sense of sight might exist detached from physical active function, it is an unnatural and in general an impossible isolation. These two powers appear together both developmentally and functionally.

In particular, we could not say of this infant that he sees that one thing is *farther off* than another. This does not imply that we should say that 'for him it is all two-dimensional' or 'all flat' or that 'he sees width but not depth'. While we do not as yet apply the 'language of three-dimensional vision' to him, that does not mean that we instead apply the 'language of two-dimensional vision'. And yet there is a tendency to think that if we legislate against speaking of three-dimensional vision, then we are inevitably turning (back) towards the attribution of two-dimensional vision. But in the first place he may see or notice nothing. And even if he does see visual sensations and physical objects, there is no order of priority from two to three dimensions. Thus, not two-dimensional perception first and three-dimensional second; but an undifferentiated array of visual sensations given to consciousness in at least two dimensions first of all; and then secondly and only gradually the attentive differentiation of three-dimensionally given objects in physical space *and* the simultaneous differentiation under colour and contour concepts taken from those same objects of the constituents of the visual field of sensations. In short, while the at least two-dimensionally arrayed visual sensations appear before consciousness before all else, they are differentiated and so 'charted' and synthesised only through the differentiation and 'charting' of what is exterior – and vice versa. All such elemental raids on the unknown are at once journeys outwards into the world and inwards into the self. Now this states the usual timing in Nature as we come to perceive visual depth. Therefore if there is such a thing as a natural direction of development, it is the reverse of what many people have tended to think.

We would probably not say of a newly born that 'he can see his mother and the light she is carrying *going farther away*'. But we would say this of a child who had achieved the basic physical mastery of his immediate environment: that is, of a child who reached for nearby objects and who crawled after more distant visible objects – without first of all reaching for them. If we said of such a child that 'he can see that his mother and the light are going farther away' and were asked, 'How do you know?', it would be perfectly in order to give a reply like 'Because he could crawl after her.' We identify depth-perception through identifying act-capacities.

(c) We can see the mutual dependence of action and perception

(1) Ascriptions of active bodily power imply parallel ascriptions of perceptual power. These capacities grow up together. For this reason, I think we may say that action and perception are as such mutually dependent upon each other and implicitly present in each other's formation. It is true that the newly born we have envisaged can kick his legs *and* can see, and that we can ascribe these powers in isolation of each other. However, this does not conflict with the above claim. There are two reasons why it does not: (A) and (B).

(A) In the first place, we ascribe the power to see without as yet ascribing objects of visual perception, for we can attribute such power without as yet assuming that he can put that power to use and attentively individuate anything. Meanwhile this infant's 'just kicking', while unquestionably action, is action that may so far be devoid of meaning in that he may at this early developmental stage be unable to put such action to purposive intentional use. In that case, his kicking would be 'in itself' or senseless in a way no casual absent-minded doodling could ever manage to be in subsequent stages of development.

Such an infant's visual sensations and kickings would pass each other by like ships in the night. These two phenomena, in being unaccompanied by meaning-giving phenomena like a perceptual impression or a purposive intention, must be embedded in isolated and rudimentary psychological regions or islands of a kind not encountered later. Indeed, once the link between these as yet uninterpreted phenomena and the meaning-giving phenomena is forged, (say) visual sensation with seeing-*as* and kicking with instrumental intention, then the primal link between the two great halves of the mind – the cognitive and the striving – is of necessity simultaneously to that degree consolidated. More, inasmuch as the infant is conscious there must already exist such a bond, a state such that sense-experience can via the causal mediation of an instrumental or purposive intention cause meaningful action in some body part: (say) a causal relation between tactile perception and bodily action in at least some part of the body. This is because primitive animal consciousness necessitates an at least rudimentary body-image. For if absolutely everything in its psychological armoury related in the way we suppose held between the hypothetical infant's kickings and visual sensations, the processes of integration could never begin! There could be no crossing of such a Rubicon, allegedly separating pre-body-image-formation experience from post-body-image-formation experience, in the history of a single consciousness. There would exist no synthesising mental centre that could unify those many rudimentary psychological islands. The infant's waking on birth *is* his coming into an inheritance wherein some measure of integration obtains between at least some of his motor and tactile powers. That is, into a measure of ego development.[2]

(2) The second reason (B) why the independence of the infant's capacity to see and his idle kicking does not contradict the thesis of the interdependence

[2] The impossible concept of psychological existence *without ego* is the twin to the other impossible concept of psychological existence *with death*. Shakespeare and Poe were interested in the latter in their own different ways. Shakespeare in those plays (*Pericles*, *The Winter's Tale*) in which the cup of joy is filled to overflowing through the defeat of loss and death, Poe in those stories ('Ligeia', 'The Facts in the Case of M. Valdemar') in which the Will, conceived of as a kind of overweening Freudian Life Instinct or Spinozan Conatus, temporarily defies death even as death is about to take up or actually has taken up residence in the person. Thus, when Pericles, having heard 'the music of the spheres' ('But, hark, what music?' 'Rarest sounds! Do ye not hear?'), slips quickly into 'thick slumber', we are to understand that he harbours within a plenitude matching that of the unborn, the good dead, the immortal, in whom the ache of longing never stirs, and that this plenitude is not consistent with consciousness (which is forever striving) or even dreaming (which is forever desiring), and that in consequence his sleep is deep and dreamless. Hence, though that blissful state is induced by the defeat of death, paradoxically we must interpret this event as a rehearsal for good death and heaven. After all, man's conception of heavenly immortality is drawn from just such phenomena. Now these are, in Shakespeare, timeless, almost Platonic, states. Then by contrast with these beautiful ideas, Poe, obsessed with the living death of the buried alive, indeed with living death as such and the hate that effects it, attempts in his odious and powerful 'The Facts in the Case of M. Valdemar' (and,

of physical action and perception is this. Consider what *enables us to say* he can see and act. The main consideration is that he is an infant instance of a *kind of being* that is a conscious agent, recognisably a human being, and therefore as such endowed with the potentiality for synthesised perception and physical action. If human-sized creatures of amoeba-like behaviour and constitution were ubiquituous, we might not so readily classify an infant example of an unknown animal species as conscious. We should need to study its behaviour, and hence motor-perceptual synthetic structures, before we could identify his general type. Meanwhile another relevant evidential factor consists in the presence in this infant of eyes, which entail that he has somewhere the potential for seeing – though I should emphasise that as a type eyes are unlike (say) hands, which are material objects through which we manipulate objects, and that a creature might have eyes situated in and indistinguishable from its skin. One might say that 'eye' is not necessarily a thing-word. Therefore eyes are in a double sense identified through the part they play in a totality which includes physical action. In short, if we are to identify eyes, or seeing, or animality generally, we must in the final analysis direct our attention onto purposive action that is expressive of perceptually acquired knowledge.

These considerations return us to the primacy of behaviour as a means of detecting both action and perception. It follows that we shall identify *independent* phenomena like idle kicking and mere visual sense only through supposing that they are set in an object that as such has the potentiality for *synthesising* examples of these phenomena. We identify the genus of that object through identifying in bodily movement the applicability of a tightly meshed grid of psychological concepts of the type 'see' 'want' 'pursue' – a grid that encompasses active and perceptual concepts. I conclude that phenomena like the hypothetical infant's 'seeing' and kicking are ineffective exceptions to what is my central thesis at this point: that physical action and perception find their way into the very heart and constitution of each other. A thesis that might be expressed by saying that all seeing is given as of 'what I might in principle act upon', and all intentional physical acting-upon as upon 'what I might in principle perceive'.

as near as possible elsewhere, e.g. 'The Cask of Amontillado' – another terrible and much greater work) to depict a condition *in time* wherein death is actually experienced. This is to be understood as anything but a plenitude. On the contrary, as the experience of a lack that of necessity could never be made good: of such a loss that, the loser having lost being itself, there is nothing left in which could inhere the phenomena of the overcoming of loss (as no psychic unifier exists in the ego-less). Thus, a condition of infinite despair. Hell, its very self! For it is the actual experience of the loss of everything. Unquestionably a chilling idea, though it has its counterpart – in life. (Doubtless in E. A. P.'s life as well.) In any case, we may say that, comes psychological existence, comes want.

3. AGENT AND OBSERVER

In the previous section (2) I attempted to characterise the mutual bond that links physical action and perception. From this point on I shall concern myself with the problem which set this discussion in motion. Namely: the putative observation of one's own actions. This I take to be an impossibility – however strenuous the attempt. Indeed I judge such a project to be a form of assault upon that fundamental bond. More, as a perversion of the natural order, even as akin in ways to the phenomenon of incest!, almost indeed a sort of Oedipus Complex for Action. For a bond that lies at the very foundation of any and all forms of consciousness – in that sense not to be questioned and to that degree sacrosant, as the non-sexual tie to the sexually united parents lies at the heart of sanity and of society itself – is brought thereby into jeopardy. Then as the fulfilment of incestuous wishes has a tendency to lead to madness, so the unholy encroachment here contemplated tends likewise to call forth its own punishing 'furies'. These will become apparent only as the chapter approaches its conclusion.

(a) Involuting perception onto action tends to deprive it of meaning

(1) It typifies promises that they are kept, since breaking a promise is breaking with an institution of trust and is therefore ultimately dependent upon the perpetuation of that trust. And engaging in bodily action that has no immediate dependence upon perception of the environment, say the idle kicking of this infant, is ultimately dependent upon the existence of acts that do so depend upon sense perception: that is, upon meaningful intentional purposive action. For if an action is intentional and purposive it typically takes place in a climate that has over a period of time been created by the sustained conjunction of physical action and sense-perception: namely, a fully developed animal consciousness. Thus, it typifies physical actions that they depend upon sense-perception. And the reverse is equally true. This states the fundamental order of priorities amongst these basic few elements of the mind.

What I shall now go on to claim in (2) (below), concerning the relation between physical action and perception, has I believe universal application to animality as such, even though it specifically concerns only the formative situations we have been examining. These early situations in which action and perception are interdependent, are logically prior to certain more developed situations in which action and perception drift apart and occur independently of each other. As a result, they are more revealing of the nature of both action and perception. Somewhat analogously, saying what you think and being a member of a society are each logically prior to and more characteristic phenomena than telling lies or Robinson Crusoe-dom.

(2) Then concerning those more developed situations in which physical action and perception have drifted apart, I wish to claim that if they were universal, both action and perception would lose their very identity. As we have already observed, physical actions that never occurred within the context of sense-perception would be little more than the wavings of a tree in the breeze, incapable of giving expression to higher-order rational mental states of the kind of purposive intentions expressive of rational desire. Likewise perception that was never accompanied by physical action would surely at the least be less than its normal self. Thus, someone totally paralysed from birth would almost certainly remain an '*unmarked tabula rasa*'. While it may be conceivable that one could construct for him a linguistically demarcated world of some kind, we should remember that we in fact teach language to children who have discovered both themselves and the world of which they are part, and that Helen Keller was *in the world* from the very start. By contrast, this '*tabula rasa*'-being seems merely to be poised as a potential person on its threshold.

It is not just that action and perception are antithetical. Even though this is true, it is misleading. These interdependent phenomena help to develop and reveal the full nature of one another, and isolated from each other are nothing. In particular, physical actions as such require a relation to the world which is in the final analysis given through perception: that is, if they are to have meaning and identity, and if correlatively the world is to be real and discovered for one. Therefore to disengage perception from its normal role of *handmaiden to action* and involute it onto action itself – not as I say to put it to the services of action as an accomplice in actively helping to lay before the action its object and its field of operation – would be to rob action of its relation to the environment and its object which at a formative level helps to constitute its very identity. Thus, looking at one's own actions is a logically secondary activity parasitic upon the accomplice uses of perception. For example, watching one's arm as one throws a ball is parasitic upon the situation of watching one's aim as one throws. But, further, to involute perception onto action from the standpoint of the *observer* would be to attempt something far beyond such aims. Not only would perception not be a handmaiden here: it would have to play an actually antithetical role! For what visual perception seeks in general to discover must be something that can be seen by all, such as the path followed by a body, whereas what is

visually revealed in the handmaiden use of perception in active situations is
not visible to others. I mean, the relation of hand and quest, for the agent
sees a dynamically organised world and the observer does not. Thus, the
attempt to situate one's actions in a perceptual field that is being put to uses
that actually *clash* with the typifying basic uses is an attempt that must fail.

(b) What does it mean to speak of the meaning of an action?

I have claimed that, without the sometime somewhere existence of a relation
to the world through perception, action would lose all meaning. But what
does it mean to speak of the *meaning* of action? In the passage that follows I
shall suggest an answer to that question. And in addition, bearing in mind
the fact that intentional action is the logically primary case of action, I shall
defend the claim that action is *as such* a meaningful phenomenon. I hope to
demonstrate that the exceptions to this generality are either more apparent
than real or else trivial atypical members of the kind.

If action were simply an event in the physical world, a merely physical
phenomenon in nature such as a fall of rain or the dilation of an artery,
something 'in itself' whose relation to the rest of the world was purely
physical, then perception would play no essential role as stage-setter, and
we would not think of action, as we now do, as something with meaning.
We are, perhaps, insufficiently surprised at the fact that we ask, of an action
that is clearly visible, '*What* is he doing?' Such a question lines the action up
with portraits, hieroglyphs, signals, sentences, and of course in a sense with
thoughts. It is true that there exist cases of intentional behaviour in which
we say that a man is doing no more than one sees, e.g. that he is stroking his
chin *simpliciter*. But it is important to bear in mind with what ease, how with
the slightest of alterations or merely with an afterthought, this action can
change its character in our eyes to (say) 'posturing' or 'caressing himself'.
I think there is the permanent possibility of such re-description, and we
ought not to be surprised at this if we bear in mind how it is possible for a
gifted mimic to incorporate the slightest of our gestures, and even perhaps
any of them, in an accurate satirical portrait – thereby re-describing them.
Somewhat similarly we may ask of a group of marks on an Egyptian obelisk,
'What do they say?', and be informed that they are a purely decorative use
of the hieroglyphic symbols, saying nothing on this particular occasion. (It
would be entirely different to be told that they were gashes it had received
in a fall!) Then when we say that a man is stroking his chin *simpliciter*
this is comparable to the former situation in which what might have had
a meaning in fact lacks one, and altogether unlike the latter situation in

which we are speaking of a mere 'in itself' item in the world – something in another domain altogether. In this sense completely unintentional absent-minded behaviour can be ascribed meaning. In a word, action of its nature tends towards the condition of meaningfulness.

(c) The visual world of the physical agent is not that of the observer

I shall now attempt to characterise the typical relation that holds between physical action and perception, and in particular the way in which these two phenomena interact. And I shall contrast the very different situation that obtains when perception is employed for the less typical uses of sheer observation. It will emerge how the unlikeness of these two situations is relevant to the elucidation of the problem that is our central concern, viz. the observation of one's own actions. Here I shall be making use of a familiar but little-discussed variety of 'seeing as . . .': the non-visual mode of seeing-as in which our visual experiences are *coloured* by extra-visual factors. I begin by a discussion of the visual world of a *physical agent*.

We have seen that physical action and sense-perception are interdependent phenomena. And yet it is possible to act physically in the absence of perception of the environment. However, this latter state of affairs is not what I have called 'typifying'. Perception and action are typically intertwined in the sense that perception is a kind of *stage-setter* for action. Perception reveals to the agent a world that is dynamic inasmuch as certain items in that world are *seen as* goals or dangers in relation to which one is there and then intentionally *acting*. This is perhaps the sense in which the orange that one is just about to pick seems to be saying, 'Pick *me*.' It is a dynamically organised world in that it presents us with the spectacle of our there-and-then active quests and goals and the actively chosen requisite avenues of launched behaviour. Subjectivity of vision of this kind lends itself to artistic representation. Tintoretto puts on display a supreme example of such a dynamic world of activity and passion: the lines of perspective that organise his space are at the same time the lines of his and our noblest and most heroic aspirations, urges, projects, even deeds!

What of the *observer*? What can we say of his visual experience? Well, while it is true that the world of the pure observer is one that is being actively questioned, in that I can characterise what I am looking at *as* that which I hope will display phenomena of one particular kind, and is presumably dynamic to that degree, it is nonetheless *the world* that determines the content of my experience – the expected and the unexpected. The relation of action and perception is, in the pure observer situation, to a degree atypical, inasmuch as the perceived world of the observer is one that is going its own way, that is taking its own course, and that may or may not shed a certain requisite item for which we are busy scrounging, viz. facts of a particular kind. In that world we see not our purposes but our hopes or needs or lacks. Now this is not our fundamental experience of the world. One could say that sheer observation departs from the generally and typically true maxim: 'To understand the world it is necessary to change it.' (I have in mind birdwatching.)

What happens if we attempt to insert our own physical actions into such an observational framework? Suppose I look at my hand moving towards an orange and try to see this in the manner of an observer. All I seem to see is the hand and the orange: a world of discrete objects – nothing that is the product of the union of the motor and the visual. As observer I cannot organise that hand and its goal into a dynamic unity: they are not so linked and unified, since as observer my role is that of attendant questioner. And so the one enterprise contradicts the other and the project must founder. Now if it were your hand, where I relate unproblematically as observer, then sometimes I can see that the hand is heading for an orange, even though the relation between intending-to-grasp-x and x is not a visible relation. But in the usual first-person situation in which we actively engage with the environment it is altogether different. If it is I who am reaching for an orange, then I can describe what I see as: an orange; but it is also possible for me at the very same time to describe the object as: *that for which I am reaching* – and this is an incorrigible description. Here the link occurs at the level of the description of my experience. In such a case I can say that I see my hand and the object for which it is heading, and be offering an incorrigible description: it is something that I *see*. These characterisations of what I see are altogether normal and everyday – and yet the descriptions are incorrigible. I think this obvious fact is truly worthy of astonishment. As intentions introduce the idea of a putative incorrigibility in relation to the immediate future, so they do in relation to the present visible, which can be described almost in the manner of an itinerary rather than a map. It is as if we were forever tracing out invisible roads and times upon the forever changing face of the visible – an almost Heraclitean picture.

It is not as if I saw the orange as an orange and then, bearing in mind what I am doing, as that for which I am reaching. It is not as if some of the time I lived in a world of *things*, and some of the time in a world of *intentions*. The idea of such a world of things is a myth, a myth designed for a species of Observer Beings, a world calculated to stultify all action through the extremity of its power to inspire apathy, the apathy of the catatonic, capable of turning all action to stone by a single look. And the idea of such a world of intentions is equally mythical, as if somehow the world could manage to look literally as Tintoretto has painted it, an expressive humanised world instantly absorbing and precipitating us headlong through tracts of space with no gap between intent and achievement. We cannot separate the world of objects and the world of our intentional projects: they are one.

This dynamic concept of what is seen, something which comes into view when we describe the visible in terms of intentions formed in the light of one's anticipations, is entirely different for agent and observer. As agent I characterise what I see as: the orange I am going to get, the hand with which I shall get it, the bowl in which is contained the orange I shall get, the part of the table across which I shall move. As observer I would characterise these objects as: the orange I am looking at to see if he takes it, the hand I am looking at to see if it moves and takes the orange, the path across which I expect the hand might move if it does take the orange. In one case I was looking at the orange I was about to take, in the other I was looking to see whether he would take the orange. In one case I describe what I am looking at in terms of my intentions: I impose a particular form on the world. In the other case I describe what I am looking at in terms of what I am querying of the world and in terms of what I am ready to receive from it, and thus impose a different form. Then it is not possible that we should simultaneously impose two such opposed forms on the one perceived scene. Therefore we cannot relate as observer to our own actions.

Of course one might replace all that I have just said by a few simple and trenchant statements about the purposes of observation, the role of expectation in the case of the will, and the like. These I have deliberately avoided.

4. DOING TWO THINGS AT ONCE

I propose now to consider the suggestion that the difficulty in relating as observer to one's own actions lies in the difficulty in engaging simultaneously in more than one meaningful action: as an example, in arguing and reminiscing. After showing that the latter difficulty is not a trivial matter, and endeavouring to bring out the natural unity that typically prevails between multiple actions and perceptions, I attempt to demonstrate the impossibility of fulfilment of what might be termed Radical Narcissism. Finally, I offer reasons why the difficulty in engaging simultaneously in two meaningful actions offers a significant clue as to the real difficulty in relating as observer to one's own actions.

(a) Does observational involution deprive the action of identity or of will?

(1) When we attempt to relate observationally to our own actions they tend to grind to a halt. Then does such an activity tend to halt the action through the reduction of the action to something less than its real self, or through diverting the will into another channel? Does the act terminate through loss of meaning or loss of will?

Let us consider the first of these alternatives. To the extent that I relate as observer to my own actions, to that same extent I withdraw my concern from the object, purpose, or aim of the action, and to that extent the action loses its *raison d'être* and identity, and either ceases to be or becomes instead something rudimentary – barely an action. Here we have a rationale which seems persuasive.

Then once again: why, if I begin to succeed in relating as observer to my own action, should it simultaneously begin to grind to a halt? I am drawn at first to the answer given above. I am inclined to say that it is because the act would thereby cease to be oriented towards the aim or object that helps to define the act for what it is. And we should remember that if my action is oriented towards an object, then I myself am likewise oriented towards that object – and how can I act if I lose my goal? I am therefore inclined to say that the action ceases to be because it loses its object and thus its very identity. In a word, it fades away through a sort of de-personalisation. So at first blush it seems.

(2) But another answer is possible. I shall express the problem in this way. As I attempt to relate observationally to my own actions, either observation seems merely to skid over the surface of the act or else the act begins to come to a standstill. Let us suppose that this observational enterprise actually leads to a termination of the action. Then the two alternatives being considered are these: did the act go out of existence through losing its *object* or through losing my *will*? Did it cease to be out of atrophy or through sheer diminution? Two different ways of going out of existence: as red on a white background may grow pink and finally white, or instead faint and finally invisible. Was I, that is to say, like a walker who gradually came to a halt as he gradually forgot where he was going, or if he continues walking is now to be described as 'merely walking'? Or was I like one who slowly desists from what he is doing? Is it that I lost sight of what I was doing, or did the action simply come to a halt because I was engaged in doing something else and my will had become unavailable?

There are reasons why the difficulty might look as if it could not consist in my failing to be oriented towards the object of action; that is, look as if the act does not go out of existence through loss of object and identity. For were I to direct my observations not onto the action itself but onto the object of action, this too would interfere with the action – provided it was not integral to my purposes. And yet why so? It would not be because I was thereby failing to be oriented towards the object of action, but rather that my orienting to it in the mode of observation obstructed my orienting towards it in the mode of, say, pursuit or appropriation. But why does it thus obstruct? Is it because I lose the object of my action in transforming it into another kind? Or is it that I have to see it in two different ways at the same time? But if the difficulty is of this latter kind, then why should the observational relation pose special problems? Thus, think of the difficulty of engaging in two unrelated actions directed towards the same object: say, trying to remember the name of and simultaneously to catch a rapidly moving object. Here, too, we encounter a difficulty that seems not unlike that experienced when we try to observe our own actions. Indeed, why should we encounter trouble only when concerned with the one object? Might it not arise with several objects? Then by this time the difficulty in observing one's own actions looks merely to be that of engaging in two unrelated actions at the same time. More precisely, it may reside simply in the fact that both act and observation are two purposive meaningful acts which are obliged to occupy the very same slice of time.

(b) Is the difficulty one merely of doing two things simultaneously?

(1) Might it be the case that the difficulty in relating as observer to one's own actions is one merely of doing two things simultaneously? But what is this 'mere difficulty' that can apparently be accommodated with such ease? Of what nature is it? I believe if we examine it we shall find it to be anything but a triviality.

Why is it that we cannot perform acts like reading and listening at the same time? Is it because we can never do two acts simultaneously? But clearly we can and do, for I can tap my feet as I listen to music. Then is it because we can never do two fully aware actions simultaneously? But we can and often do, provided those acts are not too absorbing, for I can drive the car with reasonable care and simultaneously converse. And yet *why these limits*? Is it because we have so much attention to distribute and no more? In other words, is it a merely quantitative question? This would be the triviality. Well, even though there is on occasion a quantitative problem, the problem that at present concerns us is not quantitative in character, since the difficulty in the case of fully mentalistic unrelated actions is a logical difficulty. No – here it is a consequence of being a person, one person and not two, and the difficulty on such occasions is with most illumination to be likened to the difficulty in engaging simultaneously in two contradictory activities. Just as I cannot be going north and south at the same time, so I cannot be conversing and reading at the same time. I cannot split my mind in two, as if it were an apple! In the way in which one can be car-driving and talking one cannot be listening and talking. Naturally, if we dilute these activities anything becomes possible, and we can become like the chess player who plays a roomful of people 'at the same time'.

If the difficulty were quantitative then the miracle of a man who is absorbedly sculpting, painting, designing buildings, and composing poems all at the same instant in time would be like the miracle of the loaves and fishes. But instead of saying, 'It is bewildering that he can simultaneously manage to do all that', as if he were a Michelangelo, we should think of him as the most splintered of beings – or worse. Michelangelo was one great unique person, whereas this being is a monster, a monster of ordered disorder, something that might occur in the myths, but not a human being – a Minotaur of the mind! When we say that human beings and their minds are one we are affirming an essential truth concerning their nature; we are not putting forward a statistical generalisation. Men like Michelangelo are not freakish departures from human nature; they are glorious and undreamed-of realisations of it. In uniting within themselves so many diverse traits at such a supreme level, they manage to realise our highest human ideals.

If the point seems elusive, consider how you would in fact react to someone's claim to have been engaged in solving a difficult philosophical problem while he was strenuously fighting for his life in a raging mountain torrent. Consider what you would *say*, and consider *why* you would say it. Contrast the use of eye, hand, and ear on the part of an operatic conductor. Here we discover a unity in diversity which is absent in the above case. Again, we may describe a man who is dancing as he listens to music as a man who is dancing in listening – his dancing is subordinated to his listening, for without the intention of listening he would not be dancing; by contrast, the ballerina who listens as she dances is someone who is listening in dancing – her listening is subordinated to her dancing, for it is her intention to dance that causes her listening. These seemingly wayward accompaniments of activities are in fact closely knit subordinated act-parts of an actively selected totality, and are thereby unified. But nothing could unify two activities like arguing and composing unless, tautologically, they were already unified like the hands of a pianist.

The difficulty is not quantitative. I believe it stems from the fact that, being one person, we can only fully orient ourselves in one direction at a

time. This is a tautology. For if we were to pass from the word 'fully' to
the word 'completely' to the word 'wholly' and on to 'with all one's being',
thereby more and more openly announcing our meaning, it seems we finish
up with a mere circularity. And yet we should consider such expressions
as 'He is lost in that action' with seriousness. They remind us of the fact
that an activity can all but fill consciousness. And how could one be lost
simultaneously in two activities? In each case the rest of the world would
'drop away', appearing like the blur surrounding a focussed photographic
image. And how could that happen *twice* in one and the same instant?
As one's body cannot be wholly encapsulated in two distinct pockets of
physical space, so one cannot be lost in two distinct regions of mental
space. How could one be 'actively abandoned' – as one might say – to one
activity, if simultaneously one was heavily committed elsewhere? It would
be like sleeping with one eye open!

I cannot be wholly given up to an activity and simultaneously 'miles
away' – another expression we ought to take seriously. I cannot entertain two
mental images simultaneously. Who could? A god? What is the difficulty?
Attention shortage? Ineptitude at psychic juggling? I cannot be thinking
about two distinct topics at the same moment in time, nor mindedly about
one topic and absent-mindedly about the other. Any activity which involves
the mind to any great degree is liable to be incompatible with any other
such activity, for what happens in my mind cannot be absent from my
mind. By contrast, what happens in my foot can be peripheral to my
awareness, so that habitual or trifling physical actions or movements can
go on absent from the mind and pass more or less unnoticed while one
is actively engaged elsewhere. Logically necessarily, anything with a mind
that is simultaneously writing and conversing is a something that is *either*
constantly changing mental horses in mid-stream *or* that is not giving
expression to two distinct thinking processes. Whereas the one broad river-
bed can support two quite distinct rivulets, there can of necessity be but
one thinking process supported by a single mind at any moment in time.
The rest lies in the realms of mythical monstrosity!

So we shall reject the word 'merely', and say that the 'mere difficulty' is
not a result of the finite amount of attention available to all of us, but is a
direct consequence of the fact that, since each of us is no more than one
person, we can be wholly given up to no more than one activity at a time.

(2) How does the difficulty in relating as observer to one's own actions
relate to the difficulty we have been discussing? Is it different from that of
observing *another being's* actions while simultaneously one is absorbed in

a different activity? We have just seen that the latter is a genuine, indeed an insuperable difficulty when absorption is complete, proceeding from the unity of consciousness. And we have also seen that one cannot be thinking simultaneously two unrelated trains of thought. In either case – *per impossibile* – the self would have to divide in two! Thus, when either of any two distinct activities fully absorbs one's attention, or when those activites are of the type thinking, it becomes a *logical impossibility*. Therefore unless my intentional activity and the activity of observing another's actions were united under one heading, unless for example my activity was giving a description of his movements, we should have to say that it was a logical impossibility that I be simultaneously performing two wholly absorbing deeds of such a kind. And so similarly it must be in the case of one's own actions. Indeed, there is a further difficulty here. For *how could there be* such a unity in the case of one's own actions? That is, a unity which preserved the concept of observation. I would need to construct a unity between the act which I propose to observe, and the act of observing that action. Were there to be such a unity I could not be relating as observer to my own deeds, for I would be looking at some one activity of mine in the course of performing some other activity. It seems that the only way we could escape this difficulty is to make the act that one observes one's own activity of observing!

Thus, relating as observer to one's own actions necessarily implies simultaneously engaging in two activities that cannot be subsumed under one heading. And this is a decisive reason for saying that it is logically impossible for one to be fully absorbed in either activity. And yet it remains an open question whether one might relate as observer to acts of one's own if neither activity is especially absorbing. For example, it is an open question whether or not one might relate as idle observer to (say) an idle intentional act like using one's right hand to open a door. Therefore the problem posed by the simultaneity of fully mentalistic activities must be quite other than the problem which is the main topic of this chapter, viz. that of relating as observer to one's own deeds. However, the difficulty that it brings to light, which stems from the unity of consciousness, a difficulty concerning what can occur at any one moment in a single consciousness, proves to be highly relevant to that central problem – as I hope soon to show.

(c) *The natural unification of many actions and many perceptions*

The question just now examined concerns unity and division within the mind. More exactly, it concerns unity and division in *experiential consciousness*. We have seen that some experiences are of such a kind that they cannot occur simultaneously, while some others can do so. What is it that enables the latter? In the case of multiple active experiences, the answer lies in a unity that is born of the intention which lies behind these phenomena. For example, what unifies the various actions and perceptions, let us say in the case of the operatic conductor who watches closely, listens attentively, beats time precisely, adjusts the volume delicately, exhorts or encourages or controls both singers and instrumentalists, all perhaps at the same moment in time, is that they are all logically subordinated to the single activity of conducting at an operatic rehearsal. While some of these activities are parts of that activity, and some stage-setters, all are tightly and even essentially bonded, for all owe their existence to a single germinal source, the intention of conducting, which accordingly sets its seal upon each of these activities' essential description. Without these activities and perceptions the activity of operatic conducting could not exist. By engaging in such multifarious activities the conductor engages in *one single activity* in which he may be completely absorbed and lost. But, unlike the musical purist, he is not thereby completely absorbed in listening to the music; unlike the singer's admirers, he is not completely absorbed in watching her perform; and so on. His is a comprehensive or encompassing and theirs a differential or selective active relation to these same items. More, his is a dynamic-perceptual and theirs a receptive-perceptual relation to the same objects; somewhat as, even though their experiences are essentially differ-ent, the pianist who is completely absorbed in the act of peforming music experiences no less of it than the listening audience that is equally absorbed by the identical performance. For the conductor's activity is not the *sum total* of the various component activities, since at any moment the object of his concentrated attention is a single complex yet unified object – the opera from the musical side, so that all of these activities point of their very nature towards the one focal goal object. These component activities are not the self-subsistent *atoms* out of which is constructed some one active phenomenon that is, through the agency of a synthesising factor, a unity and not a multiplicity. The conductor is not a kind of juggler, performing a set of independent acts, but a man who in performing a number of distinct yet *essentially interdependent* activities manages thereby to be engaged in a single rich and complex activity that utilises the greater part of himself – body, mind, feelings, and senses.

One can see that his activity is not the sum total of these component activities if one considers that in watching the singer, he watches not so much her face and form as her movements and expression; not so much her movements and expression, as her movements and expression in relation to the music that animates them; and these in turn in relation to the drama that channels and contains them. And so he watches not so much the singer, as an aspect of the singer in relation to the needs at that moment of the music and drama. These attendant or handmaiden activities are unified and related to one another through their subordination to the overall activity of conducting. For example, listening to the music and controlling the tempo and volume are closely related to each other, and together they create a kind of musical fabric into which is woven the sound of the singer. This is a kind of world-for-the-conductor, a world constituted out of these various items which exist in his eyes, in relation to one another and in relation to him, in a manner which is completely determined by the overall activity in which he has chosen to engage.

(d) The impossibility of Narcissism

(1) The conductor cannot listen as *observer* to the music he makes, since he already listens to the music from the standpoint of *conductor*. His listening is logically subordinated to that activity, to which it relates somewhat as the painter's looking relates to the activity of painting: it is coordinated with the movements of his arms and informed with his overall purposes. Were he to listen as observer, his listening would no longer be subordinated to the activity of making music. One cannot be listening to the music one makes both from within the act and from without the act: one cannot simultaneously listen in two such entirely different ways. This is the specific difficulty which is encountered when the putative observer-sense is playing an essential stage-setter role for the activity it putatively studies. Here we have a project of observation which is antithetical to the harmonious syntheses of action and perception elaborated above.

Then once again I ask: what is the difficulty facing the observation of one's own actions? It is not that of simultaneously acting, nor that of simultaneously performing acts of which one is fully aware, nor is it like the above that of relating as observer when the observer-sense is stage-setter for the activity to which one putatively relates as observer. The difficulty we are considering is encountered in the simplest of cases – like the following. There is a difficulty in relating as visual observer to an idle intentional act like using one's right hand to open a door. Then it seems to me that the explanation of that difficulty must be along the lines which we have recently spelled out. Thus, for a man to relate as observer to his own actions would be for the act of observation to fall *outside* the unity created within the observed action: the act of observation would neither be subordinated to the act under observation, nor would the act under observation be subordinated to the act of observation of itself. We would have two proposed actions, unified neither one under the auspices of the other, nor through any overall action to which they are essentially subordinated, in which one is nonetheless object for the other!

We have just noted that the problem posed by simultaneous mentalistic or fully absorbing actions is a different problem from the main problem under investigation. And yet it provides a clue to that problem. For the difficulty in the case of such simultaneous activities is in effect the difficulty of not being two people! An impossible divide in experiential consciousness – in the Attention – is the penalty awaiting this project: something the far side of a 'fugue' within present consciousness! Then something comparable but different is the 'nemesis' awaiting the project of relating as observer to one's own actions. Here, too, the self would suffer an impossible self-division – but in a different mode. To succeed in the quest of self-observation, would in effect be to succeed in becoming two people, the being who acts *and* the being who observes that action, such that the former has to play the role of *object* for the latter! It is not a divide within experiential consciousness that is being proposed, but a split into observer and agent, and ultimately into observer and object in the world. It is *this* which is the obstacle which prevents our relating as observer to our own deeds. In so far as one approximates to such an impossible ideal of the division of the self, one is approximating to the replacement of oneself by two selves, and in a form which is tantamount to a destruction of the self in the mode of *dispersal*: oneself as awareness *and* oneself as agent in the world. The dream of observing one's own actions is the dream of the loss of the self through division and dispersal.

(2) My suggestion is, that the difficulty posed by the aforementioned extreme examples of simultaneous action is closely paralleled by *all* putative examples of observation of one's own actions; indeed, that the difficulty posed by simultaneity in these latter cases provides a clue to the main problem under discussion – that of relating as observer to one's own deeds. Thus, the supposed two acts, act and observation-of-one's-act, that are unrelated in the way of synthesiser and synthesised, are instead here supposedly related in a different way: namely, in the way of *act and object*. As already remarked, the act of observation would have to fall outside the unified act-structure required within the act that is to be observed; so that one would have, as it were, to overtake oneself: it is as if one had to encapsulate and engulf the unity or world of one's action within the world or unity created by the overall activity of observation of it. One action has to become subordinated to another, only not now as handmaiden-assistant but as *object*. It has to

play the role, in this topography, that is normally played by something in the world.

One would have to be divided into two selves, since the acts are not unified, which implies that the agent must be in the world for the observer but the observer not; and in addition, one self would have of its very being to appear as object in the eyes of the other. Further, one would be two selves and yet in the very moment of their appearing, one self would have to be engaged in incorporating the other. I say 'incorporating the other' because the very ground of the being of the agent-self is that it is locked logically in the scrutiny of the observer-self, whose being in turn is constructed upon the ground of the observation of the agent-self. It is *the nature* of one such self to see and the other to be seen! The relation of observer and observed is here an internal relation that unites and defines these two selves. And the moment this relation draws to a close these selves coalesce into oneself. Now this condition of putative fragmentation should be contrasted with the fragmentation that putatively obtained in the situation of the Minotaur-being. But it is equally unacceptable. For the very quest of the self that would destroy the self through division by dispersal – the quest of relating as observer to oneself in action – forces logically upon the agent-self the role of object in relation to the observer-self.

Over all of this might be inscribed the heading: 'The Impossibility of Narcissism'. The two internally related selves would be all that remains of oneself, assuming Narcissism to have been successful, but are in fact less separate than Siamese twins or the dual beings on playing cards. One is therefore in no position to describe the agent-self and the observer-self as true selves, as selves resulting from the fragmentation of oneself: rather, one simply describes them as *whatever it be* that results from this almost division of oneself. Indeed, since radical narcissism is an impossibility, so likewise are they. They are mere constructs.

We should infer the impossibility of relating as observer to one's own actions on two counts. In the first place, were the only objection to be one against simultaneity in action, we should in those extreme situations in which one is lost in either act, be obliged to speak of two selves neither of which is oneself, and as a result would not manage to realise an example of oneself observing one's own actions: instead we would be concerned with a further example of the Minotaur-being. But the real objection to self-observation is based on the consideration that observation of our own actions would situate them in the world in the eyes of the observer: something that splits the self in *all* cases. So in the second place – and this diverges from and goes well beyond any objection in terms of simultaneity of action – since these dual selves are internally related, it would have to be a necessary proposition that the observer-self observe the actions of the agent-self. Then it is clear that such putative entities cannot be true selves, nor for that matter can they be anything else, and the situation cannot count as the observation by one self of the acts of another self, nor as observation by the self of its own acts.

In so far as one seems to relate as observer to one's own actions one ought to have the experience of the loss of the self through division into observer and agent. Agent in the world and observer in limbo – oneself dispersed! One's acts become for one items in the world, and one observes them from an isolated world that has no point of juncture with the world. One observes one's own actions as the acts of another being in the world, and thereby one loses them and ceases to have any relation to the world. In the section which follows I will consider such a state of affairs.

5. SELF-DISPERSAL AS THE END OF THE IMPOSSIBLE PROJECT OF RELATING AS OBSERVER TO ONE'S OWN ACTIONS

Let me express this last claim in different terms, in which once again I put to use the fact that within the field of action there is a unified structure, with oneself in the centre, in which the constituents are perceived in terms determined by one's actively projected future. I have expressed this property by saying of those elements that they are part of the world that I 'project', a part of 'my world'.

If one is to relate as observer to anything then one has to be 'without' it, whereas if one is to do anything then one has to be 'within' it. Now either we remain 'within' the action we are attempting to observe, in which case we may have a completely empty and self-delusive experience of observation – comparable to Wittgenstein's example of the right hand attempting to pay the left hand money – or else we remain 'without' in some more or less serious sense and genuinely seem to observe the action. But, remaining 'without', we lose the action as ours in gaining the observation: we lose any 'withinness'. The action becomes for us a mere event in the world, and we ourselves become dispersed and lost amongst the bric-à-brac of the world: we become of the world in our own eyes – we suffer the experience of loss of identity. (I say 'experience', because no one can actually lose his identity.)

(a) Observing one's actions and experiencing a loss of agency and self

A man whose behaviour is dramatically out of keeping with his normal behaviour is to a degree liable to suffer from an experience of loss of agency.

(This suggests the existence of a positive experience of agency, which we might single out either as 'the experience one becomes aware of when the experience of loss of agency departs' or as 'how one experiences one's own agency'.)

In what follows I describe an example of the experience of loss of agency which is dependent upon the experience at the moment of action of becoming a stranger to oneself. I do so because I wish to exhibit the close links between the experiences of seeming to observe one's own actions, of loss of agency, and of loss of identity.

Let us take as our example the situation of engaging in a solitary extreme political gesture during the middle of an important piano recital. One is liable to feel, 'Am I *really* doing this?' or 'Is this *me* who is doing this?', and most significantly one is liable to have the experience of being a spectator of one's own actions. At 8.35 precisely, when all is still and the music is hushed and overwrought with feeling, one is to rise to one's feet and deliver a short speech at the top of one's voice. One's behaviour may be completely rational. One may have chosen one's moment exactly and have the most impressive political justification for one's action. It is now 8.34.50 . . . 55 . . . 58 . . . one is getting to one's feet . . . 59 . . . and there is one's voice sounding distant and flat somewhere up near the roof of the auditorium! After a time, as the hubbub slowly breaks out, that sound near the roof links up with one's own mouth, one no longer 'hears' the voice; it is now echoing in one's ears, and one is *now* engaged in addressing these people. The sense of agency returns and with it the sense of identity: one *is* the person who is in the centre of this turbulent scene, who has just created a disturbance.

At this point the voice is no longer something in the world. It is now like a gate or window or aperture through which one directly encounters these people. It is like the open road whose only meaning is that it leads to Rome.

We need to notice that the experience of loss of agency means that, between 8.34.59 and 8.35.01, 'something' began to sound up near the rafters, 'a voice', the occurrence of which is in some ways somewhat mysterious to one: one is not completely on the 'inner', so to speak, with regard to its occurrence, as one is on the 'inner', later, with regard to that sound echoing in one's ears (being of the nature of a kind of logical byproduct). True, one realises all along that one is responsible, but one has for a time no *awareness of creating*. Therefore one has no sense of *how* the voice comes into existence. And that suggests that when in more normal circumstances one does something, the will provides us with an answer as to how we effect what we do effect.

It might be claimed of this case that it provides us with a genuine example of a person's witnessing his own actions. But against that assertion I would raise two objections. In the first place, the description offered by the agent of his own experience is not the decisive test for establishing that he has related observationally to his own actions. In the second place, I shall here merely reiterate the objection raised earlier in the discussion. Namely: that the ideal of observing one's own actions is an impossible ideal, on the grounds that, were one to suppose it realised, one would be obliged to suppose the existence of two distinct yet internally related selves locked in an observer–observed relation, and this is inconsistent with their being true selves and *a fortiori* with one self's observing the act of the other.

(b) The experience alone never establishes observation of one's own actions

(1) Before I consider the significance of the above description of the 'self-observing' experience, I must first clarify the important concept of being unaware of what one is doing, since it plays a significant part in that discussion. We say on occasion that a man is not aware of some trifling act in which he is engaging, and all that we imply is that his attention is elsewhere. This is quite usual. But we may also say of a man that he is not aware of what he is doing, and be affirming something of a quite different and more serious order, in which at the very least we attribute a state of diminished responsibility. Thus, it may be to ascribe to him a somnambulist or else a drugged condition, which are conditions we would characterise as involving either loss or diminution of consciousness, an absence of awareness of his surroundings and actions, and of much else besides (including that he is thus unaware). It may on the other hand be to ascribe to him a condition of 'transport' where the attention is simply overwhelmed: say, a condition of such extremity of feeling – the extremes of joy or grief or terrible rage – that he is unable to say afterwards just what actions he engaged in during that time. Now we would not say of such a person that he was barely conscious, but we would surely say that he was barely conscious of his surroundings or of what he said or did. All he seemed to be aware of was his joy or his grief or his intense and extreme hatred.

There exists one further example of this condition which is relevant to the above discussion, which bears a similarity to the main example under consideration. It is the situation in which a person seems to be experiencing no particularly strong feelings, and is apparently awake and engaging in complex meaningful activity, and yet the activity in question happens to be bizarre in the extreme. I think that here too we would say of such a person that he was not aware of what he was doing. I think we would assume that 'he was not himself at the time', and if the condition were to persist then in the end we might come to regard it as a kind of loss of the self. This is significantly similar to the situation encountered in the experience of the political speaker at the concert.

(2) I do not believe we ever say of a man, either that he can tell he is acting because he *observes* that he is, or that he can tell of his act that it is intentional Φ through *observing* that it is. Thus, even if a man underwent such unusual experiences as occurred at the concert, in which for a moment he seemed as spectator to be listening to his own speaking, that alone would not provide us with sufficient grounds for saying that he knew what he did through observing it. For if we decide that he was aware of what he was doing, then we have decided against such an account. And we have other, more decisive, tests for establishing that he was aware of what he was doing.

One of the most important tests is behavioural. Thus, if he described his experiences as I have done, which is to say with a tinge of 'alienation', but his political speech was nonetheless full of verve and invention, we would all agree that he was a man who had at all times been aware of what he was doing. Indeed, even if the description that he gave of his experience was *completely* observer-like, for example even if he made accurate third-person comments of the kind elocutionists make, noting how at this point the voice was flat, there reedy, now hasty and breathy and so on, nevertheless if his behaviour at the time was inventive and self-possessed, we would undoubtedly say that he was aware of what he was doing and hence could not have related as observer to his own deeds. In short, the character of the accompanying behaviour seems to be of overriding importance.

But if these vital behavioural tests point in the other direction, then the situation significantly alters. If the subject's behaviour is bizarre, if he appears to have no idea that he was speaking, if his report of 'the voice' was purely that of an elocutionist, we may well come to describe him as unaware of what he was doing (in the special sense spelled out). Then if in these extreme circumstances he can nonetheless tell us roughly what 'the voice' said, should we not at long last say that he could do so because he *heard* what he said? Should we not agree that here we have unearthed the elusive case of relating as observer to one's own acts? But why so? Is it because we endorse the 'principle': since he knows what was said, yet was unaware of what he was doing, he must have discovered what he said through hearing it? But must he have? Would not his knowledge have been unimpaired even if his fingers were in his ears? Would he not have known even if his voice had been drowned in the uproar? And was not his attention wholly given up at the time to the activity of speaking? So how could he have been listening as observer?

Even though some of these cases might appear to suggest so, we are never in a position to say: his being in a bizarre state enabled him to relate as observer to his own actions. For whatever seem to be grounds for saying that he had something more than a merely odd experience and actually observed his own actions – for example, his ability to say what he did, together with many elocutionary details – are at the same time grounds for saying he was at least partially aware of what he was doing and therefore for saying that his condition of depersonalisation was only partial. This is because the account of the experience is overruled. Therefore depersonalisation cannot be the avenue whereby we may arrive at the observation of our own actions.

(c) The seeming fragmentation of the self

(1) Let us return to the political 'agitator'. I have described here the experience of a man who seems to observe his own actions and suffers at the same time the experience of loss of agency and loss of self.

This is a man whose reason leads, as it were, in a direction of which the rest of him is ignorant or in which it is unwilling to go. He is in subjection to his reason, or rather in subjection to a reason that is split off from action or imagination or feeling, and finds himself betrayed by it into a totally alien situation. It seems to him that he finds himself making a public gesture that in his eyes at that moment has the quality of exhibitionism; it seems to him that his avowed reasons for acting thus are not the reasons of this being who is acting thus, or else that his reasons for acting thus have nothing to do with the avowed reasons of the being who avowed reasons. In other words, if the avowed reasons are his, then the action is not, and if the action is his, then the avowed reasons are not.

The subsequent experience of self is almost 'Humean' in character, in that there seems to be a conglomeration of sounds, sensations, and sights, but nothing that is *oneself*! All those faces are looking in the same direction, but one does not realise that what they are looking at is oneself, for one has no awareness of one's own location. We see, here, a close connection between the sense of identity, and the most primitive possible knowledge of one's position in space. We remember the genuinely primitive cry: 'Where am I?', of a person coming out of deep unconsciousness, the sense of which is much closer to 'Who or what am I?' than to 'What room in what building is that ceiling a part of?' or even 'What has been happening?'

Common to all experiences of loss of agency is the sense of becoming a spectator of one's own actions. Common to all experiences of its recovery is the sense of one's own actions becoming so close to one, almost in the manner of one's own eyelids, that it is impossible for one to remain any longer a seeming spectator of them. Instead one seems to look through and beyond them, as if through a glass or frame. And at such a moment one relates once more directly to the world.

The experience of loss of agency and of becoming a spectator of one's own actions, when taken to their extreme limit, lead, not to the resolution of what one might call 'Narcissus' problem', but to a complete unawareness of what one is doing. Then at that point one's acts are lost to one – they become like the acts of another – given to a disintegrating consciousness.

(2) To conclude, let us ask why it is that the 'Humean' experience of dis-integration of self should accompany the experience of seeming to observe one's own actions. I shall make no more than a brief comment on this difficult question. The speaker who for a few moments seemed to hear a 'voice' came nearest to observing his own actions, but during that period was almost unaware of what he was doing. Now not to know what one is doing, in the case of a trifling bodily act, is to have distributed one's attention elsewhere, whereas in the above case the expression 'not knowing what one is doing' is the specification of a general *mental state*, the existence of which may be inferred from a subject's unawareness of the character of a *single* 'minded' action – and here we may no longer invoke the distribution of the attention as explanation. Thus, there are 'minded' actions, such as the delivering of a speech, that one cannot engage in absent-mindedly, so that an unawareness (say) of uttering shameful and grotesque things to a vast assembly, cannot be put down to his having directed his mind or attention elsewhere. Onto what, then, is his mind or attention directed on such an occasion? Onto nothing else, and hence not properly onto any-thing. Accordingly, given such an extreme situation of engaging in 'minded' action without knowing what one is doing; and bearing in mind that his reasons for thus acting cannot be rational, so that reason played small part in determining his behaviour, which in turn cannot therefore be free and self-determined; it seems evident that the more extreme such states the less happy the application of the concept of purposive intentional action. It is true that at such times the agent is 'out of his mind'. But – purposiveness

draining away – he is nowhere else. And that inevitably has repercussions in his state of consciousness.

This man is neither asleep nor unconscious, neither barely nor partially nor half-conscious. But he is not *properly* conscious, and his state is a *disturbance* of consciousness: he is unaware of what he is doing, of what he is doing to those around him, probably of who they are, and the like. These latter claims are not of an empirical nature, but are involved in the concept of being unaware of what one is doing. For the phenomena, being unaware of what one is doing and disturbance of consciousness, go together; and the phenomena of disturbance of consciousness and imperfect awareness of immediate surroundings, likewise go together. Thus, it may or may not be that we would say of someone that he is unaware of what he is doing even when he displays a keenly observant awareness of his surroundings – but I doubt if we would. And I doubt if there is any behaviour on the part of a man who is gravely announcing his conviction that he is Perseus that would convince us he was both fully aware of his surroundings and altogether unaware of what he is doing. So it is at the least generally true that the account we give of what this man perceives is one that greatly reduces the normal perceptual account, say in regard to awareness of spatial layout, of physical detail, etc. Indeed, it is seemingly as impoverished as the perceptual content of dreams. More, it is almost as if this man was a *dramatis persona* in someone else's dream! For he is devoid of interiority, is 'possessed' and irrational, and knows not why he does what he does.

This man was unaware of what he was doing, and what he was doing could not be described as *freely self-determined*. Nonetheless he was *doing* something, and doing it *intentionally*. But if his mental state deteriorated and his speech became senseless and finally became pure incoherence and formless babble, then we would describe him as raving and would speak less and less of his being unaware of what he was doing. This is because these acts are no longer capable of being synthesised into meaningful wholes, are no longer parts of synthetic structures, and can therefore support no inter-pretative re-descriptions and *a fortiori* none that can elude the awareness of their agent. For at that extreme point not only does the concept of *free action* lose its grip, but so to a degree does that of *meaningful* intentional action, and all that remains is the phenomenon of intentional action *simpliciter*. Thus, his acts tend to degenerate into a mass of senseless active atoms which cannot be unified under any projective heading, into phenomena that are akin to the senseless kickings of the newly born – mere act fragments. Now this radical condition corresponds to a break-up of synthetic act structures, synthetic perceptual structures, and synthetic connections linking parts of the self. In the end we would describe such a being as barely conscious, as hardly aware of his surroundings – and all of this through the loss of the mind alone! Yet just as the ego of the newly born must be of *some* extent, so the loss of the mind and intentional projects and the consequent loss of consciousness can never be *total*. For the mind cannot die even as the man continues to exist; indeed, the mind seems never to pass away through its own ailments. And so it is here: consciousness all but, but not quite, fading into non-existence. What, then, does this man see? It is no accident that it is like the case of the newly born infant. All we could do in order to try to answer this question would be to continue the above process of draining away awareness from what is seen, so that consciousness would fade – not through a withdrawal of attention, as in sleep – but through a loss of the identity of everything that is seen. Such descriptions would not, I think, fall far short of the 'Humean' account. Intimations of this account were already felt in cases where we seemed, perhaps, close to observing our own actions.

CHAPTER 10

Sub-intentionality and the scope of the intention

1. INTRODUCTION

Donald Davidson enunciated what might be proposed as a principle. It was to the effect that anything that is an action must be intentional under some description or other. Thus, the leg rise of reflex cannot be brought under an intentional description, whereas the unintentional act of moving one's shadow as one walks falls under the intentional description 'walking'. This principle, if valid, could be used as a *test* of being an action. But it is important to note that it could not be proposed as a *definition* of action. To do so would be to endorse a circularity, as I will now explain. It is a mistake to suppose that the sense of 'intentional' in the Davidsonian principle is the property that we oppose to extensionality. If it were, desires would be actions. The sense rather is 'intentional action'. This implies that the claim already utilises the concept of action, and is thus debarred from being a definition of action.

At best it is a necessary condition. And the *prima facie* case for this view is strong, for it seems to hold of most actions. For example, the aforementioned acts of walking and moving one's shadow: these are one and the same event, but we walk intentionally and generally unintentionally move our shadow. Then if acts which are intentional under one description can be unintentional under other descriptions, if being intentional is in this sense description-relative, a partial detachment of act from intention must be possible: in short, we can act – but so to say a-wrong. Then the question I am at present asking is: can such detachment ever be total? Are there acts which are intentional under no description whatever, however vague and attenuated the proposed description may be? Well, there exist trivial acts which look as if they might escape awareness and thus intentionalness altogether: for example, idly and unawares moving one's tongue as one drives one's car. On the face of it, such acts seem to be exceptions to the

Davidsonian principle. Let us call the (conjectured) property of being an action which is intentional under no description 'sub-intentionality'.

2. PRELIMINARY QUESTIONS

The question I am asking in this chapter is whether there exist actions which are intentional under *no* description. Before I embark on this inquiry, there are two highly relevant topics which I must discuss. The first concerns the nature of absent-minded behaviour, the second the marks of the intention and of intentional action.

(a) The nature of absent-minded behaviour

(1) What is absent-minded behaviour? A typical absent-minded action would be (say) bringing the comb which is in one's pocket to the front-door lock – while talking animatedly. What is happening here? Now intentional action *as such* makes demands upon awareness: it occupies a measure of mental space in the limited attentive arena that we call 'the Attention': it takes up *experiential space*. Indeed, sheer intentional exercise of the will, whether successful or not, makes demands upon attentive space. Then in the above chosen example of absent-mindedness, much of the attentive space was occupied by the activity of conversing. In this way the simple act of bringing one's front-door key to the lock was depleted of the 'mental oxygen' it needed to exist. This is the 'absence of the mind' referred to in the expression 'absent-minded action'. The absence was not of thought, but of awareness or consciousness.

In such situations the subject's mind is still to a degree occupied with the absent-minded act he is doing: some small measure of awareness has been granted by the mind to this act, even though it is not enough to meet the needs of the situation. The effect of this semi-starvation of attentive oxygen is that while the act performed is capable of supporting certain intentional determinations, they are fewer than the practical situation required. It is rather like our visual experience of the objects situated in the periphery of the visual field, where the objects as given to awareness have fewer determinations than those near the centre: we discern the largeness and brightness of the object situated in the peripheries, but not its triangularity and yellowness.

Now while the act under discussion was one of bringing *one's comb* to the front-door lock, it was also an act of bringing *an implement that was in one's pocket* to the lock. Then even though the agent of this act did not intend to bring his comb to the lock, he did mean to bring an implement that was in his pocket to the lock. Accordingly, the act of moving the comb must have been intentional under 'bring implement in pocket to the lock' and unintentional under 'bring comb to the lock'. In sum, the intentional act that he performed had fewer determinations than were required by an act of bringing the key to the lock, and the cause of this shortfall is that the act was not granted the quotum of attentive space which even a simple act like opening a door requires. Absent-minded acts are acts which are intentional under descriptions which invoke fewer determinations than the act-situation demands, where the cause of the deficiency lies in the dearth of attention available for the deed.

(2) Here we have one mode adopted by action in which we act in a way which escapes our attention. And one could imagine an extrapolation of the above kind of situation to an extreme, where an act is *so* absent-minded, and *so* starved of attentive space, that the determinations under which it can be counted as intentional fade away in the absent-minded mode to something approaching zero. For example, 'doing something or other with my hand', or 'doing something or other that seemed required by the occasion'. Nevertheless these actions are still intentional under these almost empty headings. And the common cause of the impoverishment of content is the near unavailability of the attention, the near starvation of the mental oxygen without which intentional action cannot so much as exist. In sum, even the most extreme examples of absent-mindedness prove to be intentional under *some* heading. No act can be absent-minded without being intentional under *some* description.

The relevance of the above observations to the problem of sub-intentionality is the following. Might it not be the case that all seeming examples of sub-intentionality are exemplifications of a similar state of affairs? Might it not be that they are all actions which are so starved of attentive oxygen as to fall under headings which are almost but not quite vacuous? If that is the situation, these acts must be intentional under these very broad headings, and so must fail to exemplify sub-intentionality. This is a serious challenge for the theory of sub-intentionality.

(b) The marks of intentions and intentional actions

(1) If we are to make headway with the problem of sub-intentionality, we need to know what are the main properties of intentions and intentional actions. Before I list those properties, I would emphasise that the intention is that in the light of which we so describe an act as to reveal its goal or *meaning*. In addition, I think we should understand this concept in a broad

enough sense to allow for relatively negative non-purposive re-descriptions of the kind: 'just expressing myself'. The following seem to me the most significant properties of the intention/intentional action in self-conscious subjects.

   (i) The intention has an act-object.
  (ii) The intention is a practical commitment to action.
 (iii) It is future-directed, and sometimes also present-directed.
 (iv) At the time of intentional action one knows of the act.
  (v) At the time of intentional action one expects its next phase.
 (vi) The intention is capable of rationality.
(vii) The reasons for the intention are those of the intentional act.
(viii) The intention expresses act-desire and belief.
 (ix) The intention, along with the act-reasons, is part-cause of the inten-
       tional act.
  (x) The intention is the agency of control over action.

   In sum, the intention is a practical commitment, on the basis of act-reasons, to the performing of action that extends in part at least into a future that one immediately expects, and it has the power immediately to initiate and halt such action.

(2) In the light of the above, I suggest that if we are to discover whether some phenomenon is an intentional action, then we should address the following three questions:
   (i) Does one know of the phenomenon under some description or other?
  (ii) Does it occur for act-type reasons (allowing for the negative sub-variety
       of being judged unexceptionable)?
 (iii) Is the immediate future of the phenomenon expected?

3. PUTATIVE EXAMPLES OF SUB-INTENTIONAL ACTION

There exist various seemingly active phenomena, all occurring near the peripheries of awareness, whose general character must be examined if we are to make progress with the question of sub-intentionality. I have selected four exemplar cases, each realising a different attentive situation. They are:
A. Idly drumming one's fingers on the table as one talks.
B. Playing a note on the piano with one's left little finger in an extremely
    rapid musical passage.
C. Humming tune X to oneself, barely aware of doing so.
D. Idly and unawares moving one's tongue in one's mouth as one drives
    one's car.

For convenience, I shall single out these cases under the following labels: 'Consent', 'Collectivity', 'Specificity', 'Primordiality'. I discuss them in this order.

A. Consent

Idly drumming one's fingers on the table as one talks
Drumming one's fingers as one converses mostly is a case in which one allows a simple inclination to have its way. Such activity usually has no aim – not even the aim of letting one's restlessness express itself. Then how can the activity be intentional? It is intentional *through having one's consent*, and in an unthinking mode (unlike the consent a pianist might give to idly drumming with the fingers of his recuperating hand). Usually one unthinkingly, but nonetheless actually, judges such trifling behaviour to be 'unexceptionable' 'harmless enough', and so forth.

In sum, one is aware of the act, unself-consciously judges it unexceptionable, is unsurprised by what happens next, and might reply to the query 'Why were you doing that?' by saying, 'I just felt like it.'

In the light of these considerations, I think it clear that typical occurrences of this phenomenon are intentional activities.

B. Collectivity

Playing a note on the piano with one's left little finger in an extremely rapid musical passage
(1) I will begin by filling in the details. Suppose that over an interval of one second, between times t_1 and $t_1 + 1$, an activity with the left hand occurred of playing a musical passage of ten notes. And suppose that midway through at time $t_1 + \frac{1}{2}$ it involved the movement M of the left little finger L, an event occupying $\frac{1}{10}$th of a second. Then the following observations concerning this case are pertinent.

  (i) If an act of moving L is to have occurred, then at the time of the movement of L *one must have been able proprioceptively to perceive L*.
  (ii) If an act of moving L is to have occurred, then at the time of the movement of L *one must have been able to move L*.
  (iii) I am assuming that at each moment of the second-long interval *only one finger* of the left hand is in motion.
  (iv) I am assuming that over the second-long interval *ten* finger movements of the left hand occurred.

(v) One was aware of the *synthetic activity* of 'playing the musical passage for the left hand' between times t_I and $t_I + 1$.

(vi) An *intention* of performing such a synthetic activity caused that phenomenon.

(vii) The movement of L, which occurred at $t_I + \frac{1}{2}$, was a *single event*.

(2) Of what is one aware between times t_I and $t_I + 1$? My first inclination is to liken this situation to the instantaneous visual perception of a collective, in which the totality is noticed and no one of the collected visibilia is noticed. That is, it is to say of this case (B) that in the rapid flurry of finger movements *the single movement M* of the little finger L was simply not noticed. And it is in addition to claim that if *an act of moving L* did occur, that act was one of which the subject was wholly unaware. As I say, my first inclination is to propose the visual perception of collectives as a model for the performing of the complex rapid physical activity of moving ten fingers, and the perceivability of each collected but unperceived visibilium as a model for what obtains in the case of each act of finger-moving.

However, certain considerations make this comparison unacceptable. Notable differences exist between the two cases. After all, in a mere instant of visual perception as many as *fifty objects* (e.g. fifty faces) might be simultaneously present in one's visual field, each item at that moment being visually discernible to one whose gaze was fixed. Nothing like such multiplicity is realised in the case of the activity with one's left hand in the musical example in question. Here at each instant we are concerned with the movement (and moving) of a *single finger* of the left hand. This is a far cry from supposing that fifty separate movements might be either noticed and/or executed in an instant.

A more accurate visual comparison would be with the temporally successive visual perception, within the space of a second interval, of ten separate small neighbouring lights of diverse colour: each light being not merely perceptible to one, but perceived. And surely something of this kind is feasible. Fifty visibilia is too many, two presents no problem, and it may be that ten comes close to the limit of human powers of attentive differentiation. In sum, I find no reason for supposing that the playing of a particular note in a rapid musical passage relates to the attention as do each of the fifty clearly visible faces in a crowd one glimpses for a brief instant. The model of visual 'collectivity' is clearly inapplicable.

(3) It is salutary to recall that the conditions necessary for perceptual awareness are relatively few. We require no more than that the item in question be

noticed, which is to say attentively spatio-temporally differentiated under some description or another. We do not require that it be identified as of the kind it is. As remarked earlier when discussing absent-mindedness, the heading under which an item comes to the attention can be broad to the point of near vacuousness: 'something or other' 'something dark' 'something moving', and so on. Provided the vacuousness is not total, so long as the heading has content, that suffices for the perception of the item. Then I would like at this point parenthetically to observe that the theory of sub-intentionality runs the risk of taking as its model for intentional action, perceptual examples of a more developed kind than are necessary for sheer awareness. What one is inclined to describe as a 'sub-intentional act' may sometimes be an act occurring on the very margins of awareness, in which the individuating heading is near to but not wholly vacuous. Then it must be emphasised that sub-intentionality requires something other than nearly vacuous headings. It requires that the object not be noticed *under any heading whatsoever*. And that is a truly stringent requirement.

(4) One additional comment on the present pianistic example. The inclination to posit the visual parallel is probably fostered by the decision-situation in this situation. Did one decide to play that particular note? It seems certain that nothing resembling a 'snap decision' to play that note occurred. Then did one at any time decide to play that note? I think one did – though non-individuatively – when one decided at such and such a moment to start playing the musical passage. I think one had the intention of playing that note, not under the heading 'playing note N in bar one', but under the collective heading 'playing each of the notes involved in the musical passage' (or some such). Then the lack of a decision which takes the playing of this note as its sole object, the fact that the act is only collectively singled out in the decision, is liable to make one feel that one did not intend to do this particular deed, and intended *only* to do a 'collective deed' – rather as one might see *only* a collective object like a crowd – as if at each moment one was not in control of what one was doing (as one does not notice each face in the crowd). This is an error, for while there are collective decisions and sights, there are no such 'collective deeds'. The moving of L is an individual act over which one has complete 'say' – for one may decide to stop at *any* point in this musical passage – even though the moving of L was decided upon only under the cloak of a collective heading. Intentions have a continuous act-expression over a continuous period of time, and at each instant a novel sector of the act remains to be done – intentionally. (After

all, the fingers do not 'take over'.) This is what is happening in the present case. I conclude: the act is intentional under 'finger-moving'.

(5) And yet how can one so easily dismiss the possibility of 'collective action'? Well, I do not deny the existence of complex acts which are constituted out of distinct acts, or complex acts which express collective decisions. What I reject is the possibility of complex acts which are constituted out of distinct acts to which one relates as one does to each distinctly visible face in a momentary sight of a totality of faces given purely *qua* 'crowd of faces'.

Consider the example of a person with a hundred arms playing a hundred pianos. (A sort of Percy Grainger phantasy!) At time $t_1 + \frac{1}{2}$ the little finger L_5 of hand 5 strikes the keyboard. Might this movement be a distinct act of which the pianist was unaware? Now as things stand with humans, proprioceptive awareness of limbs is a necessary condition of limb-moving. Then would this principle apply to the supposed act of moving L_5? Or would we instead relate attentively to this supposed act as we do to (say) face 5 in the momentary glimpsing of a crowd of faces? If the former, one must have been aware of the act, which will in turn have been intentional under some description; if the latter, we must be in the presence of a sub-intentional act.

On what grounds could we judge the moving of L_5 an action? If the reply is, that we have active power over L_5, we must demonstrate that this moving of L_5 is unlike the movements of normal respiration, since in normal respiration we do not utilise an inhering active power. If the reply is, that an intention set all hundred fingers in motion, we need to demonstrate that the movement of L_5 and the other fingers is not an active complex of inactive phenomena collectively caused by an intention. (As happens all the time.) Then I see no reason for abandoning the above principle whereby proprioception is necessary for bodily action, in which case the movements must either be unnoticed and inactive or noticed and intentional. Either way, no sub-intentional act occurs. Of course, with vastly improved attentive power, one could realise a parallel situation to that which obtained with two hands.

C. Specificity

Humming tune X to oneself, barely aware of doing so
What is of interest in this case is, that the subject is aware of his activity but unaware of its specific character. That is, when the subject realises fully what is going on, which is to say notices that he is humming tune X, the propositional object of his noticing is not that he is performing an activity,

or that he is performing the activity of humming a tune, but that he is humming *tune X*. Then when we say he is *aware* of this phenomenon – which we do without qualification – we posit a relatively unambitious conceptualisation on his part: more ambitious than 'doing something or other', but less ambitious than 'humming tune X', so that there is conceptual space available for his making a discovery concerning this action, which is to say for 'noticing-that . . .' However, this does not mean that there is conceptual space for a simple noticing-of the act, which would imply that at the time of action he was simply *unaware* of the phenomenon – under *any* description.

There can be little doubt that this activity of humming a tune is intentional. It is true that one did not decide to do it, so that the intention must have appeared of its own accord in the mind. And yet how could it have done so, if intentions are oriented towards the future? How can the future enter into an activity which occurs without thought? Well, we find such a thing in the case of certain inclinatory activities whose object is *merely indefinitively processive*, such as tapping one's feet or drumming one's fingers; for an activity can project no more than an immediate short-term homogeneous future, something of the order of 'more of the same', and nothing beyond. Here it is useful to remember the 'short list' of simple tests of intentionalness which I proposed earlier. They were:

(i)   Does one knows of the phenomenon under *some* description?
(ii) Does it occur for act-type reasons (allowing for the relatively negative sub-variety of being judged unexceptionable)?
(iii) Was the immediate future of the phenomenon expected?

The activity of humming a tune satisfies these tests. One is vaguely aware of this event, for the event is an experience and therefore known of under *some* description. Meanwhile, so far as reason is concerned, the variety of reasons operative in the case of activities of this kind is of the non-rational variety of mere inclination ('I felt like it'), which is perfectly consistent with the act being intentional. Finally, there seems little doubt that one knows what is coming next as one hums the tune: not what is coming five seconds down the line, which would require a measure of self-consciousness that is not present, but one knows what is coming here and now. Stopped in one's tracks, one could say what it would have been.

D. Primordiality

Idly and unawares moving one's tongue in one's mouth as one drives one's car
(1) *Activeness (1)*. This is far and away the most persuasive example, so far as the theory of sub-intentionality is concerned. All the other examples

can in my view be comprehended as intentional once one appreciates that active purely inclinatory phenomena can be given to consciousness under almost indeterminate headings, and that this is consistent with their being intentional. However, idle tongue moving of the type under consideration appears on the face of it to be resistant to this defence of intentionalness: the reason being that it seems to escape awareness completely.

I shall break the discussion of this phenomenon into two parts: an inquiry into the action-status of the phenomenon, and an inquiry into its intentionalness-status. I do so because the answer to these two central questions is by no means immediately apparent. I begin by asking the question: why believe that this tongue-moving is an action? A first minor reason in favour is of a linguistic order, namely the fact that when we notice what is going on with our tongue, we say, 'I noticed that I was moving my tongue.' And it is important that we do not say, 'I noticed that my tongue was moving.' This last is what we would say were we to notice an eyelid twitching 'of its own accord'. However, while this linguistic consideration rules out that particular comparison, it does not prove that such tongue-moving is an action: after all, we attribute breathing to the subject rather than to his body, yet there are compelling reasons for judging breathing to be inactive in character.

(2) A second much stronger reason for believing that this phenomenon is an action is, that a necessary condition of the variety of tongue-moving under consideration is that at the time of the moving *one be able proprioceptively to perceive* tongue movement. If for some reason one could not, if one was at that moment incapable of directing one's attention immediately proprioceptively onto that organ and its movement, we would surely say that the tongue must have been moving of its own accord. By contrast, we do not require of breathing that the subject be able to perceive the phenomena in chest or lungs: breathing continues under deep anaesthesia, a state which cannot support proprioceptive or any other perception. Now while this necessary condition of this particular variety of tongue-moving does not prove that proprioception of the tongue is going on at the time, it strongly suggests it. And it distances tongue-moving from the autonomic phenomenon of breathing, which is such that in the state of consciousness, an unused active power continues to inhere side by side with sheer automaticity. Idle tongue-moving must be adjudged different in kind from both the twitching of an eyelid and the autonomic phenomenon of breathing.

Then *why is it* that proprioceptive *perceptibility* is a necessary condition of the familiar variety of tongue-moving? Far and away the most likely explanation is that *proprioception* must be a necessary condition of the phenomenon. What other explanation can one propose? In other words, proprioception must be occurring at the time – however marginal to the Attention. The mind must reach out to the limb in question in the mode of concrete immediate awareness, if this variety of tongue-moving is to occur. Then if proprioception is a necessity, why so? It is not so in the case of breathing – then why here? Again, far and away the most likely explanation, bearing in mind that proprioception is a necessary condition of bodily action as such, is that this variety of tongue-moving is a bodily action.

Finally, we note that *contemporaneous active power* over the tongue is as necessary a condition of the phenomenon as is contemporaneous proprioceptive perceptibility. Then if one goes on to ask why such active power over the tongue should be a necessary condition of this phenomenon, we find once again that far and away the most likely explanation is that such active power is a necessary condition of *any* activity of tongue-moving. And this also is a good reason for supposing that this variety of tongue-moving must be an action.

(3) A third and final reason favouring the judgement that unawares tongue-moving is an activity is, that when we notice it we can halt it, and by doing nothing: that is, we can halt it *immediately*. This suggests that the act-power to move the tongue – which is as necessary to the phenomenon as is proprioceptive perceptibility – must be mobilised at the time. And yet it does not prove it, since this same property is present in the case of breathing. For while breathing goes on 'of its own accord' prior to one's noticing it, the moment we do notice it we can as in the case of tongue-moving halt it – by doing nothing. Nevertheless, this property of tongue-moving distinguishes this phenomenon from cases of the type of laughter. In laughing, as with mere inclinatory activities, we do what we do because we feel like it – and yet laughing is not an activity. However, whereas we are able immediately to stop tongue-moving, we cannot immediately stop laughing. We try to stop laughing by doing such things as thinking of disagreeable matters: that is, mediately.

In sum, it has emerged in the discussion of the present case (D) that idle tongue-moving is different in kind from the *merely bodily event* of the twitching of an eyelid, from the *autonomic phenomenon* of breathing, and from the *semi-helpless inclinatory phenomenon* of laughter. Meanwhile the type of the *description* we give of the phenomenon, and the fact that both proprioceptive *perceptibility-of* and *act-power-over* the tongue and its movment are at the time of its occurrence strictly necessary conditions of the phenomenon that we know being the kind it is, together constitute a strong case for the thesis that such idle tongue-moving is an activity.

D. *Primordiality: intentionalness (2)*

(1) If this phenomenon is active, is it intentional? One's first assumption is that it cannot be, because at the time we seem to be completely unaware of moving the tongue. Let us begin this discussion by considering this latter claim.

One usually cannot answer the question: have you been moving your tongue in your mouth over the last minute? This seems beyond doubt. Then compare: could one answer the same question concerning tapping one's feet to music during a film? I am of the opinion that, while one would be unable to speak of specific time intervals such as a minute, one might well find oneself in a position to say that one was vaguely aware of tapping one's feet during some of the time the music was thumping away. By contrast, we can do nothing of this kind in the case of idle tongue-moving. Then could it be that at each instant one was aware of the *activity*, but unaware of any *interval of activity*? Might this be the extreme situation for action in which synthesis across time has contracted infinitesimally close to zero: an awareness such as to leave no recollection of any temporal span? That is, knowledge at the time which leaves no memory? As daydreaming drifts from instant to instant, with no long-term project afoot, might the idle moving of one's tongue be the limiting case for intentional structures of this sort: the extreme case in which the short-term spans contract to next to nothing more than sheer moving? But if it were so, how could it be both intentional and completely detached from orientation to the future? Well, it might plausibly be replied that the very concept of activity, being processive in type, is such as *already* to project an immediate future the same in kind as the continuous present. After all, there is no such thing as an instantaneous process.

(2) These are difficult and seemingly recherché questions. And at first glance one would give a negative response to these extreme suggestions. Then whatever the truth on this matter I think it near certain that if such tongue-moving is intentional, it will have to be through being the limiting extreme in which the projected future contracts to whatever is the experiential equivalent of an infinitesimal. Knowledge without recollection! At best, something on the edge of these extremities.

And yet is it so? One fact points towards an affirmative answer to this question. Earlier in section D.(1) (above) I advanced considerations in favour of the theory that this activity necessitates proprioceptive perception. But perception is an experience, and there are no unconscious experiences – even though there are experiences about whose character and content one can be ignorant. It might therefore be argued – given that idle tongue-moving of the kind under discussion necessitates proprioception of such movement – that momentary awareness and knowledge of the phenomenon must have occurred at the time which leaves no recollective residue whatsoever. After all, when we notice that the process is going on, we are in direct contact with it, and prior to that instant it must have been equally accessible, even though not brought to full self-consciousness.

But if we notice that the phenomenon is occurring, something must have changed: a state of self-conscious knowledge has appeared which must have been preceded by a different knowledge. But what kind of knowledge could have preceded the self-conscious knowledge? Now while this is a serious difficulty for the thesis that one is aware of this idle activity, a lesser version of the same problem can be raised concerning the process of tapping one's feet to film music – and yet an unself-conscious cognitive awareness must undoubtedly have accompanied one's vague attentive awareness of that phenomenon. What kind of cognition can it have been? One speaks here of vague awareness, and we mean an experience in the outer suburbs of the Attention, of minimum intensity and slight conceptual definition, together with knowledge of comparable impoverishment. Then whatever we wish to say of these latter phenomena, they are unquestionably realities, for at the time one truly was vaguely aware of the activity of foot-tapping. Accordingly, in the later cognition of full recollective self-consciousness, one must at that later point know what one earlier knew, only at this later stage *under additional conceptual determinations*, so that the knowledge must have undergone instantaneous development at the time of the event of noticing that it was occurring: it must have acquired further determinations, taking place now in a context of full self-consciousness. Accordingly, if one knew of tongue-moving at the time of the activity, it must have been under the most impoverished of conceptual headings – leaving not a trace in memory. It must have occurred at the outermost edge of the universe of the Attention.

4. CONCLUSION

What are we to conclude? I believe that I must retract the theory I had proposed in the earlier version of this work, and conclude that the concept

of sub-intentionality is simply invalid. I think that at the time I had failed
fully to grasp just how near to complete vacuousness an awareness can
be. Once one gives this idea its full weight, it copes rather easily with
most of the examples (although the case of tongue-moving still seems to
present problems). In addition, I think I had not fully considered the fact
that intentions can appear in the mind both in the absence of a decision
and without self-conscious 'vetting': tapping the feet to music is a fair
example. The main flaw in my reasoning lay in using a middle-of-the-road
example of intentional action as a yardstick of the phenomenon as such: as
Wittgenstein would say, I was living on a one-sided diet.

Meanwhile, even when I proposed the theory of sub-intentionality, I had
no illusions about the closeness of action and intention. I recognised that
it was a necessary property of the will that it instantaneously and infallibly
obeys 'instructions' from the intention. This property of the will is unique –
no other mental phenomenon is or could be at one's immediate beck and
call. For the will is essentially infinitely open to control: one has merely to
decide and therefore intend to start or stop a willing, and necessarily the
decision takes effect. It may be difficult to decide – indeed, one's act-desires
may fail to obey one's judgement – but if I really do decide to now start or
stop willing, then start or stop of necessity I do. And while there may be
some doubt as to the reality of my decision, it is certain that a real decision
to now act/now stop acting – and therefore a genuine intention directed
to the immediate present – is infinitely endowed with the power to effect
its aim of willing/stopping. To be sure, this infinite effectiveness does not
operate any further than the will – for example, in so far as act-mechanistic
progress is concerned – but the will must obey.

CHAPTER II

Voluntariness and the volition

I. THE THEORY OF THE VOLITION

(1) The main topic in Part III of this work is the nature of bodily action. Then the received traditional theories of bodily action tend to be volitionist in character. This chapter is devoted to the question: is the theory of the volition correct? I begin with a statement of the theory. Now the word 'volition' is a philosopher's term of art. Accordingly, there will inevitably be a stipulative element in any statement of that theory. And yet enough has been said about volitions, whether of an approving or disparaging character, to enable me to spell out a theory of bodily action which has two virtues. First, it is as close as we are likely to get to a statement of the doctrine adopted by traditional self-styled 'volitionists'; second, it is a plausible and natural account of the nature of bodily action. I take the theory to be as follows.

Whenever a bodily action occurs, which is to say a phenomenon most philosophers would describe as a 'voluntary bodily action', then a certain V occurs which is endowed with the following traits. V is an *event*; an event which is sometimes described as an '*act of the will*'; which is *psychological* in status; and that is, in a sense I shall shortly explain, situated in the '*inner world*'. In addition, if the voluntary act in question is a bodily act Φ of φ-making, then V is the *cause of* φ. Finally, if Φ gives expression to a desire and intention, then V is the effect of the desire and intention. Accordingly, the event V is said to be causally sandwiched between the psychological progenitors of the act Φ – viz. an act-desire and an intention to Φ – and the willed event φ.

(2) To complete the specification of the theory of the volition I must explicate what is meant by 'inner world' in the above statement. This is because the supposition that the volition is situated in the 'inner world', in some sense of that expression, is an important part of this theory. And

there are many precedents for such a rendering of the volitionist thesis. For example, Locke in characterising the will speaks of 'a power to begin or forbear, continue or end, several actions of our minds and motions of our bodies, barely by a *thought or preference of the mind* ordering, or as it were commanding, the doing or not doing of such a particular action. This power is what we call the Will. The actual exercise of that power, by directing any particular action or its forbearance, is that which we call *volition or willing*'[1] (my italics).

The sense which I propose for 'inner world' is stipulative, and prompted by the main conclusion of the succeeding chapter 12 (which is that bodily actions are psychological events). Then I believe that we have the over-whelmingly powerful intuition that events like acts of kicking cannot be located in anything one would call an inner world, whereas by contrast both primitive psychological phenomena like sensations and more developed mental phenomena like mental images lie hidden within. Then what principle unites pains, images, and forgettings, in one class, and excludes kickings? It cannot be that one kind of phenomenon is experienced and the other not, for pains and kickings are experienced and forgettings are not. More to the point, it cannot be that one is unperceivable by sense organs and the other not. The reason I say this is, that it presupposes the falsity of Physicalism, whereas the proposed distinction between 'of the inner world' and 'not of the inner world' can be drawn without adjudicating on this wider issue. Thus, if some version of physicalism is true, it may be possible to set eyes upon brain events which constitute the phenomenon of pain. Then since bodily acts are visible, the test cannot rest on the possibility of perceivability.

Yet bearing in mind the natural intuition that bodily actions cannot be set in anything one would call an 'inner world', and taking the hint that the stipulation should be determined by the possibility of a perceivability that can be known prior to establishing the truth-value of physicalism, I suggest the following purely stipulated sense for 'inner world'. An item x is located in the inner world if (i) x is psychological and (ii) it is not the case that there exists some bodily non-psychological item y which is such that it is *a priori* given that y is a part of x. On this test pains and thoughts and the volition as traditionally conceived all turn out to be, while kickings and talkings prove not to be, situated in the inner world.

(3) That completes my statement of volitionism. Then a last complication before I turn to a discussion of voluntary action. It is clear that most

---

[1] *An Essay Concerning Human Understanding* II, ch. 21, 5. Oxford: Clarendon Press, 1950.

doctrines that travel under the name 'volitionism' are naturally wedded both to the use of the cognate expressions 'voluntary' and the term 'action'. Thus, volitionism usually goes hand in hand with talk of 'voluntary action', and therefore also with talk both of 'involuntary action' and 'reflex action'. While it has no binding need of doing so, it yet naturally does. And there are reasons for this. For such a style of speech tends to keep company with a particular theory concerning the nature of bodily action that is cast in terms of the volition. Now this is why the version of volitionism stated above will generally find itself *embellished* with this theory. Again, not necessarily, but again almost always. Then for this reason I shall for much of the time during the ensuing discussion make the assumption that such an embellished claim is our topic. Precisely what the embellishment is will emerge in due course.

When in the course of this chapter I speak of 'volitionism', I shall have in mind the simple unembellished theory. But I will at the same time mostly take that volitionism to adopt a stance on the nature of action that is all of a piece with its natural commitment to a terminology of 'voluntary', 'involuntary', 'reflex', 'action'. In short, I shall for the most part be examining an *embellished* volitionism. This links the theory intelligibly with issues that determined its very being. And it has the virtue of enabling me to engage in a critique of a terminology which is covertly selling a theory of bodily action. This chapter is in effect a kind of 'exposé' of this state of affairs.

2. VOLUNTARY ACTIONS

(a) The theoretical advantages of volitionism

What do volitionists believe to be the theoretical advantages in postulating volitions? I think they take themselves to have discovered the answer to an important question: 'What makes voluntary actions voluntary?' To which the volitionist replies: their volition origin does. That is, the volitionist believes there is something special about voluntary actions, and it lies in their having a special *origin*, viz. a volition. This problem he thinks volitionism resolves. But more. Volitionism can claim a second asset. For volitionism endorses the theory of the reality of the will, which it takes to be a psychological phenomenon of the inner life. And this will be accounted an additional merit by many, for it is undoubtedly natural to suppose that when we perform such voluntary acts as walking and talking, something psychological occurs that is active in character. Witness the number of philosophers who have thought as much. Then in supposing that the situation in voluntary action is of this character, and so in opting for a distinctive event ('willing') element in voluntary action, volitionism eschews that total reliance upon the applicability of a battery of conditionals that is so characteristic of neo-behaviourist analyses of the will. This some will judge to be a further asset.

Thus, a central task allotted to the volition is to explain the existence of the vastly familiar usage in which we say of some limb movement ϕ: 'I did ϕ.' For the theory assumes that there exists an event link between me and certain ϕs that is such as to enable me to say of that ϕ, 'It was *voluntarily done* by me.' The act of the will is conceived to be a distinctive interior psychological event that is such that, in a special sense of 'responsible', not identical with but underpinning many examples of moral responsibility, I can be said to be *responsible* for certain limb movements (etc.). The above several assertions give us the why and wherefore of the volition.

(b) What is a voluntary action (1)?

(1) What is a voluntary action? Well, we do not have a definition ready, but the voluntary act seems easy to define by example. Thus: walking, talking, kicking, all count as voluntary actions; whereas the following do not: falling through space, leg rise that is caused by a blow beneath the knee, shivering caused by the cold. But now we would like to know the principle of membership of the class of voluntary actions. Then could it be that we shall discover that principle by seeking the principle of membership of the complementary class, viz. that of involuntary actions? Might this phenomenon more pellucidly reveal what distingishes the two kinds of phenomena? But we then face a problem. For the use of 'involuntary action' normally observed is such that leg rise in response to a blow beneath the knee counts as a paradigmatic example. But that is also accounted a 'reflex action'. Then what is the relation between 'involuntary actions' and 'reflex actions'? Before we can answer this question, we must be clear on what is meant by a 'reflex'. A reflex is said to occur when a bodily phenomemon y ('the response') is physically caused by another bodily phenomenon x ('the stimulus') in accordance with a neurologically based regularity. It follows on the above usage that a reflex *action* must be a bodily phenomenon that can on occasion be immediately voluntarily chosen, which happens on this occasion to be caused by a 'stimulus' in accordance with a neurologically based regularity. These stipulations are such that an example of a *mere reflex* would be the pupil of one's eye contracting in bright light, while an example of a *reflex action* would be leg rise resulting from a blow beneath the knee.

Then how are involuntary actions related to reflex actions? It seems that the latter form a sub-class of the former. For there must be other types of 'involuntary actions' besides the reflex variety. After all, no one would describe a 'passive act', such as occurs when someone lifts one's left arm, as a reflex of any kind, and yet no one would call it voluntary. Now in none of these usages do we discover the raw material for a definition of 'voluntary action'. And in any case, any such definitions would be viciously circular, inasmuch as the stipulated definition of 'action' – which is certainly neutral as between voluntary and involuntary and reflex and passive action – relies in the final analysis upon an intuitive understanding of 'voluntary action'.

(2) The attempt to define 'voluntary action' by defining 'involuntary action', and doing so through appeal to the concept of 'reflex', has proved unsuccessful. Accordingly, we must now meet the problem head on and look for whatever is common and peculiar to voluntary actions. That is, to walking, pushing, talking, etc.

What can it be? Might it be that the act is caused by a decision to act? But that has the unwelcome consequence that certain acts that we would describe as both rational and intentional emerge as involuntary: say, hurling oneself out of the way of a bus. Now this 'self-hurling' counts, not merely as voluntary action, but as intentional rational instrumental voluntary action, since one was trying to instrumentally produce a rationally desirable state of affairs, viz. non-collision. But the intention state it expressed was one whose onset cannot have been identical with any decision event, since the onset of the state signalled the end of no condition of uncertainty over what to do. Thus, acts that we describe as voluntary need not owe their existence to decisions.

Then must the voluntary action be the expression of an intention to do such a thing? Clearly not, since there exist unintentional acts which are voluntary acts, such as touching an electrified wire – thinking it neutral. And yet this act was intentional under 'touching the wire'. Then might it be that a voluntary act is an act that is intentional under *some* description? We have seen that this is true, but we also saw that this necessary condition cannot be a definition, since it already uses the concept of voluntary action.

(3) Thus, neither decision-origin nor intention-origin is definitional of 'voluntary action', even though the latter is a necessary condition. Then what is the correct definition? Well, what do we understand by 'He acted completely voluntarily'? Freedom? Might it be that all acts that are voluntary are acts that their agent *need not have done*?

Now there exist terrible acts which are such that, while one could not in normal circumstances bring oneself to perform them, under certain extreme conditions one must and will do such a thing: for example, take one life to save a thousand lives. In this specialised sense a man in the first situation is not free to do such a deed, and in the second is not free not to do it. Nonetheless in either case his act or his abstension is intentional and hence voluntary. Thus, the voluntary cannot merely be the *non-compelled*. Then might it be that a voluntary action is an action that *unconditionally* we need not have done? That is, an action Φ will rate as voluntary if the following *unconditional assertion* is false: 'I had to do Φ.' On this test the aforementioned terrible act performed under the compulsion of extreme conditions emerges as voluntary on the grounds that the compulsion derived from no more than the attendant conditions. The capacity for choice still existed and was exercised.

But a difficulty arises when we come to consider the complementary class of acts. Thus, when on this test is an act involuntary? When the capacity to choose has gone. That is, when 'I had to do Φ' applies unconditionally, which is to say in what might be called *end-of-tether situations*,[2] such as occur when a man hanging onto a spar in the ocean has in the end eventually to let go. Here the element of choice is no longer discoverable: a psychological pressure of a simple non-rational kind is certain in the end to ovewhelm all resistance, thanks to the intensity and duration of the force and the state of the being upon whom that force is brought to bear. Then are these all but wholly unfree acts voluntary? To the extent that the correct description of what happened at the end was 'He let go', rather than 'His fingers slipped', it is certain that they are voluntary. Indeed, they are that *before all else*! After all, why did he let go? Because, despite all that he knew and all else that he wanted, he wanted, indeed longed, overwhelmingly wanted, to let go. That overwhelming psychological pressure, far from robbing him of the capacity to *perform* a voluntary act, robbed him instead of the capacity *not* to perform a voluntary act. Then is the act rational? But how could it be? Only desire finds expression in these acts. Pure force determined them and reason is helpless and completely disarmed. Yet the force, being a longing to act, finds expression in action: in action – despite all else! More, these most extreme members of the species may paradoxically be singled out as paradigmatic examples: they display the type in all its purity. Thus, these supremely voluntary actions enable us to drive a decisive wedge between the concepts of free rational voluntary action and voluntary action, and to

[2] See P. Herbst, 'Freedom of the Will', *Mind* LXVI, 1957, 1–27. Edinburgh: Nelson.

separate out the concept of the voluntary in a pure state. In sum: we have here a non-rational voluntary act that is all but totally unfree. So, despite the unmistakable overtones of 'willingly', 'of his own free will' (etc.), 'voluntary' does not mean 'free', whether it be a conditional or unconditional freedom. The link to freedom is a blind alley.

(c) The extreme generality of the concept of a voluntary action

(1) It should by now be evident that I entertain a very generous conception of the voluntary action. For example, it will be noted that I am in disagreement with those philosophers who – in identifying 'voluntary action' with 'act that is freely performed' or with 'act that is decided upon' – use 'voluntary action' to delimit what I would characterise as sub-categories of the phenomenal kind that I am calling a 'voluntary action'. I believe they each single out a species of a true genus, whereas I think I have named that genus itself. It is the genus willing, or action. Clearly, the difference is not verbal. We differ over a point of substance. At bottom we differ over the existence of a particular kind. I believe, and presumably they do not, that there is one kind of event that encompasses the vastly heterogeneous array of items listed immediately below. That is, the kind action.

(2) According to me, the range of voluntary actions is vast and encompasses such heterogeneous phenomena as the following:

Making a speech

Idle unnoticed tongue-moving during sleep

Looking around automatically and unthinkingly upon hearing one's name called out

Jumping out of the way of a bus

Signing a false and degrading 'confession' at the point of a gun

Typing 'thought' when you meant to type 'though'

Calling out under extreme torture

Writing a love letter

Absent-mindedly bringing a comb from one's pocket to the front-door lock

Etc.

The range is great. And it may be further augmented by the following interesting sub-variety. Namely, by those high-speed deeds in which the subject 'before he knew what he was doing' 'finds' that he has just acted. For example: one turns one's head and sees a snake a few feet away – and finds oneself over by the door! An hiatus in consciousness mediating those two awarenesses, precisely because of the dearth of self-awareness during action.

And the range includes habitual acts like putting one's foot down on the clutch as one changes gear. And skilled acts like driving one's car around the Place de la Concorde. And irrational acts like insulting a policeman. And so on.

In sum: while there are chosen, intentional, decided upon, free, rational, voluntary actions, there exist many other examples of the species. Thus, there also exist habitual, automatic, absent-minded, barely noticed, conditionally compelled, uunconditionally compelled, unintentional, undecided upon, skilled, unskilled, basic, instrumental, constitutive, non-instrumental, non-rational, irrational, mad – voluntary actions!

(d) What is a voluntary action (2)?

What makes the voluntary action voluntary? Surely, as the name suggests, it must be something psychological. But what? Thinking of the vast range of heterogeneous items falling under the heading 'voluntary action', one might understandably despair of finding anything that is at once psychological and common to all examples. For consider. It is not that the voluntary act is an act that is caused by a decision now. Nor that it is caused by a sometime decision. Nor by a rational consideration. Nor by its being not compelled unconditionally. Nor by its being not compelled conditionally or unconditionally. Nor by its having a psychological cause. Nor by its having a desire cause.

Counter-examples exist, as we have seen, to every one of these suggestions. Then is it that the concept of voluntary is malformed? But that can hardly be. Do we not know to include: walking, talking, letting-go-of, looking around, calling out, jumping-out-of-the-way-of? Do we not know to exclude: falling, sleeping, waking, sneezing, shivering, glimpsing, desiring? While problem cases exist for the concept, such as laughter and breathing, we can in the first place give decisive reasons for excluding these phenomena from the class of actions, and in the second place agree on a list of unproblematic examples both of voluntary action and of events falling outside that class. Does not that strongly suggest that we are dealing with a determinate concept?

Then it is at this precise point that the theory of the volition comes forward, offering its services. It will do justice to our intuition that when voluntary action occurs, something that is psychological and common and peculiar to voluntary actions likewise occurs. And to the intuition that the voluntary act is endowed with a distinctive experiential character. And to the intuition that the voluntary action has a distinctive psychological origin. And it offers to do all this even as it does full justice to the evident heterogeneity of the items falling under 'voluntary action'. The solution offered by volitionism to these matters is simple. There is indeed one psychological phenomenon common to all cases of voluntary action. Namely: the volition. And there is a special experiential character to all voluntary actions: the common presence of the volition. And there is a common and peculiar cause of all voluntary actions: the volition. Why not? Volitionism affirms that the willed is caused by the willing-of.

3. THE DILEMMA

(a) A statement of the dilemma

(1) Thus, the volition seems to meet several related demands. First, it matches up to the intuition that, in contra-distinction to the account cast solely in terms of conditionals that tends to be offered by neo-Wittgensteinians, the physical voluntary act Φ of ϕ-making has a *richer inner life* than the mere conjunction of seeming-ϕ and knowledge that an intention to ϕ-make is at this instant directed to a present 'now'. Second, it matches our intuition that this additional richness consists in the occurrence of a *distinctive inner event*. Third, it *brings order* into the bewildering multiplicity of voluntary acts. Fourth, it offers an *explanation and analysis* of the voluntariness of voluntary acts, and so purports to say how it is that, in a sense of 'responsible' that underpins some examples of moral responsibility but is identical with none, a subject can in a pre-eminent familiar sense be said to be responsible for those bodily movements that are voluntarily done and which most volitionists would describe as voluntary actions. (For traditional volitionism claims that the voluntary is voluntary through being caused by a volition.)

This theoretical account is in sharp opposition to another theoretical position, one that in part encompasses the views of Donald Davidson, to the effect that the voluntary act of ϕ-making does not derive its act-status from any event of the kind of an 'act of the will' or 'volition', but comes rather from ϕ's owing its existence – no doubt in suitable regular mechanistic manner – to an intention and presumably also to an act-desire and belief. In sum: volitionism and 'intentional extroversion', as I shall call this latter theory, both accept that the voluntary act Φ of ϕ-making owes its voluntary status to the fact that the origin of ϕ is of a certain kind, but differ significantly regarding the nature of that origin.

(2) 'It is the volition origin that confers the property of voluntariness upon voluntary acts,' say volitionists.

Now the following objection tends to be urged against this theory – an objection which has its counterpart in sense-datum theory – which takes the form of a *dilemma*. If it is the volition origin that makes ϕ voluntary, what of the volition itself? *Is it voluntary?* And here we have the dilemma: viz. (α) or (β)? (α) If we say that the volition is voluntary, then what makes it voluntary? (α1) Another volition origin? But we are then launched on a regress. (α2) Nothing that is of the kind of a volition origin? But how then can it explain the voluntariness of ϕ to say it comes from a volition V, seeing that V's voluntariness has a different explanation? Faced with these unpalatable alternatives, we may opt for the other horn of the dilemma. That is, (β) we may deny that V is voluntary. But this has unattractive consequences. Thus, as an argument is as strong as its weakest link, as a belief is as rational as the least rational of its determining beliefs, so we feel that the voluntariness of some physical phenomenon ϕ must be as voluntary as the closest of its immediate psychological causes. And, in any case, we naturally feel, if V is not itself voluntary, surely V must therefore do no more than 'crop up' in us? Surely, therefore, V must be an event that, not being itself willed, simply 'happens to' us? Then must not the same be said of the ϕ towards which it is directed and which it causes? If V 'crops up' in and 'happens to' us, must not ϕ also? Then what is left of the voluntariness of ϕ? Has not volitionism managed to *reduce away* the voluntariness of the voluntary? Has it not plucked out its very mystery? Does it not commit a sort of Naturalistic Fallacy in locating the voluntariness of the voluntary in an event origin? Indeed, may not volitionism be running its head up against the *irreducibility* of the voluntary?

(b) Towards a suitable statement of volitionism (A): the use of 'action' in the expression 'voluntary action'

(1) This very interesting objection is indicative of problems. And they will take some straightening out. We shall see that to a large degree the problems derive from the terminology in which the most familiar form of volitionism is couched. In short, I do not think the above dilemma exposes a fundamental flaw in the doctrine, and believe that the essentials of volitionism can be retained in a formulation of the theory which is not

vulnerable to the above dilemma-question. The following issues need to be addressed:

A. The use of 'action' in the expression 'voluntary action'
B. The use of 'voluntary' in the expression 'voluntary action'
C. The uses of 'do' in volitional theory
D. Are tryings voluntary events?

I begin with (A). Consider the expression 'voluntary action' as it occurs in the statement of volitionism and of the dilemma. Here we have an expression of a strange kind. I say so, because there are reasons for believing that this particular usage derives from a technical scientific/philosophical usage – but covertly and without acknowledgement. Whereas the use in common speech of terms like 'plutonium' and 'quark' plainly implicates their users in theoretical positions, 'voluntary action' appears on the face of it not to do so. And this is deceptive – as we shall see.

So let us ask: how did we come by the expression 'voluntary action'? I think it was as follows. During the latter half of the nineteenth century certain scientists/philosophers began to use the word 'action' in the following way: it was said to range across (say) leg movements, eyelid movements, hand movements, finger movements, and so on, and to exclude hair movements, ear-lobe movements, blushings, and so on. Then a particular vastly familiar sub-class of these 'actions' was described as comprising 'voluntary actions'. Meanwhile, there were said also to exist 'involuntary actions' along with these 'voluntary actions'. Then what was said to be the relation between these two concepts? Well, the scientist's use of 'involuntary action' was such that leg rise caused by a blow beneath the knee counted as a paradigmatic example. However, in this same usage this event would also be called a 'reflex action'. Then how do these concepts relate? We earlier noted that a 'reflex action' must on this present usage be a bodily phenomenon that can be produced in a 'voluntary action', which happens here to be caused by a 'stimulus' in accordance with a neurologically based regularity. These stipulations are such that involuntary actions and reflex actions cannot be one and the same, for no one could on the above set of definitions describe a 'passive action', such as occurs when someone lifts one's arm, as a reflex of any kind, and yet no one would call it voluntary.

(2) So much for a characterisation of a special usage launched by certain scientists and philosophers. Then what can we say concerning the sense of the word 'action' in this usage? Well, we have seen that it is such that there exist what these people would call 'voluntary actions', which consist in the active bringing about of instances of the kind in question. And this seems

to be a defining property of their term 'action'. In short, the word 'action' is to be explained through a sub-variety of itself! A strange procedure! For if one then goes on to ask, 'A sub-variety of – *what*?', it seems one is landed in an explanatory circle! It is true that the circle can be readily broken and content inserted. This is to be accomplished by instancing examples of the defining sub-variety, and examples of its complement. Thus, walking, talking, kicking, all count as voluntary actions, whereas the following do not: falling through space, leg rise that is caused by a blow beneath the knee, shivering caused by the cold. Nonethless, the oddity of the situation remains.

For a question lingers. For how does the scientist/philosopher know in the first place *which* phenomena to pick as 'actions? It seems to me that it would be disingenuous of him to claim that one *begins* by actually discovering a special kind that is exemplified whenever walking, talking, punching, etc., take place. For these latter phenomena are all examples of what established usage would call 'actions', a fact of which he cannot be unaware and upon which he leans in his definition. It is a sense which long pre-dates the sense scientific volitionists give to 'action', a sense which might at any time over the last thousand years have occurred in such relatively timeless statements as 'The dumb beasts are not morally responsible for their actions.' Then according to this established use, the rise of a leg as a result of a blow beneath the knee would not count as an action, nor would the movement of an arm that was produced by a shove. And again, the scientific volitionist must be aware of these facts.

(3) Thus he hijacks a term which is in common usage, applies it in all the situations in which that term has application, but now applies it also in situations in which it does not. And the scientific volitionist must know that the sense he gives to 'action' cannot be that of common usage. Then why lay hands upon this familiar term, and give it a new sense? And why do so when it is applied in all the situations in which the old term has application – as well as in situations in which it does not? And why define the new term through leaning upon the old? It seems to me that far and away the most likely explanation of all this is that the scientific volitionist entertains the theory of act-constitution which I called 'embellished volitionism'. That is, he believes that (say) the act of walking is identical with the event that in his novel usage is dubbed an 'action' (in this case, the movement of legs). It is said to be a special case of such an event: the case in which the cause of the event is a suitably related volition. What we have here is not so much a 'persuasive redefinition' of 'action' as a usage which introduces a *theory* into the language – without acknowledging the fact. The theory being that the

bodily action, which is to say what is here being called the 'voluntary bodily action', is identical with whatever bodily movement is suitably caused by a volition.

(c) Towards a suitable statement of volitionism (B–D): three further issues

(1) The questions B–D are less pressing, and the discussion correspondingly brief. I begin with (B): what function does 'voluntary' have in the expression 'voluntary action'? Now in common usage this word tends to be applied mostly in statements like 'He signed the confession voluntarily', and here the role of 'voluntary' is to indicate that the act of signing was not performed under duress. Thus, it has a qualificatory function, describing the action in the way adjectives like 'rapid' or 'confident' might do.

By contrast, in the volitionist usage the word has a very different role. This can be shown in two ways. First, by noting that whereas the ordinary use of 'voluntary action' does not single out a fundament mental type, in the special scientific usage this expression is taken to stand for what ordinary usage calls an 'action': in other words, to designate an absolutely fundamental phenomenon, indeed a topic fit for philosophical investigation in a 'philosophy of action'. No such claim could be made for 'rapid action' or 'confident action', or even for 'action performed under duress'.

Secondly, it follows that in so far as the expression 'voluntary action' is used in this special fashion and is at the same time inserted into common usage, we can only legitimately employ the expression if it is understood to have the logical form of a *name*, and not that of a *qualificatory characterisation*. In other words, the logical form of any acceptable use of 'voluntary action' must be akin to that of (say) 'genuine artist' or 'real gold', rather than to 'talented artist' or 'colloidal gold'. Accordingly, if in this special technical usage the word 'voluntary' is used side by side with 'action', so that 'voluntary action' is taken to designate what we all call 'actions', then it is obligatory that it be acknowledged that the word 'voluntary' is otiose in 'voluntary action'.

(2) The next question (C) turns upon a possible ambiguity in the active sense of 'do'. Now there can be no doubt that 'do' has an inactive merely causal sense, as in 'Look what the storm did to the wheat.' But there are in addition *two active senses* of 'do', to be explicated via two types of phenomena each of which we would be said actively to 'do'. Namely: an event that is *actively produced* (e.g. arm rise ϕ, broken window ϕ'), and an event that is the *active producing of* such a ϕ or ϕ' (e.g. act of arm-raising, act of window-breaking). Thus, 'do' in one of its active senses takes the *actively*

produced phenomenon as its object, and in the other active sense takes the *active producing* of the phenomenon as object. Now we have seen that in the scientific usage a 'voluntary act of bringing about ϕ' and 'a voluntarily produced ϕ' are assumed to designate the same event. Meanwhile, one might understandably have assumed that the two active senses of 'do' must designate different phenomena – although this is open to debate. But if it were true, it would follow that, even though almost any stipulation of which we are aware rates walking a voluntary action, we would be contradicting ourselves if we affirmed the following two propositions:

(p1) The leg movements of walkers are voluntary actions.
(p2) Walking is a voluntary action.

Conversely, were we to accept the claims (p1) and (p2), as do scientific volitionists and intentional extroversionists, we should be endorsing a highly contentious theory of the nature of physical action.

(3) The final difficulty, (D), concerns whether the use of 'voluntary' is such that tryings rate as voluntary in character. Now this issue may *seem* stipulative without actually being so. Thus, it may really turn upon the existence or not of a *sui generis* event-type that encompasses both walkings and talkings as well as tryings to open doors (that succeed) and tryings to raise arms (that fail). In any case, it is a philosophical claim; and yet, bearing in mind that a trying to open a door that succeeds can be identical with (say) an act of pushing or kicking the door (open), and that in general we freely choose to try irrespective of success or its absence when we do, it is difficult to deny that tryings must be voluntary events along with walkings and talkings.

But if tryings have the property of being voluntary, and walkings also are voluntary, then for the scientific volitionist the class of voluntary items threatens to divide in two! For *prima facie* trying to raise an arm is a psychological event and a limb movement is not, and it is difficult to believe that a *sui generis* trait, activeness, could encompass such ontological diversity as: psychological *and* bodily non-psychological. Accordingly, if we decide that tryings are voluntary events, as we more or less must, and if we simultaneously assume that the leg movments of walkers are voluntary actions, as has been the general practice in the received versions of volitionism, then we put the concept of voluntariness under intolerable strain.

(4) It is clear that matters have gone too far. To extricate ourselves from these confusions, the first step is to recognise the completely stipulative character of the scientific definition of 'action' whereby the action which occurs when I walk is taken to be the leg movements involved. In other

words, we must recognise that it is an open question whether the class that we populate with walkings and talkings, which we would all call the class of voluntary actions, and the class that we populate with the leg movements and jaw movements that occur when such voluntary actions occur, are one and the same. This important question is to be settled by philosophical rather than stipulative procedures.

(d) Coping with the dilemma

(1) So let us go back to the beginning. Let us see if volitionism can say what it wants to say without endorsing additional theories and without falling foul of the dilemma.

A man voluntarily raises his arm. Then the volitionist states that the reason the act of arm-raising was voluntary is that it was suitably caused by a distinctive internal event, a volition V. A formidable objection is then raised. What of the volition itself? Is the volition also voluntary? If (α) it is voluntary, then why is it? Either (α1) it is because it is itself caused by a further volition V′ whose voluntariness in turn derives from being caused by a V″ . . .; which is an unacceptable vicious regress. Or else (α2) it is voluntary for some reason other than having a suitable V-type cause; which then implies that the principle 'The voluntary acquires its voluntariness through being suitably V-caused' must have its wings clipped, ceases to be analytically explanatory, and even ceases to be explanatory! But if on the other hand (β) the volition is not voluntary, then how can its ϕ effect be voluntary? If V just 'crops up in' or 'happens to' one, why should not the same be true of ϕ? After all, it is V that is the psychological event that is causally most proximate to ϕ. But is not that to say that ϕ is not voluntary?

(2) How can volitionism meet this challenge?

Well, volitionist theory need not take the familiar form in which it is claimed that voluntary acts are voluntary because they are suitably caused by volitions. Volitionism can affirm the gist of what it wishes to say, both without committing itself to additional theories and without endorsing this problematic claim. Indeed, it can do so by making a suitably guarded statement which is cast in the old terminology.

Here is such a guarded statement. A volitionist could say that when a voluntary act Φ of ϕ-making occurs, the voluntariness of that act is due to the fact that ϕ is suitably caused by a volition. Now I can discover no reason why this claim should be thought to lay the volitionist open to the charge of covertly affirming additional ('embellishing') theories of the nature of physical action. And a similar state of affairs exists in the case of the dilemma. For I can discover no reason why the dilemma should be thought to pose a difficulty for a volitionism that takes the above guarded form. It seems to me that the volitionist who makes such a claim should without anxiety affirm the first horn of the dilemma, viz. (α). Thus, he can claim that the volition is itself a voluntary event, and this need involve him in no undue embarrassment. And he can eschew the regress through asserting that the voluntariness of the volition derives from something other than its supposedly having some supposed volition origin. Let me explain how this comes about.

(3) 'When a voluntary act Φ of ϕ-making occurs, then ϕ falls under the description "Event that is such that some voluntary act *is* its bringing about", for the reason that ϕ is suitably caused by a volition V.' Let us take this as a formulation of the more guarded and theory-neutral statement of the volitionist thesis.

Then to the challenge 'Is V voluntary or not?' such a volitionist can, I think, agree that it is. While to the question 'Why is it?', he can avoid the regress through claiming that its voluntariness derives from something other than its having some supposed further volition cause. Why not? For as we have just seen, his guarded claim is not that the voluntariness of all events derives from their having a suitable volition cause, but that the voluntariness of any voluntary act Φ of ϕ-making is due to ϕ's having a suitable volition cause. The fact that a volition is voluntary for a reason other than its having a suitable volition cause, is no exception to this rule. It would be an exception only if the volition's existence entailed the existence of some voluntary act of V-making (which it does not). His analytic account of the voluntariness of such a Φ remains. True, it leaves important questions unanswered, for it fails to provide the necessary and sufficient conditions of voluntary action. Yet the two explanations could be linked were he in addition to argue that volitions were, in a way which could in principle be spelled out, the voluntariness-conferring element of voluntary acts. That would permit him to argue for the existence of some one unifying explanation of the voluntariness of volitions and ϕ-makings that copes with the dilemma. Thus, such a guarded statement of volitionism need not be embarrassed by the dilemma.

In short, provided we put forward a version of volitionism that is neutral with respect to certain contentious theories concerning the constitution of physical action, volitionism finds no embarrassment in the dilemma. Making use of the traditional terminology of 'voluntary', 'action', 'volition', a volitionist could claim that voluntary actions of ϕ-making are voluntary because ϕ is suitably caused by a volition V; he could claim in addition that

V is a voluntary event; and it may or may not be that he will at the same time put forward a theory as to why V's suitably causing ϕ is a necessary and sufficient condition of an act of ϕ-making.

(e) A general account

(1) Then is volitionism true? I think not. Yet the thesis, to be demonstrated in chapter 12, that all actions are identical with some striving or other, brings me close to volitionism – whose error seems to me to consist, not in endorsing the existence of a distinctive psychological event that is an act-of-the-will, but in assuming that the volition is an *inner event* and that it is the *distinct cause* of the willed phenomenon ϕ.

And yet the challenge: 'Is the volition itself voluntary or not?' seemed at the time to put its finger on a painful spot. Why was that? It turns upon the concept of an event's just 'cropping up in' and so 'happening to' one. Thus, we naturally feel that it cannot do justice to the psychological dynamism of wilful action to suppose that ϕs that are willed merely 'crop up' in us. And so we look for something, say a special event interposed between us and such a ϕ, that will tie the willed event more directly to us. But will not that lead to a regress? For will not the special event, like all events, also 'crop up' in and so 'happen to' us? So we shall need another special event, and so on. Therefore, since such a multiplication of events threatens us with regress, the only course seems to be to split apart 'cropping up' and 'happening to'. Accordingly, we at this stage seek to interpose an event of *such* a distinctive character that its cropping up or happening *in* one is never its happening *to* one. Now such an event the volition is supposed to be. And such an event, I submit, the event of *striving* actually is. In the sense of 'happen to one' under consideration, striving never happens to one. Hence its voluntariness looks to be a *de re* essential property and derivative from nothing else – even though the type of its origin is a necessary property. Then for this reason, such a challenge as: 'Whence the voluntariness of the volition?' cuts no ice with striving. The volition, as traditionally understood, is in my opinion a myth, and striving is not. But they each meet the same vital need of providing an event that is so special that, howsoever compelled or mindless or automatic, its happening *in* one is necessarily never its happening *to* one. Striving really has this special character. For striving is willing. Necessarily, willing never happens to one. This, after all, is precisely the distinctive character of striving. This is its essence.

(2) It is natural to attempt to elucidate the sense of 'voluntary' by saying that when something voluntary occurs its agent *does* it, whereas when

something involuntary happens in him then it *happens to* him. But how to further explain these claims? Well, we feel that what he does must stem in some pre-eminent sense from he himself, whereas whatever happens to him comes rather either from outside or else from a part of him. But then how to explicate 'comes from he himself'? That is, how to explicate the voluntariness of the voluntary? Now these are daunting tasks. Indeed, they are perhaps impossible of fulfilment. For we may be running our heads up against the irreducibility of the property of activeness. For it may well be irreducible: that is, it may be a specific or novel event-type that is essentially and inexplicably what it is. Whether or not this is so and the type irreducible, is a matter of moment for philosophy.

Now philosophers differ on this important issue. Volitionists think: when action occurs an irreducible psychological event suitably causes a bodily event like movement; so that volitionists accept the existence of an irreducible willing. Meanwhile intentional extroversionists think: when action occurs a (reducible? irreducible?) non-willing psychological item, an intention and perhaps also a desire and belief, suitably cause a bodily event like movement; so that for them there can be no such thing as the 'irreducible property of voluntariness'. The volitionist, who speaks of 'an act of the will', should think, as the intentional extroversionist must not, that there exists an event that is essentially active or voluntary; as do I. Intentional extroversionists must think that the active or voluntary status of an event necessarily derives from its origin alone, whereas volitionists must allow that the voluntary status of the volition is essential. These are significant differences of opinion.

4. THEORIES OF THE VOLUNTARY

I now set aside the above discussion of the question: In what does the voluntariness of the voluntary consist? (which in any case I suspect is unanswerable). In the present section 4 I shall do no more than characterise the three main theories of bodily action. This is as a preliminary to resolving these issues in chapter 12.

(a) Comparing two theories of the internal scene in voluntary bodily action

There are I believe three theories worth examining on this question, and I endorse the third. Here below are the two theories that I reject, call them (X) and (Y), and the theory which I accept (Z). I begin with (X).

Theory (X)

This theory, Intentionalist Extroversion, which has been widely accepted over the last few decades, has already been sketched earlier. It opts for the following account of voluntary action. We shall suppose we are considering a bodily act Φ of ϕ-making, where ϕ is the bodily event the agent is concerned to bring about. Then according to Theory (X) the following internal phenomena occur:

(i) An intention I to act now
(ii) A desire ('pro attitude') D
(iii) A 'trigger event' T (say, the judgement 'The traffic lights went green')
(iv) A suitable mechanistic causing of ϕ by I and D and T.

Now I think there is no doubt that all these phenomena occur when voluntary physical action occurs. Then the question I am asking is: what, according to Theory (X), is immediately given to the subject in the very moment of action? The following is the answer: a compound of an Intention/Desire/Trigger Event – and a seeming awareness of ϕ. To repeat: intending, desiring, knowing, and *one experience* (of perceptual kind, viz. seeming ϕ). That is, thanks to the occurrence of a 'trigger event', such as present knowledge concerning traffic lights, the intention and desire mutate to the point of having an indexically given object, viz. Φ here-and-now. And then at that point a single experience is said to occur, viz. a perceptual experience. Namely: seeming ϕ. And that is all.

What are we to say of this account of the inner life of bodily action? That it is a tough-minded, extrovert, meagre picture that we are being offered, and that it is strongly counter-intuitive. For I think we very naturally are inclined to say that, over and above these phenomena, and far more centrally significant than them all, is the occurrence of a single distinctive psychological event of the type of *willing*.

For this we are not given on Theory (X). Instead, we are offered four separate items: intending, desiring, knowing, and seeming ϕ. Now these few disparate phenomena do not 'stitch together', let alone do so as parts of some single *psychological event*. And, bearing in mind that the perceptual experience seem-ϕ occurs in passive as well as in active situations, the one experience that on Theory (X) is said to take place on the inner stage of voluntary action is by no means peculiar to active situations. Indeed, none is. No experience that is distinctive to voluntary action is said to occur. All that is supposedly phenomenally special to voluntary action is the intention state's mutating to the point of having a here-and-now indexically given object – which is in any case a *cause* of the act and thus a separate phenomenon from it. In sum: the experience of voluntary agency must boil down to an experience of a perceptual kind. This supposedly is all that happens experientially. And it is surely an unacceptable account of the experience of agency.

Theory (Y)

Volitionism, by contrast, offers an over-rich and even introverted picture of the inner life of voluntary bodily action. For volitionism affirms that, over and above all that Theory (X) allows, there also occurs a distinctive psychological willing experience, which is set in the 'inner world' (in the sense already specified). In addition, this inner event, the 'volition' or 'act of the will', is said to be causally sandwiched between intending-now and ϕ, and by implication also between intending-now and the activation of the motor-system that culminates in the goal of limb movement ϕ. Finally, the volition is understood to be essentially active in character. Such an experience supposedly occurs whenever voluntary action occurs.

Thus, (Y) asserts that an 'inner' psychological experience that is essentially active occurs whenever a voluntary bodily action occurs, assumes that this event is distinctive to action, and claims that it sets the motor-system in action as far as the goal phenomenon ϕ. By contrast, (X) must suppose that no event that is essentially active occurs when we voluntarily act, and must furthermore assume that no psychological event-experience that is distinctive to voluntary action occurs when we voluntarily act. A major difference of opinion.

(b) The third theory (Z)

(1) I hope soon to demonstrate the errors in both of the above two theories. The third theory (Z), which I accept, is closer to (Y) than to (X). Now (Z) accepts the existence of the entire gamut of items listed in (X)'s inventory of the inner 'given' in voluntary action. Its disagreements with (X) are positive rather than negative. For it joins with (Y) in affirming the existence, whenever voluntary bodily action occurs, of an experience that is *essentially active*. In short, it accepts the existence of the contentious 'act of the will' that (Y) affirms, but differs from (Y) in the characterisation of, and the causal properties of, that event. Thus, Theory (Z), while agreeing that the act of the will is an experience, fails to locate it in the 'inner world'; and while agreeing that the act of the will is the effect of desire, intention, and any trigger event, and agreeing also that it causally explains the occurrence of the limb movment ϕ, fails to posit it as the distinct cause either of the activation of the motor-mechanism or of ϕ. For Theory (Z) supposes that ϕ is the surface tip of an event that reaches all the way back into the brain – and

mind! Namely: the act of the will. Now another name for this act of the will is 'strive'. And other names are 'try', 'have a shot at', 'attempt', 'do'. And another, on occasions of success, is 'Φ'.

In sum: (Z) agrees with (Y) as against (X) over the existence of an essentially active experiential event, an act of the will, that occurs whenever voluntary bodily action occurs. But it differs from (Y) in failing to locate this psychological event in the 'inner world', and in refusing to drive a causal wedge between the act of the will and the activation of the motor-mechanism. This is because (Z) supposes that the act of the will and the voluntary bodily action are one and the same. For (Z) is a *dual aspect* theory. Here, below, is a summary account of the situation according to this theory. The case for the theory forms the subject matter of the immediately succeeding chapter, 12.

5. THE TRUTH VALUE OF VOLITIONISM

Is volitionism right or wrong according to the dual aspect Theory (Z)? Right if it restricts itself to the claim that whenever we voluntarily act there occurs an experiential psychological event, an immediate effect of act-desire and intention, that is necessarily of the type act of the will, and that causally explains the occurrence of willed ϕ. Wrong if it adds that that event occurs in the inner world, is cause of ϕ, and cause of the activation of the motor-mechanism; and *a fortiori* wrong also if it appends to the latter claim the further claim that ϕ is the voluntary act (e.g. walk). Then since it is either the former or both of the latter two theses that travel familiarly under the name 'volitionism', volitionism is wrong. Yet since the two false theories entail the first true theory, which intentional extroversion resists, it is worth emphasising that the false theories encompass this significant and detachable truth.

(a) Attempting to salvage volitionism

Indeed, if Theory (Z) is correct, volitionism is not so far from the truth. Relatively minor adjustments will put it right. Thus: first, delete the unnecessary embellishment that ϕ is the voluntary act (e.g. walk); second, delete the requirement that the psychological event be set in the inner world; third, make the volition the causal explanation of, without being the distinct cause of, the actively 'done' bodily movement ϕ.

Accordingly, when a voluntary act Φ of ϕ-making occurs, the amended claim will be that event ϕ is voluntarily 'done' because

(i) the event ϕ owes its existence suitably causally to an event V
(ii) which is psychological
(iii) of type 'act of the will'
(iv) ϕ being the teleological-goal event in the activation of a motor-mechanism for the production of ϕ events.

This statement is, I think, correct, and comes close to traditional volitionism.

(b) The inner/outer split

But one can be too indulgent to volitionism. While volitionism has the great virtue of staking a claim for the reality of the phenomenon of willing, we ought not to lose sight of the fact that the theory suffers from the major defect of introducing a *mind/body split* into physical action. For as it stands this theory provides us with no reason for giving it the credit of interpreting the volition phenomenon that they postulate, not just as an experience, but as non-interior in kind. Quite the reverse, in fact. Not only does the traditional version of volitionism offer a theory of the will that is one-aspect in character, not only are we told that bodily willing occurs in the inner world, but we have no reason for supposing that they do not construe it as ontologically on a par with (say) the active evocation of mental imagery! After all, Locke's claims suggest as much. Such an interiorist volitionism will be closely examined and (as I see the matter) found wanting in the immediately succeeding chapter, 12.

And it is in any case all highly counter-intuitive. Striving to move a limb seems altogether more bodily and less 'inner' than is trying to evoke a mental image. In our bodily striving moments we seem to reach out beyond our minds and inner world in and through our limbs. We seem actively to appear in the very midst of physical nature. The difference between trying to produce a bodily movement and trying to evoke a mental image seems to lie, not merely in the ontological status of their object, but repercussively in the very phenomena themselves. These two modes of willing look to be different in their very natures. If we could, so to say, get no 'nearer' to our limbs when we will their movement than when we image such movement, there would be a significant sense in which we would be locked within our minds and split off from our bodies. That split almost all forms of volitionism endorse and I reject. These claims I now attempt to justify.

CHAPTER 12

The proof of a dual aspect theory of physical action

The aim of this chapter is to offer arguments for the truth of a dual aspect theory of physical action, where 'physical action' stands for acts which are bodily in character, whether instrumental or 'basic'. Thus, an internal act like phantasising that sets one's pulse racing would not on this usage rate as a physical act, whereas an act of running which has the same effect would be a physical act. Then in what follows, 'Φ' stands for the 'basic' act of -making, 'ϕ' stands for the limb movement that is immediately 'done', and 'S(Φ)' for a striving or trying or attempting to do such an act. Meanwhile, I use 'ψ' to stand for the ontological property psychologicality, and sometimes also use 'ϕ' to stand for the ontological property physicality (so that 'ϕ' is ambiguous, though not I think confusingly so). Then in attempting to substantiate my main dual aspect thesis, I shall try to demonstrate the following claims.

1. Whenever we perform any physical action, we are immediately aware of trying or striving or attempting to do some act or other.
2. That trying or striving is an event, and is of psychological ontological status.
3. That trying is distinct from and non-identical with present intending.
4. No striving that is a truly 'inner' event can be visible in a limb movement that is the distinct effect of that striving.
5. Physical instrumental tryings are sometimes physical actions.
6. Physical instrumental tryings are psychological phenomena.
7. No new ontological level 'ψ-ϕ' that is constituted out of the ontological levels ψ and ϕ exists.
8. Only four theories of physical act constitution are worth considering: the theories critically assessed below in 9–12.
9. For the basic act Φ of ϕ-making, the falsity of the theory: Causes S(Φ) ϕ & Φ = S(Φ).
10. For the basic act Φ of ϕ-making, the falsity of the theory: Causes S(Φ) ϕ & Φ = ϕ.

11. For the basic act Φ of ϕ-making, the falsity of the theory: Causes $S(\Phi)$ ϕ & Φ encompasses $S(\Phi)$ and ϕ.

12. For the basic act Φ of ϕ-making, the truth of the theory: $\sim$ Causes $S(\Phi)$ ϕ, and Φ encompasses $S(\Phi)$ and ϕ, and $\Phi = S(\Phi)$.

Each of these claims will be defended in the corresponding sections 1–12.

1. WHENEVER WE PHYSICALLY ACT WE ARE IMMEDIATELY AWARE OF TRYING OR STRIVING OR ATTEMPTING OR 'HAVING A SHOT AT' DOING SOME ACT OR OTHER

(1) Suppose that a man is seated in a physiologist's laboratory, and that scientists are investigating muscular and postural electrical phenomena in him. And let us assume that the subject has wires attached to his body at various points. Let us also suppose that on a number of occasions he has raised his right arm in obedience to an order, and on each occasion done so without difficulty. Now suppose that on the tenth occasion O_{10} the scientists turn out the light, and ask the subject to raise his right arm under these visually novel conditions. And let us assume that at that time t_{10} he obeys that order and raises his arm.

At this point the scientists turn on the light, and advance highly convincing arguments apparently demonstrating, first that his right arm had not moved at all, and second that at that time (t_{10}) they had (by the use of a special apparatus) succeeded in reproducing the proprioceptive experiences associated with right-arm rise. Indeed, let us suppose that here and now, in the lighted room, they accomplish by the use of that apparatus all that they had just claimed. Thus, upon the subject's now receiving the order to raise his right arm, his arm seems proprioceptively – though not visually – to be moving when he attempts to obey that order, and in fact budges not an iota. Note that we are assuming that on the first occasion O_{10} in the dark, when the subject successfully raised his arm, the experimentalists had *not* put the apparatus to use. Finally, let us also assume that at this stage of the experiment the subject does not know any of these facts.

(2) What would a rational subject, in a rational enough frame of mind, believe and say, looking back on occasion O_{10}, supposing him *not* to know that the apparatus had *not* been used at t_{10}, i.e. supposing him still to believe he had then been the victim of an illusion? There seems little doubt that he would believe and say something like: 'Nevertheless I did all that I could to obey', or 'I tried to move it', or 'I made an attempt to do so.' And here he would be referring, not to a negative state of affairs whereby at time

t_{10} a firm intention had apparently failed to cause arm-moving, but to a 'positivity', viz. an *event* that owed its existence to that firmly held intention to move the arm there and then. As he expresses it, at time t_{10} he *did* all that he could manage to do at that moment. Thus, it is not that nothing seemed to him to occur at t_{10}. On the contrary, this subject would be in a position to claim to know, and know with authority and in an immediate manner, not only that an active event had *seemed* to occur, but that an active event had *actually* occurred. This would be the claim most people would make in these unusual circumstances.

At this juncture the subject is informed of the full facts of the case, including the fact that on occasion O_{10} he had succeeded in raising his arm, as well as the fact that the apparatus had not then been used. Then what are we, and what is he to think, concerning the active event to which at the later time (call it t_{11}) he had referred? Do the overall facts of the case prove that event to have been mythical? Surely not. For surely at that later time t_{11} he *knew*, and with authority, that he had at t_{10} been immediately aware of an active event which may perfectly well be entitled 'an attempt', 'a shot at', 'a doing of some kind or another' – at the very least. At time t_{11} he *remembered* such an event: he remembered that *experience*. And this memory cannot have been erased through discovery of these facts. Thus, suppose that for some reason active occasion O_{10} had mattered much to this subject, and that he had taken great care to raise his arm as slowly as he could (etc.). Would he not know both with authority and immediately that the event to which he referred had actually occurred? I do not see how one could dispute the fact. In short, it seems certain that on occasion O_{10} he was immediately aware of an active event.

Then what holds of active occasion O_{10} must hold of all physical actions. We have merely to complicate the situation, adding visual illusions to proprioceptive illusions, to duplicate the above situation in the universal case. I conclude that whenever anyone performs a physical action, they must be immediately aware (in a very strong sense) of doing something or another, a sense which is not corrigible by the actual events in his bodily extremities. The subject must be immediately aware of an active event. In short, an immediately given active event must occur whenever we physically act.

(3) Here below is another path via which one may reach the same conclusion. Rather than making use here of a merely seeming case of act-illusion of the kind we have been discussing – a delusion of an illusion as one might say, I shall appeal to a genuine act-illusion. The example employed has

the advantage of dispensing with the usual somewhat wearisome resort to laboratories and mythical scientists, etc.

The following situation, which would of course be a great rarity, is nonetheless a genuine possibility. One intends to perform a simple act at time t_1: say, raise one's right arm. Time t_1 arrives, and one seems to one-self to have carried out one's intention: the arm rises, and all appears as it should. However, what actually happened was this. At t_1 and at a point p_1 somewhere along the motor-path leading from the cerebral motor-centre to arm rise, the neural message 'gave out'; meanwhile, and wildly coinci-dentally, at that same instant t_1 a chance event occurred at a later point p_2 along the same motor-path, which triggered into operation the remain-der of the motor-mechanism, culminating in the event of arm rise. In such a bizarre coincidental situation the subject must surely be unaware of the fact that he had not succeeded in raising his arm. Then it can I think be safely assumed that when he later on discovers the actual facts of the case, he would at that later point know for certain that at the earlier time t_1 an active 'doing' event had occurred of which he was immediately aware. And so on, and so forth, leading to the conclusion that all bodily acts are accom-panied by immediately given active events. The basis of that inference being, that there is no difference between the psychological situation obtaining on this occasion of failure and in a normal situation of successful bodily action.

2. THE 'DOING' PHENOMENON OF WHICH THE SUBJECT IS IMMEDIATELY AWARE IS AN EVENT OF PSYCHOLOGICAL ONTOLOGICAL STATUS

(a) *The epistemology of the active event*

(1) That the phenomenon in question was an event seems obvious enough. After all, the various descriptions which are available to the subject, such as 'On occasion O_{10} I did something or other at t_1', 'At t_1 I acted', 'At t_1 my will was active', are descriptions of events. And the phenomenon has a unique location in time. And it has an event-cause, e.g. a decision to 'act here and now at the time of this order'. And so on.

What must now be demonstrated is, the psychological ontological status of this event. In doing so, I must show that two main counter-theses are false. They are, (i) that the event is ontologically borderline between psychological and merely physical, and (ii) that the event is a merely physical event immediately causally sandwiched between psychological phenomena.

(2) The first relevant consideration is, the epistemological relation in which the subject stands to the aforementioned active event. This is immediate, and mentalistically immediate. Now there are degrees of epistemological strength within this latter category. They are exemplified in order of strength by: sensations, beliefs, and experiences; each of which in their own way falls short of perfection. Thus, sensations need in the first place to be noticed and can in any case elude awareness; beliefs and suchlike non-experiential phenomena can occasionally elude one; but the only epistemological frailties in the case of experiences seem to be of the kind of self-deception. Clearly, experiences provide us with the strongest variety of epistemological access amongst mentalistically immediately given psychological phenomena. Then into which of these three groups should we place the epistemological relation in which the subject stood to the active event immediately disclosed in the above experimental situation on occasion O_{10}? Which of the three brands of mentalistic immediacy was exemplified on occasion O_{10}?

There is much to suggest that it falls into the experiential category. Indeed, chapter 16 marshalls a strong case for the view that the active event actually *is* an experience. I shall barely mention those reasons here. But it is worth noting that the event of 'doing something or other' would find a mention if, shortly after the experiment, the subject was engaged in cataloguing the contents of his 'stream of consciousness' over that relatively brief interval of time in the laboratory on occasion O_{10}. Therefore the epistemological relation must *either* be of the kind encountered with sensations *or* of the kind found in the case of experiences. Either way a mentalistically immediate epistemological relation would be realised, a relation reserved for mental phenomena. And that suffices for my present purposes.

(b) Ontological status

(1) Apart from the epistemological properties of the 'doing something or other', and the decisive consideration that the event is of the type experience, which receives strong argumentative support in chapter 16, the causal properties of the event likewise point to its being a psychological event. Thus, this 'doing' emerged from the psychological causes intention, belief, and act-desire. And it did so with mentalistic immediacy. And one knows with mentalistic immediacy that the event emerged from these mental determinants.

So much for origins. Then the same is true of effects. For one knows with mentalistic immediacy of the occurrence of this event, and this knowledge must have its source, not merely in present intention and act-reasons, but surely also in the event itself.

(2) In sum, we have taken note of the following properties of the 'doing something or other' event which was immediately experienced on occasion O_{10}, and which is generally present in active situations. Namely: having an immediate mental cause; a cause whose type is *a priori* determined in advance as act-desire/intention; being mentalistically immediately known of; being mentalistically immediately causally sandwiched between other mental phenomena (viz. intention/knowledge); and on top of these considerations the quite decisive fact of being an experience. When we conjoin these properties with the fact that the interior version of the same event-type, such as 'doings' of the kind of trying to remember, are themselves experiential and psychological, the case for adjudging the 'doing something or other' to be of psychological ontological status seems overwhelming. No arguments exist for classifying it as ontologically borderline between psychological and merely physical, let alone for characterising it as a merely physical event that is immediately causally sandwiched between mental phenomena. It strikes me as near truistic that this event was a psychological event.

3. THE TRYING IS NON-IDENTICAL WITH AND DISTINCT FROM PRESENT INTENDING

(1) The arguments so far assembled point to the conclusion that whenever we perform a physical act of limb-moving, a psychological event of an active kind occurs which one might on the one hand describe as a trying/striving/attempting/etc., but could as readily describe as an act of the will. Now the usual conception of an act of the will is of a psychological event of an active kind which is psychologically irreducible: a distinctive 'original' of the mind in the sense in which desires and thoughts (etc.) are 'originals'; and this interpretation will generally be built into the above theory of action. Then whereas some philosophers will reject each element in such an ('act of the will') theory, some others might endorse the existence of phenomena which only partially meet the above requirements. This section examines one such theoretical position.

The theory I shall now examine and reject accepts that whenever we act an immediately given trying/striving/attempting/etc. event occurs, but claims of that striving that it is the intention 'going on' or 'continuing' into the moment of action. Thus, it *identifies* striving-'now'-to-Φ with intending-'now'-to-Φ. I shall describe this doctrine as 'Intentionalism', because the most natural way of understanding this identification is that the striving is 'nothing but' intending-'now'. In my opinion, such a theory constitutes a form of reductionism within the mind, a depopulating by one, an hegemony of the intention and indeed of the intellect. However, I shall mostly be offering reasons why the simpler theory which merely identifies striving-'now'-to-Φ with intending-'now'-to-Φ must be false. If this theory is false, so too must be Intentionalism.

(2) Here below I set out reasons why the latter theory must be false.

(i) The theory telescopes two fundamental psychological concepts/phenomena into one, thus obliterating an incontestable distinction. 'Intending-now' does not *mean* 'attempting now'.

(ii) The one is a practical commitment to a 'doing now' (i.e. to an active event taking place in the present), the other is just such an active event. How could these two be one? How could present committal-to *be* the presently committed-to?

(iii) Telescoping trying-'now' into intending-'now' constitutes an obliteration of willing, a destruction of the activeness of acting. It strands us in a frozen mental scene where commitment reigns but loses its object – and nothing moves.

(iv) Neither intending nor striving can change identity, and *a fortiori* cannot do so because their time-determination is the present instant.

(v) The two types – intending and striving – are the essential and thus also the individuating types of the two phenomena involved. Then how could these phenomena retain identity if the two types and phenomena coalesce? There are no such *individuating kinds* as strive-intend or intend-strive.

(vi) The theory that intending-'now' *is* striving-'now', is, I suggest, unintelligible, precisely because it destroys a distinction essential to the very content of these concepts. Thus, which of the two headings is supposed to determine the character of the phenomenon they describe? Does the theory imply that intendings-'now' are *active* phenomena? Or does it rather imply that strivings-'now' are *inactive*? After all, strivings are active and intendings inactive. As it stands, the theory is incoherent.

(vii) If the incoherence is resolved by telescoping trying-now into intending-now, rather than by simply fusing the two phenomena/concepts, what is left of the concept of trying-now? This is a concept we cannot conceivably jettison.

(viii) Are continuous intendings-'now' supposed to constitute an activity? If so, *which* activity? That of abiding by one's intention? But while there is such a continuity or even process, there is no such activity. *Ergo*: it is not striving.

(3) So much for the differentiation of the *concepts* involved. I turn now to the differentiation of *properties*.

(ix) Tryings are experiences: they occupy at any moment a determinate part of the limited attentive space available to us. By contrast, intendings are not experiences. Thus, at any moment I harbour many intentions, but these intentions do not jostle for attentive space in the manner of experiences. True, I do not at any particular moment harbour many intendings-'now', but the fact remains that one kind is an experience-kind and the other not.

(x) Consider an occasion of total act-failure in which limb movement (ϕ) is taking place – but for the wrong causes – and unbeknown to the subject – while a striving process ($S\Phi$) continues over that time. What is *occupying the attention* of the subject during $S\Phi$? Merely proprioceptive experience? Well, let us suppose that he *concentrates* upon what he is doing. Then what could that consist in? Merely proprioceptive attending? Such an account omits what I earlier described as the Prince Hamlet of the situation, viz. an experience which is active in nature. 'Concentrating upon one's trying' means bringing that active process into centre stage in the Attention and keeping it there.

(xi) When in the situation of total act-failure in which limb movement ϕ happens for the wrong causes, and one afterwards affirms that despite failure one nonetheless tried to Φ, one is singling out nothing so *negative* as the conjunction of an intention and the absence of its usual expression: one refers to something active, and positive, and experiential, and failing, and psychologically immediately given.

(xii) Thus, trying/attempting/etc. is essentially an active phenomenon, for it is something which we engage in or *do*. Intending is not, and irrespective of whether it is directed to 'now' acting. We cannot be *occupied* in intending.

(xiii) Tryings succeed or fail, intendings do not. And when we say that a trying failed, we are referring to a 'positive' rather than a 'negative' failing. That is, we do not mean that we *did not* Φ. While what we assert implies such a claim, we are affirming of an *active event* that it did not achieve a desired status.

(4) Meanwhile amongst the properties of tryings are the following significant relational properties.

(xiv) Tryings are *caused* by present intendings. This is evidenced in the fact that we have control over our tryings: we can stop trying, resume, try hard, try less hard, change the object of trying in some respect, and so on. These phenomena are the result of the intention standing superintendingly over the deed: they are manifestations of its *causal power*.

(xv) We frequently simultaneously intend to try *and* do intentionally try. These phenomena are invariably two and distinct, related as both cause and effect *and* as directed phenomenon and object. Then let us assume that we intend to try to move a limb that is slowly recovering, and that we are not very hopeful of success. Let us also assume the truth of the theory I am criticising: namely, that the trying-now is identical with the intending-now. Then what can be the *object* of the driving intention? Can it be that one now intends that one now intends to move or try to move the limb? Can one *intend to intend*? This absurdity is one of the penalties of telescoping concepts whose content internally depends upon the reality of the distinction. As we have noted, intentions take actions and strivings as object – not intentions.

4. NO INTERIOR STRIVING COULD BE VISIBLE IN LIMB MOVEMENTS

(a) Visibility

To see an item is to become visually acquainted with the several 'visibilia' (as I shall call them) that constitute its visual appearance, e.g. its colour, brightness-value, 3D shape. In a decent case of seeing these will all be on view, together with relational properties like direction, depth, 3D movement, etc. But objects can be seen when almost none of these properties are visible, e.g. a flock of birds appearing as a speck in the sky. All that we see here is (a) expanse > 0, (b) $\pm$ brightness, and (c) directional location at some distance. In short, we merely see 'something of some width, of $\pm$ brightness, "there" some way off' (pointing). Then apart from depth, I do not think we can shorten this short list any further, for remove any one item and you remove them all. Therefore $\pm$ brightness & expanse > 0 & 'there (perhaps some way off)', constitutes the ultimate minimum in the way of visibilia. After that – invisibility! (The fate of the wind – because neither bright nor dark, of the germ – because too small to have visual expanse, of the future – because nowhere.) All particular appearances, A1, A2, A3, . . . approximate towards this degenerate case as they are denuded of visibilia.

Now when an object is seen it must *look to be* as its visual appearance *shows it to be*. The object cannot at once be seen and retreat incognito as a mystery behind its visibilia, for in seeing objects through seeing visibilia we see them as so endowed. And however few visibilia may appear, we cannot see something without setting eyes upon some of its visibilia. Accordingly, if an object is visible it must at least look to be: bright or dark or in between, & somewhere, & of some expanse. I mention this fact because, as we shall discover in a moment, it can function in certain cases as a sort of simple litmus-test of visibility.

(b) Guidelines for distinguishing the visible from the invisible

(1) That which is invisible may at the same time be eminently detectable by visual means. Thus, while orange light is visible, ultra-violet light is not, and this property of ultra-violet light is perfectly consistent with the fact that whenever that radiation strikes some particular chemical substance the latter emits orange light. Even though we can *visually tell* that ultra-violet light impinges at some point, the radiation itself (which can scarcely be an orange ultra-violet!) remains invisible. Likewise the wind that scatters the autumn leaves. And the solitary α-particle causing a white track of tiny water droplets in a Wilson cloud chamber. And the heat that makes an iron bar glow in the dark. And the itch that is causing the dog to scratch. And the snap decision to vote 'Yes' that caused Smith's arm to suddenly rise. In a word, there is much that is invisible that can yet be visually detected in a trice. The concept of seeing easily accommodates such strains. Thus, we distinguish seeing-*of* from seeing-*that*; and seeing-x-*occur*-in-y from seeing-*that*-x-when-x; etc. So when I see the dog scratch, I see the *dog* and see *that* he itches and see him *as* itching *when* he itches – but I do not see the *itch*; and will do so only if Physicalism is true and the right brain event discoverable. Now it is not in some strained sense of 'see' that this is true: it is so in *the*, public perceptual, commonest, and certainly central sense of the term. It is simply and bluntly true that orange light and blushes are visible, and that ultra-violet light and feelings of embarrassment are not.

Then what distinguishes the actually visible from the merely visually detectable? What rules govern the attribution of visibility? How is it for example that we can see a nebula in seeing an image in a telescope but cannot see the wind in seeing the swirling autumn leaves? Why is it that we can see a skin diver who is covered from head to foot but not an α-particle as it 'visibly' crosses a Wilson cloud chamber? Well, seeing is already from the start mediated by light and sensation, and in certain cases that mediation is extensible. These cases are of two kinds, exemplified by the nebula on the one hand and the diver on the other. Namely: those cases wherein an existent appearance is transported, and those wherein an appearance is borrowed.

The first cases occur when, thanks to the reliable transportation through space of existent visibilia, an appearance that physical circumstances have rendered inaccessible is reconstituted once again at a new site. It is in this way that we permit seeing to be via periscopes, mirrors, telescopes, and microscopes. Thus, in all these cases it is as if the viewer mutated spatially on a kind of 'magic carpet' – rose, turned, went and grew, went and shrank – at the end of which one recreates the normal viewing situation wherein one makes the visual acquaintance of the visual appearance of the in any case visible item. For these 'extensions of the senses' *recover* rather than confer appearances.

But the second class of cases consists of those in which a mediator *shares* its appearance with a hitherto invisible item, and here an appearance is actually conferred upon what might otherwise be without an appearance of any kind. In these cases we validly transfer the visibilia of the mediator onto the mediated, thanks to the reliable preservation in the mediator of visibilium-type properties that causally derive in the first place from the mediated. As an example, properties like shape and position, which must obtain in but need not be visible in the mediated prior to mediation. Take the case of a perfectly clear invisible block of glass that is rendered visible through being covered by a coat of fine blue dust. Here the blue of the dust transfers onto the glass because the dust and glass surface spatially coincide and the glass surface causes dust-adherence. In short, regularities linking visibilium-type properties rather than actual visibilia, first in the mediator and then in the mediated, play the central part in licensing the transfer of visibilia from mediator onto mediated. Once these requirements are met, the visual appearance of the mediator *is* that of the mediated.

And so we must not say, 'The invisible glass is made visible through utilising an appearance that does not belong to it', but 'The invisible glass is made visible through acquiring an appearance that belongs to something else.' In short, the dust's appearance *becomes* simultaneously the glass's appearance, for nothing can 'falsely' be made visible. The appearance is shared – without being divided.

(2) Then under these conditions the glass *actually looks to be* blue and round and 'there' (where rightly or wrongly it shows). As we have already remarked, when an object is visible it looks to be as its appearance shows it to be. This is a fundamental truth of visual perception. Indeed, it is a principle of kinds. That principle can help us to delimit the visible from the invisible, merely through appeal to our unstructured knowledge of whether or not an object looks to be a certain way, without requiring of us that we explicitly invoke the rules governing the divide.

Thus, the nebula that shows as a point of light in the sky actually looks to be bright, of some expanse, 'there' some fairish way off. And the diver looks black ('a dark figure') and human-shaped ('like a man') and to be entering the water ('there'). By contrast, the α-particle looks neither white, nor thread-shaped, nor of some expanse, and is in many ways like a distant tank crossing a desert, throwing up vast clouds of sand as it goes, which visibly signal the object's presence but wholly conceal it from view: plainly a 'seeing-*that*' in the absence of a 'seeing-*of*'. (If it were a seeing-of, *what words would be left* if we were actually to glimpse the tank itself amidst the swirling sand?) Then it is because the α-particle looks neither white nor thread-shaped that we class this vastly smaller than an invisible virus item as invisible. And so it is with the other examples of invisibility. The autumn wind that swirls the golden leaves does not itself look golden or serpentine-shaped. The ultra-violet light does not look orange. The heat in the iron bar does not look red. And the tank looks neither sandy coloured nor 100 metres high!

(c) The visibility status of supposedly internal strivings

My immediate aim is to show that truly internal psychological phenomena like itches and decidings cannot *visually appear* in their bodily expression. Clearly, those bodily movements cannot mediate as do telescopes and mirrors; for if the internal item has a visual appearance of its own prior to mediation, doubtless it is a brain-ish appearance which is of course not reduplicated in limb movements. Accordingly, the movements would have to mediate through conferring an appearance not possessed before, i.e. mediate as did the blue powder or the diver's suit. (Whereupon if Physicalism is true the internal item, a visual Jekyll and Hyde, would have two grossly dissimilar visual appearances!) But either way the psychological item would have to *share the visibilia* of its mediator, and therefore in these respects *look to be* precisely as the mediator looks to be, e.g. pale/moving/'there' (etc.). Then this makes it certain that itches cannot become visible in the scratching movements they cause. For if they did the itch would actually *look* as the arm movements look! and look to range over a space that encompasses the space of the arm movements! The absurdity of these suggestions merely corroborates the fact that scratching, in correlating with no more than *quale*, and hence with no visibilium-type property of the itch, lacks the law-like base that would license transfer of the visual appearance of the arm movement onto the internal event.

The same is true of the decision-to-vote-'yes'-by-now-raising-my-arm. No visibilium-type property of arm movement associates with a visibilium-type property of the decision. And can anyone seriously believe that this internal event *looks* as the arm movement looks, or looks to range over a space that encompasses the arm movement? Then all that we say of itch and decision holds equally well of bodily strivings – *if they are internal.* Now it is my belief that many physical instrument strivings (like trying to start the car by turning a crank) are visible. And that basic physical acts (like arm-moving) are also visible. Indeed, I believe these 'two' events are often the same event. Then the point of the above discussion is to show that if trying to start the car by turning the crank, and moving an arm, are visible phenomena, they cannot be internal events; while if they are internal events, they must be invisible (until we see the brain phenomena they may be). Trite and obvious these conclusions may be, but they are of considerable importance to the ensuing discussion.

5. PHYSICAL INSTRUMENTAL TRYINGS ARE SOMETIMES PHYSICAL ACTIONS

(1) I turn now to a discussion of instrumental trying, for an elucidation of its nature sheds great light on the problem of the constitution of physical action.

First, a word on *instrumental action.* The Anscombe–Davidson theory, which I endorse for reasons I elaborate later, identifies the instrumental act (Φ') of ϕ'-making with the whole act-event (Φ) that causes ϕ'. A simple comparison will help here. Thus, while being a red light is not being a signal, for these are different properties, what has the property of being a red light may also have the property of being a signal; and clearly the latter property is dependent on and partly in virtue of the former. Analogously, while being an arm-raising is not being a signalling, what is an arm-raising may also be a signalling; and the latter property depends on and is partly in virtue of the former. After all, instrumental act-content is determined merely through an act's effects, so the instrumental act-heading must be extensional, inessential, and secondary to some primary and essential active heading. Now if we provisionally define 'basic act' as 'act that is the immediate willing effecting of some desired bodily ϕ', then 'basic' and 'instrumental' must be opposed, and being basic or instrumental will be description-relative traits. Most non-interior acts are identical with some basic act, and most basic acts are identical with some instrumental act. Then note that some act-headings can be used basically *or* instrumentally, intentionally *or* unintentionally, physically *or* mentally, e.g. 'arm-raising'. Thus, I might basically raise my arm, or raise one arm with the other, or cause my arm to rise by a mental act which triggers an apparatus which effects arm movement, all of which would count as acts of the kind arm-raising. So much for instrumental action.

(2) From our present point of view, *instrumental trying* is a much more significant phenomenon. This event differs from instrumental action in that it must be intentional, done for 'one's' act-type reasons, and intentionally directed beyond itself. Since it may *wholly* fail, there must be a good sense in which it need not be an action; yet it is an event that expresses act-desire, that is intended, and that is 'done', and I shall capture this syndrome of features in a merely provisional manner by saying that the phenomenon is 'active', an exercise of the will. Finally, it is directed beyond itself to an anticipated-as-possible power-line-of-the-moment, in order to lead thereby to the desired goal-phenomenon. Then my present concern is with the make-up or the *constitution* of this intentional, rationalised, 'active', intentionally directed phenomenon. And I am concerned with *physical* instrumental strivings; that is, strivings that can be directed to either merely physical or else to psychological phenomena, but that must themselves be of the same ontological type as ordinary bodily and manipulative strivings and unlike mental strivings such as trying to remember or to quicken one's pulse.

What is the constitution of a trying to start the car wherein one turns a crank, of a trying to chop down a tree wherein one swings an axe, of a trying to ring the doorbell through pressing the bell? Now the probable definition of instrumental striving is this: to try to do an instrumental act (Φ') of ϕ'-making is to do something 'active', θ, out of a desire to do Φ' and a belief that θ might cause ϕ'. Then which phenomenon is θ? What constitutes θ in the above few cases? I propose three tests for its detection: discovering the *object of reference* when we speak of such a striving; discovering what we mean by and refer to in speaking of a *way of instrumental striving*; and discovering the *visibility status* of physical instrumental strivings. Through them I hope to identify the 'active' θ that is done on such occasions. That is, determine its nature or make-up or constitution.

(3) I see a man turning a crank and ask, 'What are you doing?' To what does my question refer? What entity if any is the object of my perplexity? Clearly, the act of crank-turning. My question seeks an *interpretation* of that act. It asks: what is the intelligible-making act-heading under which the present visible act which you are performing, and that is mutually known by both of us to be the mutual topic, falls? What prompts the question is the *oddity to me* of a visible action, the fact that I cannot think of a likely meaning-conferring instrumental-complex that might contain it. This is

shown in that the agent answers by naming a wider instrumental act-type, 'car-starting'. Thus, what is hidden is purpose or meaning, while what is queried is the *overt physical deed*. Of this last there can be no doubt. There is no possibility that my question might refer instead to a covert mental deed which perplexes me. And this is proven by the fact that the agent's answer refers uniquely to the overt deed: 'Starting the car.' Then what is here highly relevant to our inquiry is that he might instead very well have replied, 'Trying to start the car', indeed that he might offer *both replies* to the one question. The ease with which one shuttles back and forth from one answer to the other, without even noticing that one is doing so, reflects one's certainty that one is speaking of the *same phenomenon* in talking of 'starting the car' and 'trying to start the car'.

Thus, it is not as if in replying, 'Trying to start the car', one takes the original reference to have *failed*, and turns instead elsewhere and inwards. But if this trying was an inward event, we should either have to interpret it in this way, or else interpret the original reference to be *either* strictly ambiguous between the visible act and some invisible event *or* as a much less determinate reference that could splay across both domains. Yet do we in asking such a question as 'What are you doing?', in such an everyday situation, conceive our reference to be ambiguous or broadly to splay across inner and outer domains, or consider it to be unsuccessful if we receive the reply 'Trying to start the car'? Surely not. Is it not certain that when he replies, 'Trying to start the car', he is in effect saying, 'That is the character of the visible deed which caught your attention and whose relation to the World of Human Purposes you could not divine', or, 'This is what I am engaged in doing in doing this deed of crank turning'? Then does not this show that he takes the reference of our question to be, unambiguously and determinately, the act of crank-turning? Does it not prove that he *re-describes* precisely that act as 'Trying to start the car'? And does not that in turn prove that in this case trying to start the car *is* the act of turning that crank, which *is* the act of moving the arm? I see no other possible interpretation of the situation.

(4) That concludes the first argument for the thesis that physical instrumental striving is sometimes a manipulative physical action like turning a crank. I turn now to the argument that utilises the concept of a *way of trying*. Thus, let us suppose that a few of us are in an aeroplane from which the one and only pilot has just bailed out. An old lady starts pleading with me to 'try and land the plane'. I survey the sea of dials and forest of instruments with dismay. How to convey one's ignorant *willingness*? How

to convey the *ignorance* of one's willingness? 'How?', I ask her, and 'What shall I do?', and these are interchangeable questions. Then does not this show that the 'how' of trying is the 'what' of doing? Does it not make clear that, whatever I proceed then to do with those instruments, will be my way of trying and therefore my *trying*? Here, by appeal to the concept of a way of trying, we have a further simple proof that some physical manipulative actions are instrumental tryings.

But some will object to the very concept of a *way of trying*, and therefore to identifying the 'how' that I perform with *any* trying. This is because of two arguments, which I now state and elaborate (prior to answering them). First, if these tryings were physical manipulations, they must be identical with basic bodily actions, but nothing counts as a way of performing a basic act and therefore nothing counts as a way of trying. Second, 'How did you do Φ'?' asks for the way or means that led successfully to an act-goal, and therefore by implication attributes a particular active power; but trying is merely a *prospective* way to a goal and can occur in the complete absence of success or act-power. Now there is no doubt the objector has a point here. I say so because in the absence of all effects, and hence of all powers, one can yet try; and this is because it is above all *origins* that determine tryings as tryings. Even if one succeeds in doing an act that is a trying, still one does not succeed in trying, for even if one fails to do what would have been trying, that very failure counts nonetheless as trying! I lunge at a button in order to try and ring a bell, and irrespective of whether I touch the button or miss altogether I yet try to ring the bell. Since success requires that some desired event happen through trying, sheer trying can be success at nothing. Trying is never a goal and never an achievement. So much for the statement of the two arguments objecting to the very concept of a way of trying.

(5) It will help us to meet these arguments, if we consider the related and more general concept of a 'way'. 'The way' is ambiguous between *the path leading to* (according as it is 'the way *to*') and *the mode adopted by* (according as it is 'the way *of* '). This ambiguity appears in action sentences. Thus, 'by' has two closely related roles in 'He did Φ' by doing Φ': (a) to indicate the *phenomenal path* that, by dint of leading beyond itself to an inessential externally related effect, led to what ensured Φ'-dom for Φ, e.g. boiling a kettle by introducing electricity into a wire, and (b) to indicate the *particular form* that, by dint of emerging from essential internally related origin, ensured the occurrence of Φ', e.g. signalling by waving a hand.

While (a) speaks of phenomenal/legal/aesthetic/etc. 'effects' that confer an additional (Φ') character on what already has being (as Φ), (b) rather says that Φ' was in the very first place incarnated as ('the word made flesh as') Φ. Contingency and necessity creep in at different places in either case. Whereas in (a) Φ need not have been Φ' but Φ' had to be Φ, in (b) Φ' need not have been Φ but had to be Φ'. Yet in either case Φ' took the form Φ, Φ' depended on Φ for its being – only differently; and it is this that legitimises the use of 'by' on both occasions.

This distinction helps to remove the second of the two objections to 'a way of trying'. Clearly, the question 'How shall I try?' asks, not 'How shall I try to try?', but 'What form shall my trying adopt?' It asks for the 'how', not of means to a goal that is try Φ', but of means to a goal that is Φ'. For there are putative techniques of doing, and techniques of trying, and they are one and the same. Thus, a necessary condition of trying to do instrumental Φ' is that one hold a particular belief: namely, that there exists some possible known act Φ that might cause the ϕ' necessary for Φ' to occur. One cannot try to do instrumental Φ' if one knows of no such Φ. 'How?' asks for just such a Φ. It seeks to know, not how to set about succeeding in trying, but how to set about succeeding in doing. It seeks knowledge that will permit the instrumental desire to do Φ' to 'discharge' or express itself in a striving. It asks for a form, mode, or manner to be adopted by try Φ'.

In the light of this discussion we can I think now see that the above two argument-objections to a 'way of trying' collapse. The first objection, which trades on the fact that physical instrumental trying is identical with a basic act and there can be no way of doing a basic act, fails to notice that our ignorance of a way of instrumental trying is no more than an ignorance of a physical context in which to insert basic action. Absurdly, such an argument would rule out instrumental action altogether! The second more serious argument has already been met. For it is above all on account of the aforementioned ambiguity in the role of 'by' that we (just conceivably) might hesitate to accept (say) 'He tried to land the plane by manipulating the controls', and thereby erroneously suppose it entails success of a kind. Once we see the mistake we can I think have no objection to sentences of the form 'He tried to Φ' by Φ', nor any objection to the suggestions, first that such tryings to Φ' are the Φs that are their form or mode, second that Φ can be a physical action. Thus, 'He tried to lower his temperature by swallowing some aspirins.' Here it is clear that a physical action is our way of trying in the sense of mode-or-manner adopted-by. Once again, it is difficult to see how we can avoid the conclusion that some instrumental strivings are physical actions.

(6) Finally, the argument from visibility. The question we are asking is really very simple. Namely: has anyone ever seen anyone try to do anything? Surely not in the case of mental trying. For example, trying to remember. Certainly, I have seen someone trying to remember – merely in the sense of seeing him *when and as* trying to remember; but then the object of perception is *he*, and *is not* the deed. But to this it may be objected that looking is a mental striving, and yet seems to be visible. But what here is in fact visible is something altogether different, for there is a purely physical sense of 'look' that means no more than 'gaze physically directed onto'. Again, there is a physical instrumental sense of 'look', in which we re-describe a bodily act in the light of its aim or significance, as when we re-describe an act of turning a head as 'he looked around at her'. But the primary sense of 'look', as with 'listen', is 'attend to . . .'; and in either case the activity is literally and wholly invisible. It is precisely not the bodily act of turning one's head under a physical description.

But what of trying to chop down the cherry tree? What of trying to land the aeroplane by manipulating its controls? Are these visible merely in the sense that trying to remember is visible? Is it merely that I saw him *when and as* he was (covertly, probably in his psyche) trying to start his car with a crank? Surely we saw him trying to start it, even if we believed he was merely exercising and so did not see him *as* trying to start the car, or see *that* he was trying to start it! Think of the question posed by a judge in a court of law: 'Did you or did you not see Mr X try to start the car?' Clearly, to respond to this question as if one had been asked, 'Did you or did you not see him try to remember?', would be evasive and absurd, and doubtless would he adjudged so by the court.

Finally, some tryings have names, e.g. 'hunt', 'search', 'flee'. And does one not literally see someone hunting for something? Do we not literally see people engaging in searches and fleeings? Yet what are huntings and searchings and fleeings but tryings to catch and find and escape? Of course, hunting and searching and fleeing do not wear their entire heart upon their visible sleeve, but then no more do paradigmatically visible acts like signalling. Are we to say that, because signalling must have a hidden intention origin that helps to make it a signalling, overt signalling is really covert? Plainly not, and plainly not with hunting and searching and fleeing.

I conclude: that some physical instrumental tryings, like trying to start a car or trying to open a door, are identical with physical manipulative actions, like turning a crank or pushing at a door. Once again, as at the end of the previous section 4, I apologise for the triteness and obviousness of these conclusions; and once again I excuse myself by emphasising that they are of major importance to an understanding of the bodily will.

6. PHYSICAL INSTRUMENTAL TRYINGS ARE PSYCHOLOGICAL PHENOMENA

My aim is to demonstrate the psychologicality (ψ) of *all* physical instrumental strivings and therefore of at least *some* physical actions. But first, what *is* 'psychologicality' (ψ)? I discuss this question more closely in chapter 14, but for our present purposes we should note the following. Ostensively the property is common to the following: thoughts, emotions, consciousness, sensations, hunger, moods, guilt, memories, and so on – and the 'so' of 'so on' is understood by us all (a fact which demonstrates that we all possess the concept). Meanwhile, it is absent from the following: digesting, having measles, heating up, falling through space, and so on. The property psychologicality turns out on investigation to be indefinable; but it is nonetheless such that all but the most primitive examples of the type are intentionally directed phenomena. This is an essential property of the property.

(a) A preliminary cautious thesis concerning the psychologicality of physical instrumental striving

While my aim in this present section 6 is to demonstrate that physical instrumental striving is a psychological phenomenon, I shall for the moment argue for a more cautious thesis. Let us use '$\int$' for 'seemingly' in the sense 'experientially-indistinguishable-from for the experiencer' (i.e. such that the subject would so describe his experience), S for strive, Φ for the basic act of ϕ-making, and Φ' for the instrumental act of ϕ'-making, where ϕ' is the instrumentally effected effect. Then my more cautious and utterly obvious claim is that whenever an S(Φ') event occurs, in absolutely *any* accepted sense of 'S(Φ')', there occurs a psychological event that falls under both 'S(Φ')' in *some* accepted sense of that expression *and* 'S$\int\Phi'$'. For example: whenever I try to open a window, there occurs a psychological event that falls under both 'try to open the window' in *some* accepted sense of the expression *and* under 'try seemingly to open the window'. Now there can I think be no doubt that whenever an SΦ' event truly occurs, there occurs an $\int$SΦ' event; so that when I really try to open the window, I at least *seemingly to me* try to do so. Then does this latter type, $\int$SΦ', entail the occurrence of the earlier mentioned type, $S\int\Phi'$? It does not, because seeming physical strivings that are merely seeming occur in dreams. Nevertheless, $S\Phi'$ entails both $S\int\Phi'$ and $\int S\Phi'$, and these last two are here identical. Then it is this $S\int\Phi'$, which necessarily occurs whenever $S\Phi'$ in any legitimate use truly occurs, that is I claim indubitably ψ. Thus, if I really try to open the window, then I really try to at least seemingly-to-me open the window, and it is this latter event ($S\int\Phi'$) that is psychological. This is my present limited claim.

Let us examine this phenomenon, $S\int\Phi'$. Here we have a genuine striving, a striving moreover which has no need of answering limb or instrument if it is to occur. It can occur, and be known incorrigibly to have occurred, even if limb and instrument prove to have been illusions, and therefore even if no visible physically overt bodily phenomenal striving takes place. This fact ensures 'privileged access' to the event $S\int\Phi'$, so that $S\int\Phi'$ manages to satisfy the all-important epistemological test of psychologicality, and in fact $S\int\Phi'$ satisfies all the usual tests, bearing in mind that in addition it must *a priori* immediately emerge from act-desire, and be immediately given as so doing, etc. Thus, $S\int\Phi'$ must be ψ. And this last is in any case obvious. It is obvious that whenever a real intentional instrumental striving occurs, there is simultaneously occurring a (possibly identical) striving that is mentalistically-immediately given to its owner and that is psychological in status. Am I not an absolute authority on the sheer existence of my own intentional instrumental strivings? And an authority also on their content or goal? Do I not immediately know that I have at least 'been active' and that the putative goal in so 'acting' was a deed which I (and I alone) immediately know of? I conclude: whenever we perform a physical instrumental trying like trying to start the car by turning a crank, then necessarily there is occurring a (possibly identical) *psychological event of striving* that is directed towards the performance of such an instrumental act. This also is obvious.

(b) A less cautious thesis concerning the psychologicality of physical instrumental striving

(1) What is the relation between these latter strivings? What is the relation between trying to start the car and trying seemingly-to-me to start the car? Surely, identity. Nevertheless, other possibilities must be considered, if only to put these important conclusions beyond doubt. Now there exists a Cartesian-ish feeling that all strivings must be inner events. It is fostered in the first place by their psychological character, together with the natural enough assumption that psychologicality *is* interiority, but it is fostered also by the existence of readily introspectible truly inner strivings like trying to

remember. Accordingly, it is easy to suppose that bodily strivings must as such be an introspectible part of the inner life. However, the facts are quite otherwise. The truth of the matter is that basic bodily strivings are without psychological '*quale*', are psychologically describable purely and completely as 'striving to – ', are not psychologistically experienced as situated anywhere in space, indeed are almost a psychological nothing! Think of an unexpected and completely failed bodily trying. Here the above psychological properties are filtered out in pure form and put on display. This phenomenon is radically dissimilar from (say) mental trying, and its supposed interiority is far from obvious. Then it must come as something of a surprise to those believing in the interiority of the bodily will to recognise that (say) turning a crank may *be* trying to start a car. But having done so, they may attempt to salvage the interiorist doctrine by opting for the theory (call it Theory α), that the incorrigible ('$S\int\Phi''$') use of '$S\Phi''$' describes *an inner striving to Φ'* that is co-present with *a visible non-interior striving to Φ'* that either *is* or else that *encompasses* a ϕ-that-is-non-deviantly-caused-by-$S\int\Phi'$ (depending on their analysis of the basic act Φ – which we saw earlier to be identical with the 'outer' visible striving).

(2) Theory α posits the occurrence of an inner striving to Φ' that is co-present with the visible outer instrumental striving to Φ'. Now in order to assess this theory, it helps greatly to spell out the corrigibility-implications of the theory. Then let us begin by making the reasonable assumption that adherents of Theory α accept that directed psychological phenomena can be brought under both referential and notional descriptions. Accordingly, Theory α must bring $S\int\Phi'$ under both a corrigible internal-&-referential use of '$S\Phi''$' (call it '$S\Phi'_{IR}$') (requiring the actual existence of instrumental object O_i to apply), and also under an incorrigible internal-&-notional use of '$S\Phi''$' (call it '$S\Phi'_{IN}$').

Then what will Theory α say about the 'public' visible and undoubtedly real *non-internal* striving event $S\Phi'$? It must accommodate the fact that *in one use* we withdraw 'starting the car' as a description of the visible bodily striving if the 'car' proves to be a dummy; and also the fact that *in another use* we retain this description of the visible striving act in these deceptive circumstances, bearing in mind that we could say of a man who is visibly scouring the landscape that we 'saw him hunting unicorns' (i.e. trying to physically capture (non-existent) unicorns). Then the first of these two 'outer' uses *looks like* a referential use, being corrigible by $\sim O_i$, and we shall call it '$S\Phi'_{OR}$', without prejudice; while the second *looks like* a notional use, being incorrigible by $\sim O_i$, and we shall call it '$S\Phi'_{ON}$', again without prejudice. Meanwhile, according to this interiorist

406   Part III: Dual aspect theory

Theory α an additional corrigibility-condition must exist for 'outer' 'SΦ''-claims. For since Theory α identifies the 'public' striving event either with ϕ-that-is-non-deviantly-caused-by-S$\int\Phi'$, or else with a complex event that encompasses both S$\int\Phi'$ *and* such a non-deviantly originated ϕ (according as it analyses basic Φ as ϕ, or else as a complex of ϕ and S$\int\Phi'$); and since one's knowledge of (a thus conceived) Φ must be corrigible by $\sim$(ϕ-that-is-non-deviantly-caused-by-S$\int\Phi'$); it follows that Theory α must imply that a *constitutive* and corrigible necessary condition of *either* 'outer' use of 'SΦ'' (i.e. referential *or* notional) is the occurrence of ϕ-that-is-non-deviantly-caused-by-S$\int\Phi'$. I shall now assemble a summary list of the situations in which 'SΦ''-claims would be corrigible if Theory α were true (for they prove to be of some importance).

(3) Given Theory α – which posits an internal striving (S$\int\Phi'$) within visible instrumental striving (SΦ') – the following examples of retraction of instrumental act striving claims would exist ('O_i' standing for the instrumentally manipulated object, and 'ϕ' for the limb movement).

 (i) Internal S$\int\Phi'$ corrigibly falls under 'SΦ'_{IR}', being referentially corrigible by $\sim O_i$.
 (ii) Non-internal SΦ' corrigibly falls under 'SΦ'_{OR}', being referentially corrigible by $\sim O_i$.
 (iii) Non-internal SΦ' corrigibly falls under 'SΦ'_{OR}', being constitutively corrigible by $\sim$(ϕ-that-is-non-deviantly-caused-by-S$\int\Phi'$).
 (iv) Non-internal SΦ' corrigibly falls under 'SΦ'_{ON}', being constitutively corrigible by $\sim$(ϕ-that-is-non-deviantly-caused-by-S$\int\Phi'$).

Thus, according to interiorist Theory α there are three ways an agent retracts a claim to be engaging in an instrumental striving SΦ'. If $\sim O_i$, he retracts the claim in two different uses of 'SΦ'', one use being the internal and the other the non-internal use. Meanwhile if $\sim\Phi$, he assumes that he was in error in claiming there to be *any* non-internal striving event. Examples are as follows.

('SΦ'_{IR}'). I vigorously crank what I take to be my car – but is a dummy. I say: 'I mistakenly thought I was trying to start my car' (re-describing an internal event).

('SΦ'_{OR}'). The same situation as above. I say: 'I mistakenly thought I was trying to start my car' (re-describing a 'public' visible event).

('SΦ'_{OC}'). My car is there all right, and my arm moves as I frantically keep on what I take to be trying to start my car; but scientists (and not I) engendered the latter stages of each of those arm movements. I say: 'I mistakenly thought I had succeeded in trying to start my car' (retracting my putative claim regarding the sheer existence of an item in the domain of the visible).

(c) Assessing Theory α

(1) So much for a statement of the interiorist instrumentalist Theory α and its corrigibility-implications. Then what are we to say of this theory? First, that it seems highly implausible to suggest that all visible physical instrumental strivings logically necessarily conceal a second non-identical striving with necessarily identical content. These 'two' events, besides necessarily sharing general type (viz. striving), and content or goal (viz. Φ'), and time of occurrence, logically necessarily have the same token psychological cause. In addition, even though both are examples of the ontological type *physical* act-striving, as against *mental* act-striving (like trying to remember), they are yet ontologically unlike, one being psychological, the other either merely physical or else a 'psycho-physical' 'ontological amalgam' (according as Theory α construes the visible $S\Phi'$ as ϕ, or else as a complex union of ϕ and $S \int \Phi'$ and endorses the concept of the 'ontological amalgam'); so that *physical* act-strivings must on this theory be ontologically heterogeneous, and this too seems implausible. Meanwhile, the very notion of an 'ontological amalgam' is highly suspect, as I bring out in the next section 7. And so on.

(2) These are very serious difficulties for Theory α, and strongly suggestive of 'metaphysical double vision'. But for the moment I will set them aside. And I will instead confine my comments to considering the claim that the 'public' visible act of instrumental striving is not a psychological event. It is at this point that the above discussion of the corrigibility-implications of Theory α becomes relevant. For if the 'public' visible act of instrumental striving is not a psychological event, that non-psychologicality must manifest its presence in the corrigibility properties of the '$S\Phi'$'-claim that such a striving has occurred. In this situation it is the decisive test.

Now according to Theory α, the claim that a 'public' visible striving $S\Phi'$ has occurred is corrigible by $\sim(\phi$-that-is-non-deviantly-caused-by-$S \int \Phi')$ (constitutively) and also by $\sim O_i$ (referentially). Consider the first suggestion. Why should we take it seriously? This doctrine is I suggest dictated, not by observation of the facts of linguistic usage, but by nothing more than the content of Theory α. For it is certain that under the exceptional circumstances of $\sim(\phi$-that-is-non-deviantly-caused-by-$S \int \Phi')$ and seeming-Φ and $S \int \Phi'$, we would in no way retract *any* claim to have $S\Phi''$d. For one thing, we would never withdraw $S \int \Phi'$ under these circumstances.

But neither would we differentially hang onto some supposed one (inner) striving claim and retract some supposed second (outer) striving claim. We would I suggest never say, 'I engaged in the inner striving (to turn the crank), but did not manage to engage in the outer striving (also to turn the crank)' or 'I engaged in one striving but did not succeed in engaging in the other.' (As if striving could be a mode of success!) What in fact we would do is the following. We would insist that we had been striving Φ'-wards, and that would be that.

So we must reject the first half of the corrigibility-implications of Theory α regarding '$S\Phi''$-claims concerning 'public' instrumental strivings. And that leaves the (undeniable) (referential) corrigibility of such '$S(\Phi')$'-claims by $\sim O_i$. But now if this example of corrigibility is to evidence *non-psychologicality* on the part of the 'public' visible $S\Phi'$, it must be construed as demonstrating that in the absence of the external instrument-object O_i, the 'public' visible event of arm-moving Φ can be *no sort of* striving Φ'-ward (else the corrigibility will be of the kind encountered in 'see –' -claims, which can always fall back upon incorrigible and evidently psychological 'seem to see –' -claims, whereupon the remaining corrigibility test for the non-psychologicality of the visible striving Φ'-wards will have gone by the board). But even worse: since the interiorist Theory α refuses to identify Φ and $S\Phi$, it follows that in the absence of the external instrument-object O_i the bodily act of Φ-ing must on this theory *fail to rate as any kind of S at all*! This is grossly counter-intuitive. Surely, one feels, if Φ that either encompasses or is caused by $S\int\Phi'$ is a trying when O_i exists, it must still rate as *some kind of S* – and with O_i-directed content, what is more – when external O_i proves not to exist. If turning the crank is a trying, it is whether or not the car is an illusion. But according to this theory it is not so. Apparently, it is only when the propitious circumstance O_i obtains that Φ manages to surface to S-dom! Thus, S-dom becomes a kind of *achievement* and even a *mode of success*, rather as if $S\Phi'$ had in some way to be well formed or well placed to be S! Can failure be an achievement? As such? Here for the second time we find that the supposed corrigibility of an '$S\Phi''$-claim that supposedly concerns a non-psychological phenomenon, carries the implication that some strivings can be modes of success.

(3) But why in any case put such an interpretation on the existence of a corrigible use of '$S\Phi''$? Let us for the moment assume that we are committed to the above improbable thesis that $S\int\Phi'$ lies concealed behind the visible outer face of a non-identical $S\Phi'$. Now we have seen that the paradigmatically interior phenomena of thought, mental image, visual

experience, etc., can all be brought under both incorrigible notional descriptions *and* corrigible referential descriptions. For example, 'Image of glass containing a Martini' can be used incorrigibly, but also corrigibly (as when I consent to re-describe it as 'image of glass containing water' if it turns out that water was in the glass that I remembered). Then there absolutely must be two such uses of 'SΦ''. For S$\int\Phi'$ is an event that is at once psychological and directed beyond itself. Thus the notional/referential distinction must apply to S$\int\Phi'$ too. Then why not give this interpretation of the undeniable fact that SΦ' is in one use corrigible by $\sim$O$_i$? But in that case why take the existence of such corrigibility as evidence of the existence of a *non*-psychological SΦ'? All the more peculiar if one remembers that this corrigible use of 'SΦ'' is supposed to have no incorrigible S-claim to fall back upon, and that S-ing becomes some kind of achievement!

Well, to this adherents of Theory α will doubtless reply that in fact we must consider *two* corrigible referential uses of the expression 'SΦ'': S$\int\Phi'$ under a referential heading that requires existent O$_i$, *and* the 'public' use of SΦ' that also requires existent O$_i$. But once again it seems that we are being dictated to by a theory that demands such usages, rather than by the observed facts of linguistic usage. For when does one in real life avail oneself, now of the corrigible 'inner' use (but *not* of the corrigible 'public' use), now of the corrigible 'public' use (but *not* of the corrigible 'inner' use)? When would I say, 'I am trying to start the car' in these two different corrigible ways? When would I say, 'I falsely thought I was trying to start the car' (having turned a crank that engaged with no car), now in one ('inner') use and now instead in the other ('outer') use? I have not the least idea. It seems that the distinction is altogether illusory, that there is but one corrigible referential use of 'SΦ'', and that it must apply to a psychological event of SΦ'-ing.

(4) But there is something else amiss with the whole idea of a non-psychological S that would not be an S were it not for an answering external object O$_i$. Namely, *what is the point* of talking of striving here at all? In general, the point of talking of striving is, I suggest, to single out those situations where act-desire 'has its way', 'goes through', 'expresses itself', in such a way as to leave it open whether or not it realises its goal-destination: it is to let us know that such a 'surge' has anyway begun. But if a 'public' visible event that supposedly conceals an 'inner' S$\int\Phi'$ can graduate to sheer S-dom *only if* answering outer physical object O$_i$ is a reality, how can the affirmation of such an S be informing us of such a 'surge'? Unless an S event

is given to its owner under some infinitely secure mere S-heading, it is difficult to see how this state of affairs could be realised. In short, the phenomenon needs to be psychological if we are to ensure this 'infinite security' of *mere* S-ing. The 'psycho-physical' or else merely physical $S\Phi'$ of the theory is precisely no such thing.

(d) A summary statement

In sum, I reject the thesis that the publicly visible intentional physical instrumental $S\Phi'$ is non-psychological, for the following reasons. This theory has to accommodate the evident ψ-dom of an event of S-ing with Φ' content whenever $S\Phi'$, together with the equally evident fact that the visible 'public' $S\Phi'$ is a physical action. Then it has no choice but to suppose the former to be either concealed behind or embedded in the latter (construed as ontologically 'hybrid'). But this theory is at once in serious difficulties. For it seems absurd to suggest that whenever we try to open a door, one S with Φ' content occurs behind or within a second S with identical content. Partly because we have no awareness of two strivings, partly because we never speak of them, partly because we cannot differentially engage in either, but partly also because everything points towards this being a case of 'metaphysical double vision'. After all, these 'two' events are necessarily of the same type, necessarily have the same content-goal, necessarily occur simultaneously, and necessarily express the very same token act-generative forces (i.e. necessarily have the one psychological cause). Thus, they each express the non-distinct desires, $D\Phi'$ and $D\Phi$-to-Φ'; and that there is a single desire-complex is all of a piece with there existing but one expressive striving falling under several descriptions. There seems no more need to split $S\Phi'$ into 'inner' S and physical remainder, or (worse) to postulate two distinct causally related 'inner' and 'outer' S's, simply because there exist corrigible and incorrigible uses of '$S\Phi'$', than there is with thought or imagery.

Then I would characterise those two uses of '$S\Phi'$', not by saying that one refers to a psychological event and one to either a 'hybrid' or else merely physical event, but that they each refer via notional-incorrigible and referential-corrigible descriptions to the one psychological (and also physical) event. And is it likely that *physical* strivings should range across 'inner' psychological strivings going on in the mind *and* either 'hybrid' or else merely physical phenomena (occurring in mind-&-body or merely-the-body respectively), and have no status of its own? And that physical strivings should only be corrigibly and inessentially strivings? And that being an instrumental striving should be an achievement and mode of success?

Everything points to the existence of only one S when $S\Phi'$. That same S will be incorrigibly given as '$S\Phi''$' (in a notional use), and generally will be heavily endowed with all of the ψ-proving traits one can propose. I conclude, that some intentional physical instrumental strivings are physical actions *and* psychological events. I conclude that *some* physical actions are psychological events.

7. THE 'PSYCHO-PHYSICAL'

(a) The requirement of full determinacy for all being

(1) We know that an intentional striving can be a physical act like turning a crank or pushing at a door. Now most believers in the interiority of the bodily will must be unable to accept that this phenomenon is a psychological event. Accordingly, the most natural course open to them is to say that this trying is an event that is constituted out of an 'inner' psychological part and an 'outer' merely physical part. The question then arises: if this complex event with a psychological part is not psychological in nature, of what ontological status is it? It is difficult to relegate it to the domain of the *merely* physical. After all, it has a psychological part, and logically necessarily is the kind of event that in the living occurs only in animals, and logically necessarily has an absolutely immediate psychological desire-origin of which mentalistically one is immediately apprised, etc. The only remaining option seems to be to say that it is an 'ontological amalgam' and of the ontological type 'psycho-physical'. This theory has been endorsed by several philosophers. What is one to make of it?

It does not seem open to us to shrug off the whole issue, and argue that here for once an event exists that has *no* ontological status. For we surely all agree, so far as *specific types* are concerned, that 'everything must be something', in the sense that 'every individual item must be of at least one type'. And must we not accept a similar principle both for ultimate categorial status and broad ontological type? In particular, in the case of an individual event the item is and must be of the one categorial status, individual event, and must be of at least one specific type, say arm-moving, but must in addition be of at least one broad ontological type, such as psychological, or physical, or psychological-&-also-physical, etc. Every individual item in existence must exhibit *full determinacy*, whether that individual be event or material object or anything else, and whether the respect be category or type or ontological status. This principle seems absolutely firm, and is in no way compromised by the existence of 'intermediate cases', which determinately fall at a specific point in a classificatory schema, viz. on a dividing line, e.g. turquoise. Just as to be turquoise is to exhibit *full* qualitative determinacy in respect of colour, so a sub-viral giant molecule that is a minuscule bit more merely physical than living matter, exhibits *full* qualitative determinacy in respect of ontological kind: it is perfectly precisely sited at some level of being.

(2) But what of items which lack a determinate nature? Cannot an item escape the classificatory schema altogether? Might there not be an event that is constituted out of such a jumble of ontological levels that it cannot manage to have a level at all? Consider the following. Suppose one were to put through a fine grinder the rubbish that we put in rubbish bins, and pack the resultant powder into small cubes. Of what type of matter would those cubes be? Presumably of no type, being a sort of material equivalent of a chance and non-significant sequence in nature. Then might not this be how it is so far as the ontological status of physical action was concerned? Might it not be that, while in all probability this event is at least ϕ (i.e. physical), and one part of it is ψ (i.e. psychological) and the other part non-ψ, the event itself is such that we simply cannot classify it as ψ or as of some other level? Ought we not to count this event as an exception to the rule: the phenomenally real is fully determinate ontologically? In short, construe it ontologically as an analogue of the 'rubbish stuff'? But the above line of reasoning is tantamount to opting for the theory that the physical action is simply of ontological status ϕ. It settles for the 'lowest common denominator': it affirms that it is of status ϕ (and notes and accepts that this ϕ event encompasses an event which is both ϕ and ψ). Accordingly, such an event constitutes no exception to the principle of ontological determinacy.

(b) The sense of 'psycho-physical'

(1) So in the ensuing discussion I will interpret 'psycho-physical', not as a mere mixture of levels that is itself *no particular level*, rather as the 'rubbish blocks' were of no material stuff type, but as a *determinate ontological type* that finds instantiation in some individual events. As an amalgam like brass is a kind of stuff, as a hybrid like a grapefruit is a kind of fruit, so it is claimed in the case of 'psycho-physical': 'psycho-physical' is said to be a bona fide ontological kind. Then the question we must now settle is whether physical action is merely physical in type, or psychological, or else of this supposedly

third kind. This is the question that I shall be considering as I embark upon a discussion of the 'psycho-physical'.

It will help to pinpoint the difficulties I experience with 'psycho-physical' if we briefly consider other specific types in which we link one kind with another via a hyphen. Suppose I ask the question: 'What is "brunch"?' If you say that it is 'breakfast-lunch', you merely *hint* at a sense. Because 'breakfast-lunch' could easily be applied to several meal types – a midday first meal of bacon and eggs – an 11 a.m. first meal of three lunch-type courses – it applies uniquely to none. In other words, the sense of 'breakfast-lunch' has not been specified: the expression is not self-explanatory, the hyphen fixes nothing. Yet some people treat 'psycho-physical' as if it were self-explanatory, as if a *new ontological kind* were here constituted with infinite pellucidity out of a simple union of ψ and ϕ. But which 'simple union'? It cannot be *conjunction*. To be sure, a definitive complex kind is determined by conjoining kinds. Thus, 'psychological and physical' is a bona fide complex kind, entailing both psychologicality and physicality of nature, but such an interpretation of 'ψ-ϕ' is explicitly rejected by those who speak of physical actions as ψ-ϕ, else they would accept that physical action is a psychological event. Their model for 'ψ-ϕ' cannot be (say) 'Jewish-American'. So the sense of 'ψ-ϕ' is not ψ & ϕ; and yet in some sense it is supposed to be a nearly self-evident product of ψ and ϕ. What can it be?

(2) Now there is nothing to prevent our concocting necessary and sufficient logical conditions for having a property we call 'ψ-ϕ': say, being one part ψ and the remainder $\phi \sim \psi$. But then that must count as an explanation of *the very sense* of the entirely novel term of art 'ψ-ϕ'. What will not have been explained, however, is why having the complex property of being part ψ and the remainder $\phi \sim \psi$ should suffice to ensure that the item in question is of a different ontological status than ψ or $\phi \sim \psi$. Above all, what will not have been explained is why that complex ontological property should count as a *new ontological status* in its own right. After all, there exist other complex ontological properties that do not do so: for example, the property of being ψ and encompassing what is $\phi \sim \psi$ (e.g. a physically analysable pain with an atomic-level event part). Then why one and not the other?

Let me elaborate this point. Thus, to be red is one property, to be round is another, to be red and round yet another; but to be red and round is not a property that goes beyond or that is *further to* the first two properties. Analogously, ϕ is one ontological status, ψ another, ϕ & ψ yet another; but ϕ & ψ is not an ontological status further to the first two. Thus, listing ontological levels or 'orders of being', we might perhaps opt for: ϕ, vital (V), ψ, . . .; but, whether or not $\square$ (x) (ψ x $\rightarrow$ ϕ x), we cannot add ϕ & ψ as a fourth, or ϕ & V as a fifth, etc. Then if 'ϕ & ψ' is not the specification of a new ontological level or 'order of being', any more than is 'part ψ & part ϕ', why should 'ϕ & part ψ' or 'part ϕ & part ψ' count as such? It cannot be that it satisfies a need for determinacy of ontological status, for whatever is 'part ϕ & part ψ' is almost certainly 'ϕ & part ψ' and therefore 'ϕ' in ontological status; so determinacy of status is already achieved. This cannot be the justification.

(3) I suggest that those who affirm that there exists an unsuspected onto-logical level, probably in some sense 'between' ϕ and ψ, consisting in being part ψ & part ϕ, are confusing an *ontological characterisation* with a *specification of an ontological status*. But what arguments can be adduced in favour of interpreting the ontological characterisation in this way? Not that it meets a binding need for ontological determinacy. So far as I can tell, the only possible argument runs as follows: 'There exists an event that is constituted out of an "inner" ψ event and an "outer" ϕ event, and that event cannot be ψ and cannot be merely ϕ, and must we all agree have determinate ontological status, and must therefore be of the ontological status – part ψ & part ϕ.' However, if this argument is to be acceptable, all of the following four principles must be true:

(P1) An event constituted out of part ψ and remainder merely ϕ, cannot itself be merely ϕ.

(P2) An event constituted out of part ψ and remainder merely ϕ, cannot itself be ψ.

(P3) Having the complex ontological property of being part ψ & remain-der merely ϕ, *is* being precisely of such an ontological status.

(P4) Ontological status can sometimes be defined in terms of other onto-logical statuses.

(c) Examining these principles

(1) In this section I will discuss several of these principles. Consider, to begin, Principle P4. At the very least this is counter to the norm, and seems precisely to contradict what we understand by 'order of being' or 'ontological level'. Normally, that an item is of the ontological level that it is, is something absolutely inexplicable in conceptual terms. No constitutive logically necessary and sufficient conditions exist for physicality or vitality or psychologicality – irrespective of their necessary links to other orders of being. For example, even if all that is ψ must be ϕ, ψ is not explicable

in terms of ϕ, being something entirely new. Then those who construe 'ψ-ϕ' as an ontological level are ready to dispense with this strong brand of novelty: here an ontology is translucently fabricated from the already given – for the first time! In this sense the new ontology has no mystery or 'life of its own'. And it is futile to argue that novelty may yet be preserved, that 'ψ-ϕ' may be an indefinable ultimate X 'lodged between ϕ and ψ' which is entailed by though not defined by 'part ψ & remainder $\phi \sim \psi$' – as if the latter connection were *synthetic necessary*! Indeed, I believe that this latter idea lies behind the suggestion that 'ψ-ϕ' is wholly self-explanatory, as if 'part ψ & remainder $\phi \sim \psi$' merely (rigorously) pointed towards the (in any case) transparently apparent but indefineable ontological level lodged between ϕ and ψ. For one thing 'being between ϕ and ψ' is insufficiently specific, and also fits 'vital' (V), for ψ arises on V & ϕ, and V arises on ϕ, and the order of development cannot be $\psi/\phi/V$ (i.e. ψ arising upon ϕ, which in turn arises on V); but in any case, the supposedly new ontological level simply cannot be some indefinable X 'between ϕ and ψ', for it *is* being part ψ & reminder $\phi \sim \psi$ – a complex definable trait which is said to be exhaustively assembled out of existing ontological levels.

(2) We have seen that some ontological characterisations like 'ψ & part ϕ' are not specifications of a new ontological level, whereas 'part ψ & remainder $\phi \sim \psi$' is supposedly both characterisation *and* specification. Then via what rationale do we determine whether event fusion leads to a new ontological level? And via what rationale do we determine that the new event cannot be of the same ontological status as its constituents, e.g. ϕ or ψ? Thus, coiners of the concept 'ψ-ϕ' presumably permit $\Diamond(\psi$-ϕ x $\rightarrow \phi$x), but disallow both $\Diamond(\psi$-ϕx $\rightarrow \psi$x) and $\Diamond(\psi$-ϕx $\rightarrow$ merely ϕx). But how is it known that these latter two propositions are false? Are there any rules to which we may appeal in deciding such elemental issues? Are there sub-principles underlying the above set (P1)–(P4)? The following putative sub-principles may be proposed.

(p1) If event e1 of ontological level L1 unites with event e2 of some different level L2, to form event e3 of some level or other L3, and L2 is 'higher' than L1, then e3 cannot be of level L2.

(p2) If e1 of ontological level L1 unites with e2 of some different level L2 to form e3 of level L3, and L2 is 'higher' than L1, then e3 cannot be of level L1 alone.

These may be combined into the single definitive sub-principle:

(p3) If two events of different ontological level unite to form a new event, the new event must exemplify a level that is different from either: that is, a new level must be realised.

I can see no reason for endorsing (p1), and therefore no reason for endorsing (p3). Thus, precisely the reasons for disallowing $\Diamond(\psi\text{-}\phi x \to$ merely $\phi x)$, and hence for accepting (p2), seem to be reasons for rejecting (p1) and therefore (p3). These are by now familiar, but I shall nonetheless repeat them here. Namely: it is a constitutive logical necessity, and hence not a mere description-relative necessity, that if a 'ψ-ϕ' event occurs in a living entity then necessarily that entity is animal; and the 'ψ-ϕ' event necessarily has immediate psychological origins in the case of a 'ψ-ϕ' striving, of which mentalistically one is apprised; etc. These considerations look like good reasons for rejecting the suggestion that the 'ψ-ϕ' striving is merely ϕ, but they look to be equally good reasons for accepting that the 'ψ-ϕ' striving is itself ψ – and hence for rejecting (p1) and with it (p3). But the very moment that we accept that the 'ψ-ϕ' striving may be ψ, all reason for insisting that the 'ψ-ϕ' is constituted out of an 'inner' ψ event and an 'outer' merely-ϕ event vanish – and with it all reason for *splitting* physical manipulative striving in two. For now we are ready to accept the existence of an event, the (supposedly 'ψ-ϕ') event of manipulative striving, that is at once ψ and ϕ without being 'inner'. And at this very moment the problem dissolves. It has been forced upon us through our unthinking assumption that psychologically *is* interiority.

(d) A further implicit principle determining the endorsement of 'psycho-physical'

(1) One other supposed principle lies behind the above sub-principles, (p1)–(p3). In any case, this particular belief plays an important part in determining the theory that there exists a special ontological level, the 'psycho-physical'.

The whole problem gets posed thus: we would all accept that an event that is supposed to encompass an 'inner' ψ event and an 'outer' merely ϕ event may well be ϕ in status; but to what 'higher'-than-ϕ category could such a 'part ψ & remainder $\phi \sim \psi$' event belong to as well? For some reason ψ is disallowed. What is that reason? It seems to me that there is an implicit endorsement of a principle to the effect that 'whatever is ψ must be ψ *all the way*', together with the belief that '*only part of* a physical manipulative striving is ψ'. Let us consider this theoretical position.

(2) Now so far as the above supposed principle is concerned, its truth or falsity must surely depend upon *which* 'way' we are speaking of. Do we mean a lateral 'way', or an internal analytic 'way'? For if the supposed principle

held *all* 'ways', we would have in our hands a simple decisive disproof of physicalism – which no one would dream of accepting. Thus, it is at least possible that ψ items are ϕ, yet no one believes that the atomic event constituents of psychological events are themselves psychological events. In short, no physicalist could accept the principle that a psychological event must be psychological in all parts of itself. Then why should it bother us that the 'outer' part of a ψ event should be $\phi \sim \psi$? I can see no good reason for such disquiet. As we travel inwards into the atomic depths of a psychological event – assuming for the moment that physicalism is true – we rapidly leave the psychological behind – which nonetheless characterises a whole of which those atomic phenomena are part. Then why should it not be the same as we travel *outwards from the mind*? Why should not such a unifying whole or totality encompass these peripheral non-psychological phenomena? Provided a principle of unification travels with us, which seems assured in the light of the mechanistic syndrome which unfolds with nomic force, a whole that is psychological looks as if it might well survive this lack of ontological homogeneity. In this last respect the psychological is to be contrasted with the physical. For the physical *is* perfectly ontologically homogeneous: necessarily, it is physical 'all the way'. But then it is an absolutely ultimate and rock-bottom category. The universe is physical, and is not psychological. No one any longer believes in wholly self-subsistent phenomenal psychological items. As soon believe in ghosts.

(e) A 'slum' of ontologies!

(1) A final few comments on the theory of the 'psycho-physical'.

If – as those who endorse the 'psycho-physical' suppose – ψ and $\phi \sim \psi$ can be assembled to form a new level, viz. 'part ψ & remainder $\phi \sim \psi$', what is to prevent our piecing together additional ontological levels? Indeed, why should we not multiply ontological levels *without limit*? For example, why not a level 'ψ-ϕ-ψ' for an event whose first part is ψ, second part ϕ, and third ψ? And so on. It seems to me that the assumption that 'ψ-ϕ' is self-explanatory, symptomatically betrays an allegiance to the idea that ontological levels can be pieced together like Meccano parts into 'ontological assemblies', or mixed together as ingredients of an 'ontological soup'. Not, be it noted, to constitute mere complex ontological properties – but determinate ontological levels of being. Is not this what we should expect once we endorse the idea that new ontological kinds can be constructed from old? For why should we stop at 'ψ-ϕ'? Indeed, why stop anywhere? But does not this suggestion bring the very idea of 'levels of being', such as we find in the physical and the vital and the psychological, into total disrepute? *What is the point* of talking of 'levels' if an endless sequence of step-formations can be passed off as additional levels? Does it not precisely reduce the concept to absurdity?

(2) A possible rejoinder to this challenge is, to emphasise that *it is fact* that there is something that is 'part ψ & remainder $\phi \sim \psi$', whereas concoctions like 'ψ-ϕ-ψ' lie in the realm of pure conjecture, and claim that this pre-empts these 'assemblies' and 'soups'. What is one to say to this suggestion? The following, as it seems to me: that while the ontological level Life could scarcely be a reality in the absence of Life empirical, while categories like Space and Time would be phantoms in the absence of the actuality of a spatio-temporal realm, the above argument is something of an oddity. To suppose 'ψ-ϕ' a true ontological level because the world contains events that are 'part ψ & remainder $\phi \sim \psi$', but 'ψ-ϕ-ψ' a mere string of words because it happens to be bereft of items that are 'part ψ & distinct part $\phi \sim \psi$ & additional distinct part ψ', is surely to lean ridiculously on empirical fact. Do we have empirical quests for already *a priori*-constituted items? And will their 'realisation' prove that the construct was more than an idle dream? Are we to go into the world armed with Blueprints for Ontological Novelties, see whether something fits, and conclude that 'here and now we have a new order of being'? If ontological reality depended in this way upon sheer empirical fact, if bona fide 'blueprints' could be assembled which the world may or may not 'realise', must there not be possible worlds in which ψ-ϕ-ψ is a reality? But if it is a reality in a possible world, is it not simply – a reality (taken in a metaphysical or ontological sense)? Then why this turning to the empirical facts of this world? Even with a true empirical phenomenon like psychologicality, there seems to be no good sense in which the empirical facts actually lend support to the thesis that there exists a special order of being: the psychological. Will types jump in ahead of ontology? Can the reality of an 'order of being' depend on the capacity of events of disparate ontology to unite in single events of a required ontological structure? This, at any rate, seems to be the argument of those who wish to stop with 'ψ-ϕ' but shut the door upon 'ψ-ϕ-ψ'.

Occam's Razor counsels us to cut down on entities; which is to say that explanatorial good sense so counsels us. Probably it also counsels us to economise with ontological levels – and most especially when these last are introduced in *ad hoc* manner to bolster a particular answer to a particular question. Philosophical thought should proceed in precisely the reverse direction.

(f) Conclusion

(1) In sum. Let us for argument's sake make the contentious assumption that a physical instrumental striving that takes the form of a manipulative act like crank-turning, is constituted out of an interior part that is ψ (& presumably also ϕ) & a remaining 'outer' part that is ϕ and $\sim\psi$. The question then facing us is: of what ontological status is this act of striving? Then to opt for the view that it has no distinctive status of its own, is tantamount to opting for the view that it is merely ϕ. Accordingly, the only conceivable possibilities are as follows: that the event of striving is 'psycho-physical'; or merely ϕ; or ψ. Consider these in order.

A. 'Psycho-physical'. If meeting the specification of being 'psycho-physical' is not just having a certain ontological character but having a new ontological status, then the theory has to face all of the difficulties raised in the foregoing discussion. Namely: What justifies our calling this ontological characterisation an ontological specification? How is it that we can here for the first time concoct new ontological statuses out of old? What is there to stop us assembling ontological statuses without limit?

B. Merely ϕ. Then this merely ϕ event has the following set of unusual properties.

    a. Its occurrence in a living object necessitates the animality of that object.

    b. It is in part ψ.

    c. Logically necessarily it must have a psychological origin

    d. that is immediate

    e. and of *a priori*-determinable type.

    f. It is known with mentalistic immediacy to have such origins, independently of 'Humean' considerations like regularity.

    g. At least part of it, and perhaps it itself therefore, is epistemologically given to its owner with mentalistic immediacy.

C. Or ψ. Which is the only possibility left, and which is faced with no such embarrassments.

(2) The upshot is that those who believe that the visible physical act of instrumentally trying is a composite of an internal trying, the movement of the limb, and perhaps also the mechanistic phenomena, are faced with two alternatives. Either they believe that the act is ontologically on all fours with the 'rubbish stuff', and of no particular status, or else they believe it to be merely physical. But how can an event that is a real event, and of a real specific kind ($S\Phi'$), and therefore no analogue of 'rubbish

stuff' so far as kinds are concerned, be *ontologically* akin to 'rubbish stuff'? Alternatively, how can a *merely* physical event encompass an interior mental event? Neither option seems acceptable.

8. THE GENERAL SCHEMA FOR ACT-CONSTITUTION

(1) We come to the main business of this chapter: the determination of the constitution of the basic bodily act – given that whenever we act a striving to do (an attempt at doing, having a 'shot at' doing), that act occurs. In the ensuing discussion I will make the assumption that, with the possible exception of (vi) and (vii) (which are in any case fully confirmed in the succeeding section), all of the following are indubitable certainties.

(i) Whenever we perform a basic bodily Φ, a striving S to Φ occurs.

(ii) The goal bodily event ϕ occurs *because* SΦ (in some causal or causal-developmental sense of 'because').

(iii) Φ occurs *because* SΦ (in the same sense of 'because').

(iv) Whenever Φ, an SΦ occurs that is mentalistically-immediately given under some description or other to the agent of Φ, e.g. as 'doing something', or as 'acting', or as 'expressing my will'.

(v) That SΦ falls under the minimal description 'S(Φ-in-$\int$ O_L-make)' (i.e. striving towards the active making of ϕ in the at-least-seemingly-(to-me)-present-limb-object-O_L).

(vi) Φ is visible.

(vii) Φ either *is* or else *includes* ϕ.

(viii) A nomic bond relates SΦ and ϕ, viz. in circumstances of motor health and physical liberty (x) (SΦ, x $\rightarrow$ ϕ).

(ix) A nomic bond relates SΦ, ϕ, Φ and activation of the motor-mechanism, M, in circumstances of motor health and physical liberty etc., viz. (x) (SΦ, x $\rightarrow$ full-activation-of-M, & ϕ, & Φ).

Now the problem is seemingly simple. What is the relation betweeen Φ, ϕ, and the S-event mentioned above in (iv) and (v)? Then the various possible theories of the constitution of Φ divide, according as they postulate SΦ as distinct cause of ϕ – or not. Those making this assumption that Causes SΦ, ϕ, may opt for any of the following three theories of Φ-constitution (hatching indicating the conjectured confines of Φ),

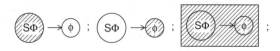

Fig. 1

and the latter theory takes two forms, according as Φ is supposed to encompass activation-of-motor-mechanism-M – or not,

ie.  or .

Fig. 2

These seem to be the only possibilities.

Meanwhile, those who deny that Causes SΦ, φ, can postulate SΦ, *either* as distinct from φ *or* as overlapping with φ *or* as related to φ as part to whole *or* related as whole to part *or* as identical with φ (and all of these structural situations are prior to postulating theories as to the constitution of Φ). That is:

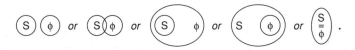

Fig. 3

The first possibility can forthwith be rejected, because it is certain that φ is in *some* causal or developmental sense *because* SΦ; but Ⓢ ⓞ allows no such sense. Likewise the second possibility, because no rational principle can be discerned whereby SΦ may extend *some* but not the *whole* distance as far as the goal phenomenon φ. Likewise the third and fifth possibilities, because φ is neither a psychological nor in-part-psychological event, whereas it is certain that SΦ is. This leaves ⓈⓅ ⓞ as the only acceptable schema for those who deny that Causes SΦ, φ. Now this general schema allows several theories of the constitution of Φ (Φ being represented once again by hatching). Then we can immediately reject the two following theories,

 and

Fig. 4

and do so on the same grounds. Those grounds are that since each theory postulates SΦ as a psychological event that is not 'inner' (because it encompasses bodily ϕ), why should not the same hold of Φ itself? In other words, the only plausible account of Φ for those who opt for the structural schema ⟨SΦ ⓞ⟩ is ⟨SΦ ⃰⟩.

(2) In sum, it has emerged that the following possibilities exist (ranging across theories of Φ-constitution *and* structural schemas for the relation between SΦ and ϕ).

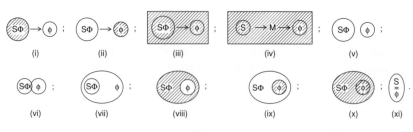

Fig. 5

And we have rejected out of hand (v), (vi), (vii), (viii), (ix), and (xi); and (iii) and (iv) are sufficiently similar to be bracketed together. And that leaves four theories worthy of attention (hatching once again indicating the conjectured confines of the act Φ).

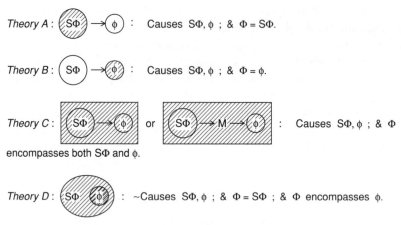

Theory A : Causes SΦ, ϕ ; & Φ = SΦ.

Theory B : Causes SΦ, ϕ ; & Φ = ϕ.

Theory C : or : Causes SΦ, ϕ ; & Φ encompasses both SΦ and ϕ.

Theory D : ~Causes SΦ, ϕ ; & Φ = SΦ ; & Φ encompasses ϕ.

Fig. 6

Theory A posits the bodily will as 'inner' and identifies the physical action and that willing; Theory B, which is the traditional view, posits the bodily will as 'inner' and identifies the physical action and the 'outer' willed bodily movement; Theory C posits the bodily will as 'inner', and the physical action as the union of 'inner' willing and 'outer' willed bodily movement; and Theory D, which is the 'double-aspect' theory that I endorse, identifies the physical action and the willing, refuses application of 'inner' or 'outer' to both phenomena, and posits the act as a psychological event that encompasses the outer willed movement. Much seems to me to hinge on the answer to this question concerning the constitution of physical actions.

9. INTERIORISM

(1) *This is Theory A (above)*, viz. Causes SΦ, φ; & Φ = SΦ; & SΦ/Φ is 'inner'. This gives an interiorist account of the bodily will, and identifies the physical action with that 'inner' phenomenon − when it is suitably causally responsible for the desired event φ. The argument against the theory consists largely in a catalogue of its unacceptable implications, which is to say in a *reductio ad absurdum*. Thus, if Theory A were true the following would hold (taking walking, swimming, running, as standard examples of physical action, and remembering that Theory A affirms that both SΦ and Φ are 'inner' (identicals)).

(i) Walking occurs always and only in the brain − if it occurs anywhere.

(ii) Running is invisible (precisely as dreams and itches are invisible). If it is ever to be seen, it will be seen in the brain (only).

(iii) No acts of any kind are visible. No one has ever seen anyone do anything. No criminal acts, like rape or murder or theft, have even been visually witnessed.

(iv) One cannot feel oneself walking or swimming. One can only feel the bodily effects of walking or swimming.

(v) Walking is never veridically experienced as going on in the legs.

(vi) Swimming is an event in the 'inner' world − like pain or dreaming.

(vii) Walking brings about leg movements, tree-chopping sets the arms in motion.

(viii) Since physical instrumental strivings like trying to kick the door down are 'public' visible phenomena, while the bodily will is here said to be 'inner', physical instrumental strivings must contain or co-exist with an invisible 'inner' striving with necessarily identical content and identical token psychological cause; accordingly, physical instrumental strivings must in this sense be double, both numerically and ontologically.

So much for *reductio ad absurdum* reasons. One other important argument against Theory A exists, set out now in (2) (below), first in (ix) and then elaborated in (x).

(2)(ix) The origins of Φ, viz. Belief re Φ/Desire to Φ/Intention to Φ, project a nomically bonded syndrome of events, almost always (say 99.99% of the time) coming together in a packet, viz. SΦ/activation-of-motor-mechanism-M-(for-ϕ)-all-the-way-to-ϕ/Φ, all of which share the same token ψ-origin, i.e. all emerging expressively from the one token act-producing psychological force-system. This is good reason for thinking these three phenomena (whether distinct, overlapping, or identical) are bonded together in one event. For to repeat: they almost always occur together, and when they do they always share the one token ψ-origin. No one much knows the necessary and sufficient conditions of event or object unity, but the above look to me likely contenders for being a sufficient set; and we seem to find such conditions at work when we unify (say) the nomically bonded parts of an oak tree, which sprang from a 'projecting' acorn, as all parts of the one natural item. This conclusion is at variance with Theory A, for Theory A postulates SΦ and ϕ as wholly distinct and united under no event head.

(x) Then if SΦ, M-activation-all-the-way-to-ϕ, and Φ, are in fact united under one event head, *what event-head can it be?* Since S$\Phi \nrightarrow \phi$, and S$\Phi \nrightarrow \Phi$ (so that it cannot be 'SΦ'); and since $\phi \nrightarrow$ SΦ, & $\phi \nrightarrow$ M-activation, & $\phi \nrightarrow \Phi$ (so it cannot be 'ϕ'); whereas $\Phi \rightarrow$ SΦ & M-activation-to-ϕ & ϕ – and no other event-heads are conceivable – then surely that event-head must be 'Φ'. Here we have another reason for thinking Φ encompasses SΦ, M-activation-to-ϕ, and ϕ, all nomically united under its conceptual cover. And this is inconsistent with Theory A.

For these reasons I reject Theory A. I think they constitute an overwhelming case against that doctrine, which strikes me as far and away the weakest of the four viable theories of Φ-constitution.

10. EXTERIORISM

(1) *This is Theory B (above)*, viz. Causes SΦ, ϕ; & $\Phi = \phi$; & SΦ is 'inner'. This theory gives an interiorist account of bodily willing, and identifies the physical action with the 'outer' willed event. By and large, this is the traditional theory, as we find it presented by Descartes, Locke, and Hume. Once again the argument against the theory consists in a catalogue of its unacceptable implications. These consist mostly in an unwelcome and wholesale 'doubling up' of entities, meanings, relations, and orders of

being, in the active situation. Thus, if Theory B is true, the following must
hold:

   (i) Whenever we physically act, there occur two distinct active 'doings',
        $S\Phi$ and ϕ; despite our unawareness of any such bifurcation, despite
        the existence logically necessarily of only one token psychological
        act-generative force-system, and despite the necessary sharing of
        psychological/moral/etc. predicate-tokens between them.

  (ii) One 'active doing' causes the other; so that trying to move the arm
        causes the act of arm-moving, and serving at tennis is brought about
        by an 'inner' trying to serve.

 (iii) One is psychologistically-immediately aware of some physical
        'active doings' (e.g. $S\Phi$), but only proprioceptively-immediately
        aware of other physical 'active doings' (e.g. Φ) – and sometimes
        (e.g. a sudden momentary striving in which ϕ happens not to be
        perceived) not even that!

  (iv) Some physical 'active doings' (e.g. $S\Phi$) have immediate psycholog-
        ical origins, while other physical 'active doings' (e.g. Φ) have only
        mediate psychological origins; some (e.g. Φ) are caused by others
        (e.g. $S\Phi$), while some others (e.g. $S\Phi$) are not; etc.

   (v) The activeness of some (e.g. Φ) is due to having an active cause
        (viz. $S\Phi$), while the activeness of some (e.g. $S\Phi$) is either intrinsic
        or derived from having an act-desire and/or intention origin. One
        important consequence of this is, that the explanation of the exis-
        tence of the property of activeness, together with its very nature,
        become highly problematic issues. (Here we have the substance
        behind certain familiar charges which are often levelled against
        volitionism. Thus, it is sometimes said that regress faces those who
        claim that the activeness of a limb movement derives from its voli-
        tion origin.)

(2)(vi) Since trying to chop down a tree is almost certainly a physical
        action, physical (as opposed to mental) act-strivings divide sharply
        in two – *ontologically* and *epistemologically.* Thus, according to The-
        ory B, physical instrumental trying must be the visible bodily move-
        ment which is non-psychologistically 'given' to its agent, whereas
        basic bodily act strivings must be 'inner' and psychological and
        'given' with mentalistic immediacy to their agent. Yet surely in
        fact all physical act-strivings are of one and the same ontological
        and epistemological status; for surely we stand in one and the same
        quasi-infallible epistemological relation to physical strivings – under

some description or other, and it is certain that ontology is not description-relative.

And there are reasons for thinking that on Theory B physical act-strivings divide in two *numerically* as well. The following considerations bring that out:

(vii) Since trying to start the car (by turning the crank) is a visible physical action, and since one who is trying to start a car knows with mentalistic immediacy that he is engaging in a striving with car-starting as its goal, Theory B implies that when we try to start the car an 'inner' invisible trying to start the car produces a *quite distinct* and simultaneous second 'outer' trying to start the car – both logically necessarily sharing the one token psychological cause. (A fantastic conclusion, it seems to me.)

(viii) And this second 'outer' striving is a striving concerning whose very existence one in his wakeful right mind can be mistaken, e.g. if the 'inner' striving-to-ϕ'-make-by-ϕ-making is co-present with seeming-ϕ and $\sim\phi$. (Equally fantastic, I should say.)

(ix) So that striving can *qua* striving be a mode of success!

Thus, on Theory B physical 'active doings', whether actions or strivings, divide numerically/ontologically/epistemologically/genetically in two. Willingly-active 'do' becomes ambiguous, as between an 'inner' will-sense of 'do' and an 'outer' willed action-sense. We seem to have here a gross doubling of entities, meanings, relations, and orders of being. Accordingly, I reject Theory B, a theory that I have treated with some seriousness, largely because it is the traditional doctrine; for any well-worn theory must be treated with respect, seeing that it has stood the test of time.

II. INTERIORISM/EXTERIORISM

This is Theory C (above), viz. Causes $S\Phi$, ϕ; & Φ encompasses & is non-identical with both $S\Phi$ and ϕ; & $S\Phi$ is 'inner'. This gives an interiorist account of bodily willing, and does not identify the physical action (Φ) either with the (supposed) 'inner' event of willing ($S\Phi$) or with the 'outer' willed event (ϕ), but construes the act as a complex event encompassing both phenomena, along with the connective events in the motor system. (A necessary condition of Φ being that the willing ($S\Phi$) and the willed (ϕ) events relate to one another non-deviantly causally.) The case against the theory consists of four distinct arguments: (A1) the argument from ontology, (A2) the argument from the nature of physical striving, (A3) the argument from mechanism, and (A4) the argument from modality (which is set out *en passant* in the succeeding section, 12). Each argument strikes me as decisive, but the joint effect is undoubtedly stronger.

(A1) The argument from ontology contra Theory C

(A1a) The ontological implications of Theory C

(1) Here in (A1a) I want to demonstrate that this present Theory C is by implication almost certainly committed to the thesis that Φ is a psychological event. Now the only conceivable ontological options are: that Φ is *both physical and 'psycho-physical'* (ϕ & 'ψ-ϕ'); that it is *merely physical* (ϕ & $\sim\psi$); or that it is *physical and also psychological* (ϕ & ψ). Then in section 7 a strong case was marshalled against the theory that there exists a separate ontological level 'ψ-ϕ' ('psycho-physical') which *is* being part ψ & remainder $\phi \sim \psi$. Meanwhile, if Theory C were true then the case against Φ's being merely physical (ϕ & $\sim\psi$) is strong from the start, since Theory C claims that the 'inner' ψ event SΦ is both part of and the essential teleological developmental core of Φ. In sum, it seems to me that Theory C is by implication all but committed to the ψ-dom of Φ. Here is a statement of the various reasons supporting this reading of the situation:

  (i) Φ is a single event, endowed therefore with determinate ontological status, necessarily at the very least part ψ, and necessitates the use of a brain.

   And the genetic and epistemological properties of Φ (as conceived by Theory C). To wit:

 (ii) Necessarily Φ has an immediate psychological cause that is mentally immediately known *of*, and mentally immediately known *to be* cause of Φ, and known *a priori* to be of the type act-desire.

(iii) Therefore the causal relation between Φ and its psychological progenitors exhibits all the marks of the special 'mental causal' relation, viz. type of cause *a priori* known in advance, singular causal relation known incorrigibly and independently of 'Humean' regularity considerations.

Thus, Φ is immediately *genetically bonded* to the ψ-system, and in the special way that is unique to the mind. Then the following consideration (iv) at least suggests that if Theory C is true then Φ may also be immediately *epistemologically bonded* to the ψ-system, and again in the special way that is uniquely mental.

(iv) Since we are psychologistically-immediately aware of SΦ (under some heading or other, e.g. as 'doing something'); and since (according to Theory C) SΦ is an essential element of Φ, and near universally sets in motion the phenomena completing the teleological goal event Φ of which it is a core part (so that a two-way nomic regularity links the two phenomena, i.e. $S\Phi \equiv \Phi$); it seems plausible to suppose that the psychologistically-immediate awareness of $S\Phi$ is one and the same phenomenon as the psychologistically-immediate awareness of Φ. While this argument is not obviously valid, I mention it in part because it helps to show how Theory C passes naturally into Theory D.

(2) In sum, if Theory C were true then Φ must be genetically bonded to the ψ-system in the psychologistically-immediate manner that is unique to the mind. In addition, there is reason for suspecting that it might be epistemologically bonded to the mind in the same manner. Taken in conjunction with the *ad hoc* and wholly unconvincing thesis that a separate ontological level 'ψ-ϕ' ('psycho-physical') exists, and the strong *prima facie* case against Φ's being merely physical if Theory C is true (since Theory C posits the supposedly 'inner' ψ event ($S\Phi$) as the essential core element of Φ), it is difficult to see how adherents of Theory C can avoid the theoretical position: Φ is of ontological status ψ.

(A1b) Deductions from A1a (above) (or 'The Principle of Cartesian Translucence')

(1) Then what follows if Φ is ψ? I think it follows that the wind goes out of the sails of Theory C; for Theory C is built upon the presumption that psychologicality entails interiority, i.e. that no psychological event could *a priori* be given as encompassing a determinately specifiable peripheral mere bodily movement. In short, if Φ is ψ then Theory C loses its main rationale, and we shall see that it mutates inevitably into Theory D.

But I will set this consideration aside, and return to the question: what follows if Φ is ψ? I think it follows that this event, already agreed to at least harbour the event $S\Phi$, must actually *be* $S\Phi$. I say so because of a Principle P_D (for Descartes) that seems to me fully in the spirit of the Cartesian insight into the mind's translucence. Namely: any ψ item that is an experience, must under normal mental cognitive conditions (awake, sane, etc.) be psychologistically-immediately experienced under some minimum self-validating near-incorrigible psychological heading H. Now if Theory C was true, and if we make the further assumption that Φ is ψ, then Φ must be a ψ item that is psychologistically-immediately experienced. Then the question Principle P_D poses is: what can be the near-incorrigible heading H in the case of Φ? Not $\int \phi$ ('seemingly (to me) an occurrence of ϕ'), which is merely a putative experience of ϕ as ϕ and not an active heading, whereas the event one is experiencing and characterising (viz. Φ) is active. Not $\int \Phi$ ('seemingly (to me) an occurrence of Φ'), for that expression has to be understood *either* as signifying Φ *or else* as signifying an experience with active internal object, but not such as to entail activeness of nature. Nor can Φ itself be the H that we are seeking, since Φ entails φ and is grossly corrigible by others. Nor can the will-heading 'SΦ' and the awareness heading '∫φ' 'fuse' and produce a new will-heading – for none exists.

We are looking for the *active 'lowest common ψ-denominator'* under which the ψ-immediately-experienced ψ event Φ near-incorrigibly falls in normal waking experiential conditions. None of the above will do. And we know that SΦ is ψ-immediately-experienced whenever Φ occurs (probably as 'doing *something* φ-wards'). Clearly, 'SΦ' alone fits the bill. It alone is a ψ-heading that is at once *not* the internal object of a putative awareness, that *is* active in type, that *is* near-incorrigibly given, and that *does not* entail the occurrence of φ. Therefore Φ must be SΦ. And that disproves Theory C.

(2) Note that the Cartesian Principle P_D, to which we have appealed, is not grounded upon any of the following five claims.
(a) Every part of a ψ event is ψ. (Which is probably false, cf. Physicalism.)
(b) No ψ-item has a non-ψ part. (Which is probably false, cf. Physicalism.)
(c) Every ψ part of a ψ item is ψ. (Which is an empty tautology.)
(d) Every ψ-event is ψ-experienced. (Which is false, cf. forgetting.)
(e) Every part of a ψ-event-that-is-ψ-immediately-experienced that *a priori* analytically and constitutively contributes to the event's being the ψ-event type that it is, is itself ψ. (Which may well be false, e.g. Φ may be a psychological heading and yet be answerable to φ.)
The correct statement of the rationale for Principle P_D must be cast in terms of experience, and takes the following form.
(f) Every part of a ψ-event-that-is-ψ-immediately-experienced that *a priori* analytically and constitutively contributes to the event's being the ψ-event type that it must near-incorrigibly veridically be experienced to be, is itself ψ and and ψ-immediately experienced.

(3) It is thanks to this latter truth (f) that we arrive at Principle P_D, which amounts to the claim that ψ-immediately-experienceable ψ-items must lie fully open to mental view in the mind. That is, there can in ψ experience be no analogue of the physical situation in which we glimpse a side of a tomato that could be *either* a whole material object that is half a tomato coming to the attention *or* a whole material object that is a whole tomato coming to the attention. Diagramatically: while the following two perfectly veridical perceptual situations are epistemically possible and visually indistinguishable to the subject:

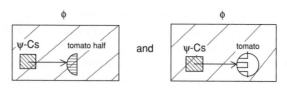

Fig. 7a

nothing corresponds to the second of these two (below).

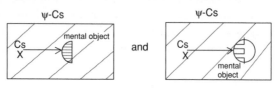

Fig. 7b

(4) Please note that we are not denying the insights of Freud. The distinction has nothing to do with the Unconscious. For what we are saying is this. The (material object) type we can veridically (visually) experience an object of visual experience to be, *can* on those veridical occasions be analytically-constitutively determined by factors (such as the presence of an unseen other material half) lying outside that experience. But the psychological type we more or less must in normal mental conditions veridically psychologistically-immediately experience an experience to be, *cannot* on those veridical occasions be analytically-constitutively determined by factors such as the presence of an UNEXPERIENCED THOUGH PSYCHOLOGICAL OTHER HALF or an UNEXPERIENCED NON-PSYCHOLOGICAL OTHER HALF.

In this sense the ψ-immediately experienceable is, like a painting or a piece of music, a pure creature of appearance. And just as it matters not that the painting is incarnate in paint stuff, so this truth remains unaffected by the fact that the ψ-immediately experienceable may be incarnated in cerebral phenomena. In either case we are speaking of an infinitely shallow and essentially *one*-sided item. Thus, what could we mean by 'the other side of the red of the pillar box'? Or 'the other side of the Mona Lisa'? Would we mean the other side of the canvas? Or of the paint? Or of 'the' front part of the paint? Take your pick, but we no more mean 'the other side of what you greatly admire' than we mean anything by 'the other side of the afterimage' 'the concealed under-side of the footache' 'the obscured interior of the headache'. It is a world of pure appearance that is our concern here.

(5) Applied to the physical action Φ (construed now as psychological), Principle P_D and its underlying rationale dictate that, if we assume

Consciousness (Cs) to be 'looking down' the deed (Φ) in the direction from-'inner'-to-'outer', then the non-psychologistically-experienceable non-psychological event ϕ cannot analytically-constitutively determine the ψ-type that the psychological event Φ must veridically and near-incorrigibly and psychologistically-immediately present to Cs. Diagrammatically:

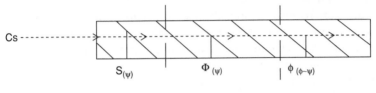

Fig. 8

Whereas ϕ is (non-psychologistically) immediately (proprioceptively) experienced, and (together with SΦ) causes us to have the experience, awareness-of-Φ-*as*-Φ, it is a causal but it is not a constitutive determinant of that experience, and this is because it is not a constitutive determinant of the psychological heading under which the experience is psychologistically-immediately and veridically given to the experiencer. In a word, ϕ cannot in this psychological situation play the role that is taken by the unseen tomato-half in visual perception.

(6) Thus, on the basis of Principle P$_D$ together with the assumption that Φ is ψ (which seems highly plausible if Theory C is true), we deduce that Φ must be SΦ (which contradicts Theory C). That is, we practise a '*reductio*', and simultaneously show how accepting that Φ encompasses SΦ leads inevitably to the view that $\Phi = S\Phi$; that is, we show how Theory C leads inevitably to Theory D. In short, we construct a bridge whereby Theory C may cross over to Theory D. (For Theory C is the last 'resistance' before Theory D.) Now that concludes Section A(1) (*The argument from ontology*), which has consisted in those considerations directed against Theory C that are concerned with the ontological nature of Φ and most especially with the suggestion that if Theory C were true then Φ would have to be of ontological status ψ. I come now to a different argument against Theory C. This is an argument based upon a consideration of the nature of physical striving. However, before I set out the argument in section (A2), I would like once more to remark that I believe the present section (A1) has brought to light the inner logic whereby Theory C passes inevitably into the 'dialectically superior' Theory D.

(A2)   The argument contra Theory C from the nature of physical striving

(1) The present argument consists in an elaboration of the (grossly unacceptable, as it seems to me) implications of Theory C, so far as the nature of physical strivings is concerned. I list them (below) in (i)–(vi).

(i) I shall assume that anyone endorsing Theory C accepts the obvious truth that physical instrumental strivings are sometimes visible (etc.), and for the many reasons already advanced in section 5 identifies them sometimes with overt actions like turning a crank or kicking a door. But as soon as they do, the following unwelcome implications (rehearsed already in section 6) confront them.

(i) One set of physical strivings must be 'inner' and incorrigible by others (viz. $S\Phi$, 'basic striving'), while another set of physical strivings – the visible physical instrumental strivings (viz. $S\Phi'$) – must according to Theory C be 'inner-outer' and corrigible by others. This is because Theory C analyses the visible $S\Phi'$ into a first part ('inner' $S\Phi'$) together with a completion (visible part) ϕ, so that such a phenomenon can become an $S\Phi'$ of the publicly visible kind only if a suitably engendered ϕ occurs. Accordingly, it will be corrigible *qua* $S\Phi'$ by $\sim\phi$.

But *why should not* visible instrumental strivings be corrigible by $\sim\phi$? After all, these strivings are identical with the publicly visible instrumental act Φ, and Φ is certainly corrigible by $\sim\phi$. Well, the fact that Φ is corrigible by $\sim\phi$ does not mean that $S\Phi'$ also is corrigible by $\sim\phi$. For even though $S\Phi'$ *is* Φ, and Φ is corrigible by $\sim\phi$, $S\Phi'$ is not corrigible by $\sim\phi$. What is here corrigible is, that the striving $S\Phi'$ *takes the form* Φ. In fact, the only known corrigibility by others for an $S\Phi'$ is that deriving from the referential use of '$S\Phi'$' – and such an insignificant variety of corrigibility exists alike with mental images – and $S\Phi$! Therefore no usage of '$S\Phi'$' exists that can bear witness to the existence of such a supposed 'inner-outer' instrumental striving.

(ii) Physical strivings must divide into 'inner' and 'inner-outer', and doubtless divide ontologically as well.

(iii) Whenever one performs an 'inner-outer' (visible) physical instrumental striving $S\Phi'$, one performs a purely 'inner' striving with identical content $(S\int\Phi')$ that expresses the one token act-generative psychological force-system, for it is undeniable that one who engages in an instrumental striving incorrigibly knows that a striving seemingly Φ'-wards is taking place. In other words, when one performs a 'public' (visible) physical instrumental striving one is supposed to be performing *two* $S\Phi'$s, one part of the other, stemming necessarily from the identical token causal source. (A highly improbable thesis, as it seems to me.)

(A3)   *The argument from mechanism contra 'The sandwich theory of the bodily will'*

(A3a)   *Introduction*

I come now to what seems to me to be an argument of some importance. I speak here of a 'sandwich' theory, because this argument is directed against an account of the bodily will wherein, 'sandwiched' between the antecedents of physical action and the activation of the act-mechanism M, is said to occur an 'inner' psychological event of willing that stands outside and 'triggers off' that mechanism. The theory is represented immediately below, where DΦ stands for the act-desire to Φ, BΦ for the associated belief cause of action, IΦ for the intention to Φ, and SΦ for striving to Φ.

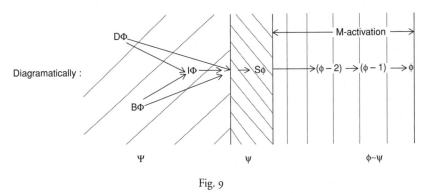

Fig. 9

Whereas the theory which I endorse (Theory D) views the situation as follows:

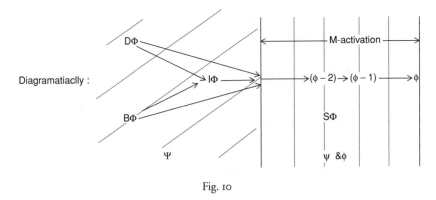

Fig. 10

Clearly, two profoundly different accounts of the mind–body relation are at loggerheads here.

(A3b)　A regulative principle

(1) I will first of all set out this third argument ('from mechanism') that is directed against Theory C, and then offer reasons in support of its several subsidiary claims. The argument begins with the statement of a principle of some importance – if true. Namely: $\Box$(S$\Phi \to$ M-activation-*some*-distance-towards-ϕ) (where ϕ is the limb movement which owes its existence to the basic bodily act striving SΦ).

Why should we endorse such a claim? Briefly: it is because *absolutely nothing* could be invoked to account for SΦ's sometimes activating M and sometimes not. For *how else but by invoking breakdown* IN THE MIDST OF M-ACTIVATION are we to explain instances of SΦ & $\sim\phi$ in situations of physical liberty? Are we to believe in an occasional 'pure impotence of the physical will'? But we seem not to make conceptual provision for such a possibility. That is, I suggest that $\Box$(S$\Phi \to$ activation-at-least-*some*-way-along-M). (Let us call such activation 'M-a'.) Accordingly, if *full* activation of M ('M-A') consists in the regular causal sequence $\phi_1 \phi_2 \ldots \phi_n \ldots \phi$, then (in physical liberty) $\Box$(SΦ & $\sim\phi_n \to$ M-a & M-breakdown). I suggest that this is a rule, and that the rule holds irrespective of whether the breakdown is superficial and muscular or profound and cerebral. For under what deep cerebral conditions would we encounter the elusive 'pure impotence of SΦ'? Hysteria? But hysteria is a mental and not a neurological illness, and in M-health/wholeness and physical liberty SΦ strictly necessitates and perhaps even *entails* Φ. Therefore no hysterical mental state can interpose itself between SΦ and M. It follows that the class of hysterical phenomena cannot conceivably harbour the missing case of 'pure impotence of SΦ'. In any case, the hysterically 'paralysed' are simply those who fail to really try (i.e. really to SΦ), when they hysterically or grossly self-deceptively seem to themselves to SΦ, the hysterical schism being intra-psychically sited between psychically 'higher' cognitive and executive centres and psychically 'lower' actualities with which putatively they are in immediate contact. It is a mode of being mentally 'cut off' from one's body.

(2) In a word, the hypothesised occasional 'pure impotence of the bodily will' seems to be a myth. This supposedly rare possibility is, I suggest, an impossibility. But I have of course not yet demonstrated this very important thesis. Let me here attempt to do so. Now it is plain from the above considerations that the 'pure impotence of SΦ' could be realised only if it is possible for SΦ to take place in the complete absence of M-activation. The suggestion is that SΦ might simply bounce back off this M. (The willing in the inner world completely not engage with the motor-system!) But do we

have truth-conditions for SΦ & ~M-a? We have truth-conditions for SΦ & ~ϕ, viz. the truth of SΦ and of ~ϕ, for both of which we have agreed verifications. Likewise for SΦ & ~(activation-of-M-beyond-m_p), viz. the truth of SΦ, and of ~(ϕ_q V ϕ_r V . . . Vϕ): the latter depending upon our determining that ϕ_q . . . ϕ is the last part of M-A, which in turn is achieved through correlating Φ with ϕ_q . . . ϕ and establishing that each element is a causally sufficient condition of its successor element in the mechanistic sequence. But the difficulty is to *break free of this epistemological mould* and discover truth-conditions for SΦ & ~M-a, i.e. SΦ in the complete absence of M-activation.

How to make this differential discovery? Now it is not that I entertain the idea that M need not be determinate in content and extent: I recognise that M, from the mere fact of being a mechanism, must have a determinate end – and beginning. Evidently we need to come by the truth-conditions for an event's counting as the very first element in M-A, i.e. for being ϕ_1. Then surely all we need to do is discover the first event in a sequence of events that terminates in ϕ and that correlates regularly with Φ. (With the proviso that there may be any number of M's to ϕ.) And is not this a task that is best left to brain scientists? Let us for the moment assume so. And let us suppose that these scientists have successfully discovered the first event ϕ_1 in the/an M-sequence, and let us further suppose that we encounter ϕ_1's absence in a non-hysterical subject who plainly is not lying when he insists that he is engaging in SΦ. Are not these the missing truth-conditions of SΦ & ~M-a? Is not this an instance of a 'pure impotence of the bodily will'?

(3) But a difficulty exists. For what of the physical form taken by SΦ? If scientists are to identify ϕ_1, it must on principle be considered only when both SΦ and Φ obtain. But why so? Might not the mechanism M be activated by a probe – rather than willingly? It may well be that it can, but if we are to ensure that M really is the mechanism of the action Φ, we are obliged to correlate it with all the cases of SΦ-and-Φ. It follows that, in the course of the search for the content of M, *physical* SΦ must always be co-present with ϕ_1. For if a rigorous law binds SΦ and the beginning of an M-sequence-leading-to-ϕ, such as could not conceivably hold between (say) thought and thought or affect and blush, must not SΦ be an event that is at once physical and psychological? (As there is no nomically regular mechanism of thought-linkage or affect-expression, precisely there is in bodily action – even to the point of a psycho-physical law that in liberty and motor-health may even be an entailment!) Then have we not a right to expect, not merely physicality in SΦ, but a regular physical type or fixed

set of fixed types? At the very least, some sort of regularly present physical phenomenon? If SΦ normally correlates with physical ϕ_1 and its successors in the M-sequence(s)-to-ϕ, how can this fail to be so?

Then if that is true, how is one to differentially distinguish SΦ and ϕ_1? I suggest that, for all that brain scientists may be able to tell in engaging in such physical procedures, SΦ might be identical with ϕ_1, or with an event whose parts are ϕ_1 and ϕ_2, or ϕ_1 and ϕ_2 and ϕ_3, etc. A sort of Heisenberg Indeterminacy Principle reigns here that legislates against the particular differential findings that we sought, whereby SΦ is to be detected in the absence of M-a – rather as if SΦ were the necessarily unique observational medium for the observation of an observed phenomenon that is inevitably disturbed in the process! In short, it seems that we lack truth-conditions for SΦ & ~M-a. That is, $\Box$(SΦ → M-a).

(4) But if SΦ rigorously necessitates M-activation, if SΦ is never in any possible world encountered without M-activation, why should we in those worlds distinguish SΦ and M-activation? Not because we say, 'M-activation occurred *because* SΦ', for we also say, 'The embryo developed a brain *because* it is human', and infant/embryo are non-distinct. Not because there may be occasions on which M-activation occurs in the absence of SΦ, for that in no way qualifies the truth that no worlds contain SΦ and absence of M-activation. Now we identify an item x as a member of an M-sequence-to-ϕ by correlating Φ with a causally bonded sequence ϕ $\phi - 1$ $\phi - 2 \ldots$, and discovering of x that it is part of that sequence, and therefore sufficient causal condition of some succeeding member and thereby of ϕ itself (in conditions of physical liberty). But whatever correlates with Φ correlates with SΦ. Then does not that imply that SΦ satisfies the test for being at least part of the M-sequence-to-ϕ, i.e. part of M-A? For what other test could one propose for an item's being at least part of M-A, than correlating rigorously with Φ and being causally sufficient for ϕ via a well-worn physical 'path' regularly used by Φ? And SΦ satisfies this test.

Then surely the only satisfactory explanation of the entailment from SΦ to M-activation is, that it is a logically necessary condition of an event's being an SΦ that it is an activation-of-at-least-*some*-way-along-M. This permits SΦ to be physical in character, explains its entailing M-activation, and explains SΦ's having the property of satisfying the proposed test for being at least part of M-A. In short, SΦ must be part of M-A. But if SΦ is part of M-A, which part? No principle exists whereby we may single out some first segment of M-A and identify it with SΦ. Therefore SΦ must be M-activation-*any*-distance-towards-ϕ. Then just as the properly visual 'seem to see' entails 'notices visual sensation', so 'M-activation that is SΦ' entails 'immediately DΦ-caused'. That is, SΦ just *is* an M-activation that is immediately DΦ-caused: SΦ *is* an (immediately DΦ-caused) M-activation-towards-φ: it is the event realised by the unfolding of this teleologically directed process. Then in motor-health and liberty the phenomenon of M-activation-*some*-way-to-φ is *all-the-way*-to-φ. That is, does not cause φ. This disproves Theory C (along with Theories A and B), and more or less takes us as far as Theory D.

IIA. POSTSCRIPT

To repeat: just as the properly visual 'seem to see' entails 'notices visual sensation', so 'M-activation that is SΦ' entails 'M-activation that is immediately DΦ-caused'. That is, SΦ just *is* M-activation that is immediately DΦ-caused.

Then here in this latter observation we have the truth resident in anti-will theories of bodily action; for it is *as if* SΦ were otiose, seeing that DΦ immediately activates M without the mediation of any will-event. But in actual fact SΦ is precisely the unique and immediate expression of the act-desire DΦ, and therefore a necessity if action is to occur. One could characterise the situation by saying that we have no need of a separate (let alone 'inner') ψ-event SΦ ('willing') to get M moving, and to suppose so would be to interpose an unnecesary 'inner' mediator between the mind and the motor-apparatus; but we have every need of the ψ event SΦ if the mind is to get M moving, and to suppose we do not would be to interpose an unnecessary 'outer' mediator (M-activation) between the mind and the surrounding environment.

I believe that the peculiar structure to be found in the physical act situation, *whereby a particular physicalist truth is for the first time openly demonstrable*, has doubly and understandably misled people. We find it hard to grasp that an overtly physical phenomenon like M-activation could be validly and immediately given as a ψ-event like willing. We tend to feel that if it is psychological then it cannot be given a physical specification. Both of the above misinterpretations of the act-situation – the positing of a separate and 'inner' SΦ *and* an M-activation-that-is-not-SΦ – which introduce incomprehensibility into the mind–body relation (for we have no rationale for a separate and 'inner' SΦ's managing to generate M-activation when it happens to do just that) – reveal the extent to which Cartesianism is embedded in our thinking, indeed is natural to thought. More specifically, the Cartesian thesis that ontological diversity entails event distinctness: a doctrine alive and kicking in the thinking of some physicalists, whose adherence to theories of a reductionist character reveals, along with their apparent readiness to tolerate event identity amidst ontological duality, a covert intolerance of *real* ontological duality in the one event. In a word, these anti-Cartesian theories are haunted by their own unconscious Cartesianism. And the explanation of this fact is: these theories are not as such dialectical.

12. DUAL ASPECT THEORY

This is Theory D (above), viz. $\sim$Causes $S\Phi$, ϕ; & $\Phi = S\Phi$; & Φ encompasses $S\Phi$ and ϕ. In the ensuing sections 1–3 I will set out and answer objections to this theory. However, before I begin that discussion, I would like briefly to say what I take to be the natural intuitively acceptable account of physical action (Φ). It goes like this. First that the act Φ is a visible phenomenon, and therefore must include the event ϕ; and second that Φ is at the very least co-present with, and perhaps even in some way overlaps with, an immediately given event (call it X) that is 'dynamic' and an active 'doing'. Now such an analysis of Φ is not consistent with Theory A, but is with Theories B, C, D. Then despite Theory D's agreement with this natural conception of physical action, it must be admitted that the theory is to a degree counter-intuitive. How can that be? Well, it may be that the natural or intuitive view is in addition that the 'dynamic' X is 'inner' in character. Accordingly, it must be the idea that $S\Phi$ can be ψ and yet encompass ϕ, and therefore that an item can be psychological in type without being 'inner', that some find unacceptable. Then here in section (a) (below) I list objections to Theory D which take off from this belief, together with the replies of one who endorses the theory. Thereafter in sections (b) and (c) I set out and reply to certain additional objections to Theory D, and in section (d) I put forward arguments in favour of the theory. Finally, in section (e) I list the theoretical assets of Theory D. (Objections are in inverted commas, replies in brackets.)

(a) Interiorist objections to Theory D

(i) '"Psychological" (ψ) means (amongst other things) "inner and private".' [We can only know what this statement means when 'inner and private' is defined. But in any case 'psychological' is surely indefinable. In particular, it is not to be defined in terms of intentionality, bearing in mind that the property 'psychological' ranges not just across thoughts and beliefs, but in addition over rudimentary phenomena like sensations and bodily actions. It follows that the only acceptable reading of the above critical sentence is '"psychological" means psychological', and that poses no problem for Theory D.]

(ii) 'ψ entails being of necessity intuitable or witnessable by its owner and by he alone'. [Some ψ phenomena like the process of forgetting are neither immediately experienceable by nor immediately cognitively given to their owner. And if Physicalism is true, then ψ phenomena will in principle be perceivable by others.]

(iii) 'All ψ items that are immediately experienced by their owner are "inner" in the sense of being quasi-incorrigibly and immediately given to their owner alone.' [But SΦ, and therefore Φ, are all of this on Theory D.]

(iv) 'All ψ items that are immediately experienced by their owner, and therefore quasi-incorrigibly given to their owner alone, do not fall under constitutive descriptions nor under type-heading descriptions that are corrigible by others.' [But in the first place if Physicalism is true ψ events will have physical parts discoverable by others, and will therefore have constitutive descriptions corrigible by others. And secondly seeings are immediately experienced ψ items that are quasi-incorrigibly given to their owner alone as 'seem see —', that fall under type-heading descriptions (viz. 'see —') that are corrigible by others.]

(v) 'All ψ items that are immediately experienced by their owner can never be ψ-immediately given to their owner as including a $\phi \sim \psi$ event part.' [But if Theory D is true, SΦ satisfies this edict. According to Theory D it is *a priori* necessary that SΦ is ψ, that it is ψ-immediately experienced, and that SΦ that is Φ includes the bodily movement ϕ; but it is not *a priori* necessary that Φ be ψ-immediately experienced as encompassing ϕ. After all, the cause of one's experiencing SΦ as Φ is the corrigible proprioceptively immediate experience of ϕ, and this implies that the ψ-immediate experience of SΦ cannot be ψ-immediately *qua* Φ. This latter claim in no way contradicts the above four claims (i)–(iv). What is novel in the position adopted by Theory D is, that what is ψ and immediately experienced can be brought under a type-heading which is determinately physical (viz. M-activation). In other words, according to Theory D both the physicality and the specific physical content of this particular ψ event are philosophically demonstrable.]

(vi) 'Whatever you say about the indefineability of "ψ", there just *has to be* some sense in which "psychological" means "inner".' [We cannot know the full *a priori* implications of psychologicality, until we have settled the truth-value of Physicalism, and brought to a satisfactory conclusion investigations like the present inquiry. Until such times we cannot assess claims like the one you make. But I suggest that your firm conviction that physical strivings must be 'inner', and indeed that all that is ψ must be 'inner', comes about in the following manner. It seems to me natural to suppose that if SΦ is ψ then it must be comparable *in very general kind* to a bodily or mental feeling like strain, and therefore that SΦ must be a possible interior object of introspective scrutiny. This idea probably derives from the fact that when we think about tryings we usually concentrate on tryings that are either mental strivings – like trying to remember, or tryings that are strenuous and accompanied by introspectible ψ items – such as occur when we attempt to lift a heavy weight. Thus, all along we have the idea of trying or striving as something at once decidedly mental, certainly introspectible, and of a distinctive phenomenal character: one thinks of straining, of a sense of effort, of sensations in one's muscles, of thoughts relating us to our goal, etc.

But the truth is that the phenomenon which we have at length been discussing is not like that. Think of a bodily trying that completely fails, and take note of its properties, for here we encounter bodily trying purely *qua* psychological event, divested of all other experienceable properties. Then it is clear from such an example that the physical strivings of which we speak must be totally dissimilar to mental strivings. For one thing they are infinitely more primitive, being present in all varieties of animal life. For another they are not *introspectible*, for there is no such thing as directing one's attention mentalistically-immediately onto one's present bodily strivings: one can *think about* the phenomenon as it is going on, but one cannot mentalistically-immediately *attend* to it. Indeed, the psychological properties of bodily striving are all but invisible. I say so because of a constellation of unusual properties. Thus, it is *nothing but* a striving to Φ. For SΦ does not *feel* either SΦ-ish or *any* way, and is entirely lacking in phenomenal character or *quale*. Moreover, it is normally neither intense nor faint. And SΦ is not ψ-experienced *as at* any body part, nor could it be; and neither is it ψ-experienced as psychologically *extensive*, unlike either bodily or visual sensations. And SΦ does not, as do such 'affective' bodily sensations as pains and tickles, *obtrude* into consciousness or distract. And one can give no psychological description of SΦ other than 'SΦ'. And so on. Strangely enough this *most primitive* of all psychological phenomena shares many properties with the *least primitive* of all psychological phenomena, the thought; for all that we have cited above to demonstrate the psychological 'invisibility' of SΦ may with equal validity be affirmed of the thought event. It, too, seems to have nothing but a content!

Then once we recognise how unlike other ψ items this ψ item is, and once we have grasped how *infinitely primitive* it is in the psychological domain, we may I suggest feel less disposed to insist in advance on its necessary interiority. This almost ineffable quasi-invisible primordial citizen of the ψ-domain is all but a psychological zero. Why *must* such a thing be interior?]

(vii) 'To say that Φ is ψ, is to make heavy weather of ψ; it is to put too much pressure on this ultimately imprecise term. Let us not surrender to a fanatical obsessive ontological pigeonholing!' [*Either* Φ is ϕ ψ *or* $\phi\sim\psi$ *or* of the *supposed ontological level* 'part $\phi\psi$ & remainder $\phi\sim\psi$' ('psychophysical') *or* it is borderline between $\phi\psi$ and $\phi\sim\psi$. There are no other possibilities. We have rejected $\phi\sim\psi$; we have examined the concept of the ontological level ψ-ϕ that is a 'hybrid' ontological level, and found it grossly unconvincing. Therefore, in lieu of $\phi\psi$, all that remains is 'borderline'. Now possibly this is possible – seeing that borderline conditions must exist between inanimacy and life as well as between mere life and conscious life. Nevertheless, it must be true or false that it is neither true nor false that Φ is ψ. Then I have already advanced reasons for the view that Φ is ψ, and hence for supposing the above proposition false. Thus, Φ necessarily constitutively involves use of the brain, Φ is necessarily at the very least ψ in part (viz. SΦ), a part which is its teleological core, and Φ has *a priori*-given immediate psychological origins and effects, etc. Let us not surrender to a careless conceptual *laissez-faire*-dom!]

(b) Objections to Theory D relating to the brain's involvement in action

Here, below, I continue with the format of objections to Theory D followed by replies to the objections. The following objections and replies concern the role of the brain in physical action. Once again, objections are in inverted commas and replies in brackets.

(i) 'Since one can be mentalistically-immediately aware of SΦ, all that is necessary for SΦ must have happened before ϕ and be confined to the brain.' [I agree. For what Theory D claims is, that ϕ is an inessential part of SΦ; and the necessary and sufficient conditions of SΦ must surely be brain events.]

(ii) 'All ψ events, if anywhere, must occur in the brain alone. For they reside entirely in the mind, and wherever the mind is must be where the brain is.' [Theory D claims that SΦ is *in part located of necessity in the brain*, and *necessarily begins in the brain*, and claims in addition that when SΦ 'expands' then it *necessarily expands systematically* along a nervous system which may perfectly legitimately be regarded as an extension of the brain, e.g. the spinal cord. Is this counter-intuitive? I do not believe it is. What, I think, would be truly counter-intuitive, would be either to locate SΦ elsewhere than in the brain, or else to include in it bodily phenomena outside the brain which stand in no systematic or nomic relation to the brain.]

(iii) 'But Theory D asserts that SΦ includes non-neurological events like finger movements. But SΦ can only encompass brain events, or at best events that are at once located in a brain extension and essentially determined by the normal working of the brain.' [But events like finger movements are events in a motor-system which is teleologically directed towards precisely them themselves, a system that begins in and is exclusively activated by the brain. Why must it be that 'whatever is ψ can only encompass brain events or events in a brain extension that are essentially determined by the normal working of the brain'? Why not 'whatever is ψ can only encompass events which either are in or are necessarily and systematically determined by the normal working of the brain'? After all, we may well allow that ψ events encompass molecular events which are not themselves ψ or even biological, so why not events that are necessarily and systematically determined by the normal working of the brain?]

(iv) 'My finger moves *because* I tried to move it. This "because" is causal; and therefore the two events must be distinct.' [But 'the tree grew because the acorn germinated' is true and causal, and yet the two are not distinct.]

(c) A modal objection to Theory D

I continue with the format of objections to Theory D followed by replies to the objections. Here we are concerned with a single argument of a modal kind, an argument which is put forward as a possible disproof of Theory D. The argument is set out between inverted commas, the reply is between brackets.

'Φ is necessarily Φ, and SΦ is necessarily SΦ. But it is not necessary that S$\Phi \rightarrow \Phi$, since some tryings fail. But if $\Phi = $ SΦ, and Φ is necessarily Φ, it must be necessary that S$\Phi \rightarrow \Phi$ – which contradicts the above. Therefore $\Phi \neq $ SΦ.'

[Suppose a man's arm is imprisoned in a rigid perfectly fitting mould m, though he does not know so, and assume that he sets out to move that arm. Instead, without budging an iota, his arm presses against m. Then he performed a single whole bodily act of m-pressing. I say so, because he could actively intentionally obey an order to do exactly what he had just done; and in each case he would have performed a single whole act. Then of that single act we can say, '*That act* would have been an arm-moving if mould m had not been there.' For (a) an m-pressing *did occur*, and (b) *would not have occurred* without m, and (c) an arm-moving *would have occurred* without m, and (d) we cannot suppose that a wholly distinct act would have occurred without m, for (e) it *under-describes the situation* to say that 'without m an arm-moving would have occupied (almost) the same space-time region as the m-pressing act', for it seems in addition (f) that we cannot but believe that a *very close relation* held between the present act of m-pressing and the hypothetical arm-moving act – surely (g) the relation of *identity*.

But may we not instead mean: an arm-moving would have occurred of which this present act would have been part? But do we mean that if m had not been present there would have occurred *two whole acts* (viz. all that we did in m-pressing *and* the act of arm-moving), one part of the other? Surely not. Surely we rather mean: an act of arm-moving would have occurred of which all that here mechanistically occurred (neurological messages, muscular contractions, etc.) would have been part. And that does not mean that *this act-event* of m-pressing would have been a whole act-part set in a *non-identical whole act-event* of arm-moving. Thus, one and only one act occurred in this present situation of constraint, and one and only one act would have occurred in the absence of m, and we can surely agree that these acts are not two perfectly distinct acts. Meanwhile we have just seen that one of these acts would not have been part of the at-least-non-distinct other act. Then how else could they be related but by the relation of identity? If we are passing from one possible world containing the whole act of m-pressing (which is an act which contains no whole act-parts) to another possible world containing the whole act of arm-moving (which likewise contains no whole act-parts), and these are not two perfectly distinct acts, how else can these (whole, non act-composite) acts be related but by the relation of identity? But may not these acts be related instead by the complex relation: non-distinct & non-identical? But then the problem becomes to discover the *type* or *character* of the non-distinctness that is to ensure this non-identity. Well, what about the relation: sharing a part? But which part? It can only be m-pressing. Thus, this suggestion returns us to the already rejected idea that the act of m-pressing would be a whole and countable act-part of the hypothetical supposedly non-identical act of arm-moving.

In the light of these considerations, and remembering that these 'two' non-distinct act-events are agreed to share the one token origin-source and the one natural teleological end, it seems certain that identity is the only possible relation in the circumstances. And this conclusion has familiar precedents.[1] I conclude that the present act of m-pressing and the

---

[1] 'Were it not for that rock on the road the skid would have been as far as the wall' entails 'In some possible worlds in which that rock is absent *this skid* (which was as far as this rock) is as far as this wall.' As we eloquently put it, 'It might have been worse.'

444 *Part III: Dual aspect theory*

hypothetical act of arm-moving must be related by the relation of identity. That is, one 'doing' would have been a 'doing' of another kind. But if '*that* act would have been an arm-moving without m', then in certain possible worlds which lack m that particular act *is* an arm-moving. Therefore in some possible worlds there exist basic act-individuals of basic act-type T_1 which reappear in other possible worlds as act-individuals which are not of act-type T_1. Therefore it cannot be an essential trait of basic act-individuals of type T_1 that they are basic act-individuals of type T_1. Therefore Φ is not necessarily Φ, even though $S\Phi$ is necessarily $S\Phi$. That disposes of the objection.]

(d) Arguments in favour of Theory D

So much for objections to Theory D. I pass now to the reasons for accepting this theory of physical action. (And I note in passing that the first two arguments which I shall put forward involve considerations which I can now offer in fulfilment of an earlier promise to advance a modal argument against Theory C.)

(i) The first argument takes off from the above modal discussion. Thus, if I wish to contract my biceps, the best way of doing so is move an arm. Then in that case I perform an intentional act of biceps-contracting, and this act *is* an arm moving, re-described in the light of its causal (constitutive) properties.[2] But whenever I move an arm I do exactly what I did on the above occasion, and we know that being an action is not description-relative. Therefore whenever I move an arm I perform an act of biceps-contracting; and once again it is clear that this act *is* arm-moving, re-described in the light of its (constitutive) causal properties. Then an act of *identical act-type* would have occurred if M-activation had halted at (e.g.) biceps-contraction (call that event ϕ'); and here again we show that on this occasion an act will have occurred by reminding ourselves of the fact that, even when the motor-apparatus is damaged in this way, the whole phenomenon is intentionally repeatable at will. Let us call this latter act Φ'', and let us suppose that on this latter occasion it was some bodily impediment i which prevented the act-mechanistic activation M-a from developing beyond muscle

---

[2] Just as we re-describe basic acts, such as moving one's right leg, in the light of its effects ('door-opening' 'moving leg shadow', etc.), generating a whole class of instrumental acts which are all one and the same event, so here we re-describe basic acts, such as raising one's right arm, in the light of its causally bonded constitution, generating a whole class of what I have called 'constitutive acts' ('contracting biceps', 'contracting deltoids', etc.), which likewise are all one and the same event. Thus, intentionally lifting a weight might be one and the same event as actively but unintentionally contracting one's biceps.

contraction ϕ''. So much for the empirical facts of the case. Let us now consider the modal facts.

We can say of the action Φ'', '*That* act would have been an arm-moving (Φ) if impediment i had been absent.' Indeed, we can say this of *any* Φ'' – no matter how close the ϕ'' involved may be to the brain. That is, Φ'' is Φ in some possible worlds, no matter how early ϕ'' may be in the act-mechanistic development M-a. Therefore of *any* Φ we can say: the act that *would have been* a Φ''-that-stopped-at-ϕ'' became this Φ. And: this Φ *might have been* a Φ''-that-stopped-at-ϕ''. Therefore as M-a unfolds act-identity stays fast. It is one and the same act-individual, so to say gathering branches, growing out from the mind and developing as far as the peripheral extremities. Then *what permits this*? Now had it been the case that $\Phi = \phi$ (Theory B), it plainly would not have been true that Φ might have been Φ''. How can we say of ϕ that *it* might have been ϕ''? Is not this a recipe for the suicide of ϕ? Thus, only *some* analyses of Φ are consistent with this persistence of act-identity as M-a unfolds. Then what is it about those particular analyses that permits the persistence of act-identity? Can it be independent of the *type* that those theories are ready to grant to Φ? I do not think it can.

Let us express the matter this way. We have seen that Φ reappears in some worlds as Φ''. We have also seen that the Φ'' that is the reappearance of Φ ranges across worlds where ϕ'' is close to the peripheral extremities and worlds where ϕ'' is close to or actually in the brain. Then *what is it* that is so reappearing in these worlds? What is the *constant* to which we are continually referring as we speak of these vicissitudes amongst a multitude of worlds? *What* is changing its spots? Not Φ. Not Φ''. It seems that if this entity reappears in some possible worlds and not others, and so has a determinate essence, some characteristic must be available for it that is independent of its world home and is yet revealed in all of its world homes. It must be an active event-type, and one that is already realised when SΦ is co-present with howsoever little of M-a. What else but SΦ itself? It alone has the minimal-to-zero commitment to success that is required for the aforementioned constant. No other active heading can shake off this commitment in this way. Only striving has this readiness for total failure that will permit ϕ'' to be as close to the mind as it is logically possible for an M-element to get. Thus, Φ must both encompass ϕ and be identical with SΦ. That is, Theory D.

(ii) A second argument in favour of Theory D closely resembles the above. But it has the advantage over (i) of not depending upon proving that Φ is not necessarily Φ. I return to begin with to the act (Φ'') that is realised when the final event (ϕ'') that occurs in the motor-development happens to be the penultimate element in a normal full M-activation (so that ϕ'' here occurs, but the normally succeeding and final event ϕ does not). This act-event (Φ'') must surely be capable of inessential alterations, and must appear in other worlds different from what it actually is in this. Then it seems that we can say of it: 'It might have involved the event in M-A that is immediately after ϕ''''. We say of skids that they might have been a little longer, of explosions that they might have been worse, so why can we not say of these Φ'' acts that they might have involved a little more or a little less? After all, they would share the one token origin and the one natural teleological goal ϕ. Why should it be essential to them that they end at ϕ'' rather than (say) a single event-element later? Whether or not $\Box(\Phi$ is $\Phi)$, it does not seem necessary to these Φ'' events that they terminate in the event ϕ''. That is, Φ'' is almost certainly not necessarily Φ'', any more than a skid to point p was necessarily to p, or an unripened fruit was necessarily unripened to the extent it was. But if Φ'' can reappear in worlds where ϕ'' is close to the periperal extremities and worlds where it is close to or actually in the brain, what is the *constant* to which we are continually referring as we speak of these vicissitudes amongst a multitude of worlds? Once again, it looks as if only $S\Phi$ can meet the joint requirements of being an active event-type *and* being endowed with the minimal-to-zero commitment to success that is required for that constant. But if $S\Phi$ can extend almost to the peripheral extremities, all arguments against extending it the whole way to ϕ crumble, and the way is open to accepting that $S\Phi = \Phi$. That is, Theory D.

(iii) So much for modal arguments. Then here is a further argument in favour of Theory D. Now we know that in the case of instrumental actions generally, the act of trying to do some instrumental act Φ' consists in the performing of some act θ with the overt purpose of generating the necessary and desired effect ϕ'. Then if θ does succeed in generating ϕ', the act θ of trying to Φ' as a result finds itself describable also as the instrumental act Φ': that is, such a trying *becomes* such an instrumental act. This rule holds both of mental tryings (like trying to call up a name, or trying to quicken one's pulse by thinking of something exciting) and of physical tryings (like trying to open the door by kicking, or trying to quicken one's pulse by running). Thus, the slogan 'The successful attempt *is* the act one succeeds in doing', holds of absolutely all *instrumental actions* – which constitutes a great part of the class of all actions – and far and away the most significant part. But in addition this same slogan holds of *constitutive actions*, for a successful attempt to constitutively contract one's biceps takes the form of a normal act of moving one's arm, and this action is identical with the constitutive action. Then since the slogan looks to be determined by entirely general considerations, such as the nature of striving and the nature of action, this is reason for thinking it must hold of actions generally and therefore also of basic bodily actions. And that is tantamount to endorsing Theory D (remembering the transparent untenability of Theory A, and the fact that of the four viable theories only Theories A and D identify Φ and $S\Phi$).

(iv) We saw in section II(A3) that we do not seem to have truth-conditions for $S\Phi$ & absence-of-M-activation. That is, it seems likely that $\Box(S\Phi \rightarrow$ M-activation-*some*-way-towards-ϕ). Then why distinguish $S\Phi$ and M-activation-*some*-way-towards-ϕ-that-is-immediately-DΦ-caused? After all, all those worlds containing the one occurrence are worlds containing the other. More, $S\Phi$ satisfies the test for an event's being at least part of M-activation-all-the-way-to-ϕ: namely, it correlates with Φ and is normally a causally sufficient condition of ϕ via the 'well-worn' path activated in Φ. But if $S\Phi$ is at least part of M-activation-all-the-way-to-ϕ, which part? No principles guide us to the choice of a part. Accordingly, it is natural to assume that $S\Phi = \Phi$ in motor-health and physical liberty. That is, Theory D.

(v) Theories A, B, C, D leave no real alternatives. Theory A is plainly false. The cases against Theories B and C are very strong. Meanwhile, I find nothing with which to reproach Theory D – short of slight counter-intuitiveness.

(e) The theoretical advantages of Theory D

So much for arguments in favour of Theory D. I shall now add indirectly to these arguments, and complete this entire discussion, by listing the theoretical assets of Theory D.

(i) Theory D postulates only one act, only one 'doing', as expression of each individuatable act-producing psychological force-system (consisting of Desire, Belief, and Intention, all directed towards the occurrence of the one token Φ).

(ii) It is the simplest answer to the problem, and avoids multiplication of entities and meanings and ontological levels, postulating one active event only.

(iii) It squares with the negative differential disclosures of introspection: for when we physically act, we seem to ourselves to 'do' only one thing; and this accords with Theory D.

(iv) It makes good sense of the thesis that whenever we act we strive or attempt to act – without having recourse to any form of 'metaphysical double vision'.

(v) Thus, it postulates no tryings *within* tryings,

    (vi) nor 'doings' *within* 'doings'.

   (vii) According to Theory D, physical tryings do not cause physical 'doings'.

  (viii) And one 'doing' does not cause another 'doing'.

    (ix) All physical strivings are ontologically on a par, whether basic or instrumental.

     (x) All physical 'doings' are ontologically on a par, whether act or striving.

   (xi) No mind-body split is obligatory – as seems at least probable were $S\Phi$ to be an 'inner' 'private' event in the 'inner world'.

  (xii) All physical strivings can be psychological phenomena.

 (xiii) No improbable theory of an *ad hoc* 'hybrid' novel and wholly analysable ontological level, consisting of being in part psychological and remainder merely physical – the 'psycho-physical' – is required.

 (xiv) Physical instrumental strivings – like trying to start the car by turning a crank – can be visible physical 'doings'.

  (xv) It allows absolutely all actions and 'doings' generally to have immediate psychological cause.

 (xvi) Yet simultaneously permits basic physical actions and physical instrumental strivings to be openly visible and 'public'.

(xvii) The almost limitless set of 'constitutive actions' (as I have been calling them) realised as M-activation occurs – that is, varieties of Φ'' as the various ϕ''s follow one another in succession during M-activation – can on Theory D all be of one and the same processive type, viz. $S\Phi$; so that the presence of a single active directed teleological process is thereby acknowledged.

(xviii) Theory D squares with the modal or essential properties of Φ, i.e. with the fact that Φ is not necessarily Φ, and is necessarily $S\Phi$.

 (xix) Theory D heals multiple rifts consequent upon interiorist theories of the will, rather in the way Spinozan metaphysics healed divides in the Cartesian world. And it does so without obvious cost.

  (xx) Finally, it is well to re-emphasise the parsimony and extreme theoretical simplicity of Theory D, over and above its other advantages. I refer to the fact that one and only one active event is postulated, that is avowedly both psychological *and* physical, that is both $S\Phi$ *and* Φ, and that extends continuously from the mind to the publicly visible physical extremities.

CHAPTER 13

The definition of action

My aim in this chapter is to define 'action'. What may we legitimately seek in the way of a definition in the case of this phenomenon? We cannot look to discover a mental constitutive definition of action, but we can surely expect to find Wittgensteinian 'criteria', by which I mean the evidential 'front' via which mankind knows incontestably of the reality of actions. However, I hope to discover more. Whereas most mental phenomena do not have necessary and sufficient conditions of existence, I think they are accessible in the case of action.

I. THE DEFINITION OF BASIC ACTION

(a) A rough preliminary list of the 'indicators' of actions and basic actions

We confidently identify actions all the time, and so must be apprised of rules governing their identification. The same is true of the important sub-class of actions called 'basic actions', which stipulatively I take to be the immediate active moving of one's limbs. Because of their simplicity, and because it assists in the wider question, I have chosen to begin the inquiry with a brief study of these actions. However, my procedure will be to first draw up a rough list of 'indicators' of acts generally and basic actions in particular, and proceed from there. They are as follows:

A. We often discover that an act occurs through learning that an event occurs which falls under an *active heading*, e.g. 'walk', 'talk', etc.
B. Actions have a *mental* origin,
C. an origin of the kind *desire to do*, taking 'desire' in a wide enough sense to accommodate simple bodily inclinations and chilly injunctions from one's conscience,
D. and they have an *intention* cause. Action is forward looking.
E. Hence the sheer occurrence of activeness does not *surprise* one.
F. One can *try* and *fail* to do actions.

G. One can *obey an order to start, stop, quicken*, etc. the movement of one's actively moved limbs, and in general to control any actively effected event.
H. Thus, one has *power* over the bodily part, and in general over the acted-upon,
I. and *exercises* that power when one acts.
J. The event occurs because one *tries/attempts/*etc. to make it happen.

Through this scattered data I hope to arrive at a definition of basic action, and then derivatively of action itself.

(b) Abbreviating the list of indicators of basic actions

We can reduce the list of indicators of basic actions as follows.

A. That the name or type is indicative of activeness depends on alternative modes of identification of activeness. In this sense, test A is after the event. Moreover, problem cases exist for action: breathing, laughter, blinking; and any valid definition ought to be able to settle the will-status of these phenomena; but knowing the name or type of the phenomenon cannot provide that answer. In short, test A is otiose and must be deleted. And let us note in passing that the logical form of action sentences is no test of activeness. We have to dig beneath the language to discover the truth here.

So much for test A. And yet this test should not be underrated, for it is our usual method of determining whether an action has occurred. The language is like a bank of knowledge, having already classed many phenomena as active or inactive. Thus, it may take much effort to discover that in witnessing certain scissors-like motions in legs one is witnessing walking, but once that has been determined one knows one is in the presence of action. Tests B, C, and D may be compressed into the single property: being ultimately caused by mental phenomena of the broad kind of act-desire/intention. Test E remains: absence of surprise at one's intentional acts. F, G, and H I shall collapse into the material basis of a power to move a limb; in short a motor-mechanism exists and is used in basic action. Test I remains, that one tries to perform the bodily movement one actively and non-instrumentally brings about. And so does test J (use of the power).

(c) Defining the basic action

In the light of the above, we can assemble a set of necessary and sufficient conditions of being a basic action.

A necessary condition of a basic act of ϕ-making is that there occurs a bodily event ϕ which is the teleological goal-event of a bodily motor-mechanism M for the active making of ϕ. A further necessary condition is that the event ϕ occurs through the activation of M. Another is that the activation of M occurred because an event $S(\Phi)$ of striving to ϕ-make occurred, being the exercise of an act-power. And this striving event was the immediate expression of an act-desire and intention.

2. THE EXTENSION OF 'ACTION'

From now on my aim will be to discover the logically necessary and sufficient conditions of being an action. The above analysis of basic action, while providing a guideline, does not reveal those definitional rules. For example, it does not tell us why acts that are unstriven for are yet acts, or why acts not governed by teleology are acts. And so on. The definition we seek must range far and wide beyond basic actions and across the following phenomena: swimming, thinking, idle unnoticed tongue-moving, talking, calling out under torture, murder by shooting, a particular moving of one's left little finger in a stormy piano passage, knocking over a vase as one gesticulates, moving one's shadow as one walks, stirring during sleep, contracting one's biceps as one moves an arm, etc. Two important issues arise: the first concerns the relation between the concepts of action and will, for we need to know what to include and what exclude in the extension of 'action', and in particular whether to include failed tryings. The second concerns the general classifications governing actions, for a definition of action must apply to all varieties of action.

(a) Action and will

(1) We speak of actions, and also of doing things. What is the difference? What relation holds between the concept of action and the concept of 'active doing'? Now two very simple tests indicate that an event is what one would call 'an active doing': (i) being a suitable answer to 'what are you doing?', and (ii) being something one can desire and intend to do. Actions satisfy these tests. But so also do tryings. Thus, both phenomena are 'active doings'. Then are these two phenomena one and the same thing? Are we just describing the one phenomenon in two different ways? More to the point: is the concept of a trying the concept of *an action*?

(2) Certain considerations incline one to say it is. Thus, tryings are events, with the same desire and intention origin as actions; and one is responsible for one's tryings; and most importantly some tryings are identical with

actions: say, trying to open the door by kicking it. However, the question is not whether a trying might be an act. Rather is it: is there an act of the type (say) 'try to open the door'?

The following are reasons why there is not. First, the schema Try (——) is such that whatever is an act can be inserted into the slot, and Try (——) cannot be so inserted. While there is trying to bring it about that one try, and in that sense trying to try, there is no immediate trying to try as there is for all actions. Second, if Try (——) was an act-heading, trying would be an act at which one could not fail. For what is it to fail to try, in the sense *unsuccessful attempt?* After all, an unsuccessful attempt is yet an attempt. 'I tried to try to Φ but failed to try to Φ' is surely contradictory. But then what sort of an act can it be that does not even in principle permit an unsuccessful attempt to perform it? Thus, one corollary of the impossibility of trying to try is the equal impossibility of failing in trying and succeeding in trying. Now when we speak of action we are as such referring to an occurrence which *is* the active producing of some event: say, an event of arm rise or window fracture. But the concept of trying/attempting, with its readiness for success at nothing, is of what need advance no distance towards any such event to be what it is. So how could it be an act-concept?

I conclude that in seeking to define the concept of action, we are not attempting to define a concept whose extension includes mere tryings. However close the concepts of action and trying may be, our enterprise is that of discovering the definition of phenomena which go beyond mere tryings and achieve the status of actions.

(b) Classifying actions

(1) I drew attention a little earlier to the multiplicity of phenomena to which a definition of action must apply. This breadth of application is of great relevance to that definition, in part determining its content. The reason is that the wider the range of phenomena that count as actions, the less specialised the requirements of the common factor of activeness. As an example: it tells us something about what an action is to know that it can be (say) instrumental in kind. It implies that the event that the act is the active bringing about of, need be no part of the act. Therefore an act must be able to satisfy one of the necessary conditions of being an act as a result of extra-constitutional factors. Equally important data concerning the nature of action itself can be gained through examining the other main categories of action. Accordingly, I shall now briefly characterise the broad

categories into which actions fall. Their content is best expressed in terms of oppositions.

(2) *Mental/physical.* This distinction is between internal and physical actions. On the one hand thinking, on the other hand talking. The distinction is between the only two possible ontological varieties of action.

Intentional/unintentional. The necessary and sufficient conditons of intentional action are as follows. An act is intentional if (i) an intention to Φ or try to Φ (ii) immediately causes (iii) a trying to Φ (iv) that suffices for Φ (v) through being an exemplification of a power to Φ (vi) that one intentionally uses. We can then oppose to this the unintentional act, which we define as an act which *fails* to be intentional.

Instrumental/basic/constitutive. This division, which applies to physical and perhaps all actions, is according to the causal positioning of the event ϕ_x that the act is the active making of. Then the event ϕ_x can adopt no more than three positions, corresponding to the above three varieties of action. An act is 'instrumental' if ϕ_x lies outside its own individual confines, and is caused by the act through the use of a power-line which leads beyond those confines: examples are driving a car, swimming, lifting one's left arm with one's right arm. Meanwhile, a 'basic act' is one in which the bodily ϕ that gives its name to the act is (i) the last part of the act, (ii) the first and immediate object of the will, (iii) the teleological causal end-point in a bodily act-mechanism (M) for the making of ϕ, and (iv) generated through use of the act-power which M helps to exist. Finally, I shall define a 'constitutive' act as an act in which the ϕ_x that the act is the making of occurs within the sequence M-activation-to-ϕ: examples are intentionally contracting one's biceps by moving an arm, unintentionally contracting one's biceps by moving an arm, contracting one's biceps intentionally or unintentionally in wholly unsuccessfully trying to move an arm. The above three broad varieties of action exhaust the field of physical and perhaps of all actions.

(3) Thus, the concept of action has a vast extension, ranging from complex intentional rational self-conscious internal actions to barely noticed senseless bodily movings. A few words now about the concept which has such an extension. We noted that the range of actions excludes mere strivings, despite the fact that strivings are 'active doings' and may be identical with some action. An important consequence of this is, that not only is being intentional a description-relative property of actions, but so too is being an action, even though actions are active phenomena and activeness cannot be a description-relative property (since tryings are essentially tryings). A

second relevant property of this 'active doing' concerns its content. Thus, despite the fact that there exist both causal and active 'doings', actions and active doings are not sub-varieties of some wider 'doing' kind that includes causings. 'Doing' is simply ambiguous between the causal and the willing senses – 'what the storm did to the wheat' / 'what Don Giovanni did to Donna Elvira'. While action strikes one as being in some sense the direct descendant of causation, as it were the type of bringing-about open uniquely to conscious beings, in actual fact action is no type of causation.

(c) All acts entail the occurrence of some event ϕ_x that is such that acts of that type T necessarily are the active bringing about of ϕ_x

(1) I would like now to gain a better understanding of the principles governing the allocation of types to action, seeing that every act must be of some determinate type. Thus, what is it that determines that one act is an arm-raising, another a swimming, a third an act of murder? All important to the answer to this question is discovering in each case the event which plays the same role in type-determination as does the event which in simpler cases transparently gives its name to the deed. It is clear that arm rise determines the type arm-raising, and window fracture the type window-breaking, but what determines that an act is a swimming or a murder, etc.? My suggestion is that simple cases like arm-raising and window-breaking point the way for all cases.

For every act there is an event ϕ_x to which it stands in the relation: the act is the active bringing about of ϕ_x. This claim runs at once into a minor difficulty posed by acts with complex event objects: say, delivering a speech. What is the ϕ_x event here? Consider a simpler case: saying, 'Clear out!' This is the single act of making two sounds, which are each token occurrences of a word. Then the present occurrence of these two sounds is the sounding of the sentence 'Clear out!', intended in a specific sense. Here we have the single phenomenon that the single act of telling someone to 'clear out' is the active bringing about of. In short, the fact that acts can have whole act-parts, and be the bringing about of complex single events with whole event parts, poses no serious difficulty for the above claim.

A second difficulty is, that sometimes an act that is the active bringing about of ϕ_x does not thereby rate as an act of some given type T, not because T is not the active bringing about of ϕ_x, but because additional necessary conditions exist for T acts. For example, while walking is the bringing about of the movement of one's body, it has also to be through the movement of one's limbs and along a surface. However, this complication is no more of a problem than the above. We need merely to observe that walking is the bringing about of a body movement that is endowed with certain additional properties.

(2) Then to repeat: common to all acts is the occurrence of some event ϕ_x such that the act is the bringing about of ϕ_x. This holds irrespective of whether the act is an arm-raising, window-breaking, swimming, moaning, car-driving, driving one's car to Oxford, or telling someone to depart. In each case some pre-eminent ϕ_x must happen, an event that is not identical with the action, but that owes its existence to the act. This ϕ_x event is not a sufficient condition of an act of type T, but may nonetheless be described as the *first necessity*. I say so because ϕ_x is such that if an intentional act T occurs, then ϕ_x must be accounted *the end* or aim of that act. An example like swimming makes this clear. Here the ϕ_x in question is the motion of the body through the water. While the active production of this event is an insufficient condition of swimming, it is surely the first necessity. That 'first necessity' cannot be limb movement, for the reason that swimming is defined as a *way* of moving the body through water, which implies that a swimmer moves his limbs *in order* to propel his body through water.

This theory implies that all act-expressions must be analysable into expressions of the form 'act of bringing about ϕ_x . . .', where the vacant slot is either left empty or else filled in by expressions of the kind of 'by doing y' or 'by doing y by doing z', and so on. It is left empty with basic acts like arm-raisings, and with simple first-order instrumental acts like window-breakings, but filled in by *a priori*-given specifications in the case of swimming, and by *a posteriori* specifications in the case of moaning, groaning, etc. Since many of the subsidiary y's are examples of the first type, and all seem to go back to such, the primary mode of physical action must be the simple act of the kind of ϕ_x-making, such as arm-raising or window-breaking. It follows that the main task in searching for the definition of 'Act of type T', and thus also of 'Action' itself, must be to discover the necessary and sufficient conditions of the occurrence of an act of type of ϕ_x-making. Once this has been discovered, the rest presents no great problem.

3. THE DEFINITION OF ACTION

(a) Constraints in defining action

Earlier I arrived at a definition of the basic bodily act of ϕ-making. However, our discussion has to range far beyond this simple phenomenon if we are to arrive at a definition applicable to the vast range of occurrences that are actions. We realise that whatever factors account for the act-status of basic acts, cannot all be factors that are necessary and sufficient conditions of action generally, even though they suggest possible answers. I then surveyed the phenomena falling under 'action', and noted that they allowed of three main non-competing classificatory schemas: mental/physical, intentional/unintentional, basic/instrumental/constitutive. Accordingly, the problem of defining 'action' now becomes that of explaining how, given the definition of basic action as a clue to the wider definitional project, there can exist (say) a mental unintentional instrumental act of ϕ_x-making, or (say) a physical unintentional instrumental act of ϕ_x-making, or (say) a physical unintentional constitutive act of of ϕ_x-making.

At first this multiplicity of act-types suggests an account of action in which the act disappears beneath a cloud of relations. And this supposition is natural enough, seeing that both origin and output are of supreme importance so far as action is concerned. In fact, however, we shall see that the idea is mistaken. We will discover properties that are necessary to action, and that are both non-relational and intrinsic to the phenomenon. On the other hand two events can in themselves be very different phenomena, indeed can be quite different actions, and yet both be acts of ϕ_x-making. It follows that no intrinsic character can be necessary and sufficient for being an act of ϕ_x-making. Here we have an important general property of actions which must be realised in the definition. In showing what the definition cannot encapsulate, it in effect constitutes a simplification of the definitional task.

Meanwhile the multiplicity of the varieties of acts of ϕ_x-making demonstrates that much else can be dispensed with in defining action. For example, the existence of unintentional acts of ϕ_x-making shows that the necessary and sufficient conditions of being an act of ϕ_x-making cannot include being caused by an intention to ϕ_x-make. And the property of instrumentality demonstrates that we may not include the condition, that ϕ_x is the teleological goal of a teleological process. Therefore, unlike the case of basic bodily Φ, the requirements of inner-outer matching prove in the case of action generally to be minimal. Unintentionalness and instrumentality enable us to whittle away at the original definition of basic bodily action to a marked degree, in the attempt to arrive at a definition of action.

(b) A parallel with visual perception

(1) We identify an item as an act of some type T in terms of an event ϕ_x which owes its existence to the act we bring under 'T', and we describe the act as 'the act of bringing about ϕ_x . . .', in the special active sense of 'bring about'. As we have seen, this sense of 'bring about' differs from the

merely causal sense of the expression. This difference in sense is apparent when we recall the so-called 'accordion effect', which is peculiar to action. If I perform an act which is the bringing about of x, which in turn causes y, which goes on to produce z, then I have done an act of 'bringing about x', one of 'bringing about y', and one of 'bringing about z', and these three acts are one and the same event. This singular fact about action, which is not to be found in the case of causation generally, must be a clue of some significance so far as the nature of action is concerned. Precisely what its import is, becomes clearer when we compare the phenomenon of action with that of perception.

We find a close parallel to the act-situation in the other main concrete point of interaction of mind and environment: the perceptual variety. Consider the visual perception of a physical object. Here noticing or seeing a visual sensation is *identical* with seeing the suitably projectively related light cause of that sensation, which is in turn *identical* with seeing the suitably originating physical object. For example, noticing a round red visual sensation, may *be* noticing a cylindrical beam of red light, which may *be* noticing the setting sun. The explanation of this transitive state of affairs is, that in perception a basis for knowledge travels down the several reliable connective causal lines in the Attention, and this fact licenses corresponding re-descriptions of the one perceptual event.

Certain features of this situation are discoverable in act-situations. One is that there is an order of priorities and dependencies. Thus, each of these relations is *by* or *in virtue of* the next in line, but not vice versa, so that whereas the sun comes to the attention through its light doing so, the reverse is not true. Another significant feature is the fact that whereas one can truly notice a visually presented object under the wrong heading, as when I really see a balloon in the sky but as an aeroplane, this measure of dislocation between impression-content and object-type is possible only because I can bring both under reduced descriptions such that a match is revealed, e.g. 'dark object in the sky'. This fact implies that nomicity can extend into the mind one stage deeper than the sensation – that it travels as far as the content of the noticing event. We shall discover close parallels to these and other features in the case of action.

(2) The following features of the visual situation provide clues to the definition of action:

A. The existence of a regular causal chain linking mind and perceived object.

B. The fact that the perceptible objects closer to the mind represent the remoter objects in the causal chain.

C. The fact that noticing any one object in that chain is noticing the other objects.
D. The fact that there is a first psychological representative, here the sensation.
E. The fact that while I can notice truly under a false heading, this is possible only because I notice truly under a reduced but true heading that accords with a causal regularity.

We discover close analogues in the act-situation. And those analogous properties of action accord with and develop what emerged earlier in the analysis of basic action. Conjoining these two 'clues', we find ourselves in a position to define action itself. I shall do so by way of a consideration of instrumental actions.

(c) Applying the visual comparison to instrumental actions

We are looking for a definition of action that will be sufficiently broad to range across mental and physical, basic and instrumental and constitutive, intentional and unintentional, examples of the kind: a definition which explains what it is that confers an act-type of form 'act of ϕ_x-making' upon actions, and reveals how the existence of a causal bond relating the act with a sequence of causally related ϕ_xs permits that one act-event to fall under multiple act-descriptions. Then the problem before us is seen at its clearest in the variety of action remotest from the simple case of basic action: the unintentional instrumental act. For example, I fire a gun which starts an avalanche which kills, and as a result the act of shooting qualifies as an act of killing. What explains this fact?

What needs to be the relation between an act that I do, and an instrumentally effected event ϕ_x that I bring about, if my act is to be one of ϕ_x-making? It must be that ϕ_x would not have occurred were it not for the act, and a repeatable regular causal relation must have governed the transaction. In a word, an instrumental act-power must have been used, and irrespective of whether it is known to the agent. For example, in intentionally utilising the power to walk, I may unintentionally be utilising a power to move my shadow. Then the comparison with perception holds on this particular count. A significant likeness between the two situations is, that in each case a possibly unknown and unthought-about causal regularity helps additively to constitute a longer more complex regularity, linking a first directed psychological event with an external item, and as a result the psychological event acquires an additional object. Just as the sun comes to the attention through and in addition to its light coming to the attention, so analogously I actively bring about an avalanche through and in addition to performing an act of shooting. And whereas the last perceptual representative of the sun is a sensation, so that it is through awareness of this psychological individual that the other items come to awareness, in similar manner the chain of act-representatives comes to an end with the basic act, and therefore comes to an end in the psychological and essentially active event of willing/striving/'doing' with which it is identical. More, it can come to an end in a failed but real attempt to perform a basic act, an attempt which relates suitably to the ϕ_x in question – and here I can discover no perceptual analogue. So much for the moment for instrumental action, intentional and unintentional. I think we can now proceed to generalise from this case to action as such.

(d) Formulating the definition of action

(1) Let us suppose that a decision triggers off the act-mechanism M-for-ϕ of a basic act Φ of ϕ-making, consisting of the mechanistic elements ϕ_a, ϕ_b, . . . ϕ; and let us also suppose that this basic act ϕ causes a sequence of events, ϕ_1, ϕ_2, . . . ϕ_n, taking place in conditions C1 such that (Φ) $(\Phi \rightarrow \phi_1$ & ϕ_2 & . . . & $\phi_n)$. Then the following acts occurred: a basic Φ of ϕ-making; (constitutive) acts of ϕ_a-making, of ϕ_b-making, . . . , of ϕ_z-making; and (instrumental) acts of ϕ_1-making, ϕ_2-making, . . . and of ϕ_n-making. Then *which events* are these acts? They are all of them one and the same event, the basic act Φ. Then since Φ is identical with striving-to-Φ $(S\Phi)$, they must also all be identical with $S\Phi$. In sum: $\Phi_a = \Phi_b = \ldots = \Phi = S\Phi = \Phi_1 = \Phi_2 = \ldots \Phi_n$.

Then what are the necessary and sufficient conditions for an act of ϕ_x-making? What rules govern acts of all varieties? The answer to this question should tell us what an action is, seeing that all acts are acts of making some ϕ_x. Then I suggest the following: an act of ϕ_x-making occurs if a willing/trying/attempting/'having a go at' doing some act or another occurs, whether internal-mental or physical-bodily in character, directed wheresoever and expressing an intention directed wheresoever; and an event ϕ_x occurs causally because of that striving, whether externally as effect, or internally as either constitutive-of or teleological goal, acting along a repeatable causal line such that, in those specifiable circumstances C1, such a striving event would be a causally sufficient condition of ϕ_x. I believe that this is what we *mean* when we say an act of ϕ_x-making occurred. We mean: a willing occurred which nomically causally was responsible for a ϕ_x event. Then ϕ_x may, though need not, have been projected by an intention directed to that specific causal line, in which case an *intentional* act of ϕ_x-making will have occurred.

(2) This tells us what an act of ϕ_x-making is. And this in turn tells us what an action is, since all acts are acts of making some ϕ_x. Then to repeat and expand: an act is a willing – causally responsible for an event – that is causally sufficient in prevailing cirumstances for such an event – as an exemplification of the causal power of such willings to be causally sufficient for events of that kind – whether as effect or constituent. That is, an action is a willing that has such causal relations to some event ϕ_x, whereupon that willing counts as an act of the type, ϕ_x-maker. A transitivity of repeatable causal relations enables the one psychological event of willing, according as it either *generates* or else *involves* but is in any case causally responsible for events along such a repeatable line, to qualify for the act-title 'ϕ_x-maker', whereupon each ϕ_x will be said to have been actively 'done' by the agent. And so there occurs a line of regularly repeatable effects or constitutents, and thus of active 'doings' and 'done-by's, travelling *outwards* and *inwards* from the agent, generating in turn a succession of act-titles for the single willing event, viz. 'ϕ_1-maker' 'ϕ_2-maker', etc.; and also 'ϕ_a-maker' 'ϕ_b-maker', etc.: a list that is in principle endless.

This state of affairs is closely akin to the perceptual situation. Just as there may exist a set of causally bonded events that are actively 'done', travelling *outwards* from the agent-subject, so there may exist a line of causally bonded phenomenal items that are 'sense perceived', travelling *inwards* towards their perceiver-subject and his attention. One is a line, not just of causing, but of causing and therefore *also* of actively doing; while the other is a line, not just of being caused by, but of being caused by and so *also* of being an attentive awareness-of/perception-of. And just as there is only one act and many events that are actively 'done', so there is but one attentive awareness and a (limited) sequence of distinct entities that are the objects of awareness/perception.

This definition of action achieves the required generality. It leaves it open whether the act is mental or physical, basic or constitutive or instrumental, intentional or unintentional.

(3) I will now in (e)(1) (below) offer a brief summary statement of this definition of action. However before I do, I wish to make a claim which enables me to provide a second definition of action. The claim in question, which received its justification in the previous chapter 12 section 11 (A3), is that a necessary and sufficient condition of an event of willing is that

an act-desire/intention find immediate causal expression in an event which consists in the activation of a power-line to generate some ϕ_x. If this claim is correct, it would follow that we can define an action in the following two ways: either as a willing that is causally responsible for an event through use of a power-line, or else as an activation of a power-line that is the immediate expression of an act-desire/intention that is causally responsible for an event through use of that power-line. The first of these definitions seems to me to be uncontentious, the second not.

(e) Circularity in the definitions

(1) The above two definitions of action prove to be circular in two respects. The definitions were as follows.

An *act of ϕ_x-making* occurs iff (i) a willing/trying/attempting/'having a go at' doing some act of ϕ_y-making occurs, and (ii) an event ϕ_x occurs causally because of that striving, (iii) along a power-line that encompasses ϕ_x, whether constitutively, or as far as the natural teleological goal ϕ, or instrumentally.

And: an *act of ϕ_x-making* occurs iff (i) a desire/intention to do some act of ϕ_y-making (ii) immediately activates a power-line as far as ϕ_x, whether constitutively, or as far as the natural teleological goal ϕ, or instrumentally.

We shall now see that these definitions are circular.

(2) The first circularity derives from the fact that the desire involved in the second definition is a desire to do. Now desires are either desires with *direct objects* (which are almost invariably act-desires: 'to do – '), or desires with *propositional objects* ('that p be true'). These two varieties of desire are closely related, and in self-conscious beings most act-desires necessitate an accompanying propositional desire. For example, I cannot want to drive to Paris without wanting it to be true that I do. However, the reverse does not hold. A man who wants the weather to clear has no desire to clear the weather. Then it should be noted that we cannot reduce direct-object desires to propositional desires, and *a fortiori* cannot hope by such means to expunge the concept of will from that of act-desire: 'I wanted to sing' does not mean 'I wanted it to be true that I sing.' The desire-to-do is essentially just that, and defies all attempts to reduce it to phenomena that can be described without recourse to the concept of activeness/'doing'/striving/etc. In sum, we cannot reduce away the presence in one of the definitions of a something that essentially falls under a description utilising the concept of will.

The second circularity derives from the concepts of 'motor-mechanism' and 'power-line', which occur in both definitions. Thus, the concept of a motor-mechanism is of the material foundation of the power to perform some physical basic act, while the concept of a power-line, which has application across both mental and physical acts, is likewise of the basis of an act-power. In neither case can the concept be specified without recourse to the concept of will. In short, once again we are involved in a circular and ineradicable reference to willing.

(f) *Conclusion*

(1) The concept of action admits of *a priori* analysis in which the act is identified with the psychological phenomenon, 'do'/try/attempt/etc. Then while the act-event is not dismantlable into mental parts, a set of necessary connections hold between the act and certain other mental phenomena. Meanwhile the physical sub-class of actions proves to be analysable into physical event-parts, although it should be noted that those mechanistic elements constitute in themselves no more than a continuity of bodily events which is insufficient for action. This is because action in addition necessitates that the first mechanistic event owe its existence immediately to act-desire/intention.

Thus, even though physical acts are physical events, the criteria for an event's being an action are in part irreducibly psychological. Meanwhile, even though the act is a psychological event, and despite the fact that there exist non-constitutive psychological criteria consisting in necessary ties with occurrent and potential mental states and events that are distinct from the act, the act itself cannot be psychologically anatomised and in that sense psychologically explained. Then the above is a broad statement of the ontological situation which prevails in the case of physical action. In sum, the situation is this. Even though physical actions are constituted out of physical events, the concept of physical action cannot be explained in physical terms. And even though actions as such are identical with the psychological event of 'doing', and necessarily related in determinate ways to other mental phenomena, the concept of activeness cannot be explained in mental terms. It is irreducible.

(2) Finally, we must distinguish the necessary and sufficient conditions of action from the *essence* of action. If we understand the essence of action to be that to which we constantly refer when we trace all intelligible references to the phenomenon we bring under 'action' through all conceivable factual and counter-factual situations, then the essence of an act of ϕ_x-making

proves to be different from the necessary and sufficient conditions of an act of ϕ_x-making. As emerged in chapter 12, the essence of an act (Φ_x) of ϕ_x-making is the event of trying/striving/'having a shot at' doing whatever (ϕ_y) deed one is endeavouring to do when one performs the act (Φ_x) of ϕ_x-making: it is an event of directed psychological activeness. This is the unchanging 'it' that appears in all of the possible worlds in which the phenomenon can take its place. In this specific sense, the essence of action is the event of willing.

4. TESTING THE DEFINITION OF ACTION: FOUR PROBLEM CASES

(a) The will-status of breathing

(1) The above two definitions of action state all that is required if a ϕ_x-making act is to occur. Then while from the point of view of psychological explanantion this is a discovery of little moment, being circular in character, it is an insight into the concept of action. Moreover, it helps to resolve the question of the will-status of the following problematic cases: breathing, laughter, blinking, and thinking.

Let us consider the phenomenon of breathing. How to determine its will-status? But first, what *is* breathing? It is a vital process causing gas-intake that involves the use of a physical apparatus which exists in order to cause intake of needed gas. Therefore breathing must be able to occur in plants and animals of all kinds, and highly diverse phenomena might rate as examples of breathing. In some animals it might be as automatic and involuntary as heat-intake, while in some others it might (like drinking) be in control of the will (so that we might perhaps take five or six gulps of air a day, rather as we drink water). Indeed, in some animals it might sometimes be one and sometimes the other. Therefore breathing has no will-status *as such*, even though particular examples of breathing do.

(2) My topic is human breathing, a phenomenon which cannot be *a priori* necessarily of one will-value or the other. Then there can be no doubt that human breathing is sometimes inactive. For example, the breathing of the deeply unconscious. It is not possible that in this state bodily act-desire to breathe could be repeatedly caused as the lungs repeatedly empty. Even though sensations and physical desires occur in sleep, deep unconscious-ness is inconsistent with phenomena like thirst, restlessness, sensations, and the variety of desire that sets our limbs actively in motion. While mental events and even experiences may occur in this state, such body-directed

phenomena may not. Therefore the breathing of the deeply unconscious cannot be caused by bodily act-desire/intention. It follows from the definition of action that in the deeply unconscious breathing is inactive. This gives us reason to suspect that breathing as such must in humans be inactive.

(3) My main concern is the will-status of conscious human breathing. Two things suggest that it might be active. First the fact that it may perhaps be the case that when we are conscious we breathe because we *feel like* breathing, second the fact that one has *absolutely immediate control* over breathing. Then let us examine the phenomenon more closely.

One is inclined to say that when one obeys an order to inhale and exhale, one is voluntarily breathing. But on such occasions *what more* does one do but actively desist from stopping breathing, actively choose the rate of breathing, and actively attend to the phenomenon? But when I raise an arm I do not actively desist from inhibiting action: I simply do not inhibit anything, I *do* do a deed, and I perhaps choose a rate. Then my suggestion is that there is no analogous '*do* do' open to the will with breathing. What would it be, on top of the powers of inhibition and rate-control, to insert or withdraw from the situation the use of this supposed power?

This account is confirmed by the facts. The relevant powers available to human subjects are as follows:

(i) One can intentionally stop breathing.
(ii) One can intentionally breathe at a certain speed.
(iii) One can intentionally stop stopping breathing.
(iv) One can intentionally stop choosing to breathe at a certain speed.

And that is the full complement of our powers, the full extent of our control over breathing.

Then compare and contrast with the above the following:

(i) One can intentionally stop walking.
(ii) One can intentionally walk at a certain speed.

But what would we mean by

(iii) one can intentionally stop stopping walking, or
(iv) one can intentionally stop stopping walking at a certain speed?

The two situations are disanalogous. Intentional walking is not intentionally stopping stopping walking, whereas all that is open to the will in breathing is intentionally stopping stopping breathing, which is merely the chosen cessation of an activity, and not the chosen embarkation upon activity. Therefore what happens when we stop stopping breathing, in other words the normal occurrence of breathing, cannot be an activity. And our linguistic practices seem to bear this out. Thus, while we say such things as 'Breathe in' 'Breathe out slowly' 'Hold your breath' 'Stop holding your breath', we do not in the same sense say, 'Breathe', 'Resume breathing', for the only sense we could give to this latter request is 'Stop stopping breathing', whereas the sense of 'Resume act X' is not 'Stop stopping X-ing.' In sum: all that intentions determine here are preventions and timings, as well as the cessation of or desisting from such exercisings of the will, but they never determine the coming into being of the process so controlled. While both measures of control exist in the case of action generally, in the case of breathing only the former exists. This unusual state of affairs is the source of the puzzle over the will-status of breathing. It is plainly of survival value that a process as central to life as breathing should be the office of an automatic bodily system rather than the mind, and yet at the same time should remain sufficiently within the control of the mind to eschew life-threatening situations like choking.

(4) In this discussion the definition of action has been of use in the following way. It enabled us to appeal to the rule that the necessary and sufficient conditons of physical action are that an act-desire/intention immediately activate a motor-mechanism for action. Then in the case of breathing the fact that one was operating against a compulsion rendered this condition impossible of fulfilment.

(b) The will-status of laughter

(1) Laughter shares with breathing some of the features which make these phenomena problematic from the point of view of the will. In each case a bodily act-mechanism is activated in a phenomenon which seems nonetheless not to be active. On the other hand, laughter differs from breathing in certain significant respects. Most importantly, it differs in having an obligatory 'inner life'. Thus, it shares with action, as breathing does not, an obligatory origin in a direct-object desire: a desire-to-do (in some sense of 'do'). And it differs again from breathing on the count of control, for whereas the phenomena involved in breathing resemble action in being immediately controllable, those of laughter do not.

This last property is enough to prove that laughter is not an action. For in the case of laughter, and in a way that is reminiscent of breathing, the point of application of the will is at best the negative one of stopping rather than the positive of acting. But whereas in the case of breathing the power of stopping is immediate and sure, that of laughter is indirect and uncertain. We can at best try to stop laughing and by one means or another, but in the case of breathing we simply stop and by no means. In this regard breathing is exactly like action, for when we act we likewise do not try to stop, we simply stop if we so desire. Problems can arise over the control of the desire, but once the governing desire is the negative one of stopping action, stop we do. And we do, without trying to do. Unlike action, stopping is no achievement, which is why there is no trying to stop. After all, there can be no failing with stopping, as there can be with action. This real but negative event, which is as much within our control as action itself, is on this count asymmetric with action. In stopping action there is no analogue of the event (ϕ_x) that action is the active bringing about of. Nothing is risked or assayed in this phenomenon.

(2) One fallible but useful indicator of act-status is what one might call 'the Stage Test'. Namely, is an actor's version of the phenomenon a real example of the kind? If it is, the phenomenon is usually active. Thus, stage walking and coughing and smiling are real examples of their kind, and these phenomena are all actions. Then I suggest that on this count laughter emerges as inactive, for a stage laugh is not a real laugh. Like laughter it is the making of a bray, but it lacks the requisite inner life of laughter, for it fails to emerge from a feeling-like laughing. As a result of this lack we would say that in ordinary circumstances a phenomenon identical with the stage occurrence would be accounted insincere. By contrast, there is no such thing as insincere laughter, any more than laughter can be sincere.

A second indicator of the will-status of a phenomenon is the character of its origin. And unlike the Stage Test, this test is decisive. Now the necessary inner life of action includes direct-object desire. And the same is true of laughter. Indeed, without such an origin the activation of the laughter motor-mechanism would be a mere spasm of the body that issues in a bray. Here we find important common ground with action. Moreover, laughter is like some actions in that it emerges from a desire to do which is a simple feeling-like doing, which in either case is a desire which is not rational. For many and perhaps most feeling-like desires are non-rational desires. This also is common ground.

Now one might at first think this common ground with action a reason for judging laughter an action. However, these similiarities ought not to blind us to a major difference: that the object of an inclinatory act-desire is an act which has rational instances, which in turn implies that the act-desire in question must have rational instances. By contrast, the desire to laugh has no rational instances. Whereas I can rationally (e.g. prudentially) or non-rationally (e.g. merely inclinatorily) want to drink, I cannot rationally want to laugh. (Though I can rationally want it to be true that I laugh.) The desire to laugh is *as such* non-rational, the desire to drink is not. It follows that the phenomenon which the desire to laugh engenders can have no rational occurrences. But anything that is an action must in principle have rational occurrences. I conclude that laughings do not constitute a sub-class of the class of acts of braying: namely, those whose origin is a helpless non-rational urge to bray. Here we have another proof of the inactiveness of laughter.

(3) In sum. Laughter is a phenomenon occurring in a body-part over which the will has sway, the physical constituents of which can be produced by the will, with an immediate origin in a feeling-like desire which like act-desire takes a direct object ('to do'), but which is unlike act-desire is not being directed to action (i.e. to active 'doing'). Then whereas both act-desire and the desire to laugh immediately activate a motor-mechanism, in the case of laughter that activation is not immediately controllable, being only indirectly and uncertainly responsive to intentions. The motivating desire to laugh shares with many feeling-like act-desires the property of being non-rational, but unlike them is of necessity non-rational, and the same therefore must be true of laughter, which as a result cannot be active. This inactive phenomenon is never rational, meant, immediately controllable, sincere, intentional or unintentional, striven for or failed at, and so on.

The definitions of action include the requirement that the act be the immediate expression of act-desire/intention, and immediately responsive to the intention. On both counts laughter emerges as inactive. By the indirect or roundabout means of appeal to the other criteria, it emerged that the 'desire to do' operative in laughter must be a desire (merely) to inactively 'do'. It is not an act-desire.

(c) The will-status of blinking and the rationale of our overall findings

(1) One is rarely aware of blinking. And yet it continues as long as our eyes are open. Then as with breathing and laughter, there exists here a motor-mechanism one can utilise at will. This happens when one chooses to blink. But does one usually activate the mechanism at will?

The following is why not. It could be that blinking is caused by sensations of discomfort in the eyes, so that it might even have a psychological cause of the type desire. Yet it does not have a cause of the type act-desire. But how to show this? The considerations that tell against blinking being active, and hence circularly against the desire's being act-desire, turn on the issue of power. For even though in blinking we utilise a mechanism over which we have control, at the time of blinking that power is not used. And the evidence for this is: that one does not know when exactly the next blink will occur; and one might *await it*; and then *find* oneself blinking; and find moreover that the blinks come *in a packet*, not of one, but two or three or more! And not only does one not employ a power in determining when, and therefore that, and even how many; but because one is unaware of the stages in the blink, one is incapable of exerting any power over the phenomenon once it has begun. So neither the that, nor the when, nor the how many, nor the way, is determined by one's capacity actively to determine phenomena of the kind of the blink.

To repeat: though an act-mechanism is activated in blinking, and possibly even activated by desire, that activation is not the exercise of an act-power. Therefore any motivating desire cannot be an act-desire. This account of blinking finds corroboration in the fact that blinking generally is necessary, automatic, repetitious, stereotyped, unnoticed, and the exercise of Nature's purposes alone.

(2) The three phenomena we have examined are natural syndromes, whose contents and boundaries are shaped by Nature's hand. And they are all problem cases for the Will. For even though in all three cases a motor-mechanism M exists for the willing producing of some phenomenon ϕ, and in each phenomenon M is activated and ϕ occurs, nonetheless the ϕ-making is not active. An event ϕ occurs in organs over which the will has control, but in each case the will proves to be inoperative.

The reasons are as follows. The necessary and sufficient conditions of an act of ϕ_x-making are no more than two: (a) that a desire/intention to do a ϕ_y-making act (b) should immediately activate a power-line as far as ϕ_x. It follows that if these three problematic 'acts' are inactive, it must be because of failing to satisfy (a). And they can do this in any of three ways: (i) through lacking a psychological cause, (ii) through lacking a desire cause, (iii) through lacking an act-desire cause. Now while it is uncertain whether all three phenomena satisfy (i) and (ii), it is clear that they all fail to satisy (iii). Then my main interest in this issue has been to heighten the significance of the clause in the definition of action which states that the operative immediate cause of action must be an *act-desire*. And in addition to demonstrate the circularity of the definition, and in that way the ultimate *indefinability of will*.

(3) The existence of inactive 'acts' does not merely teach us that a set of physical events can constitute an active event only if they can be so ordered that (i) some first ϕ_a causes some next ϕ_b . . . generally up until the teleological goal event ϕ, and that (ii) the whole phenomenon owes its

existence to an immediate act-desire/intention cause. They show also that there can exist causally bonded syndromes of events which can on some occasions constitute an active event and on other occasions not. That is, that two occurrences of the very same causally bonded sequence can be such that on one occasion they unite as parts of *one active event*, while on the other occasion they fail to do so. The question then arises: might ϕ_a $\phi_b \dots \phi$, given some requisite non-act-desire origin, unite as parts of some *one non-active psychological event*? But the only psychological event that can span the mind-body divide in this fashion is bodily willing. Thus, it may be that we are obliged to endorse the claim that two events can be physically indistinguishable, and, because of the diversity of their origins, one and only one falls under a psychological heading, viz. willing. I shall pursue this question later in this work.

(d) The special case of thinking

(1) For anyone who is conscious, and on pain of stupor or daze, there must be an answer to the question: 'What are you thinking of?' That is, the interior phenomenon to which one refers in replying to this question is a necessity for consciousness, however outward or inward the direction of one's attention. A racing driver navigating a patch of oil will think to himself such simple but real (admonitory) thoughts as 'To the right! Drive to the right!', equally as much as Rodin's 'Penseur' is engaged in an inwardly directed process of thinking. In fact, the relation of thinking to consciousness is even closer than that of necessary condition, for these two non-identical phenomena invariably accompany one another. And yet there can be no doubt that the state of consciousness is an inactive phenomenon! This paradoxical fact seems to raise difficulties for the claim that the thinking process is active in character.

Despite the necessity of thinking when conscious, we can choose what we think about. However, we *cannot but* make such a choice: that is, when conscious the object of our thinking will have been chosen or endorsed by us – even though we have no choice but to do so. Then if we conjoin the aforementioned properties of thinking, we find we are faced with a situation in which, even though we must choose the *object* of an actively directed process, we cannot choose to engage in such a processive phenomenon *independently* of choice of object. This is in contrast with the usual state of affairs. Normally when we choose the object of an active directed process, we choose to engage in an activity whose content it is. If I choose to eat cake, I choose to eat; if I choose to walk to Rome, I choose to walk; and it is difficult to find exceptions to this apparent rule. By contrast, if I choose to think about tennis, I do not choose to think. Here we find a major singularity in the process of thinking. It generates a problem concerning the will-status of the phenomenon, which I now consider.

(2) The following considerations suggest that thinking may be an inactive process. The main consideration, as was noted above, is that we can neither choose to think nor choose to stop thinking. This property of thinking makes the process appear even less within our control than the inactive phenomena of breathing or blinking. After all, there is such a thing as holding one's breath and stopping oneself from blinking, whereas there is neither 'stopping one's thinking' nor 'resuming one's thinking'. Thus, although in the case of thinking one might be inclined to deduce from the existence of choice of object that the process itself must be active, this argument is invalidated by the simple fact that there is no such thing as choosing to think or not think. In effect the point is made in *Waiting for Godot*, when Lucky's putative obedience to Pozzo's order to 'Think!' takes the form of a senseless word-salad. The helplessness of thinking is a consequence of the fact that consciousness is purely cerebrally caused.

Meanwhile, the following considerations point to the opposite judgement, viz. that thinking is active. A first simple fact is, that when (say) we are engaged in private ratiocination, we would reply to the question 'What are you doing?' by saying, 'I am thinking.' Moreover, if one was ratiocinatively thinking, one would do so by the active use of words, which strongly suggests that this linguistic activity must be making possible a closely knit non-identical active thinking process. And in fact there can be no doubt that, even though the inner life continues to throw up unanticipated events as our limbs do not, one is in broad control of its direction of movement, and in particular of the thinking process. After all, there is no such thing as absent-minded thinking, for thinking *par excellence* lies at the centre of experiential awareness, and has of necessity to do so. In sum, it is impossible seriously to entertain the view, when we are thinking about a chosen topic, that this particular examples of thinking could be anything other than active in character. It is not open to us to doubt whether *this present process* here and now going on is active. I conclude – rather bluntly – that thinking must be an activity.

(3) Whenever we think we are thinking about some X, engaging in an activity, and doing what we choose to do, so that thinking must be an activity. But if that is the situation, must it not be a 'compelled activity'? The ground of this claim being, that one cannot choose not to think *and*

that one has to think. I believe we must accept this judgement. Thinking is necessitated, and therefore thinking is a compelled activity. However, this claim is put in perspective when we contrast this phenomenon with three other examples, of compelled activity.

(i) Neurotically compulsive behaviour, e.g. compulsive handwashing.

(ii) Samson at the mill with slaves.

(iii) Continually finding oneself humming a particular tune.

In each case we would in different senses speak of 'compelled activity': in (i) of an irrational force ('I feel I must . . .') having its way, in (ii) of a rational prudential force ('It is better than death') having its way despite counter-considerations, and in (iii) of near inevitability irrespective of any resolve one way or the other. Accordingly, if thinking is compelled it is so in a different sense from these phenomena. In thinking one yields to no force of any kind even though one acts out of desire, and although thinking is like some examples of humming music to oneself in being an inevitability, there is a significant difference between the modes of inevitability. Thus, while one can temporarily choose to stop humming a tune, thinking lies beyond all choice, choice here being inconceivable. It is compelled in a sense that wholly transcends the case of unawares humming a tune.

One might attempt to resist the conclusion that thinking is compelled activity by protesting that action precisely is the one phenomenon which cannot happen to one. This is indeed true, but the claim is not that the activity of thinking happens to one. Rather, what happens to one is that one is thinking: not the thinking, but the fact of thinking. Unlike the compulsion of the obsessive it does not compromise reason, unlike that of prudence it is not a limitation upon freedom, and unlike subliminal humming it is not in conflict with self-determination. While we think because of purely cerebral causes, each example of thinking occurs for whatever reasons persuade us. For in general our thinking is for reasonable reasons, even though paradoxically we are obliged by the state of our brains alone to think and for no reason. Finally, the necessity of thinking constitutes no limitation upon anything.

Waking to consciousness is finding oneself in a state in which one is and has no choice but to be actively thinking. Consciousness condemns us to mental activity, rather in the sense in which J.-P. Sartre claimed we are condemned to be free. In either case we are talking of the condition of wakeful self-conscious consciousness. Thinking is an irreducible part of that state.

CHAPTER 14

Defining the psychological and the mental

The following emerged in the foregoing discussion. First, that all physical actions are strivings; second, that we relate epistemologically to strivings as we do to experiences; third, that all physical actions encompass the willed surface bodily phenomenon ϕ. Now is not that an unusual state of affairs? In particular, does it not make physical action look as if ontologically it must be something of an oddity? For what is its ontological status? Are physical actions merely bodily phenomena? Or are they instead psychological in type? If the latter, as we have suggested, might it be that physical actions occupy a special place within the realm of the psychological, a site at the very end of the less mental end of the psychological spectrum – as near to the *merely physical* as the domain of the psychological will permit? So I suspect, but need to look more closely at the facts before making a judgement on the matter. These questions lead me here in chapter 14 to attempt to define the ontological concepts involved. Meanwhile, the problem that set this all in motion, namely the ontological status of physical action, forms the subject matter of the next chapter, 15.

I. UNCERTAINTY OVER THE ONTOLOGICAL STATUS OF PHYSICAL ACTIONS

(1) One's first intimations are that physical actions are psychological phenomena. Many facts suggest so. To begin, the philosophy of action is part of the philosophy of mind. More important: all actions originate from mental causes, and do so with that internal connective pellucidity characteristic of 'mental causation'. Furthermore, if one had to say what was the prime manifestation of mentality in a living object, one would select physical actions: more specifically, physical actions which are interpretable in terms of other psychological phenomena, like belief and desire, with which they are intimately linked. Finally, and most important of all, we have seen that all actions are identical with strivings, and that strivings are of the status,

472

experience: taken together, these considerations seem to demonstrate that the ontological status of physical actions is psychological.

Second thoughts make this conclusion appear questionable, and suggest that physical actions must be non-psychological in character. Thus, actions divide into mental and physical actions, and there is surely an ontological difference between visualising and chopping down a tree. While it seems evident that the former phenomenon takes place in the mind, it seems equally evident that the latter does not. Then how could tree-chopping fail to be non-psychological? This theory receives a measure of confirmation when we recall that whereas mental acts like visualising are at once invisible and given epistemologically with authority to their agent, physical actions are neither. These considerations suggest that, despite the set of properties marshalled in the previous paragraph, visualising must be mental, as delivering a kick is not. Then that in turn seems to imply that delivering a kick cannot be mental, and must in consequence be relegated into the domain of the merely physical.

(2) Third thoughts are that there must be *some* sense in which physical actions rate as psychological: after all, we have just encountered what looks like a demonstration of their psychologicality, a proof based on the fact that all physical actions are identical with a striving, a striving of which one is mentalistically-immediately aware. And so we find ourselves torn between two incompatible alternatives. We are faced with two putative entailments of which it seems that one must be accepted and the other not. They are: (A) Tryings must be psychological, bodily acts are tryings, therefore bodily acts must be psychological; (B) Bodily acts cannot be mental, bodily acts are tryings, therefore tryings cannot be mental.

What is the resolution of the problem? Which prevails out of (A) and (B)? I think the correct answer is that both do and neither does. Let me explain. In the light of the considerations advanced in chapter 12 supporting the theory that all physical actions are identical with some striving or other, it is I think inconceivable that we settle for the doctrine that physical actions are merely one biological event amongst others, no different ontologically from digestion. I think we have no choice but to opt for the thesis, that in *some sui generis* and non-stipulative sense of 'psychological', physical actions rate as psychological.

Then how are we to deal with the clash between (A) and (B)? I think we reject it. For (A) and (B) employ the terms 'psychological' and 'mental' – unreflectively. What is needed is, if not new terms, at the very least a close look at old ones. Accordingly, if we could manage differentially to refurbish the terms 'psychological' and 'mental', we might find ourselves in a position both to do justice to the aforementioned ontological unlikeness and bypass the dichotomy: (A) or (B)? This definitional enterprise is the subject matter of the remainder of this chapter.

2. DELIMITING THE PSYCHOLOGICAL

(1) What is the defining criterion of psychologicality? What *is* the property psychological? If there is such a thing, it should be equally present in pains, forgetting processes, thought events. What can it be? What property do these phenomena uniquely share with dreams, hunger . . .?

It cannot be the property: being intentionalist; for after-images lack this property. It cannot be the property: being concept-dependent; for pains lacks this property. It cannot be the property: being belief-dependent; for hunger lacks this property. It cannot be the property: being individuated for the subject along a purely temporal axis; for sensations lack this property. It cannot be the negative property: not having an *a priori*-given physical expression or physical part; for bodily strivings lacks this property. It cannot be the property: capable of having an immediate psychological cause; for sensations lack this property. It cannot be the property: being a content of the stream of consciousness; for forgetting processes are not. It cannot be the property: being private and invisible and at best located only in the brain; for physical actions are none of these. And so on.

Then is it a myth? Does the concept of the psychological do no more than arbitrarily bring together under one heading a variety of items of disparate status? I think not. After all, do we not know what to insert and exclude in the sequence: thought, pain, dream, belief . . .? Do we not know to include anxiety and debar digestion; joy and not birth . . .? Then what principle is at work here? It does not consist in some specific relation. Nor in the possession of a particular logical property, such as intentionality. Nor in general in anything that is not in itself purely and simply the property of *psychologicality* – such as invisibility or spacelessness or privacy. In short, psychologicality is *indefinable*.

(2) Nevertheless, there exist simple necessary and sufficient conditions for an item's being psychological. These can be discovered if we remember that psychologicality in a living object entails the animality of that object. Other properties like (say) that of having blood do not ensure animality in the bearer, since it is possible that (say) vegetables contain blood,[1] so

---

[1] 'The next day the seed potatoes were full of blood.' From J. M. Synge, *The Aran Islands: Plays, Poems and Prose*, London: Everyman's Library, Dent, 1972, 251.

that having blood or being formed out of flesh cannot even be sufficient conditions of animality.

Then I suggest the following logically necessary and sufficient conditions for an item's being psychological. An item is psychological in character if it possesses a property P; which is that *de re* essential property of some events and states which is such that all animals and no non-animal living object in any conceivable life system in any possible world possess the somewhere potential for items endowed with P; and no item can lack P and necessarily ensure animality in its living owner. This unambiguously demarcates this unanalysable type. It delimits it without defining it.

What we have done here is this. We know of one important and necessary property of psychologicality: namely, that it necessarily distinguishes animality from all other forms of life, viz. vegetable, cellular, viral, bacterial, etc. Thus, 'X is an animal' and 'X is living and has the somewhere potential for supporting psychological phenomena' are logically equivalent. Therefore without attempting to dismantle psychologicality, we can both put its reality beyond doubt and precisely delimit the class of psychological items. This is the next best thing to a definition. It shows that there truly does exist a realm encompassing pains, forgetting processes, hunger, dreams, etc. This realm I shall call the Realm of the Psychological. I symbolise it by 'ψ'.

3. ONTOLOGY AND THE MIND

(1) There can be no doubt that psychologicality is a true ontological level, a new plateau in Being. The contents of the World made a definitive leap when psychologicality appeared: a novelty in the strongest sense of the word came into existence at that point. Then the question I wish here to ask is: might there be ontological diversity *within* the realm of the psychological? Two natural candidates are: the ontological level corresponding to self-consciousness, and the level of what I shall call 'mentality'. I consider them now in order.

When I speak of self-consciousness, I imply the inherence in the bearer of a mutually entailing set of properties: self-knowledge, rationality, the capacity to think, etc. This new phenomenon surely constitutes an 'ontological novelty' within the ontological development, consciousness/psychologicality. It is a true development and not just a complexification, and if anything merits the term 'higher' this mutation in Being must be deemed a change from 'lower' to 'higher', just as is animality in relation to vitality. I see nothing stipulative in such a claim, for this particular divide within the psychological can be spelled out with precision in *a priori*-given terms. Meanwhile the concept of 'higher' can be explicated *a priori* through appeal to the fact that psychologicality arises on the ground vitality, just as vitality arises on the ground physicality.

The development of the self-conscious variety of consciousness involves the appearance within the mind of *novel phenomenal kinds*, kinds which are unique to the new type of being. The most notable example is thought, but one could in addition instance novel events in which the mind turns back upon itself, such as attending to a sensation, or novel affective phenomena like remorse or anguish or even hate. Meanwhile, along with these novel phenomenal kinds occur *novel transmutations* in 'old' kinds: for example, when in visual perception (say) one sees an object as an instance of the conceptually given type, chair. The acquisition by a mind of the battery of concepts that is involved in language-acquisition cannot but wreak change in all those phenomena which utilise concepts. In sum, we note here the arise within the mind of two novelties internal to the development of self-consciousness, one the appearance of new kinds, the other the transmutation of 'old' kinds. Both developments may be described as ontological mutations. New orders of psychological being, and not just new phenomenal types, enter existence for the first time, phenomena which are internal to the development of the ontological level self-consciousness. In short, the arise of self-consciousness is an ontological development.

(2) The second property that I wish to consider I have called 'mentality'. What I have in mind is the fact that there seems to be a relatively sharp break between most of the contents of the mind and a certain few other psychological phenomena in which the body makes its presence overtly felt. I think there is a case for describing the former phenomena as properly mental, and the latter as merely psychological. I instance as examples: dreaming on the one hand, and toothache on the other. There are compelling reasons for speaking of ontological difference here, even though both phenomena are examples of the type psychological. It seems to me that dreams are 'higher' phenomena than, and therefore developmentally remoter from the merely physical realm, than are sensations. It remains actually to demonstrate that this difference is something more than a difference in degree: that is, that the 'relatively sharp break' of which I speak (above) is a reality.

Before I address this issue, one theory of the mind's contents ought to be mentioned here: a theory which in my opinion is mistaken. It consists in the supposition that there exists a class of developed 'higher' mental phenomena which occur in humans and are yet simultaneously 'fit for angels'. Thus, one might believe that whereas toothaches and hunger and bodily strivings could not intelligibly be predicated of a being essentially lacking in physicality, thoughts and aspirations and knowledge might be so predicable. If this is understood to say that in one sector of the human mind occur phenomena which might in principle occur in a bodiless mind, then there is a sense in which it must be false. While it is plain that bodily sensations are necessarily putatively of some body-part, and overtly unfitted to enter the supposed angelic mind, there exist in my opinion ineradicable links between the most interior mental phenomena in any animal and its body, a mental connective tissue internal to those mental phenomena. To be sure, this is not to say that thoughts and knowledge *as such* are incapable of occurring in a bodiless mind. Rather, that the variety occurring in animal minds could not do so.

One relevant phenomenon in this regard is affect. Most affective states have a corresponding physiognomy – a fact which cartoonists put to good use. In this way affect links us to the body as (say) thought does not. Of their very nature affective states tend to reveal their presence in the body, sometimes in the form of actions prompted by act-desire, but often in phenomena like change of blood flow or rate of respiration, and of course in whatever goes into the constitution of a physiognomy. Now the general connection between emotion and bodily expression is surely *a priori* necessary, even though the particular ties seem not to be. Thus we know that emotions express themselves differently in different peoples, and presumably also differently in different peoples in different historical eras. Indeed, reports like 'His face went white with rage' and 'His face was purple with rage', remind us that the one and same emotion can express itself differently even in the one individual.

I would like now to set down what what I understand to be the impact of – more, the essential presence of – the body within the mind, taking my cue from the example of emotion. Now there is in the first place a good sense in which emotions are internal phenomena: after all, emotions generally take a thought-given object, and people can keep their emotions to themselves. Nevertheless we have just seen that there exists a causal relation to the body which is part of the essence of emotion. Then I suggest that what holds here of emotion holds also, though at a greater remove and non-expressively, in the case of more paradigmatically interior phenomena like thought and image and belief. In short, full interiority co-exists with *a priori*-given links with the body. It seems that the body makes its presence felt throughout the farthest reaches of the mind. I hope to demonstrate this truth in the succeeding chapter, 15.

4. DEFINING THE MENTAL (I)

In this section 4 and also in section 5 I address myself to the defining of 'mental'. There will inevitably be an element of stipulation in what is proposed, since the sense of 'mental' is less exact than the sense of 'psychological'. However, the distinction which I draw in this definitional enterprise is not, I believe, marked by the same imprecision. My point of departure in this enterprise is that physical actions must be rated as psychological events.

(a) A paradigm of the mental: the thought-event

What are we to say of the evident ontological unlikeness of the acts of tree-chopping and trying to remember? If, as is now claimed, the former is psychological, into what supra-psychological heaven are we to elevate the latter? Yet nothing, at least in this region, seems 'higher' than the psychological. Then how are we to do justice to so evident a difference? The resolution of the problem, which is achieved without demoting physical action from the Domain of the Psychological into the domain of the merely biological, takes the form of drawing a line within the psychological realm, thereby delimiting two closely interrelated regions: a line distinguishing those psychological phenomena which are fully mental in character, and those whose full mentalism seems in doubt. It is into the higher of these regions that we set the act of trying to remember, and into the lower that we set the act of tree-chopping.

Thus, the distinction that I have in mind requires to be drawn, not between the psychological and some supposedly loftier realm, the properly mental, but between the *merely* psychological and the *properly mental subsector* of the psychological. That is, between the non-mental psychological and the mental psychological. So that if we symbolise 'psychological' as 'ψ' and 'mental' as 'Ψ', then we are distinguishing $\psi \sim \Psi$ from $\psi\Psi$, i.e. $\psi \sim \Psi$ from Ψ.

As a preliminary to drawing this distinction, I shall take a paradigmatically mental phenomenon like the thought-event, and list those of its properties which seem relevant to its being classed as mental in character. Given this list, we should find ourselves in a position to single out certain psychological phenomena which measure up only partially on this yardstick of mentality.

   (i) Intentionalist
   (ii) Concept dependent
   (iii) Belief dependent

(iv) Not governed by tight type-type psycho-physical law
 (v) Being holistically and intelligibly related to the contents of the mind
(vi) Not having an *a priori*-given physical expression or physical part
(vii) Not given as at a location in space
(viii) Individuated purely temporally
 (ix) Capable of having an immediate psychological cause
  (x) Capable of having immediate psychological effects
 (xi) Mentalistically immediately cognisable
(xii) A content of the stream of consciousness
(xiii) Situated, if anywhere, exclusively in the brain

No doubt this list omits features of importance. Equally clearly, some of these properties cannot be necessary for mentalism: thus (xii) would rule out beliefs. Yet despite these flaws, phenomena like an image, or a dream, or a passing thought, satisfy all the tests, while a phenomenon like falling through space satisfies none. Clearly, they must be some sort of a guide to some sort of psychic-ality.

(b) Demoting sensations from the mind – into where else?

(1) How do pains and visual sensations fare on this preliminary account of the mental? Singularly poorly, for they fail to satisfy all or nearly all of tests (i)–(ix).

The most important test surely is (i): intentionality. In all probability sensations fail to exhibit this vital trait. Thus, bodily sensations seem not to be 'of' some body-part in the sense in which (say) fear is 'of' snakes or a mental image is 'of' the Eiffel Tower. The sense of 'of' in the case of bodily sensations is more accurately given by an 'in', a spatial principle of individuation. For example, being given as a pain 'in' the elbow does not imply that the pain itself is essentially of that body part: it is no part of what the pain *is*. After all, two indistinguishable pains could be present in each elbow. In this sense the sensation does not represent an object as the above mental states do, and I assume that the received concept of 'intentionality' posits just such a representational property. Furthermore, visual sensations like (say) a red after-image are given merely directionally: they do not 'aspire' to some (bearer) object. These considerations make it improbable that sensations meet the requirements of intentionality. Whether we should say the same of an awareness of the sensation is a different question into which I will not here enter.

(2) Thus, both bodily non-perceptual and non-bodily perceptual sensations differ from paradigmatic mental phenomena on numerous counts, and in

particular on the important intentionality test. And this strongly suggests that they be excluded forthwith from the category of the mental. And yet we must not forget that, while the event of falling through space satisfied none of tests (i)–(xiii), sensations measured up on all of the counts (x)–(xiii). And how do we do justice to that? For is it not a matter of some significance? Why allot more weight to *failing* to satisfy (i)–(ix) than to *succeeding* in satisfying (x)–(xiii)?

Let me express the matter this way. Thinking of the fact that they fail to satisfy (i)–(ix), it is natural to exclude pains from the realm of the *mental.* Yet if we push pains out of the mind, do we push them into no more than the *physico-biological world?* But that rides roughshod over every intuition we have. Then what realm do they inhabit? Now we shall answer this question only when we understand what we mean by 'realm', and in particular by 'the realm of the *mind* '. Then I think we so use 'in the mind' that 'x is in the mind' = 'x exists and x is mental'; so that 'x comes into Smith's mind' = 'x is mental & x comes into existence & x is ascribable to Smith'; and 'Smith has a mind' = 'Smith is such that x's that are mental can be ascribed to Smith'. In short, the mind, rather than being a mystic quasi-spatial container, is a non-spatial logical container of items of the kind mental, somewhat as the number system is the logical home of items of the kind number. The 'realm' or logical container inhabited by an item is determined by the type of its inhabitants.

Then what is the logical container of pains, itches, etc.? Not the mind, apparently. Not the body either, for that also contains events like digestion. Thus, mind and body are unacceptable logical containers of sensations. And yet there must be such a container, for there is such an ontological type as the type exemplified in sensations and perhaps other bodily oriented psychological phenomena. It seems therefore what we need is not a word, but a characterisation of that conjectured type. Then my suggestion is that the type is psychological non-mental – a type which we are in the process of defining. The present delimitation is therefore of a realm within a realm.

(3) Let me once again briefly link these findings with the theory of action. I hope to demonstrate in the near future that the act of trying to remember falls into the category mental psychological, and the act of tree-chopping into the category non-mental psychological. In this way we manage to hang onto the important truth that all actions are psychological phenomena, while simultaneously doing justice to the evident ontological unlikeness of mental and physical actions.

5. DEFINING THE MENTAL (2)

(a) Intentionality

(1) This present section is concerned with attempting to provide necessary and sufficient conditions for 'mental' (Ψ). My way of going about this task will be to single out – within the set of properties listed in section 4 as present in phenomena one would naturally describe as 'properly mental' – those properties which seem to *distinguish* phenomena of this type from 'merely psychological' ($\psi \sim \Psi$) phenomena. Then bearing in mind that Ψ appears to range over thought events, belief states, and forgetting processes, but to exclude pains and visual sensations, I suggest the following as tests for an item's being of Ψ status. A phenomenon is Ψ if it is:
   (i) Psychological
   (ii) Intentionalist
   (iii) Not given as at a location in space
   (iv) Individuated along a purely one-dimensional temporal axis
   (v) Not governed by tight type-type psycho-physical law
   (vi) Holistically and intelligibly related to the contents of the mind
   (vii) Lacking an *a priori*-given physical expression or physical part

(2) Let us take a closer look at these tests. I begin by briefly commenting on what is probably the most important of the tests, viz. (ii) intentionality. Now I understand this complex property to conjoin the properties (1) being object-directed (whether to a singular or propositional object), (2) indifference to the existence of the object/truth of the proposition, and (3) referential opacity.

So far as (1), being object-directed, is concerned, we have seen that this concept raises a problem. The example of bodily sensations showed that to satisfy (1), the essential description of the item *itself* requires completion with an object-expression. Thus, while fear cannot just be fear but has to be of —— or lest ——, and pain has to be of —— or in ——, the fear is *in itself* of its object whereas the pain is not *in itself* of some given body-part. The second property, (ii), marks an important distinction between superficially similar sentences, e.g. 'He seeks El Dorado' and 'He sees El Dorado', which have different structural entailments. The third property, (iii), opacity, can readily be misunderstood. Assume that I(s) is an intentionally used sentence, where s is the object of the phenomenon being characterised. Then it is not that I(s) & s = s_x → I(s_x) is false. Rather is it that, while this entailment is a reality, it does not entitle us to put I(s_x) to here-and-now intentional use.

That is, from the fact that I(s) designates an item *as* it was given to its owner (creator, etc.), and s = s_x, it does not follow that I(s_x) also designates the item *as* it was given to the same owner (creator, etc.). In any case, the above property is what I propose to bring under the description 'the property of opacity'. And this gives us a workable concept of intentionality for defining Ψ.

(3) Then how does intentionality relate to the first of the two concepts under scrutiny, viz. psychologicality? Well, the example of sensations makes it clear that intentionality cannot be a necessary condition of psychologicality, while meaningful phenomena like drawings make it likely that it is not a sufficient condition either. What of the relation between intentionality and mentalism (Ψ)? It has frequently been claimed that intentionality is the defining mark of the mental. I shall not enter into this question any further than to note that all of the items which we locate within the mental sub-sector of the psychological exhibit intentionality, so that I strongly suspect intentionality to be at least a necessary condition of mentalism. Then I am here engaged in supplementing this important property with several other properties in the attempt to define (or 'fix') 'mental'. The aim is to arrive at a set of necessary and sufficient conditions for 'mentality'. The remaining tests are set out below.

(b) Tests (iii)–(vii): individuation/psycho-physical law/bodily expression and parts

(1) We individuate mental phenomena along the one-dimensional axis of time. Whereas one can have two instances of believing p, provided they are separated by time, one cannot at any one time twice believe p or twice have the same thought-event. This principle of individuation holds whether we are thinking of the contents of the stream of consciousness (which is to say experiences), or states that lie outside experience (such as the knowledge of one's name), or processes and events which are not experienced (such as either the process of, or else the discontinuous event of, coming to forget some fact or experience).

Thus, mental items are individuated without reference to space. This holds irrespective of the truth-value of Physicalism, a theory which would identify all of the above with cerebral phenomena in space. Then how does this property of the mental relate with the fact that we do not experience mental phenomena as located in space? It is surely one and the same trait. For example, if we could experience visual experiences as happening in front of one, this should allow for the possibility that one might simultaneously have an indistinguishable visual experience happening behind one, and such a thing is not possible. If one had two pairs of eyes, one in front and the other behind, one might be able to have two visual fields, and be able to switch attention from one to the other. Indeed, one might have visual awareness of both visual fields simultaneously, and do so even if those visual fields had visually indistinguishable contents. But the claim that one might at some one moment in time simultaneously see different visual fields containing visually indistinguishable contents, is not the claim that one might at some time have two internally indistinguishable visual experiences. After all, in the situation imagined above one could point in different directions to two distinct instantiations of the same visual appearance, just as one might point to two 'look-alikes', either in the one visual field or in different ones. Such a thing is not possible in the case of visual experiences: we cannot point at visual experiences. Visual experiences do not line up in space, as do visible objects or entire visual fields (which might stand side by side before one in different directions).

(2) The next test to consider is the pair (v)/(vi): the inapplicability of tight type-type psycho-physical law to the mental, and being holistically and intelligibly responsible to the contents of the mind. Then so far as this claim is concerned, I am content at this point to refer the reader to the argument marshalled by Donald Davidson in his very creative paper, 'Mental Events'.[2] In this paper Davidson advances considerations which tell strongly against the existence of tight psycho-physical type-type laws for entities like beliefs, i.e. Ψ entities that are holistically responsible to the rest of the mind's contents; and his arguments have application, not merely across evolutionary systems or species, but within the one individual. Whereas, for example, there exist regular causally sufficient conditions for the occurrence of (say) pain, such as the sudden sharp insertion of a pin into the skin, we know of none such for a particular thought-event or particular image, and so on. While it may be that no law governing sensation ranges across all possible animal species or life-systems, the science of anaesthetics reminds us that within each species the occurrence of sensation is type-type law-governed. We cannot *a priori* say what form those sufficient conditions will take, but we can *a priori* say that they must exist.

(3) The last of these tests (vii) is: not having an *a priori*-given bodily expression and/or physical part. But first, which psychological phenomena have a bodily expression? Taking a liberal reading of 'expression', I would

---

[2] In L. Swanson and J. W. Foster (eds.), *Experience and Theory*, London: Duckworth, 1970.

say the following: physical act-desire, physical act-intention, physical act-striving, certain but not all sensations, and most emotions and/or affective states; and it is difficult to think of further examples. Then which of these expressions are *a priori*-given? The first three seem likely candidates, but since this is part of the overall theoretical claim that I wish to make, I will set them to one side. Amongst sensations, the tightest connections are between itching and scratching, and pain and bodily agitation. These links are close, but I cannot discover any justification for deeming such expressions *a priori*-determined, even though it is hard (say) to imagine an intense itch not generating an urge to scratch. It is surely intelligible to suppose that there might exist some species of creature in which the sensation generates no such impulse.

(4) The second half of the above test (vii) is the negative property: not having an *a priori*-given physical part. Then while this may not be the most important indicator of mentalism, for our present purposes it has an obvious interest – which I bring out in the next chapter.

6. CONCLUSION

(1) The conclusion that I draw from the foregoing is this. Within what I have called the Domain of the Psychological, a small group of phenomena emerged which seem in some sense to be different in kind. These are those psychological items which have a peculiarly close and overt relation to the body. It is a relation which can be delineated with precision in *a priori*-given terms: for example, in that they each have a spatial and not merely temporal principle of individuation. Now this property – singled out by Kant as the differentia of 'outer sense' from 'inner sense' – is of such major significance that one is inclined forthwith to characterise the divide as ontological – and with justification. In any case, these few phenomena are so out of step with the rest of the phenomena which populate the Domain of the Psychological that, rather than stipulate a special term for the latter more typical occupants of that domain, it seems to me that it may be better to reserve the established term 'mental' for those typical occupants, and describe the exceptions in terms which take note of their deviation from the psychological norm. That is, describe thoughts, emotions, beliefs, desires, intentions, memories, and so on as 'mental', and sensations and bodily actions as either 'psychological non-mental' or 'improperly mental psychological'.

(2) The summary situation is as follows. The proposed definitional marks of the mental (Ψ), which were assembled in Section 5(a)(1), consisted of the following properties:

(i) Psychological

(ii) Intentionalist

(iii) Not given as at a location in space

(iv) Individuated along a purely one-dimensional temporal axis

(v) Not governed by tight type-type psycho-bodily law

(vi) Being holistically and intelligibly related to the contents of the mind

(vii) Not having an *a priori*-given physical expression and/or *a priori*-given physical part

Meanwhile the proposed marks of the 'improperly mental psychological' ($\psi \sim \Psi$) took the form of a set of sufficient conditions (noting in passing that (f) was not necessary, even though of considerable significance in the present context).

(a) Psychological

(b) Non-intentionalist

(c) Given in spatial terms

(d) Individuated spatio-temporally

(e) Governed by tight type-type psycho-bodily law

(f) Having an *a priori*-given physical expression and/or *a priori*-given physical part

There is an element of imprecision in these 'working definitions'. While I do not consider the sense of 'psychological' to be anything other than perfectly precise, I do not believe that the same can be said of 'mental'. I also appreciate that the tests (i)–(vii) of 'mentality' may well be a case of 'overkill'. I think tests (i)–(iv) or tests (i)–(v) would suffice.

CHAPTER 15

The ontological status of physical action

"When the body is sad the heart languishes."

Albert Camus, *The Fall*

I. INTRODUCTION

(1) I return to the original question. What is the ontological status of physical action? I begin by retracing the natural dialectical progression of this question.

Is the physical act a psychological phenomenon, or is it merely physical? One's first inclination is to suppose it psychological. Thus, it has of necessity a psychological origin to which it relates with that internal pellucidity characteristic of mental causal connections. Most important, it is identical with some striving or other, and since ontology can be description-relative only in the sense of being description-revealed, and because striving must surely be rated a psychological phenomenon, physical action it seems must likewise be psychological. So, at first, it appears.

Second thoughts take us in the opposite direction. For we know that actions divide into mental and physical actions: for example, visualisings as against kickings. These two phenomena are markedly dissimilar, on the score of public visibility, epistemological authority, immediate localisability, and sheer interiority, and such differences point overwhelmingly to the existence of ontological unlikeness. Then this gross ontological dissimilarity, taken in conjunction with the evident fact that visualisings (etc.) are psychological phenomena, strongly inclines us to relegate bodily actions from the psychological domain into the domain of the merely physical.

Thus, we are torn between: (A) tryings are mental, bodily acts are tryings, therefore bodily acts are mental; (B) bodily acts are non-mental, bodily acts are tryings, therefore tryings are non-mental – and neither conclusion seems satisfactory. Then 'third thoughts' say that we must sidestep this

486

dichotomy – without collapsing back into the doctrine that bodily acts are *merely* bodily events. That is, we cannot but suppose that in *some* sense the first position must be correct, even if in *some* sense the second position must also be correct. And this was the 'state of play' when, early in chapter 14, I took my 'cue' from this idea and proceeded to refurbish the senses of 'mental' and 'psychological', hoping to show that it was the existence of dialectically opposed ontologically diverse orders of being that underlay the seeming contradictions of (A) and (B).

To repeat: we have 'third thoughts' to the effect that the considerations in favour of classifying bodily acts as in *some* sense 'psychological' or 'mental' constitute an overwhelming case. Above all, the fact that they are identical with a striving and that we relate epistemologically to bodily strivings as we do to experiences generally. This is a formidable, indeed surely a decisive argument. After all, the only serious reason for dissent lies in the ontological dissimilarity of physical and mental acts. But the distinction between 'psychological' (ψ) and 'mental' (Ψ), elaborated in chapter 14, is capable of doing justice to this distinction, which it simply takes in its stride. Accordingly, it seems that we should settle for the doctrine: the ontological status of mental actions is Ψ, and of bodily actions is $\psi \sim \Psi$.

(2) Indeed, at this point the scales may well fall from one's eyes. For precisely *over what* is one arguing in disputing whether physical strivings are psychological in nature? While psychologicality is a *sui generis* property, are we not in danger of erecting a *mystique* of the psychological? For does not the property of being known, not merely immediately and quasi-incorrigibly, but in the way we know of experiences generally, finalise the matter? What more does one require? I submit that we need no more, for the reason that, while we can stand in all sorts of epistemological relations to psychological items, it is a *logically sufficient* condition of psychologicality that we relate epistemologically to an item as we do to (say) thoughts and images.

To miss the fact that it is a logically sufficient condition is to construe this test as on a par with the litmus-test for acidity or alkalinity. Ultimately, it is to endorse the theory, not merely that psychologicality is a natural-kind property, which after all one assumes it must in some sense be, but that it is significantly akin in logical character to *a posteriori*-given natural kinds like heat or light or water. Whereupon the tests of 'mentality' (i)–(vii) produced in chapter 14 will be taken to be no more than a 'royal flush' of 'epistemological markers' of a property whose essence is hidden from view yet accessible to depth empirical inquiry. In short, tests (i)–(vii) are here interpreted as *mere symptoms* of the psychological! It follows that one might pile symptom upon symptom, swelling the list of tests to (i)–(1000 + vii) – without actually *entailing* psychologicality, and psychologicality proves to be something of which, in Locke's terminology, we have as yet a merely 'inadequate idea'. Indeed, as gold can travel in the deceptive garb adopted by colloidal gold, so the non-psychological might deceptively appear under just such a 'royal flush' of 'symptomatic markers' as above!

This Bad Metaphysics of the psychological – a product of Physics Worship – conceives of psychologicality as something whose essence is concealed in depth. But in fact this property is indefinable, and its essence is known when the use of psychological words is learned – which is what one would expect in view of its philosophical significance. By contrast, mankind actually lifted the veil and discovered the essence of heat and gold through protracted scientific inquiry millennia after fixing the referent and the use of their designating expressions. Then in reaching the conclusion that we stand epistemologically in the identical relation to physical tryings as we stand to mental phenomena like thoughts and images, we have no farther to travel to reach the conclusion that physical tryings are psychological phenomena. It follows, since *all* physical actions are *some* trying or other, and ontological status is not description-relative, that all physical actions are psychological phenomena.

2. PRECISELY FIXING THE ONTOLOGICAL STATUS OF THE BODILY WILL

(a) The tests for ψ and Ψ

(1) We accept that physical actions are psychological events. And that coheres with the distinction drawn in chapter 14 between ψ and Ψ, for thanks to this distinction we can do justice to the gross ontological unlikeness of visualisings and kickings, and do so without needing to demote the latter into the merely physical domain. We simply classify the first as Ψ and the second as $\psi \sim \Psi$. For there is much to support the thesis that physical actions are, not merely psychological, but $\psi \sim \Psi$ as well. And yet we shall now see that this more differential thesis faces a difficulty. This is because *prima facie* a variety of ontological classifications seems possible for phenomena as heterogeneous as intentional, unintentional, actings, and tryings, of either 'basic' or instrumental type – even as we accept that they are all of them psychological events. Might not some of the more interiorist of these phenomena be not merely psychological in status, but Ψ as well? Accordingly, the subject matter of the present

section 2 is the determination of the precise ontological status of bod-ily/basic/instrumental/intentional/unintentional/actings/tryings. Thus, I am here concerned with a wider issue than the ontological status of *bod-ily action*: it is the determination of the ontological status of the *bodily will*.

(2) I hope soon to demonstrate that the bodily will as such is $\psi \sim \Psi$ by appeal to the conclusions reached in chapter 14. There I defined the properly mental (Ψ) as: (i) ψ; (ii) intentionalist; (iii) not mentally given as at a location in space; and thus (iv) individuated along a purely one-dimensional temporal axis; (v) not governed by tight type-type psycho-physical law; (vi) being holistically and intelligibly related to the contents of the mind; (vii) not having an *a priori*-given physical expression or physical part. This list can I think be trimmed down to (i)–(iv).

In sections (b) and (c) (following) I apply these tests for mentalism (Ψ) to the above variegated set of bodily active phenomena. Then since intentionality is of such importance as a test of mentalism, let us first briefly review the intentionality-status of the above phenomena. Thus (α) '*basic acts*' are extensionalist because (say) arm-raising necessitates an arm rise that is the object of this event. (β) *Intentional 'basic-act' tryings* are intentionalist, since both referential opacity and indifference-to-existence obtain. (γ) *Instrumental actions* are extensionalist, since to count as an instrumental ϕ'-making an act needs merely to cause ϕ' along a 'power-line', so that instrumental act-content is determined independently of one's intentions/beliefs/concepts. (δ) *Instrumental tryings* are intentionalist, being directed towards an intentionally given effect that need not occur.

In sum: all *physical act* headings, whether basic or instrumental, whether intentional or unintentional, are extensionalist. And all *intentional tryings*, whether basic or instrumental, exhibit intentionality. So much for inten-tionality. I now put these findings to use in determining the ontological status of the above physically active phenomena.

(b) Intentional bodily striving

My aim is to demonstrate that the ontological status of the bodily will is $\psi \sim \Psi$ in the case of all of the above bodily activities, and to do so through appeal to the tests (i)–(vii) (above) of mentalism. Only intentional basic bodily strivings and intentional instrumental bodily strivings seem to have much chance of satisfying those tests. So I begin by applying the tests to an intentional basic bodily striving.

(i) It is psychological.
(ii) And it is intentionalist.
(iii)/(iv) But it fails test (iii) and (iv). This physical event has an *a priori*-given location in space, namely the site of motor-mechanistic activation, and must be spatio-temporally individuated.
(v) And it fails test (v). Since the event of trying is identical with activation of the motor-mechanism, and the motor-mechanism is a regular syndrome which occurs whenever we act, a regular sequence of mechanistic events must occur whenever an intentional basic bodily striving occurs.

In sum, intentional basic bodily striving fails tests (iii)–(v) (at least), and according to those tests must be deemed non-mental psychological ($\psi \sim \Psi$) in status.

(c) Intentional instrumental bodily trying

(1) Consider an intentional instrumental bodily trying in which one attempts to signal by raising an arm. Here, too, we find that the tests (i) and (ii) of mentalism are satisfied. However, this phenomenon fails at least two of the other tests. They are: (v) not being governed by tight type-type psycho-physical law, and (vii) not having an *a priori*-given *physical expression* or physical *part*. We shall see that bodily instrumental trying fails these conditions of Ψ-dom because of being endowed with the following properties:

(A) It is governed by tight type-type psycho-physical law.
(B) It has an *a priori*-given physical expression.
(C) It has an *a priori*-given physical part.

(2) (A) *Psycho-physical law*. We are discussing physical trying, and it is important to note that seeming to oneself to physically try is an insufficient condition of trying. A dreamer can seem to himself to try to run, but it is an illusion that he tries (else his legs would move). This is because bodily trying, in conditions of physical liberty and bodily health, is a strict sufficient condition of the body event. In short, if it is a real and not an imagined bodily trying that occurs when one seemingly attempts to move one's signalling arm, this event must be nomically related to the desired bodily event. If the bodily event does not occur, either external or internal constraints have prevented it.

(B) A priori-*given physical expression*. A real bodily trying to move a putatively signalling arm has an *a priori*-given physical expression, viz. the activation of a bodily mechanism for the production of arm movement.

(C) A priori-*given physical part.* We saw in chapter 12 that there was no conceptual space for a trying to move a limb which occurred without activation of the motor-mechanism for the movement of the limb (however far that activation progressed). Indeed, it emerged that the trying and the activation were one and the same phenomenon. Accordingly, the failed trying has an *a priori*-given bodily description, and thus an *a priori*-given bodily part.

In sum, while intentional instrumental bodily trying passes tests (i) and (ii) of proper mentalism (Ψ), it fails the other tests. I conclude that the phenomenon is $\psi \sim \Psi$ in status. And since this was the most favourable case for the opposing thesis, I conclude that the bodily will *as such* is $\psi \sim \Psi$.

(3) It may come as a surprise that so seemingly mental a phenomenon as, say, a fully intentional and completely failed trying to signal that is wholly private to its agent, should be ontologically on a par with, say, an idle tongue-moving that is performed during sleep. But it is so. Thus, *all* bodily actions and *all* bodily tryings are psychological non-mental ($\psi \sim \Psi$) in status. In short, the bodily will is $\psi \sim \Psi$. By contrast, imagining and trying to remember and listening are psychological mental (Ψ) phenomena. It follows that our original intuition of a gross ontological dissimilarity between mental actions and bodily actions is vindicated: it is the evident difference in ontological status of the mental and the bodily will. And so too is the intuition that the bodily action rises above the ontological ruck of the *merely* vital, let alone the *merely* physical, phenomenon.

3. THE UNIQUE STRUCTURE OF THE BODILY ACTION

(a) Determining the ontological structure of the bodily action

(1) Suppose a pin-headed dinosaur twiddles a toe that is at the far end of its 50-foot body. What is the ontological status of the single event, toe movement, that takes place 50 feet from its tiny brain? Well, that dinosaur *might have* died the ultimate brain death 0.01 seconds before the toe began moving at t_I and even as the neurological message was on its way from the brain. But if it *had* died before t_I that toe movement would not have been a psychological event, for no psychological event can occur that belongs to no simultaneously existent being. Therefore *that* toe movement in the live dinosaur – that might have been in the dead body of the dinosaur – cannot be necessarily psychological. Therefore *that* toe movement is not psychological. (A conclusion that is in any case obvious.)

Now in chapter 12 we saw that the act of kicking encompasses the event of leg movement that its occurrence entails. And we now know, first that kicking is of the ontological status (ψ), second that leg movement is of the ontological status physical non-psychological ($\phi \sim \psi$). It follows that the psychological event of kicking must encompass the non-psychological event of leg movement. But it is inconceivable that the psychologicality of kicking could derive from nothing more than the mere conjunction of two non-psychological events. But kicking analyses into leg movement and whatever remains when leg movement is subtracted from kicking, and we know that the former event is non-psychological. Therefore the latter 'part-event' (as I shall call these merely potential slices of a whole event) must be psychological in status. And since it does not encompass leg movement, it cannot be identical with kicking. Accordingly, the psychological event of kicking (Φ) divides in the following way: into a last part (ϕ) (viz. leg movement) that is non-psychological, and an earlier part (Φ') that is both psychological and non-identical with kicking; that is, into a (non-ψ and *a priori*-given) ϕ and a (ψ) part-event Φ' such that $\Phi \neq \Phi'$.

(2) This structural situation is unique in the ψ-domain. For example: neither image nor desire nor pain divides into two such ontologically dissimilar and *a priori*-determinable parts. Then note that what is here unique is not that a psychological event should encompass a non-psychological event. After all, if almost any version of Physicalism is true, thought-events must encompass non-psychological molecular events. What is not found elsewhere in the ψ-domain is the *structure* that obtains here. There is no possibility that (say) a thought-event and a bodily act could be structurally isomorphous. A thought-event θ cannot be divided into an *a priori*-determinable non-psychological molecular event m and a psychological event θ' which is such that $\theta \neq \theta'$. *A priori*, this structure obtains only with bodily action.

It seems to me a matter of great significance that this structure is unique to bodily action. The unique role of bodily action as a bridge between inner and outer – one end immediately flush with the mental intention, the other end lodged amidst the bric-à-brac of the merely physical realm – is made possible thereby, the ψ event of bodily action being at once endowed with an immediate Ψ cause and a surface goal event-part ϕ that is non-ψ. This unique ontologically impure structure is internal to the fact that the mind has in bodily action an *immediate mediator* between itself and the rest of nature, a precious something without which it would exist in an impossible condition of radical isolation. It is this truth that Magical

Volitionism, according to which a supposed volition immediately and so to say magically generates an event on the body's surface, so grossly misrepresents. Magical Volitionism misrepresents the character of this crucial immediate connection between inner and outer, replacing a causally immediate link that holds between a Ψ event and a $\psi \sim \Psi$ event that is endowed with a surface and *a priori*-given non-ψ event-part ϕ, by a magically causal immediacy that is said to hold between a mythical Ψ event and that same ϕ.

(b) The psychologisation of the entire animal body

(1) Psychological events cannot occur outside the brain. And yet the above structural theory proves that events occurring outside the brain can be parts, indeed necessary parts, of immediately experienced psychological events. For example: a fairly large, public, visible, bodily, non-psychological, event, finger movement, occurring a yard away from the brain, can be a necessary (though inessential) part of a psychological event that is as immediately experienced as a thought, viz. a striving to move that finger (that succeeds), i.e. an act of finger-moving. Why not? It comes as a jolt to have to accept such a proposition; but not, I think, as more. In particular, it fails to force upon us any new conception of the psychological. A new image, perhaps, a new set of beliefs, no doubt, but hardly a new belief as to what the psychological *is*. For the property psychologicality is what the empiricists would call 'simple'. I have no theory as to its constitutive nature. Hence no theory to change in the light of these facts.

(2) Now it has seemed natural to suppose that anything that is a psychological event must occur in the mind. And yet since the mind is the logical rather than spatial or occult container of Ψ events, $\psi \sim \Psi$ events cannot be lodged therein. Therefore rather than locate sensations in the mind, we ought instead to employ the concept of a logical container of ψ items – 'The Domain of the Psychological' – into which we fit both Ψ and $\psi \sim \Psi$ items. Therefore the Mind must be accounted a sub-section, indeed the central core sub-section, of the Domain of the Psychological. Then the thesis that some ψ events have event parts that occur outside the brain – which *is* the organ in which occur all physical events internally contributory to the occurrence of Ψ items – leads to the following theory. Since the physical site of psychological items extends beyond the brain, we may say the same of the Domain of the Psychological. And that is to say, that the location of that of which the mind is a central core part extends throughout the body.

It spreads beyond the brain to the farthest reaches of the nervous system, albeit peripherally and inessentially. Indeed, it spreads farther, because the movement of a kicking leg is not an event in the nervous system, but is part of the ψ event of kicking. Thus, the Domain of the Psychological must have 'outposts' in the body, 'frontier stations' as it were, radiating out from a central legislative centre. It will encompass the limbs, indeed the entire body seeing that a man can flex his body – but fail differentially to include (say) the ears. In short, *a priori* the Domain of the Psychological necessarily ranges over a spatial region that at least includes the spatial surface envelope that the living animal body presents to the world. In this sense, the Domain of the Psychological and the body are in their entirety inextricably intertwined. And since the Mind is the core sector of the Domain of the Psychological, this constitutes an added tightening of the bond between Mind and Body.

(c) *The psychological depths of the bodily action*

A priori the ψ event of limb-moving Φ divides into the non-psychological event of limb movement ϕ, together with the psychological part-event residue Φ' (wherein the psychologicality of limb-moving resides); and $\Phi \neq \Phi'$. An odd relation! Indeed, it promises to be odder still. For this psychological part-event residue Φ' must itself divide up into, say, non-psychological muscle-contraction ϕ' together with a new psychological part-event residue Φ'': a process that cannot but keep repeating itself. That is, the unusual event totality that is the bodily act has a part that is non-psychological and a remainder part that is psychological; and the part that is psychological in turn has a part that is non-psychological together with a remainder part that is psychological; and so on all the way back to brain (and mind). But it is important to note that none of these psychological parts is a whole or individual event: they are what I have been calling 'part-events'. Thus, this account in no way commits me to the doctrine that arm-raising splits into two events, one psychological, the other non-psychological. Rather, I recognise that the event divides into an individual non-psychological event (arm rise) *and* a psychological non-individual part-event (striving); and that the latter psychological part-event divides in the same way; and so on. Thus, I recognise that irrespective of where we draw a divide in this complex event-totality, the earlier part will be psychological, non-autonomous – and striving, while the later part will be a set of autonomous (i.e. whole) mere bodily non-psychological events. And this holds no matter how small the first part, which thereby confers its psychological character upon the totality that extends as far as the surface of the body. The totality derives its psychological character from its earlier segments, no matter how early they be. Therefore the brain, the seat of the mind, must be the necessary determinant of the psychological ontological status of the bodily act.

(d) The ontologically asymmetrical line of development of the bodily act

In sum: the psychological event of limb-moving (i) encompasses an *a priori*-given non-psychological whole event ϕ, (ii) is divisible into the latter event together with a psychological non-autonomous part-event, striving, (iii) a process which keeps repeating itself, (iv) the event of limb-moving extending from the brain as far as the limb extremity, (v) being an occupant of an ontological domain whose instances range over a region of space that incorporates the space of the body surface. Then the sequence of those non-autonomous active psychological part-events – thought-slices out of a developmental process that is complete only by the final member – together constitute the process of directed striving: *the very surge of the will itself*!

We can see from this account how a striving can be identical with an arm moving and yet given epistemologically *both* in a psychologistic quasi-incorrigible manner as striving *and* neither psychologistically nor quasi-incorrigibly as arm-raising. For however far the trying process extends along the time-line running from its beginning to its termination, it will yet be a trying and of psychological status; while only if it extends the entire distance sufficient to encompass the event ϕ on the body surface will it be identical with arm-moving. That is, only then will it be *successful*. Thus, while bodily striving aims at something, it does not aim at an event lying at a causal remove from itself, but pursues instead a certain *character* for itself. It aims at development into a potential: it seeks *fruition* for itself. And this is achieved through the earlier sectors of the trying process causing the later sectors, a causation that occurs within the event, along the naturally appointed pathways of the body, terminating in a kind of *figure-head phenomenon*, viz. the goal event ϕ. Then because its goal is not located at a causal remove, the desire-originated hiatus in bodily willing must lie within the very willing itself, for what is in question in bodily willing is the degree of development of the willing event. In the light of this account it becomes clear how it can be that the physical extent of the striving or willing event is not psychologistically given. What is thus given is merely a willing directed *towards* a bodily extremity. It is not thus given *how far* it extends.

4. THE MIND'S BODY AND THE BODY'S MIND

(a) The $\psi \sim \Psi$ systematically causally relates to the non-ψ remainder of the world: for example, the sensory half of $\psi \sim \Psi$ relates thus

(1) Sensations must have non-psychological causes. One reason why we should endorse this claim is that we would never believe in the existence of a sub-class of pains immune *as such* to the action of analgesics. Then if sensations *a priori* necessitate non-psychological bodily causes, there must exist psycho-physical regularities and thus also a science governing their occurrence. And the same situation holds in the case of bodily actions. For there is a difference between a merely apparent and a genuinely successful attempt to move a limb which is moving, and the difference lies in the absence or presence of a regularly acting psycho-physical mechanism. In short, here too psycho-physical regularity is a necessity.

(2) Let us now examine the sensory part of the $\psi \sim \Psi$ domain. Sensations have bodily non-psychological causes, and systematically depend upon a sector of the brain that is open to causal influence by the rest of the body, and thus open to systematic influence by the environment. For sensations are systematically causally sensitive to those environmental phenomena that suitably and regularly perturb the neural pathways for the sensation. For example: within the body to limb damage, which leads to pain; or to movement of nearby objects directly in front of one, which generally leads to the movement of visual sensations within the visual field. In short, the sensory part of the $\psi \sim \Psi$ realm is a sort of 'frontier post' of the mind where, through relating regularly to phenomena in the non-psychological part of the world, and therefore through the mind's use of a kind of sense-instrument, $\psi \sim \Psi$ phenomena appear in immediate consciousness which can be automatically interpreted by the mental apparatus in the light of one's prevailing beliefs.

These sensory phenomena occur in that $\psi \sim \Psi$ marginal region of the mind in which it faces *immediately outwards* to the environment. Therefore both the sensations and their bodily causes must in general either structurally or qualitatively match certain simple structures or qualities of certain external phenomena, and doubtless in those which are of primitive importance to animals. For example: movement is the simplest manifestation of animate life, and the visual field and retina are such that certain ψ phenomena, say the movement of a sensation on a sensory ground, are regularly caused by just this important phenomenon. Therefore the fact that psycho-physical law governs visual sensations is entirely consistent with their functional explanation, viz. as instant source of spatio-temporal and qualitatively differential information concerning the environment. If the mind is to know of its environment, there has to be that in immediate consciousness which is capable of such regular determination.

This is why causal independence of the Ψ system, and law-governed causal dependence upon the physical setting, are necessary features of the sensory sector of the $\psi \sim \Psi$ realm. This 'frontier post', if it is to be systematically responsive to the extra-ψ environment and feed sensory data to the central information-legislative Ψ centres, must be causally determined by bodily regularities *and* free of influence from the properly Ψ mental centre. And we have seen that it is.

Indeed, it is one of the marks of a *sick* system, not that the inner (Ψ) realm should act as immediate cause of sensation (for that *a priori* is impossible), but that some Ψ condition should in the receptor centres in the Ψ domain determine what is seemingly the type of event that is in normality generated by the 'frontier posts'. For example: a *mentally originated* seeming-to-oneself-to-see-blue (say) when blue is not in the visual field. That is, not an hallucinatory sensation, for there is no such sub-class of sensations, but an hallucination *as of* having some sensation. Alternatively, the hysterical case of seeming to oneself to have a pain when there is none. Here the Ψ centre which receives messages from the 'frontier post' must be all of a dither – red lights flashing as it were – even though 'all is quiet on the western front'. The trouble (which is 'back home') resides in the responsiveness of the Ψ receptor centres to certain Ψ-hysteric strident influences. In short, the subject is mentally ill and physiologically normal.

(b) Hysteria and disturbance in the $\Psi / \psi \sim \Psi$ relation

The hysterical symptom is a disturbance of that part of mental function that relates to the sub-mental $\psi \sim \Psi$ part of the mind. This is so even though the trouble lies, not in the 'frontier post' itself, but in that sector of Ψ that links that 'frontier post' with the Ψ receptor centre that is geared specifically to the 'frontier'. For hysterical symptoms are not, unlike obsessional and paranoid phenomena, the fruits of damage to *thinking* mental function. Rather, in hysteria the damage occurs to such elemental and so to say animal mental functions as those of *perception* and *bodily action*. Thus, the typical hysterical phenomena studied by Freud were hysterical blindness, hysterical paralysis, etc. And it is important to note that an hysterical blindness is neither a true blindness nor a negative hallucination. It is not a blindness because the visual apparatus may be completely intact. And it is not an hallucination for the reason that hallucinations are illusory seemings that are caused, not through pathological impairment in the relation between the ψ 'frontier outpost' and the Ψ receptor centres that are specifically geared to the latter, but through the latter receptor centre's being open to causal influence at the hands of certain other parts of the Ψ domain – an influence which is manifestative of a general impairment in the sense of reality.

Then my claim is that hysteria is a purely mental non-neurological illness that is characterised by a disorder in the relation of Ψ and $\psi \sim \Psi$, which is such as to generate phenomena in those two centres, the Ψ centre and the $\psi \sim \Psi$ centre, that are marked by the fact that the normal two-way causal processes between Ψ and $\psi \sim \Psi$ are disturbed. Thus, if a certain Ψ phenomenon, call it Ψx, is normally the cause of a certain $\psi \sim \Psi$ phenomenon, call it $\psi \sim \Psi$x, i.e. Ψx $\rightarrow$ $\psi \sim \Psi$x, then here cases of $\sim\Psi$x & $\psi \sim \Psi$ occur, e.g. hysterical vomiting. If Ψx $\rightarrow$ $\psi \sim \Psi$x normally, then cases of Ψx & $\sim \psi \sim \Psi$x occur, e.g. hysterical paralysis. If $\psi \sim \Psi$x $\rightarrow$ Ψx normally, then cases of $\psi \sim \Psi$x & $\sim\Psi$x occur, e.g. hysterical blindness. If $\psi \sim \Psi$x $\rightarrow$ Ψx normally, then cases of $\sim\psi \sim \Psi$x & Ψx occur, e.g. hysterical pain. That is, there are four distinctive types of hysterical phenomena: hysterical vomiting, paralysis, blindness, pain; and whereas hysterical vomiting is a true vomiting, the paralysis and blindness and pain are unreal. Thus, in hysteria the two-way causal relations between the Ψ mental centres and the merely $\psi \sim \Psi$ are disturbed, and since the latter $\psi \sim \Psi$ phenomena relate regularly to the body and environment, the relation of mind to body and physical environment is likewise disturbed. In short, hysteria is an illness that is symptomatically characterised by disturbances in the relation of mind and body, and generally also thereby disturbances in the relation to the environment. Yet it is a true mental illness: a disorder that is entirely confined within the mind proper. That is, within Ψ. (See Figs. 11 and 12.)

(c) The mind's body and the body's mind

(1) The primordial division within the animal of mind and body is internally reflected in the Domain of the Psychological (ψ) at least twice over.

First, it is reflected in the major divide in ψ that has so interested me, i.e. between the $\psi\Psi$ and $\psi \sim \Psi$ realms, say between thoughts (etc.) and sensations (etc.); for it has emerged that the latter but not the former strictly necessitate bodily non-psychological ties of several kinds, including being individuated in body-relative physical space. Second, it is reflected in a division, now in Ψ alone, between those Ψ functions which are to a degree detached from the immediate concretely given here and now,

Normality

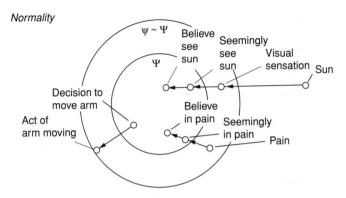

Hysteria (1)
(Blindness)

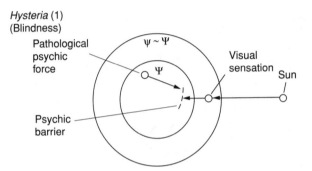

Hysteria (2)
(Paralysis)

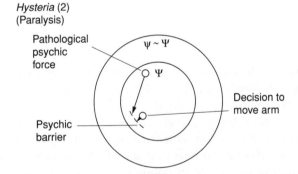

Fig. 11

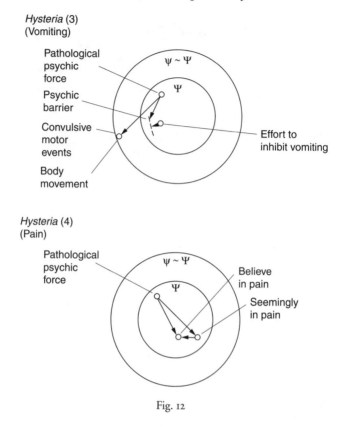

Fig. 12

such as thoughts and beliefs and images, and those Ψ functions expressly concerned with individual concrete causal interactions between the Ψ and the merely bodily realm, such as decidings-to-bodily-act and seemings-to-see and intentions-of-bodily-acting. Then the location of obsessional symptoms is, not the first of these latter two properly Ψ regions, but both regions of Ψ and exclusively so: that is, it is in the Ψ domain *simpliciter*; while the location of the hysterical symptom is in both Ψ and $\psi \sim \Psi$ regions: that is, it is in the ψ domain *simpliciter*. In sum, the location of the real trouble in each of these two mental disturbances is to be found in the Ψ domain of the mind (though no doubt in different sectors). Cause and cure lie there. For both obsessionality and hysteria are true mental illnesses. And one can see how these two neurotic conditions, which so engaged Freud's attention between 1894 and 1914, constitute in a sense a symptomatic reflection of the ontological diversity in the mind that has emerged in the course of this discussion.

Then in the light of the above considerations we might coin several slogans. We might first of all say: 'The mind has a body.' And we would mean that the Psychological (ψ)/Merely bodily ($\phi \sim \psi$) division within the animal repeats itself within the Domain of the Psychological as $\psi\Psi/\psi \sim \Psi$. Then we have just seen that this elemental cleavage of spirit and flesh repeats itself twice over in the ψ realm: first in the $\psi\Psi/\psi \sim \Psi$ divide within the realm ψ; but second again in the higher properly mental realm Ψ. (And threatens to continue doing so in increasingly 'higher' realms, though it is extremely unlikely that these 'realms' are the scene of ontological novelties.) We may therefore secondly say – if we may call the 'higher part' of the mind 'the mind's mind' – that correlatively 'the mind's mind has a body'. And what we mean here is: that there exists a region containing properly mental events that are concretely and causally directed towards the bodily extra-psychological sector of the world, e.g. a seeming-to-see-a-balloon or an intention-of-grasping-a-balloon. Indeed, it necessarily follows that by contrast 'the mind's mind has a mind'; which is to say that there exists a region of the properly mental region of the mind that is *not* so devoted to concrete extra-psychological phenomena: namely, the region that contains such items as mental images and general beliefs. In this way it becomes clear that any attempt, along somewhat Cartesian lines, sharply to mark off the Ψ from the $\psi \sim \Psi$, as if an angelic-type consciousness were lodged in a psychic totality whose outer regions alone bore witness to the embodiment of their owner, must be doomed to failure. Such a divide cannot but be mythical. For the reality of the body makes its presence felt, perhaps throughout the entire mind, certainly in a great deal more than that sector, the $\psi \sim \Psi$, that is specifically related in nomic and spatial manner to the flesh.

(2) A companion slogan for the body can at least match the first of the above slogans for the mind. Thus, it seems that the mind/body division repeats itself, only once so far as I can tell, within the body, so that we may with some justification – but without ontological illusions – speak of 'the body's mind'. For the special attunement of certain ψ events to extra-psychological bodily events, necessitates that there exist within the body certain extra-psychological events that are especially attuned to the psychological. For example: retinal phenomena, hormonal phenomena, happenings in the motor apparatus. In Albert Camus's beautiful novel *The Fall*, the melancholic hero, prone as he seems to tubercular flare-ups and mood swings, observes at one point that 'when the body is sad the

heart languishes'.[1] And I take him to be speaking of the close communion between 'the body's mind' ('the sadness of the body') and 'the mind's body' ('languishing or prostration of the spirit').

5. ANIMAL AND SPIRITUAL MIND

(a) The internal influence of the body on the mind

We have seen in the course of this discussion that the mind divides into two distinct but closely tied domains: $\psi \sim \Psi$ and $\psi\Psi$. Now it may be that there is a sense in which the former physically tied $\psi \sim \Psi$ domain stands ultimately in a relationship of *dependence* to the latter more mental $\psi\Psi$. For a bodiless entity endowed with a purely spiritual consciousness, and so without $\psi \sim \Psi$ items like bodily sensations and strivings, say an angelic or demonic consciousness, is not *obviously a priori* impossible. But the reverse, I think, clearly is. Namely, an entity lacking the somewhere (even lost!) potential for supporting anything more than $\psi \sim \Psi$ items. The world could not be such that these were the only ψ phenomena that any entities in their essential depths could support. That is, all possible worlds in which the only ψ items are $\psi \sim \Psi$ items are members of the class of possible worlds in which minds exist and fail to realise their generic potential. Thus, possibly the Ψ realm has an autonomy not possessed by the $\psi \sim \Psi$, possibly the $\psi \sim \Psi$ owes its existence non-causally to the Ψ. It depends whether the concept of the purely spiritual consciousness – which is incidentally not that of the *dis*embodied consciousness – is coherent. If it is not, the dependence of $\psi\Psi$ and $\psi \sim \Psi$ must be mutual. The answer to this problem is not immediately obvious one way or the other.

From what has emerged in the previous section 4 we can I believe know that there *has to exist* in us something that is akin to $\psi \sim \Psi$. If we are both *actively to alter* and *concretely to be aware of* the physical environment, it must be so. For the only method of *legitimising* both our motor and perceptual experience, and thus ensuring that willing or perceptual contact is actualised between a subject and the extra-ψ environment, is through the use of physical mechanisms linking the body with his experience. That is, via psycho-physical law. For if a man's sensations were haphazardly determined by his body, and hence also haphazardly by his environment, how could he learn of and therefore how be aware of his environment through sensation? After all, a healthily functioning sense organ is necessarily that

---

[1] Translated by Justin O'Brien. London: Hamish Hamilton, 1957, 33.

through which physical information can be acquired. Thus the obtaining of type-type psycho-physical law, which along with space is the primary encroachment of the body into the mind, is *guaranteed* by the fact that the mind concretely transacts with the extra-mental sector of the world. In sum: Grice's version of the causal theory of perception,[2] and my own version of the causal theory of action,[3] ensure the existence of psycho-physical law at these two select places in the animal mind. Meanwhile Donald Davidson has, I believe, demonstrated the impossibility of tight psycho-physical law relating properly mental (Ψ) items and the body.[4] We are led inevitably to the postulation of a psychological sub-domain that is such that all of its contents stand in nomic relation to the body. That is, to the $\psi \sim \Psi$.

In short, the inner–outer transaction between Ψ and the physical realm necessitates the existence of a kind of $\psi \sim \Psi$ armour surrounding the central holistically knit Ψ core: agency and perception require such a mediator element. For the anomalousness of the mental ensures that Ψ can be concretely directed onto the environment only through being directed *immediately* onto such a strange hybrid go-between as $\psi \sim \Psi$: that is, immediately onto bodily strivings and sensations. These two primordial psychological phenomena prove to be Jacob's ladders in reverse: devices whereby the 'higher' spiritual (Ψ) may distinctly and reliably commune with the 'lowly' merely physical ($\phi \sim \psi$).

This immediate linkage between Ψ and $\psi \sim \Psi$ looks to have significant repercussions throughout the entire extent of Ψ itself. For it seems that the mind must everywhere bear the mark of its own evolutionary history; and since the developed body must have preceded the fully developed mind, it follows that the 'mind's body' must be the direct representative of the past within the mind. That is, the past of the species must make its presence felt throughout the mind precisely through $\psi \sim \Psi$ making its presence felt in the mind. Thus, the intrinsic presence of the past in the mind *is* the intrinsic presence of the body in the mind. In short, I believe on developmental grounds that the presence of the body must be intrinsically evident throughout the mind. And in a sense not claimed by Mind-Brain Identity theorists. In any case, we shall see that it is so. Now I shall pursue this theme in sections (c) and (d) below, but to do so it is necessary that

---

[2] 'The Causal Theory of Perception', *Proceedings of the Aristotelian Society*, supplementary vol. xxxv, 1961, 121–52, London: Harrison.

[3] See chapter 4, sections 1–3 (in vol. 1 of the present work). Also 'The Limits of the Will', *The Philosophical Review*, LXV, 1956, 443–90, New York: Ithaca.

[4] 'Mental Events', in L. Swanson and J. W. Foster (eds.), *Experience and Theory*, London: Duckworth, 1970, 79–101.

I first briefly review the progress of the ontological inquiry that I have almost concluded.

(b) *Recapitulating the dialectical progression*

In this and the previous chapter I have traced the development of something like a dialectical progression on the topic 'the Ontological Status of Physical Action'. It moved thus. From initially supposing the physical act psychological; to supposing it non-mental; to supposing it psychological non-mental. Each thesis depending on the fashioning and use of a more differential concept than was available to its predecessor thesis. Thus, the original opposition of bodily and psychological proved to be misconceived. Comprehension of this fact liberated a new concept of the psychological: one that permitted psychological phenomena to range over the entire body. And it was precisely this enrichment of the concept of the psychological that enabled me to differentiate out from within itself the realm of the properly mental psychological, viz. Ψ.

That dialectical movement has occurred in the above progression is revealed, first in the differentiation of new concepts out of old, second in the fact that this makes possible the representation within each novel thesis of all that the earlier rejected thesis had discerned. Thus, the original thesis that the act is psychological-i.e.-mental is accepted, in that we judge it psychological in type, and rejected in that we judge it to be non-mental. Therefore the new thesis cannot be identified with the old. Yet thanks to the development of the twin concepts, of the psychological that can encompass the extra-cerebral, and the mental that is spacelessly intentionalist, the dialectical progression is a development of what lay slumbering in incipient form in the original thesis and antithesis, viz. that the act is psychological-i.e.-mental/that the act is bodily. And so the progression is at once a process of differentiation, and of vindication and recovery of the *past*. For in this negating procedure nothing is ever lost, and duly finds itself represented in the more developed moment that succeeds it. The final synthetic thesis employing differential concepts that enable it both to state and to subordinate the hitherto undifferentiated insights embedded within the preceding theses and antitheses.

This dialectic feeds upon distinctions. For at each stage one attempts to do justice to a particular contrast, even as each contrast inevitably cries out for a successor contrast that will display a hitherto neglected order of being: an order of being that can only now be differentially discerned. These successive contrasts, in *the dialectic of physical action* recently

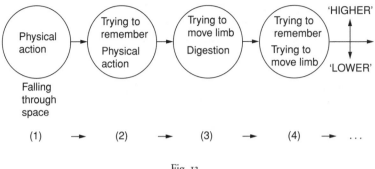

Fig. 13

elaborated, were as follows. First, between physical actions and merely physical events such as falling through space; second, between physical actions and events like trying to remember; third, between events like trying to raise an arm and mere somatic extra-cerebral phenomena like digestion; fourth, between events like trying to raise an arm and trying to remember; fifth, between specifically physically potent events like deciding-to-move-a-limb and imagings; sixth, between systematically physically potent events like deciding-to-move-a-limb-this-instant and merely specifically physically potent events like deciding-to-move-a-limb; and so on. In short, the dialectic moves on, and displays the full richness of psychic being as it does. And these oppositions lead naturally to the formation of a theory of *grades of psychic and physical being.* Some of genuine ontological order, others not. But all assisting in the full revelation both of the nature of physical action and of the mind to which it owes its existence. The development of these successive contrasts, the circles representing the phenomenal boundaries of the animal agent, is represented diagramatically in Fig. 13; while Fig. 14 is a quasi-ontological map of these various orders of being.

(c) Continuing the dialectic into the (Ψ) mind itself

(1) Let me express the advance of the dialectic thus. We begin with the elemental notions of mind and body. At that early stage certain Cartesian surrogates are not inconceivable. But it then emerges that the *mere presence* of the animal body necessitates a body-oriented sector of the mind: 'the mind's body' ($\psi \sim \Psi$); to which we oppose 'the mind's mind' ($\psi \Psi$): an ontological distinction. And it seems that we can continue drawing analogous distinctions, now based on causal properties that might appear to

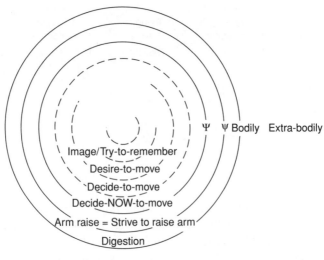

Ψ   Ψ Bodily   Extra-bodily

Image/Try-to-remember
Desire-to-move
Decide-to-move
Decide-NOW-to-move
Arm raise = Strive to raise arm
Digestion

Falling through space

Fig. 14

indicate ontological diversity but which almost certainly do not, within the mind's mind ($\psi\Psi$).

In particular: we might stipulatively take 'the mind's mind's body' (ψ $\Psi \sim \Psi'$) to encompass those Ψ items that are specifically and causally and nomically linked to the mind's body. For example: the decision to this instant move a limb – which necessarily causes a striving to move a limb. Now such psycho-psycho laws, (say) (decision-this-instant (etc.) $\rightarrow$ (striving-this-instant (etc.)), entail the existence of psycho-physical laws governing the highly specific Ψ item in question, viz. (decision-this-instant (etc.)). And yet such a highly specific psycho-physical law is not a properly general type-type psycho-physical law, for it fails to imply that any psycho-physical laws hold generally for act-decisions as such. In sum: constituents of the 'mind's mind's body' ($\Psi \sim \Psi'$) exemplify a merely specific psycho-physical law that cannot be generalised to the generic types involved. Nonetheless, the items in the 'mind's mind's mind' ($\Psi\Psi'$) do not obey psycho-physical law under restrictions of any kind. However, distinctions of the same general type can still be drawn within the latter domain ($\Psi\Psi'$). For even within $\Psi\Psi'$ we may continue the dialectic by differentiating out what we stipulatively designate as 'the mind's mind's mind's body' ($\Psi\Psi' \sim \Psi''$), which we take to encompass those Ψ items that specifically and causally but non-nomically are geared to 'the mind's mind's body', e.g. the intention of moving an arm, and oppose to them items like mental images which are not so causally geared. And so on.

These conclusions have significant implications for the mind-brain relation. Thus, it follows from the existence of the law linking intending-*now* with striving-*now* that we must be able to say of that ($\psi \Psi' \sim \Psi''$) item, bodily intention, that it is a something such that if its owner knows that the putative instant of its object has arrived, then necessarily a phenomenon occurs which nomically relates to a brain event. That fact automatically causally binds the bodily intention generally to brain phenomena. And this bond is perpetuated as the dialectic advances. For as we peel off layer after layer, travelling away from the mind's body inwards towards the mind's core, $\Psi \Psi' \Psi'' \ldots$, we continue to discover diminishing yet undeniable traces of that original tight nomic relation between mind and body even as the overall holism of the mind increasingly makes its presence felt. And the evolutionary history of the animal mind almost certainly ensures that no mental item will detach itself from this development. In short, a kind of Theseus' thread continues to link the more quintessentially mental regions of Ψ with the merely biological parts of the body. Therefore the dream of splitting off a *pure kernel core* of Ψ that is absolutely unrelated causally to the body looks impossible of fulfilment. *A priori*, the very heart of the animal mind, whether or not a rational self-consciousness, seems not to be that of the putative bodiless angelic or demonic consciousness.

(2) We continue drawing distinctions within the mind which reflect the original primordial distinction between mind and body. This might seem to be reason for scepticism over the possibility of a purely spiritual consciousness (and hence for the supposition that $\psi \sim \Psi$ depends upon Ψ). For that original elemental distinction apparently leaves its mark even in the higher reaches of the higher half of that primordial divide. Thus, the mind looks to be irremediably 'infected' with the body. It follows that, if we are to postulate the possible existence of a spiritual consciousness, we would do well to look elsewhere than to the human mind as indexical paradigm (*à la* Putnam). That is, we should not unreflectively say: 'I mean *this* sort of thing' (demonstratively defining human mind) 'in spiritual form.' And neither should we attempt indexically to explain what it is that we mean in speaking of 'angelic thinking', i.e. by characterising it as '*this* process in purely spiritual form'.

Then can an entity of the richness of the mind be other than indexically specifed? I think it can. I suggest that something has a mind iff it has the somewhere potential for supporting intentionalist phenomenal items which are temporally yet spacelessly individuated. Alternatively, merely for supporting any kind of psychological item. Therefore the angelic mind may well survive the difficulties posed by the 'body-infectedness' of existing Ψ systems. But precisely for that reason angelic minds would need to be immeasurably unlike human minds. And not merely in the sense in which the minds of animals in other evolutionary systems may be unlike those of earthly creatures. We postulate in angelic consciousness the absence of a vastly general feature that transcends evolutionary differences, viz. 'body infectedness'. Thus, their consciousness would need to be incapable as such of opening out onto the physical *qua* physical. At best it would be self-consciously aware of itself and its mind's contents: spacelessly but temporally concerned with – who knows what? Extreme, yet possibly not impossible, requirements.

(d) The evolutionary history of self-conscious mind

Somewhere in the remote past a momentous differentiation occurred between the *living* and the *inanimate*. Later, an equally momentous differentiation appeared within the living object between *the brain* and *the rest of the living object* (which *was* the development of the potential for consciousness, i.e. for ψ). Yet this latter differentiation could not have happened without simultaneously multiplying itself within the 'higher' (ψ or cerebral) half of this distinction; which, in this sense, bears traces of its historical ancestry. For the animal mind is of necessity attuned to the body, both as passive receptor of messages-from *and* active influencer of phenomena-in; and since sense-impression and bodily act-desire, which are Ψ, in general causally link with sensation and the bodily will, which are $\psi \sim \Psi$, this attunement cannot but breed the $\psi\Psi/\psi \sim \Psi$ divide within Ψ. Then this latter new divide, reflecting the original division of mind and body, finds itself reflected again and again within the very depths of the mind. For as we have already observed at several points in the discussion, the mind is 'infected' with the body, and in all probability the 'infection' spreads to its very core, $\Psi\Psi'\Psi''$ . . ., which is probably therefore *at no point* of the type of angelic or demonic. That is, we can set up a linked hierarchy of Ψ functions within the mind according as they relate to $\psi \sim \Psi$ and so also to the body – as when we deem the decision-to-move-a-limb *now* as causally at less of a remove from merely biological events than the mere decision to move-a-limb sometime, and the latter as at less of a remove than the mental image of moving-a-limb – and this causal connective tissue, albeit in increasingly anomalous form, seems to spread up from the body throughout the entire mind. Now since we have so far been assuming that we are as yet concerned merely with non-rational animals, there seems little doubt that we can link absolutely *all* of the mind's mind's mind's . . . phenomena readily with the body at this stage in evolutionary development.

Then at some later point in evolutionary development there took place upon such a corpus of essentially bodily oriented animal-type properly mental (Ψ) phenomena, the third and equally momentous development in the world's history. I mean the advent of *self-consciousness*; and with it the coming into being of rational, general, modal, concept-dependent, truth-sensitive thought, i.e. of anything that is truly worthy of the title 'thought'. A turning point, to be sure, but one that, in being integrally founded upon such a psychic corpus, almost certainly bears intrinsic witness both to its *history* and its relation to the *body*. As 'the degree and type of a man's sexuality reaches to the highest peaks of his spirit',[5] so too in all probability does the body make its presence felt in these causal terms in the most abstract thinking of a man. Yet whether this is so of absolutely any conceivable mind is, as was earlier observed, not immediately obvious. But one supposes so. Thus, desire and memory, which are essential attributes of any self-conscious consciousness, necessitate a causal foundation, and it is hard to see how this could avoid being in at least an analogue of body. And while this is merely a reason for supposing them embodied, that body must, one assumes, make its presence felt within the mind. For otherwise the body would be a sort of millstone around the mental neck of its owner! Then that would imply that the mental structure we have traced in this discussion, viz. ψ, $\psi\Psi$, $\psi\Psi\Psi'$, $\psi\Psi\Psi'\Psi''$ . . . , must be the *a priori*-given structure of any mind anwhere anytime anyhow. And that would in turn imply that Ψ would have no ontological priority over $\psi \sim \Psi$: their interdependence would be total. This, as it seems to me, is in all probability the lie of the land. But I cannot pretend to have actually demonstrated it.

In any case, I believe that the proper differentiation within the human being of these dialectically revealed realities, viz. body/mind/mind's body/mind's mind's body/ . . . , is the only true path to the resolution of the *false opposition* that is erroneously based upon the *real distinction* between mind and body. For until we undertake that task, there is nothing in our conception of the mind that indicates that it can be the mind of what is endowed with a body. Until we draw these distinctions, our conception of the mind is of a something that may *for all we know* have angelic modes.

---

[5] Friedrich Nietzsche, *Beyond Good and Evil*, fourth article *75, translated by Marianne Cowan. Chicago: Gateway Edition, 1965.

But such a putative instance of mind is of necessity *not* the mind of what can be endowed with a body. It follows that the drawing of these dialectical distinctions is a prerequisite of our being in a position to understand how the mind can be of what is endowed with a body. That is, of understanding how mind can integrate with body. In this sense the mind–body problem has a dialectical resolution. The present and the previous chapter constitute an attempt at such a resolution. Mind-brain identity theorists seem to be unaware of this problem.

CHAPTER 16

Dual aspect theory and the epistemology
of physical action

I. THE THIRD-PERSON EPISTEMOLOGICAL IMPLICATIONS
OF DUAL ASPECTISM

(a) Dual aspect action theory

In chapter 12 I put forward a dual aspect theory of physical action. The theory began with the claim that whenever we perform a physical action an event of the type 'act of the will' occurs, an event which we might designate by the use of such words as 'strive', 'attempt', 'try', 'have a shot at' – even merely the term 'do' (understood in a special active but highly familiar sense). An important second element is then added: namely, that the act of the will is a psychological event. And a third additional and highly contentious claim is that the above 'strive', 'attempt', 'try', 'have a shot at' doing some action is on occasions of success the same event as the act itself.

The next fourth ('outer') element in the dual aspect theory, more exactly the variety of dual aspect theory advanced by me, is concerned with the act considered from a physical standpoint. Now we know that a necessary condition of an act falling in 'basic act' mode under a description like 'arm-raising' is that the event of arm rise be linked via act-mechanistic neuro-muscular regular links with earlier stages of a single motor-process, a process leading back to the mental antecedents of action that triggered it into being with absolute immediacy. This fact led me to the following claim, which I advanced at several places in chapter 12. Namely, that the event of acting and/or willing is one and the same as the full activation of the motor-system. It should be noted that the claim is not that the event of *willing* activates the motor-system. Rather, it is that the immediate *act-progenitors*, act-desire and act-intention, activate that system, and that this activation-syndrome falls simultaneously under 'try', 'strive', 'do', 'will', and finally by the end of the motor-process also under 'arm-raising' or 'walking' or 'talking' (as the case may be). The claim I made was therefore that no matter *how far* activation of the motor-mechanism has progressed, it will fall *already* under the psychological concepts of 'willing' or 'striving' or 'doing' – provided it was immediately caused by act-desire and intention. And that by implication is to say that *something has already been done* by whatever moment in the developing process one happens to select, even if the process were to grind to a halt in its very first stages.

One fills in the final part of the theory as follows. Each enlarging sector of the motor-process, which falls already under 'try', 'strive', 'do', and 'will', proceeds to cause the next stage of the process, and finally to cause the (so to say) crowning event of (say) arm movement. Then although whatever slice of the activation-process one selects must fall already under the concept of 'willing'; and although that process-slice proceeds to cause the next stage of the motor-process and ultimately arm movement; this is not to say that the event of willing causes arm movement. Rather, the theory claims that the event of willing physically develops, in naturally appointed causal manner, to the point at which it incorporates the event of limb movement, and completes itself in so doing. A natural, vastly common, and perfectly normal complex physical phenomenon is at that moment realised, which falls at the same time under a set of active concepts like 'try', 'move arm', 'ring bell', and so on. Then to repeat: since willing is identical with arm-moving, and arm-moving incorporates arm movement, it is not that willing causes arm movement. It does not cause this event, even though arm movement owes its existence through a sequence of causal relations to the phenomenon of willing. The developmentalist character of the theory, together with the criteria for event-identity, disallow such an interpretation.

(b) Dual aspect action theory and Physicalism

(1) My concern in the present chapter is with the epistemological implications of this theory. I have described the theory as 'dual aspect' in type, but it is important that we understand the sense in which the expression is applied in this context. It is an ontological theory, but it is essential that we distinguish it from other ontological 'dual aspect' theories. For example, certain non-reductionist versions of Physicalism could perfectly well be described as 'dual aspect' theories in one sense of that expression. Thus, some philosophers might say of a given cerebral phenomenon that it falls at one and the same time under a psychological concept like (say) 'seeing' and under a physical cerebral concept. This theory is dual aspect in an ontological sense of the expression. And it has epistemological implications that would further incline one to describe it as 'dual aspect'. If one could

manage to identify particular psychological phenomena in cerebral terms, the subject of (say) a visual experience would in principle be able to see through mirrors an event which he immediately experienced as a visual experience with a cerebral object. He would be able to see an event that was the seeing of itself. Physicalism in one of its forms is therefore ontologically and by implication also epistemologically dual aspect in one sense of that expression.

(2) The theory of bodily action which I set out earlier is dual aspect in both of these senses. However, the theory differs in two important respects from a merely Physicalist dual-aspectism. For one thing, it arrives at a physical analysis of the psychological event of trying without depending on Physicalist Theory. It so to say constructs its own local Physicalism for bodily actions, and does so on the basis of philosophical arguments which have no application elsewhere in the mind. Thus, it involves in the particular all that the Physicalist position claims in general terms. After all, the dual aspect theory which I endorse asserts, amongst other things, that bodily actions are psychological events and also physical events. And if this is true, it must in principle be possible for an active subject to see or feel an event which he immediately experiences as action, just as it would be on the Physicalist account. In each case an epistemologically dual aspect thesis follows on the heels of an ontological thesis.

But it is not merely on the count of justification that the dual aspect theory of physical action which I endorse parts company with Physicalist dual-aspectism. It differs in its actual sense, for it differs in its analytical or constitutive content. And it is this content which justifies the application of the epithet 'dual aspect' in the sense reserved uniquely for physical actions. What I have in mind is the fact that according to this theory the physical constitution of a particular psychological event – uniquely the event of physical action – is given *a priori* in physical terms. The dual aspect theory of physical action is constitutively specific in physical terms as Physicalist doctrines are not. And this inevitably has epistemological implications which go well beyond those implicit in Physicalism. They are to the effect that there exist specific *a priori*-given physical directives for identifying a psychological event in physical terms. We have merely to single out the entire process of mechanism-activation that culminates in the event of limb movement, the theory being that in so doing we will be picking out a psychological event of type willing. Such a dual aspect action theory is the only doctrine I know of which on purely philosophical grounds offers a specific recipe for identifying a psychological event in physical terms. Not only does Physicalism not do so, it is a theory which is perfectly consistent with all sorts of quasi-Cartesian interiorist analyses of physical action in which the act is identified at one and the same time with an interior event and with unspecified purely cerebral phenomena. Physicalism is consistent both with interiorist theories of the will *and* with the dual aspect theory that I have sketched.

(c) *The perceptual and proprioceptual relation between agent and act*

(1) In this first Section I have been concerned with the physical content of bodily actions according to dual aspect theory, and by implication with the third-person epistemology in their case. Now such forms of epistemological access must be available also to the agent, relating to himself so to say in the third-person mode. In whatever way others can see and hear and even tactilely feel the movements of his limbs, so too can the agent himself. However, one mode of perceptual access is reserved for the agent alone, namely the proprioceptive mode. And it is clear that this mode of awareness is of central importance so far as physical action is concerned, indeed in a general sense must be essential to the very phenomenon of physical action as the others are not. True, the use of a mirror in shaving demonstrates that the epistemological feed back in physical action can be distributed amongst the senses, and it may even be that a bodily act might occur in the absence of proprioceptive awareness of the body. However, it seems certain that it could not in general do so. Proprioception is in general essential to physical actions, and occupies a unique position in physical act situations. If the mind is to be able to act physically, it needs *nothing more* than proprioceptive awareness of the presence and position of a limb over which the bodily will has sway. We cannot say the same of sight or of any other sense: it is simply not true that the will needs nothing more than (say) visual awareness of the presence and position of a limb over which we have control. This asymmetry between proprioception and the other senses is irreducible.

Thus, a mode of perceptual access to the active limb exists which is unique to the subject, and which cannot therefore be characterised as a 'third-person' epistemological relation, despite being perceptual in character. And there can be no doubt that this phenomenon plays a quite special and indeed essential role in act situations. One has merely to consider what would be the effect upon one's physically active life of a complete proprioceptive blackout: for most creatures in most situations it would lead to a quasi-paralysis. While proprioceptive perception of one's actions does not inform one that one's will has been active, it nonetheless plays an essential role in enabling action. It gives to the bodily will its immediate target-object, functions generally as a corroborative causal condition of one's knowing that one's endeavours are so far successful, and informs one of what next to do to complete one's active project.

(2) But it is one thing for proprioception of the active limb to be a *necessary condition* of action, it is another for it to *be* perception of the act. And this dual aspect theory implies (as do certain other analyses of physical action). And yet despite the essential epistemological contribution on the part of proprioceptive perception of the act to the successful performance of intended action, such a mode of awareness fails to deliver the full measure of information concerning one's own present actions that normally exists in the course of successful intentional physical action. And this is true of perception generally.

For example, perceptual experience of all kinds, whether proprioceptive or otherwise, can do no more than perceive the *outer segment* of the act. It cannot perceive the full extent of the deed, in particular has no awareness of its inner physical boundaries, and for these reasons cannot be *perceptually individuative* of its perceptible event-object. But secondly sense-perceptual experience of physical action is unable to detect the sheer occurrence of *activeness*. What it does perceive, namely movement in part of the body where the will has sway, is evidence that action is going on. But no more than that. It is in the first place not proof, and secondly it is neither needed nor used by the agent in order to know that his will is active. While it is at all times for the agent an inference that bodily action is occurring, which is to say that successful action is here and now taking place, it is no inference that willing is occurring, that he is trying or attempting and so forth, which is of a wholly different order from the above and which is known immediately.

(3) This observation leads naturally to the third element of epistemological shortfall on the part of perceptual experience of one's own physical actions. Now according to dual aspect theory the physical act is almost invariably immediately proprioceptively perceived. Then while proprioceptive experience is attentively immediate, even though causally mediated by kinaesthetic sensations, the brand of immediacy realised in proprioception falls short of the strong immediacy that one meets with in the mind: that is, immediacy of the kind encountered with beliefs and sensations and experiences, and the fact that simple unproblematic proprioceptive illusions

are possible as with the other senses confirms the fact. Here we have an additional epistemological shortfall on the part of perceptual experience of physical action, to be added to the fact that it is neither individuative of its object, nor identificatory of its activeness of character.

I have described these epistemological shortcomings on the part of perception as 'shortfall'. Why so? Are the latter goals realised in physical act situations? Are they realised therefore non-sense-perceptually? And are they necessary for the occurrence of action? According to the dual aspect theory the answer to each of these questions is in the affirmative. The claim is that one is aware of the act *qua* single event, and aware of it *qua* active in type, and aware of it moreover in a mode of immediacy that enables the act to be immediately related to the rest of one's mental life. After all, a typical act-report might take the form, 'I was aware of raising my arm as a signal of assent.' And yet it must be acknowledged that these accomplishments cannot be effected under *physical-act headings*, for we do not have mentalistically-immediate awareness of physical acts in physical-act terms. (If we did, dual aspectism would be a mere datum of experience, rather than a philosophical theory.) Illusion is just as possible in the case of one's own physical actions as with sense perception: one can seem to oneself to be raising an arm, which is in fact rising and apparently as a result of a contemporaneous striving directed towards just such a phenomenon – and no act of arm-raising be taking place. Thus, the *immediate data of experience* are cast neither in *pro* or *contra* dual aspect terms. Indeed, it is because of the gap between the data of immediate experience and the physical act as given in physical-act terms that we must turn to philosophical argument – rather than introspective experience – to discover the truth of the matter.

2. THE FIRST-PERSON EPISTEMOLOGICAL IMPLICATIONS OF DUAL ASPECTISM

(a) First-person awareness and dual aspect action theory

The dual aspect theory supposes that whenever we act, an experiential identification of the act takes place which satisfies the aforementioned requirements. While it is not possible for this to be accomplished sense-perceptually, according to the theory at the time of action an identification of the act occurs in mental terms under the concept 'will' which at one stroke individuates its object as one event, types that event as active, and does so in a way that has a right to be described as mentally immediate.

Now in the normal course of events such an awareness of the act in mental terms is accompanied by proprioceptive awareness of the act, and this fact has I believe caused some philosophers to deny the very existence of the active mental event: the proprioceptive experience tends to mask the psychological character of the event, as well as one's mentalistically immediate awareness of it. And yet there can be little doubt that in an exceptional situation of total failure an active psychological event would be openly encountered, which must be present on occasions of success. For example, it would be disclosed if in some normal-seeming circumstances one tried to move a limb – which failed to budge an iota. Looking back, reporting that 'I tried to move the limb at that moment', one would be referring to an active event which here came to consciousness in the complete absence of the usual kinaesthetic sense-perceptual experiential accompaniments. This highly exceptional situation lays open to view a mental active event which must be present on normal occasions of success. And I say it must be present on those occasions because just such a psychological event would have come to awareness had the limb *not* moved, and the absence of limb movement cannot have *caused* that event, nor can the presence of limb movement have *altered* its psychological properties.

Then the content of the dual aspect theory of physical action can be expressed in terms of the aforementioned experiences. The claim by the theory is that the active psychological event of which one is immediately aware on occasions of total failure, is in normal situations of active success both *present* A N D *is one and the same event as* that given in non-individuative and non-identificatory form in proprioceptive experience which is attentively immediate in a mode of immediacy which falls significantly short of the immediacy encountered in the mind. It is not that there are two events, one psychological and epistemologically immediately given, the other non-psychological and bodily which is given sense-perceptually, and that the latter hides the other: it is rather that there occurs one event whose *mental character* and *mentally-immediate accessibility* tends to be obscured by one's normally present proprioceptive experience. So, at any rate, the dual aspectism which I endorse would have it.

(b) Experiencing the act

(1) I would like now to consider the nature of the phenomenon that was given to the active subject on the occasion of total failure. That is, I wish to ask several questions concerning the active psychological event of which retrospectively one would be aware as one looks back on such occasions.

The first question is, whether the event one refers to in saying 'At that moment I tried to move the limb' was *experienced*. Well, if the event actually occurred, one would surely know so. How would one know? Certainly not inferentially. In particular, not on the basis of an inference of the following kind: 'I know that I intended to act at that instant, nothing happened in the limb, therefore I must at that instant have tried to move it': that is, an inference based on the existence of a firm absolutely contemporaneous intention to act at the moment of failure. While the inference is valid enough, it is not used by the subject as his way of knowing of the event. The knowledge of which we speak is immediate in a sense inconsistent with the use of inference. Meanwhile it is not quite like the brand of immediate cognitive access that we have to many non-experiential mental phenomena: say, to one's intention of visiting Spain next month – the kind of immediacy relating us to the present existence of our beliefs and memories and long-term desires. Thus, while one has mentally-immediate access to beliefs, one can nonetheless readily enough imagine momentary inaccessibility of a belief in a way one cannot the sheer existence of present experience. True, one might self-deceive concerning the character of an experience, but it is difficult to imagine sheer ignorance of the existence of well-defined present experience. No phenomenon is epistemologically closer than present experience. Then my suggestion is that this is how we stand in relation to the above example of completely failed trying. And in fact it is surely truistic that the event in question was experienced. It is obvious that it would find a mention if one were cataloguing the contents of one's inner experiential life of the last few minutes. It would find a mention as the intention of visiting Spain would not.

(2) Thus, the completely failed event of trying to move the limb must have been *experienced* at the time it occurred. What I wish now to discover is *the character* of that experienced phenomenon. To begin it helps to consider the spatial properties of this failed trying event as given to the experiencing active subject, and to compare them in this regard with sensations. Now in general we may say of bodily sensations that they are experienced as in body-relative physical space, and as at particular body-sites. For example, we experience a twinge of pain as a toothache, a tickle as situated on one's ankle, an itch as on one's scalp, whatever their actual literal physical site. This property of sensations enables us to have two qualitatively indistinguishable sensations at the same point in time: say, a dull ache in one's left thumb and a dull ache in one's right thumb. While one cannot have two such sensations simultaneously in the same body-site, since body-sites individuate bodily

sensations, one can simultaneously have them in different sites. The spatial framework individuates them in the first place, and the temporal framework does so secondly.

Consider now the event of trying to move an arm whose psychologicality was revealed nakedly to view on an occasion of total failure because of the complete absence of kinaesthetic experience. We shall see that the situation here is significantly different in the above respects from that realised with sensations. Thus, where was that psychological event, of which one was immediately aware, experienced as taking place? One is perhaps inclined to say that one experienced it as being at the felt location of the arm. However, it seems to me that to do so would be to confuse the site of the *immediate target-object* of the will, with the *event of willing* that is directed at that place. This finds corroboration in the following. Whereas two qualitatively indistinguishable sensations can appear simultaneously in our consciousness, thanks to the fact that we individuate sensations spatially, there is no way failed attempts to move one and the same limb in the identical way could do the same. There is no way two such events with identical objects could be given simultaneously, or therefore given at different places in experienced body-space. This is not because events of this kind are given at the felt body-site of the target-limb and spatially individuated through that criterion (which is the situation in the case of bodily sensations). Rather, it is because there cannot be two such simultaneous events. I can simultaneously fail to move left and right arm, but I cannot simultaneously fail to raise one and the same arm in two different presentations. The event in question is exhaustively specified by time, type, and object-content. Space finds no place in that specification: the phenomenon is simply not experienced as in body-space. *A fortiori* such a phenomenon cannot be simultaneously experienced at two spatial sites. This property – along with several other properties which I will now spell out – is closely relevant to the experiential status of the event in question.

(c) The spaceless character of the purely mentally given active event

(1) How would one *describe* the active event? What *description* would one give of the phenomenon one recalls when one recollects the event of striving as nakedly revealed to view on an occasion of total failure? I ask because I think the answer brings to light a character which is inconsistent with spatial individuation, the reason being that the epistemological data seem wholly exhausted by content. It is a character which strongly suggests that the event in question is of the type experience.

Let us suppose the failure-event occurred completely unexpectedly. Of what would one be aware at the moment of failure? To be sure one would be aware of affective experiences of the type surprise, shock, alarm, and suchlike. However, these are merely consequences of the occurrence, products of one's awareness of the event. But what would one say as a description of the event itself? It is something very simple. Merely 'I tried to move my arm – in an upward direction – at normal enough speed' (with perhaps also a reference to intensity of striving). But what of *quale*? What of felt or experienced character? But what conceptual room is there for variation of this sort? What conceptual space for an array of diverse *quales*? In fact what room for *quales* of any kind? For all that we are speaking of is, an object-directed phenomenon of type 'try', a given object, say an arm movement with a limited few properties, and no more. This event seems wholly exhausted by its type, content, and perhaps also intensity. While it has the accidental attribute of happening when it does, everything else seems essential: take away the type, change the object in any respect, and it is simply a different animal. And in fact it may well be that the total absence of *quale* is the cause of the widespread 'blindspot' regarding the will. This strangely simple psychological phenomenon occurs whenever a successful example of limb-moving occurs. For psychologically speaking there can be no difference between the occasions of success and failure – apart from proprioceptive experience.

To recapitulate the properties of this phenomenon. The mentally immediate awareness of the event has as internal object something which is exhausted by type and content. For what that event *is* seems exhaustively given when we conjoin the type strive with the intended object, limb movement of some variety. Meanwhile the concept of *quale*, of phenomenological character or 'feel', lacks application. Most important for my present purposes, amongst the data there is no such thing as spatial *extent*, such as we encounter with bodily sensations; nor *directional* properties, of the kind we find with auditory or visual sensations; nor bodily *site*; and so on. Thus, there seems to be no way in which space could have an individuative role in the case of this phenomenon. It is given to its owner in terms which are completely exhausted by its content and position in time.

(2) One final observation before I draw a few deductions from the above. I have suggested that the event filtered out for view by complete failure, of type trying/striving/attempting and directed to limb movement, enters the catalogue of phenomena one would list when setting out the contents of experiential consciousness at the moment of complete failure. Then although if dual aspectism is true, that one and same event will on occasions

of success be proprioceptively experienced, in fact will be perceived and in that perceptual sense 'felt', it is not 'felt' in a psychologically-immediate mode. We feel our pains when we perceive them, which is to say when we are aware of them, but I do not think that in situations of total failure we *feel* the event of trying to move the limb in question. Thus, a psychological event occurs which is directed to a part of the body whose presence one proprioceptively feels, but the awareness of that psychological event is not a mentally-immediate experience of the type: *feeling* that phenomenon. It seems on the face of it to be no more than the *having* of it. This suggests that the awareness in question must be non-perceptual in type. And it lends weight to the supposition that the concept of *quale* lacks application to this phenomenon, since any distinctive *quale* of bodily striving ought, one assumes, to fall under the concept of 'feel'.

3. THE EXPERIENTIAL STATUS OF WILLING

(1) These observations suggest an answer to two closely related questions: What is the *general type* of the psychological event of trying to move a limb? What is the general type of the *awareness* of that phenomenon? The following considerations clarify the nature of the problems expressed in these two questions.

I claimed that the event of trying, filtered out for view in purely psychological form in a situation of total act-failure in the complete absence of kinaesthetic experience, is *experienced* by its agent. One knows of its occurrence, not through inference from the firmness of a contemporaneous intention which failed, and not just mentalistically-immediately (in the way one knows one's beliefs). One knows of that trying mentalistically-immediately, and in the strong mode one knows of present experience.

But there is more to be said on this matter. The observations immediately below will enable me to spell out with more precision just what it is that we mean when we say of that trying that it was experienced. And they shed light on the nature of the *awareness* of the event of trying. For it is not *prima facie* obvious whether these latter are the same thing. It could on the one hand be that an experience that was active in nature occurred and immediately caused knowledge of itself. Alternatively, it could be that an active psychological event occurred which immediately caused an experience of awareness of itself, and that the awareness experience caused knowledge of its active psychological object.

(2) The two possible model situations are as follows.

A. At a certain point in time a thought crosses one's mind, causing knowledge of itself.
B. At a certain point in time a sensation occurs, causing an event of noticing of itself, which in turn causes knowledge of the sensation object of noticing.

In either case knowledge occurs which is based on experience, but only in the latter case are there *two* phenomena which are experienced, viz. the sensation *and* awareness of the sensation. In one case an experience occurs which is of such a nature as to engender knowledge of itself; in the other case an experience takes another psychological item as its experienced object, and is such as to engender knowledge both of itself and of that psychological object. The question we must decide is: which of these two models fits the situation in which complete motor-failure filters out for view the active event of trying in purely psychological form? What the question boils down to is something simple. Namely, is the active psychological event that was laid open to view itself an experience? Or is it the immediate extensional object of an awareness experience? Was the experience that led to knowledge *active* in nature? Or was it instead of a *perceptual* character, viz. the awareness of one's own activeness?

(3) It seems to me that the data uncovered in section 2 point to the former answer. It suggests that the active psychological event revealed in the situation of complete failure is an experience. That is, when one casts one's mind back to that situation and says 'I tried', one is recalling one phenomenon and not two phenomena given immediately in experience. Thus, it suggests that there exists an experience which is one and the same thing as trying to move a limb. An obvious conclusion, one might think, but I disagree. What is obvious, once one has engaged in the requisite thought-experiments, is that on such occasions one is in the presence of an active psychological event that is in some familiar sense given immediately in experience. But it is not obvious in what way it is thus given. My suggestion is that the active event is given in experience merely in being an experience.

The aforementioned data which lend support to this reading of the situation consists in facts of the following kind. Namely, that the event laid open to view on the occasion of total failure was:
  i. active,
  ii. not given at a point in body space,
  iii. not given as of some spatial extent,
  iv. not given in a direction,

v. not capable of being simultaneously accompanied by a second psychological phenomenon of identical type and object,
vi. not endowed with a phenomenology, being
vii. entirely determined by type and object-content (and perhaps intensity).

   Properties (ii)–(v) characterise experiences generally, and much else that
is mental but not an experience. But they do not characterise the immediate
psychological objects of awareness experiences, viz. sensations. To return
for a moment to the example of sensations mentioned earlier: while the
two simultaneous qualitatively indistinguishable pains in one's two thumbs
were each experienced in spatial terms, the *experiences* of those pains were
not so experienced. This is in line with the supposition that the active
psychological phenomenon under discussion is of the type: experience.

   (4) The above arguments have taken the form of characterising the way
the event of striving is given experientially in situations of total failure.
I shall turn soon to explanatorial considerations which point to the same
conclusion as above. But before I do so there are a few relevant observations
to be made concerning *mental actions*. The first is, that none of the above
questions can be seriously raised in the case of mental actions. For one
thing theories of the will are rarely cast in terms of mental action: they
are encountered in the form of a theory concerning the origin of active
bodily movements. Moreover, there is no highly exceptional situation in
the mind that would count as an analogue of total active failure in the
case of bodily action, and even if there were it would not act as a filtration
agency laying open to view an active mental phenomenon whose existence
has been questioned by some. In any case such a device is simply not needed
as support for the doctrine of the reality of the mental will.

   This is because the reality of mental willing is beyond dispute. No one
can doubt that there exist mental occurrences which are active in nature,
nor can many people be disposed to offer analyses of these phenomena
in which that active character is reduced to the simultaneous presence of
an initiating intention and its desired goal-event. Everyone knows that we
do such things as try to listen, and succeed and fail in varying degrees;
that we try to remember names, and sometimes succeed and sometimes
not; and it is clear that the trying in question is an irreducible process of
trying. Then the point I want to make here is, that mental acts of all kinds,
whether listenings or visualisings or thinkings, are all *experiences* and pretty
plainly so. For one thing, they are phenomena which are individuated in
a purely temporal framework: they are such that two incidents of trying
to remember the same name, phenomena which from the point of view

of the experience were qualitatively indistinguishable, *must* have occurred at different times. Moreover, when we come to report the occurrence of the active experience in question, we do so merely through having had the experience, we do not base the claim upon the existence of a further distinct awareness-experience (of 'inner sense'). And they find a place in any narrative of the 'stream of consciousness' at the time. And so on.

Then although there are significant differences between willings of the latter mental ilk and those directed to limbs, the fact that the mental variety is of the type experience is evidence that the bodily variety is also. True, the differences between these two examples of the will are great. For one thing, the bodily phenomenon is primitive in the extreme, since such willings must be present at the very lowest point of the psychological life of animals of the very simplest kind, yet probably differ in no significant respect from the bodily willings of rational self-conscious creatures. (For I can see no reason for supposing our bodily willings to be different from those of other animals.) By contrast, exercises of the mental will must mutate radically as we move up the evolutionary ladder, and constitute a great deal of the inner life of self-conscious subjects. Nevertheless, both of these phenomena give immediate expression to act-desire and intention, and are subject both to control and meaning-giving at the hands of their intention source. And they are each of active type. And so on. I mention these facts in support of the theory that the event of striving that is encountered in physical act situations is of the type: experience. Then if it is, the event of striving must be given epistemologically in the first person in the absolutely immediate mode of experiences. And the same must be true of the bodily action with which it is identical.

4. EXPLANATION AND PERCEPTION

(1) Explanatorial considerations support this interpretation of the facts, as I hope now to show. The explanatorial issue to be resolved is, how at the time of action an agent *knows* that his will is operative: that is, knows he is doing something or another (at the very least). The question we have been asking is, whether his knowledge is an immediate effect of willing/trying/striving, or arises through the mediation of an awareness experience. The answer should settle the question we have been asking concerning the generic character of the bodily will. If the knowledge is an immediate effect of the phenomenon of willing, then the willing must be an experience; if it is experientially mediated it cannot be.

I shall approach this problem by asking a preliminary question concerning our cognitive attitudes towards our own future willings. Let us suppose a man is about to perform an intended action, for example is racing across a room to extinguish a flame. What explains his believing that his will is about to be actively engaged? Why does he think he is about to do something? The obvious answer is, the presence of an intention. It entails such a belief, and simultaneously causes it. However, the desire that the flame destruct, and the belief that it may be physically within his power to effect that event, must also determine his belief in the impending occurrence of activeness on his own part. After all, the intention is to perform an act with a *desired* and *possible* end in view: the commitment to future action is not a *blind* commitment. It is not as if the inducements to action cause a commitment to future action which simply puts those inducements behind it, so to say a rigid and unthinking pointing of oneself action-wards!

Thus, both the intention as well as the situational belief and act-desire cause belief in a future willing. Then what happens to these causal forces at the time of action? Consider specifically the intention. If the intention causes knowledge of willing immediately before willing occurs, why should it lose this power as willing begins? And yet it is surely also clear that the event of willing must cause knowledge of itself, and do so through being experienced by its agent. But if it does do so, what causal role can there be left for the intention? But in fact the situation which obtains in present action can be no different in the relevant respects from that obtaining regarding future action. For just as knowledge of future intended action is not through being aware of a blind commitment to future action, so knowledge of present willing is not through being aware of willing in mental isolation: it relates us to a willing to which of necessity we are intentionally committed. And to a willing we desire to do and believe may be physically capable of success. In short, these several causal agencies – experiencing the event of willing on the one hand, and the intention, desire, and belief on the other – are not *opposed* agencies, nor do they relate to one another as *contributory conditions*. They are all necessary conditions both of the present intentional action and of our knowledge of it. No one of them could be causally operative in engendering such knowledge in the absence of the others.

(2) The question we have been attempting to settle is: what is the mode in which willing is experienced? This question leads naturally to a further question: under such circumstances what *cognitive role* would be open to a *distinct experiential event* of the type awareness of willing? What cognitive

role would be open to an internal experiential event of the type *immediate perception* of the will? The foregoing observations help us to answer this question. It seems to me that when one is engaged in action no cognitive role remains for the supposed immediate perception of willing, that the explanatorial space is already fully occupied by the intention/situational-belief/act-desire (and in a different mode by willing itself). These several phenomena guarantee knowledge of present intentional willing without need of a further agency. The explanatorial context in which willing occurs is such as to nullify *any cognitive role* for immediate perceptual experience of itself. But whenever perception occurs a cognitive role must be realised, whether or not we know of it or put it to use. The deduction I think we should make is, that since no cognitive role is available for the putative perception, the possibility of immediate perception of the will must automatically be nullified. This adds explanatorial weight to the previous arguments in support of the claim that we 'just know' of willing when it occurs. That is, for the inexistence of any distinct awareness experience. Thus, the act of will generates knowledge of itself simply through being an experience: awareness of willing is no different in this regard from awareness of thoughts and emotions.

The overall conclusion is that the act of will is of the generic type: experience. It must therefore be given to the subject mentally-immediately *qua* experience *and* perceptually *qua* perceptible. More precisely, the physical action will be given to the acting subject in the following several ways. Mentally-immediately *qua* experience; attentively-immediately and uniquely and necessarily in proprioception *qua* physical event in space; and possibly also attentively-mediately and wholly contingently to the other senses. It comes therefore as at once infinitely close *and* as an event appearing in the physical environment. Why not? This phenomenon occurs on the frontier of mind and body.

5. A RESIDUAL PROBLEM

A problem exists for the dual aspect theory of bodily action which follows on from the earlier considerations regarding the individuation of bodily actions and strivings/tryings/'doings'. It has been argued that bodily strivings that completely fail, and which occur therefore in the complete absence of limb movement and proprioceptive experience, are psychological events that are given spacelessly to their agent. They are said to be purely temporally and aspatially individuated by him: that is, to be singled out by him by their type (strive) & object (e.g. arm-raising) & time (e.g. midday); and by that alone.

Meanwhile it has been argued that bodily actions are one and the same event as the above striving event, and also that bodily actions are individuated spatio-temporally. Thus the act is said to be spatially individuated, and the striving is not, and yet they are said to be identical.

Can these claims be reconciled? Well, consider the following situation. Let us assume that at some time t_I one experiences a passing thought θ_I. Then θ_I will be individuated by one in purely temporal a-spatial manner. Now let us assume that Physicalism is true, and that one is looking through a mirror at the part of the brain in which thoughts occur, and let us suppose that at t_I one catches sight of thought θ_I as it occurs. Then one will individuate the event one visually witnesses in spatio-temporal terms. Accordingly, one individuates the one event θ_I a-spatially *and* spatially at the same moment in time. One individuates this psychological event a-spatially in the absolutely immediate psychologistic mode reserved for experiences *and* simultaneously spatially in the mediate mode of perception. Now this is a wholly intelligible 'thought-experiment', and poses no particular problem for the understanding Then so it is, I suggest, in the case of one's own bodily actions. Just as it is no part of the psychologically immediate datum that the θ_I event is the cerebral event one sees, so it is no part of the psychologically immediate datum that the striving event $S\Phi$ one psychologically immediately experiences includes the physical event ϕ one prorioceptively perceives. Nonetheless, it is the one event coming to the subject in two different modes: experientially-immediately *and* perceptually-mediately.

PART IV

From mind to body

Introduction

In Part III I investigated bodily actions, and put forward a theory of this phenomenon. It was a dual aspect theory in a sense of that expression which differs from the sense which would find application if certain non-reductionist versions of Physicalism were true. These two theoretical positions are significantly different in that dual aspect action theory, on the basis of purely *a priori* reasoning, posits a specific physical characterisation ('activation of a mechanism for the generation of the bodily movement ϕ') of an event which it brings at the same time under a psychological concept ('striving to ϕ-make'/'act of ϕ-making'). And this is something which Physicalism – at least in its present forms – does not do. None of the characterisations posited by Physicalism of any given psychological event affirm anything more than that it has a physical character. Conversely, dual aspect action theory arrives at its conclusion without appeal to Physicalism.

I. THE SENSATION

The situation in the case of the sensation is both interestingly similar to and different from the above. And the comparison between these two phenomena is illuminating. Dual aspect theory of the kind applicable to bodily actions does not hold of sensations, even though the relation of this phenomenon to the body is both close and overt. What we discover in the case of sensations is that a causal psycho-physical nomicity governs the occurrence of sensations of all types, whether they are bodily sensations like tickles or pains, or non-bodily perceptual sensations of the kind of visual or auditory sensations. In all cases the nomicity in question takes the following form. In the first place, there exist of necessity regular physically sufficient causal conditions for the occurrence of any sensation type. And secondly, whenever a sensation occurs its occurrence is of necessity causally determined through its exemplifying just such a regular sufficiency. These causal conditions allow the possibility that for any sensation type there may be a variety of regular paths into existence. Then while we know *a priori* in the case of any given sensation that there exists such an exemplified causal sufficiency, we cannnot of course know *a priori* what that path is.

So much for the *origins* of sensations. What of their *constitution*? Can we know *a priori* anything concerning their make-up? For example, can we know *a priori* that sensations must regularly be endowed with some given physical constitution? I believe so, even though we cannot offer *a priori* any characterisation of that constitution. All I think we can know *a priori* is that *some* physical constitution is a sufficient condition of the sensation. I suggest that the existence of regular causally sufficient physical conditions for the occurrence of any given sensation, necessitates in turn the existence of corresponding regular constitutively sufficient physical conditions. The necessary existence of causal psycho-physical law seems to imply such a conclusion.

2. THE BODILY ACTION

The sensation is one of the two great mediators between the psychological realm and the physical, between the mind and its containing environment. The other is bodily action. What is the existential situation with bodily action? Here, too, psycho-physical nomicity universally governs the occurrence of the phenomenon. But in this case the universal physical conditions determining existence are *constitutive* rather than *causal*. They take the form of sets of causally connected events, each set being a sufficient constitutive condition of bodily action, provided that set is immediately caused by the required mental phenomena. The immediate causes of action are psychological, and I know no reason for believing that there exist regular causally sufficient physical conditions for the occurrence of bodily actions. On what grounds could one assume that, corresponding to such mental phenomena as belief, intention, and act-desire, occur regular physical conditions jointly determining the act of the will?

There is a second noteworthy difference between action and sensation. For as we saw in section 1 (above), in the case of bodily action, though not with sensation, we can provide *a priori* a purely physical characterisation of the event, viz. 'mechanism for the occurrence of an act of ϕ-making'. That is, we can give a purely physical *constitutive description* of the bodily act. For even though the description 'mechanism for the occurrence of an act of ϕ-making' makes use of the concept of action, which is a psychological concept, nonetheless a motor-mechanism is a physical phenomenon and 'activation of a mechanism' a physical description of that phenomenon. Now it is not just that we know *a priori* that the purely physical event ϕ of limb movement is *part of* a psychological event – which already is a unique property amongst psychological phenomena, and surely of great significance. We are in possession also of a recipe for discovering the entire physical make-up of this psychological phenomenon: we empirically uncover the mechanism operative in the generation of the limb movement ϕ that some act is the making of, and in so doing we are laying bare the physical parts of a psychological event, viz. the event of striving/of physical action. We can do no such thing in the case of any other psychological phenomenon.

3. THE IMPLICATIONS OF THE SPECIAL STATUS OF BODILY ACTION

(1) What may we deduce from this special property of bodily actions? This is the question which concerns me as I set out on the present Part IV. My intuition is that whatever it be, it is likely to be of some moment. Despite the closeness of the tie between mind and body in both sensations and bodily actions, there are I believe reasons for suspecting that it might be particularly close in the latter case: more, that this proximity might be of a special order, and such as to shed light in a fundamental way upon the mind-body relation. Now we have seen that dual aspect theory does not hold in the case of sensations. Despite the primitiveness of the phenomenon, despite its necessary links with the body (spatial, individuative, causal), the sensation has to be classed as 'internal' in character, even if not an event of the 'inner life'. Thus it is not a publicly perceptible entity; it manifests its presence only indirectly; and we have no *a priori*-given recipe for identifying its physical parts. While bodily action is an equally primitive psychological phenomenon, it differs on all of these counts, and in any case clearly is in no sense 'internal', let alone a denizen of the 'inner life'. After all, this phenomenon is visible.

The question I shall be investigating here in Part IV is whether there is some respect in which the bodily action *a priori* and overtly unites mind and body. Now in one respect its double aspect status already accomplishes such a thing. But I think we should be looking for something more. For to repeat my suggestion: it is that the bodily action is a bridge between mind and body as the sensation is not. I suspect that in its case the commitments of both sides of that 'bridge' to each other are uniquely overt. We know that the physical action is pressed 'flush' against its mental causes, which are at once fully interior and capable of taking highly meaningful form. Then while it is true that the sensation is likewise also 'flush' against whatever meaningful interpretations happen to be placed upon it in perceptual experience, the fact that one relation to the mind is from origin to originated and the other from cause to its repercussions, is I believe charged with significance.

(2) These intuitions are bolstered by the following fact. The prime evidence of mentality, of the reality of the psychological realm in general, and of its existence and contents in particular cases, consists of bodily actions of one kind or another. True, the actions are for the most part instrumental in type, and are physical actions in meaningful physically presented situations, and thus presuppose an awareness of the environment which is made possible only through perception which is founded upon sensation. Nevertheless, those sensations are a background phenomenon, whereas it is in the acts themselves that the presence of the mind and its contents is revealed. It is they that we interpret. Here, for the one and only time, the mind comes out into the open. Literally!

The mind internalises the environment in the form of perception, and imposes itself upon the environment in the form of physical action. In one case the causal flow is from outside to inside, in the latter case it is the reverse – but is of a special and indeed unique order. Then this is how it comes about that here in Part IV I choose to discuss the inner-to-outer causal 'flow'. I hope to understand how it is that from the earliest cognitions and the first stirrings of desire, a causal continuity is set up which culminates in the occurrence of bodily movement and environmental change. And I hope in so doing to trace a translucently clear passage from mind to body, and bring out how uniquely in this phenomenon both mind and body overtly posit each other. In this way I shall aim at dissolving the opposition of one to the other, revealing in its stead an internal mutual dependence.

CHAPTER 17

The antecedents of action (1): from desire to intention

A familiar *causal sequence* is this. A particular *act-desire* springs up in a man. Whereupon he begins to wonder whether to perform the act. He engages in a procedure of trying to *decide* whether to do so, and this necessitates reaching a decision on some matter of fact. Then the instant in which resolution of his factual uncertainty occurs, is the instant in which resolution of his practical uncertainty occurs, which is the instant in which a certain *intention* takes up residence in his mind. Now the instant in which he judges the time ripe for the expression of that intention, is the instant in which both intention and act-desire begin expressing themselves, and their expression consists in a *striving* – a 'doing'. Finally, the process of striving is one that in the body tends naturally to lead to the occurrence of the *willed event*. Most of these phenomena stand in causal, and for the most part mental causal, relation to one another. Then it is these six topics: causing, desiring, deciding, intending, striving, acting – that provide the subject matter of the present and succeeeding chapters. My aim is to trace a pellucidly intelligible thread leading from the penultimate causally significant antecedents of action to the willed bodily phenomenon ϕ. I begin with a brief sketch of the distinctive peculiarities of mental causality.

I. MENTAL CAUSALITY

(a) Defining 'mental causality'

What is 'mental causality'? It is causality – in the mind. But what is it for causality to be 'in the mind'? Let us suppose that some event α_1 causes some event α_2, and that this is an example of what people call 'mental causality'. What does this imply? Well, we at least mean that α_1 and α_2 are mental, and that α_1 causes α_2. Yet we must mean more. For think of the following. Let us assume that $\alpha 1$ is noticing a nearby wasp, that $\alpha 2$ is annoyance, and that causally sandwiched between them are $\beta 1$ (= alarm), $\beta 2$ (= giving a start), $\beta 3$ (= spilling one's coffee), $\beta 4$ (= noticing the state of one's coffee). Then here the mental event $\alpha 1$ caused the mental event $\alpha 2$, yet this would not rate as an example of 'mental causality'. Why not? Is it because the causal relation between the two mental events is mediate, i.e. such that other events causally interpose? By no means; for mental causal chains, such as associative threads, undoubtedly exist. All that is needed for causality to be 'in the mind' is that a causal relation exist between mental phenomena that is *not* causally mediated by *non*-mental phenomena. That is a logically necessary and sufficient condition.

But how to keep the physical non-psychological out of *any* such causal transaction? Thus, suppose one grows choleric on receiving a minor insult. Then if anything rates as an example of mental causality, this does. Yet might not one's rage be assisted into being by the fact that one has not eaten for ten hours? One's empty stomach here caused the psychological state of hunger, which in turn caused such a psychological state as irritability, which played its part in giving awareness of the insult that extra cutting edge in producing this ugly mental conflagration. Empty stomach here generates a kind of mental petrol (irritability) for a mental match (insult). Then the thesis of the mental causal origin of this example of rage is, that this phenomenon can in principle be wholly explained in terms of precisely such mental factors. Therefore when we say of a causal relation between two mental items that it is 'not causally mediated by non-mental items', we cannot suppose that physical non-mental factors have *no* part to play in the genesis of the mentally caused item. Rather must we suppose that if they do, it is by bringing about or supporting a psychological something that plays its part in an autonomous psychological causal explanatory framework. We must assume that an *entirely psychological explanation* is in principle available for the mentally caused item.

I conclude that the following familiar causings must be mental causings: growing angry upon being insulted; experiencing a mental image of clouds upon hearing someone speak of the sky. This is because the two causally related items are almost certainly not causally mediated by what is non-mental. And the following must be non-mental causings: experiencing a tingle upon catching sight of something fearsome; a brain probe evoking a mental image. This is because, in the first case a physical non-mental item must causally mediate such causing, while in the second case the cause is non-mental.

(b) The peculiarities of 'mental causality'

(1) What is so special about mental causality? The first thing to note is, that 'causality' has its usual sense in 'mental causality'. Mental causality is merely causality in – and, so to say, across – the mind. Thus, it is the same relation as holds between lightning and thunder. And yet it has certain peculiarities because of being set in the mind.

Those peculiarites are in part epistemological. For when one mental item causes another mental item, immediately and *a fortiori* without causal mediation by a non-mental item and therefore 'mental causally', it is frequently possible for their owner to stand in the following interesting epistemological relation to this singular causal relation. He knows of it; immediately; and with mentalistic immediacy. That is, amongst the *given psychological data* of the moment may be, not merely that he is angry, not just that he believes Mr X called him an idiot, but that he is angry *because* he believes he was thus described. In short, a causal relation joins the psychological phenomena it relates as a *structural element* of the stream of consciousness. The stream of consciousness may internally be ordered both temporally *and* causally. I do not just experience one mental item and also another; I do not just experience one mental item and then another; I can experience mental items *as* before and after and *also* as giving-rise-to and emerging-out-of one another.

This epistemological peculiarity goes hand in hand with a second epistemological oddity. Since we are unlikely to know governing law-like regularities cast in mental terms, e.g. 'Whenever I think I am called an idiot I grow angry', it follows that in the mind one can know singular causal propositions with mentalistic immediacy, and hence with near incorrigibility, without one's knowledge being based on a regularity. While this does not entail that such singular relations are not law-governed, it is significant that strong knowledge of a causal relation can be obtained otherwise than via the standard epistemological approaches. In extra-mental physical nature, where we employ either 'Humean' or probabilistic considerations, we are in this respect epistemologically at a disadvantage.

(2) Now the above are the epistemological peculiarities displayed by *some* examples of mental causality. But *some* of these latter examples exhibit a further peculiarity. This concerns, not the *existence* of a causal relation, but its *rationale*. I shall dub this property 'perspicuousness'. Thus, with a wide-ranging variety of psychological types there exist *a priori*-given internally

intelligible mental causes. Then in such cases the internal rationale of the immediately given singular causal relation comes with the awareness of that relation. It wears its explanatory heart upon its sleeve.

Examples of 'perspicuousness' are these. That grief is occasioned by belief in the loss of the greatly loved. That anger is occasioned by belief in the obtaining of something to which one takes serious objection. That belief that p should be occasioned by belief in the existence of what counts as good evidence for p. That desire that a pain should stop should be occasioned by the fact that the pain has the property of being undesirable. When grief, anger, belief, desire, have such origins, then both the existence *and* the rationale of a causal relation are immediately given.

But how widespread is perspicuousness? Are there no non-perspicuous mental causal relations? There are indeed: there are even 'anti-perspicuous' mental causal relations! Thus, a madman laughs at the greenness of the grass: a young child is overwhelmingly upset by the fact that it is snowing: you are astonished to discover that the time at which you have awoken is 8 a.m.; etc. Yet these are not, properly speaking, suitable counter-examples with which to disprove the thesis that all mental causal relations are perspicuous. For they only serve to highlight, and ultimately depend upon, the phenomenon of perspicuousness. For in all these cases we say: 'I do not understand it'; *and cannot rest content.* Thus, when confronted by the anti-perspicuous, we pursue understanding by searching for what perspicuously explains. For example: a seeming absurdity in the greenness of grass: a hidden significance in the falling of snow: a dream-derived assumption that the time is now midnight. Once such factors are uncovered the mind can rest easy; *and only then.* Hence the anti-perspicuous is fated to give way to the perspicuous. Therefore we can hardly turn to the anti-perspicuous as a disproof of the supposed universality of perspicuousness. That 'disproof' is accomplished (in section (c) following) via different phenomena.

Is the discovery of a perspicuous origin merely the discovery of what the scholastics called the 'formal object' of a phenomenon? As the past is the formal object of memory and the tangible that of touching, might the seemingly absurd be the formal object of amusement? Could the seriously objected-to be the formal object of rage? There are two comments that I would make here. First, though sometimes the formal object exhibits perspicuousness, perspicuousness cannot *be* having a formal object. For the concept of perspicuousness has a wider range of application than that of formal object, seeing that belief on good evidence is internally intelligible as belief on no evidence is not, and desire for the cessation of such absolute undesirables as nausea is not desire for what is a formal object.

Second, that some perspicuously given objects are formal objects does not imply that these pellucid perspicuous explanations are trivial and in need of supplementary aids. It does not rob them of explanatory force. The most we can say in support of such a view is, that the explanatory enterprise is not concluded upon our discovering the perspicuous and perhaps formally explanatory cause-object of the mentally caused item. For example: we will want to know *why* the greenness of grass seemed absurd, and *why* confrontation with the seemingly absurd should have provoked amusement, and so on. Such explanatory enterprises can no more come to a *decisive end* in an individual mind than can the subject Physics be 'wound up'. The holistic character of the mind here makes its presence unmistakably felt. Therefore perspicuousness in the psychological realm is but one aspect of an explanatory situation that, viewed from a different standpoint, say that of Freud, a pre-eminent representative of holistic thinking, presents a less tidy picture than one might at first suppose. Yet it is not to be dismissed lightly. It remains a significant reality.

(c) The limits to these peculiarities

(1) Thus, mentalistically-immediate knowledge of a singular causal relation, together with its own internally intelligible rationale, can obtain concerning mentally causally related items, and in the absence of a known regularity. Yet absolutely none of the above needs hold of the mentally causally related. Indeed, it is in no way certain that mental phenomena which are immediately juxtaposed will be causally linked. For example: I hear the word 'Zanzibar', whereupon a mental image of St Paul's swims into my head. Now these two mental phenomena may be causally related via the following path. I was yesterday reading how when Wren was designing St Paul's he met a traveller from Zanzibar, and . . . and . . . And yet it is perfectly possible they are not causally related at all; it is possible that the temporal juxtaposition of hearing 'Zanzibar' and visualising St Paul's should be without causal significance. Thus, it might well be that, just as you began speaking of Zanzibar, a strong desire to revisit St Paul's was welling up within me and evoking imagery. And it is important to note that in neither case is there any firm guarantee that the subject will be mentalistically apprised of the causal situation. This obtains only if an *additional psychological datum* exists. Namely, one cast in the form, 'Experiencing x made me think of y.' Say: 'Catching sight of St Paul's made me think of the fact that Wren met a man who hailed from Zanzibar.' However, the existence of a causal relation between hearing the word and having the image does not *necessitate* the

existence of such a further psychological datum. As noted above, one can be in complete ignorance as to the mental causal situation.

In sum, with mental phenomena like thought events and mental images and perceptual impressions, mental juxtaposition can exist in the absence of a causal relation, and mental causal relations can obtain without our knowing of them. Moreover, when one knows of them one need be aware of no rationale of the causal relation. In fact the concept of perspicuousness has *no* application to phenomena of precisely this type.

(2) *Of what type?* I shall answer this question by giving an explanation of the property they share. That explanation turns upon the fact that the phenomenon of perspicuousness in the psychological realm is intimately related to the existence of our capacity to provide reasons for some psychological items which are '*our reasons*'. That is, considerations which caused the psychological item through appeal to the faculty of reason.

Now in this very important respect mental items fall into three distinct categories: (i) beliefs, desires . . .; (ii) emotions, surprise . . .; (iii) thoughts, images . . . . Consider them in turn.

(i) Beliefs are often held because of reasons which are 'our reasons'. Yet clearly sometimes they are not. Thus, the reason but not my reason for my thinking Smith a better philosopher than Jones is, that he talks louder and more often than Jones. Then when the operative reasons are 'my reasons', they exhibit the perspicuousness that characterises a good argument; so that the origin of such a belief is internally intelligible. More: the origin of such a belief can be such as to make the belief rational; and precisely for this reason beliefs can also be irrational and downright mad.

(ii) But while I have 'my reasons' for affective phenomena like rage, astonishment, and interest, these reasons can never be *good* or *bad.* Therefore the phenomena themselves can never be wholly determined by reason. Therefore the phenomena can never be rational. Thus, it is a mistake to suppose that believing you have been insulted is a good reason for rage – in the sense in which believing Big Ben says it is midday is a good reason for thinking it midday. In short, these phenomena exhibit perspicuousness, but never rationality or irrationality – though, of course, one might stipulate as 'irrational' a rage that derived from an irrational belief. What is important is that *this latter bond* can never be rational, for that suffices to ensure that the affective state cannot in any serious sense be called rational.

(iii) Then it is precisely this element of 'our reasons' that explains why perspicuousness has the limits it has in the mental causal realm. For there is no such thing as 'my reason for having the thought θ enter my mind'; nor even, despite the voluntary character of visualising, 'my reason for having an image of Paris enter my mind'; nor any 'my reason for seeming to see a larger moon at the horizon'. While one can mentalistically and quasi-incorrigibly know of such singular causal relations as 'Hearing the word "Budapest" made me think of the Danube', one is never mentalistically apprised of an internal rationale of these causal relations. This emerges in the fact that the concept of 'anti-perspicuousness' has no application here, so that there can be no such thing as an unintelligible instance of such a causal relation. Thus, it seriously perplexes us that a man should laugh at a shadow. But why should it seriously perplex us that catching sight of a shadow should make us think of laughter, or tears, or anything else? And it does not.

(d) The situation with action

Then let us now remark a significant fact. This is, that action itself, and therefore all its mental causal antecedents, is of the first psychological type, viz. type (i). Namely: not merely can we offer 'our reasons' for these items; but these reasons can be good or bad reasons; so that the phenomena they causally determine can, in an absolutely middle-of-the-road sense, be rational or irrational or mad. This holds of desire, belief, decision, intention, striving, and willing.

It therefore is the case, not merely that mental causal relations hold between such items, and not merely that we can know of them with *mentalistic immediacy* in the absence of known Humean-type regularities. In addition: these phenomena enter into causal relations that are marked by the property of *perspicuousness*, and they themselves can be *rational or irrational or mad*. In short, they exhibit to a marked degree all the peculiarities of the mental causal relation.

2. DESIRE

A brief word on desire. When action occurs, it is in the final analysis this phenomenon that underlies all of the workings of the act-generative mental machinery. For deciding, intending, striving, willing, and choosing, all require a foundation in desire. It is for this reason that I begin this discussion with an account of desire.

While desires range over desires-to-do (e.g. swim), desires-to-'do' (e.g. laugh), and desires-that-something-happen-or-be-true (e.g. that one's toothache stop), my concern here is solely with the first type of desire. Then what underlies such desires? Under what conditions do act-desires occur? No doubt imponderables always play a part in their generation, but all instances of self-conscious act-desire necessitate the seeming absence, at least of a stage of an action, and also of the object or event whose absence that act is designed to overcome (if there be such). In this sense the act-desire is directed towards the negation of a negation.

But precisely towards what is act-desire directed? Now I have heard it said that the natural expression of desire is phantasy. Is this true? It may perhaps be true of propositional desire, but it is not so in the case of act-desire. Certainly, act-desire in the very young shows an enhanced tendency to elicit phantasies of the desired. Yet bearing in mind that the infant ego is underdeveloped, this seems merely to demonstrate that action and act-desire necessitate a certain measure of ego-development if they are to so much as exist; so that the starved infant requires an ego of some sort if the mental distress occasioned by food absence is to take that form of felt absence that is an act-desire; and *a fortiori* if acting or willing are to result. After all, since acting or willing is *par excellence* an ego process, act-desires must *par excellence* be ego phenomena. Thus, it must be because the infant ego is rudimentary that act-desire tends to elicit phantasy; indeed, such an immature ego condition ensures that the act-desire itself will take immature form and have an enhanced tendency to generate phantasy rather than will. (For desires as well as egos can ripen.)

Then my suggestion is that the natural expression of act-desire is, not phantasy of fulfilment, nor act of fulfilment either, but a striving-towards or trying-to-perform an act of fulfilment. Now this says something more than that it tends to cause such a striving. For it stands in just such a relation to knowledge of itself – which cannot possibly rate as an expression. But the reason I say that striving is the unique expression of act-desire is that act-desire is of the nature of a force-towards striving. This shows in several ways. Thus, if striving does not supervene upon the occurrence of act-desire of reasonable intensity, then we are generally obliged to invoke the workings of some prevention device. And the phenomenon of striving both gains its energy from, and tends to exhaust in so doing, the motivating act-desire. And when act-desire does cause striving, it does so immediately, inexplicably or ultimately, in the manner of a force. Indeed, bearing in mind that act-desire is quantitatively variable, that it acts immediately on its agent owner, and tends to generate in its owner a unique expression effect that drains it of its energy in so doing, it may not be too much to say of it that it *is* a mental force.

3. DECIDING

Not all intendings are the outcome of decidings. Thus, I see a cup begin to topple off the table and lurch forward wildly in an attempt to catch it; and this instrumental act-striving, like all instrumental act-strivings, necessarily gives expression to an intention, viz. that of trying to catch the cup. But this intention came into being both because of and in the very same instant in which I became aware of the toppling, so that there was no instant in which I was uncertain what to do. Then this last tells us why no decision was reached in forming the intention that found expression in my act. For a necessary condition of a decision is, not that an active procedure of deciding be carried out, but that an uncertainty as to what to do should find resolution in the formation of an intention. For deciding what to do is such a coming-to-intend to do something. Thus, decidings form a sub-class of comings-to-intend. Namely, the class of those comings-to-intend events that resolve a state of uncertainty over what to do. So clearly, not all intendings emerge out of decidings. Yet equally clearly many do. The phenomenon of emergence from such a process is my present object of investigation.

(a) Deciding-that

(1) Is deciding an activity? We incline to the view that deciding-to-*do* is an activity. But is it really so? To settle this matter it is salutary to consider the deciding that occurs when we reach a decision on a matter of fact. This is instructive for two reasons. First, most decidings-to-do depend upon decidings-that, and since we wish to understand the former, it is judicious that we understand the latter. Second, the activity status of deciding-that is more readily accessible than that of deciding-to-do, and might provide a lead to that of deciding-to-do.

Now there can be no doubt that there is an active procedure of *trying to make up one's mind* on a question of fact. The existence of the order: 'Try and make up your mind on that matter' attests to the fact. But note: the order, and the activity, are not, 'trying to make up the mind *that* p', even though we describe the successful outcome as 'I made up my mind that p.' Rather they are 'trying to make up my mind – one way or the other – as to whether p'. To repeat: one is not trying to make up one's mind that p – even though one succeeds in making up one's mind – and makes up one's mind that p; and this shows in the fact that there exists no intention of 'making up my mind that p'. So the activity is trying to make up one's mind *whether*, and this is the doing of what one hopes might, and in order that it might, generate an event of cognitive commitment. Then this ratiocinative activity, if it is successful, will cause an event of cognitive commitment, one way or the other, which is the event the procedure is fishing for so to say in the dark of the mind, an event that signals the completion of that procedure.

Now while the procedure of fishing for this event of cognitive commitment is actively or willingly carried out, the resulting event of cognitive crystallisation is not itself willed. After all, we know from chapter 1 that belief is never willed; and it is in any case clear that a successful trying-to-make-up-my-mind-whether-p that leads to belief in p is not an activity of making-up-my-mind-that-p; and equally clear that we do not bring the ratiocinative procedure to a conclusion with a short sharp act of willing belief! In sum, the will takes a back seat in the formation of cognitive attitudes. Yet while cognitive commitment is not willed, the event does not come upon one like *a blow between the eyes*!; for, unlike such a phenomenon, one has a measure of *responsibility* for acquiring a cognitive attitude, inasmuch as one has 'one's reasons' which one is thereafter prepared to 'stand by' and actively to defend. In other words, the cognitive crystallisation that terminates ratiocination emerges neither from *one's will* nor from the opaque and automatic workings of that sector of one's mind that determines phenomena like sense impressions, viz. one's *understanding*. This intermediate explanatory positioning – for both belief and intention – whereby responsibility obtains without choice – is the main source of the puzzle over the activity status of deciding-to-do. And one may add that the existence of responsibility without choice internally depends upon one's continuing ability to exercise choice so to say *at a remove of one* in a causally relevant field: namely, in being able at any point actively to reopen the issue concerning which cognitive commitment now reigns.

In sum: the activity situation is this. There is a preceding process which is essentially active, which falls essentially under 'trying to decide whether', which when successful falls inessentially under 'deciding whether'; and, because there can be no intention of 'deciding-that', this essentially active process can never be subsumed, essentially or inessentially, under 'deciding-that'. Yet when this striving process is successful it generates a distinct discontinuous essentially inactive event of cognitive crystallisation, and this inactive event falls under 'deciding-that'.

(2) To repeat: there is an activity of trying to decide whether p that may inessentially prove to be an activity of deciding whether p; and an essentially

inactive event of cognitive crystallisation that is a deciding-that p, that may bring this activity to an end; but there is no act of deciding-that p. Herewith the problem of the activity status of deciding-that dissolves.

And yet this way of resolving the problem turns upon our distinguishing as separate phenomena, the active process of trying-to-make-up-my-mind-whether and the inactive event of coming-to-believe-that. And this may be queried. After all, the event of cognitive crystallisation *completes* the preceding activity. Does not this suggest that the crystallisation event is merely the last part of the procedure of 'trying to make up my mind whether or not p'? Then may not the resolution of uncertainty lie after all within our power? But to say that crystallisation completes the procedure does not mean that it is the *last part* of that procedure. Think of the relation between looking-for and catching-sight-of. The latter event completes, is caused by, and clearly is distinct from the preceding process. Yet why is it not accounted the last part of a successful looking procedure? I can think of two reasons why not. First, the looking that succeeds should then be describable as an activity of finding; which it is not. Second, the catching-sight-of event should relate in tight mechanistic fashion to the looking process, as a willed arm rise relates mechanistically to the active process which precedes and culminates in it; and it does not. Now both objections apply in the case under consideration, viz. a successful trying-to-make-up-my-mind-whether; so that the active process of fishing for cognitive commitment must cause without encompassing the inactive event of crystallisation. And in exactly similar manner a trying-to-remember process may cause and fail to encompass the event that brings it to an end, viz. recollection.

(b) Deciding to do

(1) The activity status of deciding-to-do is the same as that of deciding-that. Here too an active procedure that at best both falls essentially under 'trying to decide whether to do' and inessentially under 'deciding what to do', is followed by an essentially inactive event of 'deciding to do'. In short, there is no activity of 'deciding to do Φ', where Φ is an act, even though there is an event of deciding-to-do-Φ. This receives confirmation in the fact that there is no order: 'Decide to raise your arm.'

Then what is the relation between deciding-that and deciding-to-do? Let us approach this question by considering the account of the relation propounded by believers in the Gide-ean *acte gratuit*. This I take to be an act one performs *intentionally* and yet for *no* reason; and therefore not even for the negative reason that one wished to and saw no harm in.

Then the decision to do such a deed of 'pure freedom' must be understood to emerge out of the blue: to rest on nothing but the agent himself! Those endorsing such a theory should readily believe that deciding-to-*do* is easily detachable from deciding-*that*, i.e. accept that one might decide that p, where p is all propositions relevant to the desirability of doing Φ, and then, over and above all such persuasions of the intellect, opt for the doing or not doing of Φ. In short, leap ahead of and clear of *all* intellectual supports! Whereupon 'I did Φ because of p', must here be taken with a grain of salt, for it must be understood merely to indicate the last landmark of the intellect from which the will projected itself forward: the tip of the mind on which one stood poised before the free leap of the self-determining agent!

I, however, see the link between deciding-to-do and deciding-that as tighter. And I suppose such disembodied 'freedom' to be mythical. As bodily willing and the use of bodily mechanism are not to be opposed, so it is with deciding-to-do and deciding-that: the Gide-ean account polarising these phenomena rather as Magical Volitionism separates mind from body. Consider a concrete case. Let us assume that a jury of one is trying to decide whether or not to bring in a verdict, Guilty, and assume that the mind of this law-abiding citizen is concerned with but one issue, viz. *is it certain* the defendant committed the crime? Then I suggest that the time during which he was trying to make up his mind on this question of *fact*, and the time during which he was trying to make up his mind what to *do*, would be one. For I suggest that the enterprises would be identical. Not as a matter of necessity, but as a matter of familiar fact. For he may have entered jury service simply assuming and accepting – and without making any such decision – that one enterprise hinged completely on the other.

(2) The two enterprises, trying to decide whether or not p, and trying to decide whether or not to do Φ, are here but one enterprise. But that does not imply that the event that completes the first enterprise is the event that completes the second. These events must be two and distinct. For the event that completes factual rumination is cognitive crystallisation, the onset of cognitive commitment, whereas the event that completes practical rumination is the onset of practical commitment, which is the onset of an intention state. But no coming-to-believe can, under any description, be a coming-to-intend, even though these ruminative procedures are the one procedure under different descriptions. In short, the incident of 'deciding whether' is necessarily distinct from the incident of 'deciding to do', even though these two milestones are reached along the same road.

And so three distinct phenomena must be crammed into the one instant. Namely: the termination of the theoretical/practical ruminative procedure; which is distinct from, and the terminus of the cause of, the event of cognitive crystallisation; which is in turn distinct from and cause of the event of practical commitment. Note, in conclusion, that deciding does not as such require the occurrence of a preceding process of rumination; for a man can go to bed undecided and wake to a state of decision, without there needing to be rumination during sleep. All that may be required is that the mental dust should settle. In any case, that practical uncertainty should give way to practical commitment. Deciding is the resolution of doubt.

(3) Thus, while a man may do what he hopes may bring about his deciding to do, deciding to do is not and never can be an activity. In this sense we may say that, while the will can strew incentives before itself, it cannot directly determine its own direction. Indeed, were it to be able to do so, the floodgates would break and the will carry all before it: mind, reason, sanity, world itself! Yet a responsibility for willing exists, of a different kind, the responsibility of reason, which is to say the responsibility to standards, which one's judgement can never shake off. This mode of responsibility is such that the will has after all an opening of a kind in determining itself; for it has the power to renew the active processes that lead to the will's determination at the hands of reason; so that responsibility-to-reason links at a remove of one with responsibility-for-will. Therefore while the responsibility for the direction taken by the will is not (so to say) of the infinite variety that we call willing, it is yet real even though of a lesser and finite order.

4. CHOOSING

(1) We are all familiar with choosings that are *acts of selection*. The selected item can either be an object, an abstract entity, an event, an act by another, an act by oneself . . .; and it is chosen *as* something or other. Thus, in choosing one is confronted with a set of items, and one then performs a selective act wherein one particular item is singled out from a range of possible alternatives as pre-eminent in some respect. For example: one chooses an apple as the apple one will eat; a performance by oneself in a play as one's best performance in a decade; a certain number as the number in someone's head. Choosing in this sense is an act that is a singling out of an item, from possible alternatives, as a something or other. This provides us with a lead in the ensuing discussion.

(2) My present concern is with a closely related type of choosing. Namely, in the choosing of *an act to do*.

But why in the first place is mankind interested in the concept of act choice? I think we are interested in an important property of certain acts, viz. in the fact that they are acts for which in a certain special sense the subject must bear *full responsibility.* Now the concept of intentional action is unequal to the task of ensuring that the subject is in this sense responsible for some phenomenon. For think of high-speed reactions in sport, e.g. a sudden catch off the bat in cricket. These are instrumental strivings, hence necessarily intentional and re-describable in the light of that intention, and yet they may give expression neither to decision nor to thought. They are, to a degree, automatic and unthinking, and, even though intentional, decidedly not what one would call paradigmatic examples of responsible behaviour.

Therefore if we are to capture this feature of some behaviour, we need more than the mere concept of action; more than the concept of intentional action; and, since not all responsible behaviour issues from decision, something other than the concept of decision. Then I think the need in question is met by the concept of *doing something by choice.*

I think that our interest is in the continuing causal power that an hypothetical process of practical deliberation could exert upon an act that is unfolding itself. For we single out chosen behaviour as behaviour which gives expression to deliberation and which would therefore grind to a halt were one's mind to light thoughtfully upon another choice. It follows that chosen behaviour must be intentional action; such that the agent is aware of alternative possibilities; such that he would strive to perform were deliberation instead to opt for them; which implies that chosen behaviour can be neither automatic nor helpless. And it is a sufficient but not a necessary condition of chosen behaviour that it is expressive of a decision. After all, one can embark upon considered action without needing to be resolving practical uncertainty in doing so.

(3) Then what precisely *is* the choosing of chosen behaviour? It is possible that the usage of 'choose to do' is unsettled (though whether or not it is, is a matter of no great moment). Thus, it may be that we sometimes use 'choose to do' interchangeably with 'decide to do'. For it may be that usage will permit our saying: 'He chose to defy me but later changed his mind.' In that case choosing is deciding to do – the onset of an intention that resolves doubt – and chosen behaviour the action expressive of that decision – and no more than a sub-variety of fully responsible behaviour. But I think the most firmly established usage is such that 'He chose to defy me' has different entailments. Namely: he defied me; and did so intentionally; and that act

was expressive of a choice. Then what on this interpretation is the *choosing*? It could either be the ratiocinative mental phenomena that determined the chosen behaviour or else the chosen behaviour itself. It is of no importance what we say on this issue of mere speech practice, for the word 'choose', unlike 'desire' 'intention' 'act', singles out no *sui generis* irreducible type, choosing. Yet I incline to the view that his 'choosing to defy me' was his chosen act of defiance.

5. INTENDING

(a) Introduction

In what does the importance of the intention consist? Inasmuch as the intention lies at the heart of the concept of action, and action for reasons stressed in the introduction to volume 1 is of a particular importance and especially at this point in the development of ideas, intention is a topic of some moment. And in so far as the intention lies at the heart of our concept of freedom, and freedom is a great and perennial theme, the intention is again of the utmost significance. But there is a third string to its bow, little emphasised in the past, which seems to me of some interest. Namely: it is the final and decisive necessary condition for the coming into being of *all* those events and objects in extra-mental nature which have a *meaning* or an *interpretation*. Thus, it is a striking fact that, given any artefact of any type anywhere anytime, it must in the final analysis link up with some mind via some intention somewhere sometime. Indeed, the whole world of intelligible items that we, as city-dwellers, and in any case members of a specifically *human* world inhabit, is the direct product of the intention. For while all properly human creations ultimately originate out of thought and desire, be it cityscape or world of words, and even though it is itself abetted by willing, the intention is that Ψ item through which the Ψ domain extends the realm of the mind into the merely physical sector of the world. In this way the intention is the *favoured intermediary* between Ψ and the rest of the world: the very last causal representative of thought before $\psi \sim \Psi$ and $\sim\psi \sim \Psi$ physical items become the bearers of meaning. In short, a messenger from on high, a Mercury, or Hermes, or Archangel Gabriel figure, whereby the mind stamps its image on the face of the globe.

Then what are intentions? In particular, are they *entities*? and are they *irreducible*? and *what* are they? Let me launch this discussion with a few preliminary intuitions, which I hope soon to vindicate. Thus, as a finger and its owner can point meaningfully across space towards an object that may not be there, so the intention and its owner are aimed like a bow across time towards a future act that may not eventuate; and somewhat as a sentence relates to the world that may make it true, so the intention relates to the act it may make happen: the one concerned with what is *there*, the other with what it will *produce*, and the likeness between the two is captured in the ambiguity of 'mean', viz. 'means that x is so' 'means to do y'. Now to me the intention has the look of being a kind of plan, taken in a sense that manages to encompass the twin elements of agency and certainty. For above all else the intention seems to be a condition of – the die being cast – every doubt dispelled – *practical commitment*.

Then here are some basic facts about intentions, which conduct us naturally into the problem posed in Section (b) below. First, intend Φ (i.e. IΦ) ↛ Φ, for 'He intended to Φ, but forgot' is sometimes true. Second, so IΦ ↛ Know Φ (KΦ). Third, in self-conscious beings IΦ → Believes he Φ possible (B ◇ Φ), for 'I intend to swim the Atlantic but know it is impossible' is incomprehensible. Fourth, and IΦ → BΦ. Now to this last it might be objected, both that the future is always uncertain, and that in any case I might change my mind; to which I reply, that though no future event is absolutely certain, knowledge and rational conviction yet obtain about the future, e.g. that tomorrow will dawn; and my resolute certainty concerning my future deeds is entirely consistent with retention of the (in my eyes almost certainly not to be used) capacity to change my mind. After all, should I seriously add the riders 'unless something untoward happen' and 'unless I change my mind' to 'I shall now jump into this pool and save your drowning infant'? Then once we remove these two obstacles, viz. the irremediable uncertainty of the future, and one's refusal to abrogate one's capacity to change one's mind, the way lies open to grasping the obvious fact that 'I firmly intend jumping into this pool but am not convinced that I will' is unacceptable. Fifth, and taking desire in the generous sense of 'pro attitude', it is clear that IΦ → Desires he to Φ (DΦ). In sum: IΦ ↛ Φ, ↛ KΦ, → B ◇ Φ, → BΦ, → DΦ. Now with these few elementary facts as our aid, let us approach the topic of intention afresh.

(b) The irreducibility of intentions

(1) What is it to intend? Well, we know that some acts possess the property of being intended. This suggests that being intended might be a *quality of* or way of doing an act, and that to intend is to perform an act endowed

with this quality. But this must be false. For one can harbour intentions one never expresses. In short, besides intentional acts there also exist intentions.

Then what *are* intentions? And are they *entities*? For an intention could be an objective reality without being some one anything, rather as a storm is no more than the sum of its scattered but objective rainy, windy, lightning parts. It could be objective, distinct from the intentional act, and yet a mere concatenation of psychological items. Then three main possibilities are: that the intention is an *unanalysable* psychological entity; or an *analysable* psychological entity; or a mere *concatenation* of psychological entities.

If the first of these three theories is false, if it is false that the intention is an unanalysable psychological entity, far and away the most likely account is, that its logically necessary and sufficient conditions are (i) that one *desires* to do Φ, and (ii) *believes*, perhaps immediately and on no evidence, that Φ will occur. For we have just seen that $I\Phi \rightarrow D\Phi$ and $B\Phi$, and it is difficult to see what more is needed to ensure $I\Phi$ than $B\Phi$ and $D\Phi$. So might it be that all there is to intending is, desiring-to-do-Φ and immediately believing in the future occurrence of the act one intends? So it has been claimed. But if this were so, intending would in all probability be a mere concatenation, for in all probability the belief and desire would fail to unite under any heading, and that would be to say that strictly the intention would be nothing! Then if we are to make any headway on this issue, and more generally on the relation between $I\Phi$ and $B\Phi$ and $D\Phi$, it is essential that we come to understand the *origins* of $B\Phi$ and $D\Phi$ in a situation in which one intends Φ ($I\Phi$). These questions I now consider in (2) and (3) below.

(2) *The origin of BΦ*. What is the origin of the $B\Phi$ that is entailed by $I\Phi$? Assuming that $I\Phi$ itself derives from some instrumental/technical belief Bt, together with a 'pro attitude' desire $D\Phi$, only two serious possibilities exist: (i) that both the belief $B\Phi$ and intention $I\Phi$ spring simultaneously into being out of the technical belief and desire, or (ii) that the belief $B\Phi$ derives immediately from the intention. Concerning (i): it is certainly true that Bt & $D\Phi$ must at least at *some* causal remove lie behind $B\Phi$, presumably as particular necessary conditions. But we want the *immediate* origin of $B\Phi$. Then could it be Bt & $D\Phi$? But since $B\Phi$ is often rational, and no belief that is directly caused by desire can be rational, it could only be the *knowledge* (K) that Bt & $D\Phi$ that one might suppose might be the cause of $B\Phi$. But neither Bt & $D\Phi$ nor K(Bt & $D\Phi$) could ever be *my* reasons for holding $B\Phi$. Thus, K(Bt & $D\Phi$) could at best be a mediate cause of $B\Phi$. And that mediation would surely have to be $I\Phi$.

I conclude that IΦ causes BΦ. That is, intending immediately generates belief in the forthcoming reality of the intended act. Now it will be admitted that this claim has an odd ring to it. Then it seems to me that this is due to the conjunction of the following properties of the situation: that IΦ both causally and transparently entails and explains BΦ; but most of all it is because IΦ does not function as 'my reason for holding BΦ'. For where else does one encounter such a strange epistemological state of affairs?

Well, we certainly find it with the *cogito*. Were it not for the fact that I am here and now conscious, I would not at this instant know I now exist. Such knowledge derives from my state of consciousness. For consciousness, which is not a cognitive state, which has a non-mental cause and which can be removed with a hammer, at every instant entails knowledge of one's present existence. Then this knowledge is immediate, transparent to its owner, and of a quite different content from its cause, and the resultant belief is both rational and not due to 'my reasons'. One's judgement is, so to say, completely bypassed in this utterly pellucid transaction. Then as present consciousness relates to knowledge of one's present existence, so the intention relates to belief concerning the occurrence of intended Φ. And why should not BΦ come from IΦ? Practical commitment necessitates cognitive commitment. It is simply not consistent with cognitive 'sitting on the fence'.

(3) *The origin of DΦ*. It has emerged that IΦ → BΦ & DΦ, and that IΦ causes BΦ. But what is the origin of (the) DΦ (that is necessitated by IΦ)? There are two situations: (i) where the desire precedes and continues with the formation of the intention, and (ii) where it comes into being only as the intention does – being an higher-order act-desire of the kind Abraham acquired only when he formed the intention of sacrificing Isaac. Now clearly (i)-type desires have variegated origins, and are in any case the cause of rather than product of the intention, but what of these higher-order (ii)-type desires? While we explain these desires to Φ in terms of one's reasons for intending-to and doing Φ, nonetheless such desires would not have existed without the decision to do Φ. Thus, IΦ must immediately cause such a sub-variety of DΦ, in such a manner that the origins of IΦ are the origins of that DΦ. It, too, is a transparent example of causation that is much akin to the *cogito*.

(4) *The constitution of IΦ*. Then bearing in mind that IΦ → BΦ & DΦ, four main theories may be entertained about the psychological constitution of IΦ.

A. $I\Phi = B\Phi$
B. $I\Phi = D\Phi$
C. $I\Phi = B\Phi \ \& \ D\Phi$ – *either* fused as one state *or* as a mere 'concatenation'
D. $I\Phi = I\Phi$ (irreducible)

Let us examine these theories in order, making use of the above findings concerning the origins of $B\Phi$ and $D\Phi$.

(A) This is obviously false, since intentions are not true or false, and since $I\Phi$ causes $B\Phi$. Yet this theory has one minor virtue. For the intention is with some illumination to be likened to a cognitive commitment. The intention state is a true analogue of certainty, translated so to say from the cognitive domain of truth into that of practice. For to intend is to be in that condition that can supplant a condition of *practical irresolution*, i.e. a state that finds its natural expression in a bewildered exclamation like 'What on earth shall I do?'

(B) There is no possibility of Theory B being true if $D\Phi$ is a desire that precedes the formation of $I\Phi$. After all, forming an intention is not acquiring a second desire to Φ. And as for those higher-order desires that only come into being with the intention, they could not actually *be* the intention, seeing that the intention causes such a desire in the transparent manner of the *cogito*. And is it, after all, credible that a resolve should be something as uncommitted as a mere desire? No matter in what relations we suppose such a desire to stand, those same relations cannot manage to inject into its heart that element of commitment that is so central to the intention. Desire precisely is no form of commitment to its own expression.

(C) But if $I\Phi$ causes $B\Phi$, and causes those $D\Phi$s that come to be only with $I\Phi$, and is itself caused by all other $D\Phi$s, then $I\Phi$ must be distinct from both $B\Phi$ and $D\Phi$; and *a fortiori* can be neither a 'loose' nor a 'fused' combination of both. And how in any case could intending be no more than believing action will happen and wanting to so act? A peculiarly helpless and fatalistic view of one's future projects!

(D) And that leaves D. Which, in any case, is in full accord with the aforementioned basic intuition that the intention is a condition of practical commitment. And why should not $I\Phi$ be irreducible? The mind teems with such irreducibles!

(5) *A few general traits.* Then what is the intention? It is a phenomenon that is distinct from both the occasioning desire and the originating technical beliefs (seeing they are its cause), from both the desire and the belief that are entailed by its very existence (seeing they are its effects), and from the

intentional act that may emerge from itself (seeing it may not happen). We know that it is neither a quality of nor way of doing the act, and that it can exist in the absence of the act. It is not a process, or an event, or an experience. So what is it?

It is an unanalysable psychological state that endures and that is directed towards the performance of an action. Concerning that act-object we may say: it cannot lie in the past and must at the very least have some part of itself set in the future; it must be given as of a certain kind; and it need never occur.

And we may say of the intention itself: it can lapse and be replaced by a rival intention; it is not an immutable entity that of a sudden ceases to exist as it finds expression, but undergoes transformation both prior to and during expression. After all, we do not by magic find ourselves at the right time and place for expressing an intention, but actively stage-manage matters towards that end; which implies that the intention acquires *further determinations* before expression, e.g. becoming the intention of 'doing Φ *over there*' and *in a moment*'; rather in the way the one persisting portrait may gain in detail as it progresses. More, during the course of expression the intention both *unwinds* and acquires *differential practical and temporal determinations* in so doing. Thus, a swimmer halfway between England and France no longer intends to swim from England to where he now is, but still has the intention of swimming from England to France and at this very moment has the intention of now swimming from where he now is to France. In sum, the intention before and during action is in a condition of flux. Though not itself a process, it is in perpetual and processive flux, like almost everything else in the mind. And – and this is something I should like to emphasise – the intention is always *time sensitive*. That is, the intention to do Φ always has the determination: intention to do Φ at time t (howsoever vague may be the specification of t). Necessarily.

(c) Intentions and the future

(1) Intentions intimately relate with the future. This is not just because life is a state which manifest its presence in directed processes, and hence something that is moving towards what as yet lies in the future. Rather is it because this movement in time is in the case of the mind *internalised*. 'We live life forwards, but only understand it backwards', wrote Kierkegaard;[1] and the forward movement to which he referred was that of desiring and

---

[1] *Concluding Unscientific Postscript*, translated by David F. Swenson, Princeton University Press, 1953.

striving towards the future and possible. For the most primitive expression of our animal status is to be found in that item which, in the course of the evolutionary process, determined the very existence of animality, and that necessarily is directed future-wards. Namely: intentional action.

But we know that action takes intentional and unintentional form, as well as forward-looking instrumental and merely local meaningless bodily form. Does not that suggest that the primitive expression of animal status lies, not in striving towards *future action*, but in striving merely towards *action*? It does not. For one thing, whatever is an action is intentional under *some* description. For another, action is as such *causally sensitive* to the intention. For action evolved as a device for spanning reaches of space-time with a view to overcoming need in a manner that utilised the store of information genetically and experientially embedded in the knowledge-system – and this can be achieved only through the good graces of the intention (operating in an instrumental context). Therefore the intentional and future-oriented instrumental action typifies the encompassing genus, action, as both unintentional and merely bodily senseless action do not. Indeed, the essential causal sensitivity of action to the intention must be the constitutive realisation of this developmental rationale of action. The primitive expression of our animal status must lie in our being driven into action – by a seeming awareness of lack – that is directed towards the overcoming of lack. That is, by an intention towards the possible and future.

Let me now express the matter a little differently. The most primitive and telling evidence, and hence also the most primitive and telling manifestation, in the most primitive of animals, of their animal status, lies in their *organised acts*: that is, acts wherein one sector of the deed links intelligibly via knowledge or information across a stretch of time with another. For example: not the idle waving of some insect leg; but the systematic pursuit of its prey. And such acts are future-oriented and instrumental. Therefore at the most fundamental level, animality, action, intention, are exclusively concerned with the future (albeit via the agency of the present).

(2) But I shall now complicate the picture. For we shall here see that, even though the future retains its position of pre-eminence, the past must be fitted into a fully comprehensive account of this situation.

Thus, with the advent of self-consciousness the situation alters. It was Freud's great achievement to demonstrate that our capacity to relate in desired manner to the future, which is to say to lead the life to which we aspire, depends to a significant degree upon the character of our relation

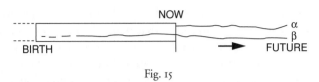

Fig. 15

to the past. In this respect his approach was in contrast with the existentialists, whose prime interest lay with the future. Since Freud's concern was not merely with the characteristics of an 'authentic existence', but at once causal, naturalistic, practical, he stressed one fundamental feature of the intentional behaviour of self-conscious beings. Namely: that it is not merely *towards*; not merely towards and *in fact* coming-from; but that it is internally and in any case avowedly *from-towards*. That is, the life of the self-conscious being is, so to say, painted upon a temporal canvas, one end stretching back to the womb, the other end moving into the unrealised future; and ideally consistency and integration characterise the structure *in toto*. Diagramatically, the characteristic fundamental human project is, not α, but β (Figure 15).

A simple example demonstrates this truth. Thus, midway through a sentence, I cannot be performing the intentional deed that engages me unless I have, not merely *some idea* of what I shall do *next*, but some idea also of what I have *just done*! (The same can be said of absolutely no act of a non-rational creature.) Then Freud brought to our notice the fact that, rather as an aeroplane may become disoriented through a malfunctional relation to the directional beam emanating from the aerodrome it has just left, so an 'inauthentic' relation to our past can obstruct our capacity to project and execute a future. In sum, with self-conscious creatures the past enters internally into the intention as it does not with the unself-conscious. This shows in the fact that we bring human intentional acts under *essential past-determined descriptions* which continue to apply *midway* through the act, say 'striving to swim from Dover to Calais', but never so characterise the intentional deeds of the non-rational (who never look back over their mental shoulder).

So here in (2) we have complicated the original thesis, that the intention is primarily concerned with the future. But I shall now in (3) by and large vindicate that claim.

(3) Thus, despite the essential link with the past in the intentions of the self-conscious, the intention is nonetheless before all else oriented futurewards. This fact can be brought to light if we consider the question: what is implicit, concerning past and future, in a present-tense attribution of an

intention? What are the *temporal implications* of 'He has the intention of doing Φ'?

I shall suppose the subject's awareness to be veridical, and so omit bizarre cases like that in which, delusively identified with Brutus, a man has an intention that he brings under the description, 'intention of stabbing Julius Caesar in the year 44 BC'. Then the first implication is that Φ is not in the past. And the second is that Φ can be in the future. This asymmetry already highlights the intention's link with the future. And the bond shows in another way. Thus, while it is true that the man swimming from Dover to Calais retains that intention even as he is midway through the act, the subordinate intention whose content gives the remainder of the intention yet to be expressed is exclusively directed *future-wards*. In sum: whenever there exists an intention, not merely can it not be towards what lies entirely in the past or present, not merely can it be towards what lies entirely in the future, and not only must it be towards what has a sector in the future, but the as yet unexpressed sector of the intention has to be *exclusively* directed towards an act-part whose beginning point is no earlier than the present.

But is it certain that an intention cannot be directed towards an act located entirely in the present? It is: the requirements are too extreme; for the act would need to be not just wholly spontaneous, but, at least in the experience of the agent, temporally extensionless. But I know of no act whose interior is non-processive: that is, an act which is not an activity. The only conceivable candidates must be acts which are structurally akin to the act of touching: that is, mere non-autonomous end-points of temporally extended activities like reaching. But there can be no such thing as an act of touching simply on its own.

(d) Intentions and predictions

Thus, the intention is before all else future-oriented; even though, because self-conscious creatures can envisage acts in temporal *extenso*, the act-object of the self-conscious can in part lie in the past. This capacity to range in thought temporally across an intentional act – the mind shuttling between a vanished past and a merely projected future – is one of the great advances made by the self-conscious over the unself-conscious condition. It makes for an entirely different order of purposive behaviour. It permits us to create active event edifices in which we plot time as we do space with objects. It allows for a (synthesised or assimiliated) history as well as a (merely lost) past. And in this sense it enables us to take possession of our past.

Then is the report of an intention a *prediction*? Well, what do I mean when, informing you of what I intend, I say, 'I will do Φ at time t'? But what do I mean when, speaking of someone else who we know intends doing Φ, I say, 'He will do Φ at t'? Well, do I mean anything different when, speaking of a somnambulist, I say, 'He will walk on the parapet tonight', than when I use the same sentence in speaking of an acrobat? Surely not. Yet surely I make a prediction in the case of the somnambulist; that is, make an assertion to the effect that the future will contain a certain event. And surely I make the same claim in the first and third person. So surely I likewise make a prediction when, speaking of an act Φ that I intend, I say, 'I will do Φ.' I mean: 'Φ-by-me will happen.' In short, usually when I intend, and let you know of the fact that I intend, I do so without mentioning the intention. I normally do so merely by predicting one of my own actions.

It follows that my utterance is rendered true, not by the existence of an *intention*, but by the occurrence of an *act*, viz. Φ. And you contradict my assertion, not by denying my intention, not by saying that 'You do not mean to do Φ', but by saying, 'You will not do Φ.' For to repeat: when I say, 'I will do Φ', speaking of an act that I intend, I do not say that I intend doing Φ, and do so only when I say: 'I mean to do Φ', 'I plan to do Φ', 'I intend doing Φ' (which are present-tense psychological reports and not predictions). Yet it is certain that, thanks to speech conventions, I normally imply that the Φ act that I am predicting is one that I intend, and so normally imply the present obtaining of a future-oriented internal state. That is why, when I say, 'I will punch him on the nose', it is entirely natural for you to say, 'You *will not*: I am sure you have *no intention* of laying a hand on him.' That is, deny my prediction and reject its unspoken pragmatic intention implication.

In sum: the intention use of 'I will do Φ' is a prediction, made true by an act, is not the report of a present intention, and pragmatically implies the existence of a present intention; while the report that 'I intend to do Φ' is not a prediction, and is made true by the presence of an intention state, for it reports the existence of that state.

(e) Intentions and explanation

(1) It is a fundamental fact about the intention that it is invoked *in explanation* of behaviour. For certain acts, say approaching a car or swimming in the Channel, can be made intelligible only by attributing an intention to the agent, e.g. to start the car, to swim from Dover to Calais. Then we here invoke an intention in order to explain an act, not in the light of a future

that *eventuates*, but of a future that is *projected* by the intention state. Such an explanatory function provides a lead to its very existence.

(2) This property of intentions helps explain why there are intentions. To bring this out, and grasp the type of explanation that the intention provides, consider two claims in which we at least seemingly explain the present via the future: 'The bee is moving in the direction of the flower because it is going to feed upon it', 'The dog is crossing the room because it is going to eat its meal.' How do these two explanations differ?

When we say: 'The bee is moving because . . .', we explain a present event by reference to an hypothetical future event; as we do when we say that 'The bird is building a nest because it will soon lay eggs.' Such utterances explain only if there exists a *natural regularity* linking events of this kind. And yet bearing in mind that we should hardly claim that 'It is winter because it will soon be spring', this hypothetical future event can explain the present only if there exists a *natural purpose* which is the rationale of the existence of events of the first kind. In short, we must be invoking a functional explanation. Thus, the future hypothetical event explains, not by implying hidden causal agencies, which are cause or effect of the present action and which would lead somehow regularly to the future act, but by demonstrating the contribution that the regular non-accidental conjunction of such events makes to something or other, e.g. functioning of wireless, perpetuation of species, flourishing of individual life. Then in this way it may provide a *lead* to the causal explanation of the occurrence of events like the first event. For example: the nature of a designer's intention, the workings of evolutionary selection, and such like. But it is not strictly required to be explicit on this further issue.

(3) What of 'The dog is crossing the room because it is going to eat its meal'? Here we mention one event, predict a second event, and explain the first event by predicting the second. But *how does* predicting the second event explain the first? This remark does not wear its explanatory heart upon its sleeve. Thus, it cannot explain *simpliciter*, as 'x caused y' *simpliciter* explains y, and it is in any case clear that the second predicted event cannot explain through being the cause of the first. Then can it be that 'It is going to eat its meal' describes an intention that causally explains the first event? While that takes us closer to the truth, it is still unacceptable; for it cannot at one and the same time be both a prediction and a description of an intention; and we know it is a prediction.

Now 'The dog is crossing because . . .' offers an entirely different kind of explanation from that given by 'The bee is crossing because . . .' For with the coming into being of the intention a *new type of explanation* comes upon the scene, and clearly the first of the above two explanations does its work with the assistance of the concept of the intention. Thus, if we call the present act Φ and and the future hypothetical act Φ', then the intention explanation has the following characteristics. Unlike the functional explanation invoked to explain the bee's movements, (i) there is no natural purpose in Φ-occurrence, for these explanations are in order when Φ has nothing to do with the functioning of anything; (ii) Φ acts have no regular effect or sequel, let alone the regular effect or sequel Φ'; (iii) Φ' acts have no regular cause or antecedent, let alone the regular cause or antecedent Φ. In short, the explanation would be unintelligible if there were no more to the situation than the factors thus far mentioned, viz. Φ, Φ', no regular connection between Φ and Φ', and no contribution made by Φ' to the perpetuation of anything. But there *is* more to the situation. Namely: an unmentioned but implied state that is endowed with certain essential causal powers, viz. the intention.

So how does the intention find its way into the explanation? Well, the statement, 'He does Φ because he will do Φ'', asserts something of the form: '(act x occurs) because (act y will occur)'. Thus, it explains the present by characterising the future, and makes no mention of the intention. Yet pragmatically it implies the existence of an intention state, I(Φ'). Then how does 'He does Φ because he will do Φ'' relate to 'He does Φ because he intends doing Φ''? Well, what do these two sentences say? It seems to me that the latter sentence states the cause of Φ; but that the cause has to be understood as intention-of-doing-Φ'-by-means-of-doing-Φ; so that the full statement that is likewise merely implicit but nonetheless understood runs as follows: 'He does Φ because he now intends doing Φ' in the future by the means of doing Φ in the present' (a formula that holds good for the self-conscious, while the formula for *all* creatures is: 'He does Φ because he now intends Φ' and Φ seems to him to be the way to do Φ''). Therefore, 'He does Φ because he will do Φ'' must be understood pragmatically to imply: there exists an intention state, directed towards Φ'-doing, directed towards present Φ-doing, causing this Φ act, suchwise that Φ falls under two descriptions, viz. 'Φ' 'striving to make Φ' possible'. In sum: the mere prediction of the act does not explain the present action; and the hypothetical future event explains only in so far as it pragmatically implies the existence in the present of a true causal agency pointed in its direction, viz. an intention with just such a content.

(4) One last comment. I contrasted the bee's situation with the dog's, assuming in the former, but not the latter, the existence of an

explanatory regularity, and supposing that a regularity links bees' moving-towards-flowers-they-have-descried (Φ) with eating food (Φ'). More precisely, we recognise that the 'because' of 'The bee is crossing because . . .' applies only if a regularity obtains, whereas the 'because' of 'The dog is crossing because . . .' can be applied in the absence of any such.

Yet this account of the 'because' of intentional action is a little deceptive, even though strictly correct. While no regularity need link Φ and Φ' acts generally, *these particular* Φ and Φ' acts can be brought under the descriptions 'striving to make Φ' possible' and 'Φ''' (respectively), which are such that *under these descriptions* the two acts have a tendency to accompany each other. Again, while intention-of-doing-Φ' states, $I(\Phi')$, have no general tendency to produce Φ acts, that same intention state also falls under '$I(\Phi'$ by $\Phi)$', *as it becomes fully determinate*, and under this description the causal agency, $I(\Phi')$, does show a tendency to generate both Φ and Φ'. Indeed, in suitable conditions, such as those of health and no impediment to Φ'-doing, such an $I(\Phi')$ can be linked closely with both Φ and Φ'. Thus, the intention explanation, which initially appeared entirely dissimilar from the functional explanation, for it seemed *completely particular* and implicitly to invoke the presence of a state that may never be repeated, turns out likewise to rest on a generality (cast in psychological terms). While the intention may be said to make possible a measure of individuality, in so far as it permits the expression of desires that need not be generic to the species, it yet remains a relatively primitive citizen of the mental realm. This shows in the aforementioned property.

(f) Causally defining the intention

(1) I described the intention as a 'psychologically irreducible state'. Then since a cerebral investigation cannot explain its having the character it has, how is this item both to harbour within itself and make felt elsewhere a distinctive nature of its own? It seems to me that the intention is a something that must to a large degree be determined by the psychological relations in which it stands; which is to say that these relations must all but necessitate its having the constitutively unanalysable character that it has. But *which* relations precisely? Miss G. E. M. Anscombe[2] characterised intentional actions as the class of actions to which the concept of the agent's reason has application. Now this is no doubt true of the acts of self-conscious beings; and the intention shares such origins with its expression act; yet since the unself-conscious can intend without having *their* reasons for so doing, and

[2] *Intention*, Oxford: Basil Blackwell, 1957.

since in any case the intention enters into other important relations, and because I think its *effects* are at least as revelatory of its nature as are its origins, I believe that if we are relationally to characterise it we shall need a wider set of relations than are given by the origins of the intention in self-conscious creatures. Indeed, I think the intention is best characterised via its *causal psychological relations generally.* With this in mind, let us ask what are the psychological causes and effects of the intention.

(2) The intention is *caused by* the causes of what it itself causes when it finds expression. Namely: it is caused by those of the causes of its active expression that, in the self-conscious, travel under the heading 'the agent's reasons for action'. For whatever were my reasons for doing intentional act Φ must have been the causes of my intending to do Φ. That is, the intention derives from act-desire and technical/prudential/etc. beliefs. This claim can be generalised to accommodate the acts of unself-conscious beings by replacing the latter clause by a wider a-rational formulation.

What of its *effects*? In the self-conscious the intention necessarily causes knowledge of itself – in whatever part of the mind; and together with this, belief in the impending occurrence of the intended Φ; and, when the desire to act is an higher-order desire that only comes to be with the intention, that desire also. Yet much more important is, not what it *actually* causes in the self-conscious, but what it *necessarily tends to cause* in all and any creature. That is: not the act itself, but striving to do it. If $D(\Phi')$ represents desire to do Φ', $S(\Phi')$ represents striving to do Φ', $K(I(\Phi'))$ represents knowledge of the intention, and if $B (\Phi \text{ to } \Phi')$ represents the technical belief that Φ-doing will suffice to ensure Φ'-doing, then the causal network that helps to define the intention may diagramatically be represented as in Fig. 16. Then to repeat: the most important of these are the origins, and the potential for causing striving. For these are universal amongst all animate beings.

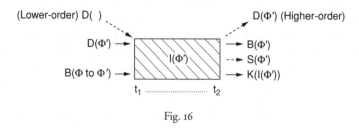

Fig. 16

But *how can* intentions cause striving? For do not an agent's reasons completely explain the act? And is it not certain that the intention is not one of those reasons? Well, clearly the intention is not a reason: for one's reasons consist in the factors which persuade one to the task through appealing to one's reason; and to intend *is* to be thus persuaded. Yet it is obvious that the intention causes intentional willing. And so a man's reasons cannot be *the* causes of the act. Instead, they are those causal factors that were efficacious through appealing to his reason. Thus, like the desire to do Φ, the intention of doing Φ is a something that is specifically apt for the generation of Φ – only in a different way. For the desire acts as a *force*, which finds its intentional expression when the supervisory agency of the intention concurs, while the intention acts as a controlling *supervisory agency*, that gives its consent to the expression of what wrested that consent from itself, and performs its appointed task when the judgement concurs. In sum, the intention is a higher-order mental (Ψ) state that is caused by what prove to be one's reasons for any striving in which it finds expression, and its causal power is neither of the consideration-type nor of the forcing-type, but of the supervisory-type.

(3) Indeed, reason could not play a determining causal role in action, such that the act can rate as rational, unless the intention state causally engaged in the generation of the act. But why so? Why could not one's reason be converted to the doing of the deed, say at t_1, and the motivating desire and the technical (etc.) beliefs generate the act, say at t_2, and the act count as rational despite the absence of an intervening intention state? But how under these circumstances would that rational event at t_1 causally engage with the striving at t_2? After all, desires and beliefs can non-rationally cause acts. In fact, the intention is a device whereby these latter two items can non-accidentally fuse as causal factors *in such a way that* the very fact that they *convert* one's reason is causally operative. Thus, it is not just that both desire and belief cause the act; it is that they work in causal consort because at the very time of acting they are converting one's judgement to the doing of the deed. That is, they are there and then continuing to bring about that practical commitment that *is* intending.

We can now offer a general characterisation of that irreducible psychological state, the intention, in terms that are provided by its causal properties. The intention is a psychological state, generated by desire and belief, causing knowledge of itself, belief in the occurrence of its object, and any higher-order desires to do that deed, and tending to cause striving at the appointed time. It is not a consideration appealing to the agent's rational side, but is of a supervisory higher-order nature, and endowed with the power of permitting reason to cause acts immediately through causing that – viz. the intention itself – which likewise causes the act immediately. Thus, it is like a catalyst in Chemistry, making possible a causal relation, but virtually disappearing from it. A match-maker that brings together: first reason, belief, desire; and then the deed. Finally, it is through the two-sided nature of the intention, product of the belief-system and judgement yet tending to generate a striving wherein the judgement is manifest, that the intention acquires its strangely mixed character: as *sense-giver of* / as *practical commitment towards*. A duality directly reflected in the ambiguity in 'mean'. For we should never lose sight of the fact that we both *mean to do* certain acts, and *mean something by or in* doing them.

(g) The ultimate rationale of the intention

(1) I asked: what is the intention? And answered: it is a psychologically irreducible *sui generis* psychological state. I then decided to psychologically characterise it, not by psychological anatomisation, which is an impossibility, but by psychologically anatomising its causal surrounds. Thus, we endeavour to cope with the question 'What is the intention?' through asking 'What is its causal role in the mind?', and that is to ask 'What is its office?', and that in turn asks 'Why is it there at all?' or 'What is the ultimate explanation of its existence?' or even 'Why did it evolve?' In a sense, there is no more to say if we are to elucidate its nature. Psychological analysis gives way to natural history. And we reconstruct natural history – rather as did Freud – through mapping contemporary causal dynamics in the mind (albeit in the course of *a priori* philosophical analysis)

Now while act-desires primarily concern the *mere doing* of a deed, the intention is primarily concerned with the doing of a deed *for-this and thus-wise and elsewhere and above all later*. Its simplest and most primitive manifestation is as follows. At $p_1 t_1$ creature C has need of material stuff α; and α will be present at $p_2 t_2$ and α-ingestion requires Φ-doing; and later at t_2 C is to be found at p_2 Φ-doing; and a significant non-accidental link relates C's needs at $p_1 t_1$ and C's actions at $p_2 t_2$. That link is the presence of a temporally continuous intervening mutating intention state.

(2) The intention is akin to a catalyst-like state-device that has the express function of permitting instantaneously responsive *information systems* to bear upon the practical problems of meeting a machine's needs. The evolutionary shift from merely vital to animate necessitated the development of a phenomenon equipped with just such causal properties. Then this

infinitely enlarges the repertoire of successful need-fulfilling measures, and does so through utilising genetically acquired, past-experience-acquired, and present-experience-acquired knowledge: that is, innate knowledge, memory knowledge, and perceptual knowledge. (And in very primitive creatures like insects, perhaps through precursors of these phenomena.) It is an inner 'set' supervening upon the causal interaction of representation of seeming lack and the deliverances of relevant sectors of the knowledge system, such that at some particular time and place, possibly here-and-now and any-old-how, but characteristically *elsewhere and later and thus-wise*, a phenomenon *will happen* that stands some kind of chance of redressing the lack. This state is essentially geared to present and future and is causally sensitive to the past, and this is so because the event it is designed to bring into being is determined by the knowledge and understanding, and, when the creature is rational, by the reason of the animal agent. Indeed, this state might be said pragmatically to justify the very existence of the animal's awareness of spatio-temporal positioning, and thus of the rational animal's awareness of space and time themselves. That is, I think it may properly be claimed of the intention that its close links with *elsewhere*, and above all with *later*, lie at the bottom of the presence in animals and therefore in explicit form in man of an awareness of space and above all of time. More, the intention state justifies and explains the very existence of the animal's knowledge and memory and perceptual systems: in short, consciousness itself! For if the only acts we performed were purely stranded in the here and now, which is to say acts like unawares tongue-movings, then from the point of view of behaviour we would be no superior to plants or amoebas.

(h) Intentional action as the rationale of action and consciousness

Let us by 'function' mean 'natural purpose', and by 'natural purpose' mean 'playing that role which is such as to contribute towards that of which it is an element best realising its nature as of the type it is'. Then we must suppose that it is the common function of all that is part of an organism first and foremost to *perpetuate and promote its life*. Now since the superiority of the animal condition over all other vital forms lies precisely in the animal's capacity to bring the contents of its perceptions, and any other cognitive or innate capacities, to the task of meeting its vital needs, and since this is uniquely accomplished in intentional action, the specific function of animality must be to bring *intentional action* into being. This phenomenon has life-enhancing virtues which determined animality's appearing in the evolutionary stream. It follows that intentional action must provide the rationale for the existence of action itself. In short, since animality exists to make intentional willing possible, willing must exist to make intentional willing possible.

Thus, while desire and will are the originating force and mental thrust that are mental representatives of the organism's having-need and response-to-need, the intentional action must be responsible for having-need and response-to-need finding such *mental representation*. Therefore both the (active) genus of which the intentional action is a species, and the very forces (of desire) which bring them into being, in the final analysis owe their being to the item they encompass and engender, viz. intentional action. From the point of view of evolution, which is a point of view that lays bare the *natural hierarchy of primary vital functions*, we may say that it is only because such a life-enhancing phenomenon as intentional action came to be that desire and will came to be: that is, their 'selection' reveals their roles in nature. Now since desire and will have predecessors in the evolutionary process, viz. having-of-need (e.g. of water in a plant) and response-to-need (e.g. osmosis in its roots), from which they evolved as ontologically higher representatives, and since they are themselves of primary importance to the phenomenon of life, will and desire must in this sense count as psychological representatives of life itself. But the intention, by contrast, must be the representative of that which singles animality out in evolution, inasmuch as it is the source of the capacity to put an information map of a sector of the world at the service of fulfilling these vital drives.

Therefore while the will provides the rationale for the *existence* of animality, since intentional will is that for which animality exists, the capacity for knowledge and awareness must be what at bottom *distinguishes* animality from all else in creation. This is because it is the differentia of the novel species of item that is responsible for the development out of the stream of life of the very genus that encompasses that species, viz. the genus will. That is, knowledge/information-using is the distinguishing mark of that species of willing that provides the rationale whereby desire and will emerged out of need and response, viz. intentional willing. To be sure, consciousness is originally 'a servant of willing',[3] as is evident when one remembers the limited range of knowings we may attribute to primitive examples of animality; yet it is because it is a servant of *knowledge*-using willing that consciousness counts as *the* great novelty in the world's history

---

[3] See Arthur Schopenhauer, *The World as Will and Representation*, I, Book 2, #18, translated by E. F. J. Payne, New York: Dover, 1969.

that is ushered into being with the appearance of animality. This emerged in the distinction, which I earlier drew in chapter 14, between ψ and Ψ: a distinction such that knowledge and perception counted as Ψ, while bodily action and purely bodily originated need states like thirst and hunger were lodged in the more primitive and a-conceptual domain of $\psi \sim \Psi$.

Then this is how we come to the conclusion that, while intentional action is a mere sub-category of action, it not only is the most significant and characteristic sub-category, it actually provides the rationale for the very existence of that of which it is a sub-category. Analogously, the brain is but one organ in the body, yet it is not only the most significant and even essential organ, it actually provides the rationale for the existence of that of which it is a mere organ part, viz. the animal body. And the analogy is no accident. For the body exists so that a willing might exist that utilises certain central powers of the brain part of that body, viz. for knowledge and awareness, i.e. in intentional action.

Thus, it is not just a *necessary condition* of an event's being actively done that events of that kind should be susceptible to the causal influence of the intention. This functions as the *decisive test* of action (as Wittgenstein pointed out). That is, not that the act *be* the expression of the powers of intentional self-determination, but that it *can* be. That is, that it be the type of item which it *makes sense* to ask someone to do. That is, do choosingly. That is, intentionally as a result of deliberation. And so here again we find that the intention is located at the very heart of action. It is not just that, as Donald Davidson observed, whatever is an action is intentional under *some* description. More important still is the fact that the causal sensitivity to the intention is the decisive test of being an action. In any case intentional action lies at the heart of action in that it provides the rationale for action itself.

(i) What makes the intentional act intentional?

(1) Then if the intention exists in order to make possible intentional action, how does it accomplish this task? What makes the intentional action intentional?

Certainly not the mere *temporal conjunction of an act and an intention with matching content.* For if I intend to kill Smith at p_1t_1, and by chance kill him at p_1t_1, my killing of him rates as unintentional. Nor even the occurrence both of an intention, an act of matching content, and an immediate causal relation between the two. Thus: I intend killing Smith, shoot at him and miss, but cause an avalanche that kills him; yet my act of killing was unintentional. More is obviously needed than the above. And it must be such as to make success non-accidental.

What more? The following provides a clue. A champion can rationally intend and a novice irrationally intend to hit the bull's-eye on a dart board; but while they both can succeed in doing what they tried and intended doing, only the champion's act counts as an intentional hitting of the target. Why so? At first glance the reason seems to be that the champion possesses, but the novice lacks, the power to do what he tried to do. Is this acceptable?

(2) But a difficulty arises which causes me to modify this claim. Thus, if a skilful sniper kills a man, then no doubt he both meant to kill him (i.e. intended such an act), meant to do that act (i.e. intended that very act), and therefore killed on purpose (i.e. performed an intentional killing). However, the above act is intentional even if he succeeds only 90 per cent of the time at such a distance, and so cannot do so *at will.* Therefore the type of power that needs to be exercised in intentional action need not be such that one can at will perform such a deed. Yet bearing in mind that the successes of a terrible shot must be written off as flukes, some sort of power must be exercised. What is the way out of this difficulty?

I suggest the following rule. The power exercised in intentional action must be such that the content of the causative intention was significantly causally contributory to the success of his trying: that is, that the intention was *to do* Φ so relates to Φ-*doing.* Now when the content is thus significantly contributory but not an *absolutely sufficient* condition, so that he cannot do the deed at will, then I think we must be dealing with a law that links trying and success in optimum display conditions, not categorically, but *statistically significantly.* Namely: given the presence of optimum display conditions, then try Φ→Φ (x per cent of the time). This is the sort of power that we attribute to a good – though not perfect – darts player; for when he hits the bull, as per intention, this was neither a choice nor a fluke; for both Lady Luck, and his powers, each played their non-negligible part in his success. Then are there degrees of intentional behaviour? There are not; but the class of intentional acts must have vague edges; for we characterise acts as intentional only when the power that found intentional expression was of non-negligible extent. That is, when the power made a causally significant contribution to the success of trying. That is, when it was no fluke. And the class of flukes, like that of bald men, has vague edges.

(3) Let me now try to state the main necessary conditions of an act's being intentional.

We have seen that an intentional act must be the exercise of a power that is significantly contributory to the success of trying. Then must one know of the power that finds expression in the act? By no means. And irrespective of whether it be a general power, like the power to swim, or a particular power, like the following. Thus, I approach and intend to try to open a window which is unlatched but which I think latched; and try to open it, and do, and intentionally. Then in that case I had the power to open the window, I utilised that power, and therefore intentionally performed the act that utilised that power, despite my ignorance of its existence. Now this example has the added merit of demonstrating that to perform an intentional Φ-doing one need not have an intention to do, but one must at least harbour an intention of *trying to do* Φ.

And the intention must find expression in the deed. But what is the expression of an intention? Not just an act that it causes; nor even an immediate psychological effect of itself, seeing that it non-expressively and immediately causes knowledge of itself. Rather, it must be the *unique act which the intention can immediately cause*, viz. striving to do the Φ act that is the object of the intention. Then how does this concept, expression of an intention, relate to the aforementioned concept, utilisation of a power? I think as follows. If a man has a power P that is either to do Φ or (say) do Φ 90 per cent of the time, then there must exist standard conditions C for the expression of that power; and anyone with P who in C tries to do Φ must do an act that has a 90 per cent chance of being a Φ act; and it is when success obtains in such circumstances that the power has been put to use. Now we know that tryings to do Φ can flukily manage to be Φ acts, and whenever this happens such a Φ cannot be the expression of a power to do Φ. It follows that the utilisation of a power P to do Φ must be those expressions of an intention of trying to do Φ that are both Φ acts *and* Φ acts for the reason that they are exemplifications of a law that applies to the agent. That law is: (in C) (trying to $\Phi \rightarrow \Phi$) (with either categorical (100 per cent) or merely statistical (say, 90 per cent) force).

(4) I shall now assemble a sufficient set of necessary conditions of intentional Φ-doing. Thus:

  (i) An intention of doing Φ or of trying to do Φ
 (ii) must immediately cause
(iii) a trying to do Φ
 (iv) that succeeds
  (v) and that is expressive of a power to do Φ,
 (vi) a power that is at least expressible in a statistical law-like claim that involves a non-negligible percentage figure.

That is, an intentional trying must have occurred that was the successful utilisation of a non-negligible statistically given power. And we may add the following rider: that the aforementioned negligibility appears *pari passu* with the property of flukiness; so that if it was not a fluke that the sniper killed his quarry then it was an intentional act of killing.

(5) In sum. He intentionally Φ-ed $\equiv$ An intentional trying to do Φ occurred that was the successful utilisation of a non-negligible statistically given power to do Φ; which is to say, that an intention of acting or trying immediately caused a striving that was successful through being the exemplification of a statistical law, where the probability is non-negligible and might even be of value 1. This is how the intention fulfils its appointed role of making an act intentional.

CHAPTER 18

The antecedents of action (2): from intending to trying

or

The mental mechanics of willing

I. THE LOGICO-NOMIC RELATION BETWEEN INTENDING AND TRYING

(1) It is time to discuss the relation that holds between intending and the phenomenon towards which it is directed: the event of trying. It is my contention that a law exists which governs this relation. Since the law relates two psychological phenomena, I shall dub it a *psycho-psycho law*, to be contrasted with *psycho-physical law*, examples of which are the laws relating (say) sensations with their bodily causes. The law in question is to the effect that an entailment *and* causal bond relates occurrent knowledge that the indexically singled out instant of that knowledge is the instant at which one intends acting, and an event of trying. That is, knowing of some 'now' instant that 'now I intend to act' both entails and generates trying to act.

This is not to say that knowledge of present intention is the 'trigger' of intentional willing, let alone that it supplants the intention as causal agency. Rather, it is to be understood to claim that the occurrence of both phenomena entails and is a causally sufficient condition of willing. While it seems to me that it is not possible for one to be intentionally acting and ignorant of one's present intention, or for an intention to have as object an act whose time is given as 'now' in the absence of knowledge of that intention, it is possible that these claims may be contested. It is for this reason that I have chosen to express the law in the above form, viz. that knowing of some 'now' instant that 'now I intend to act' both entails and generates trying to act.

One point of major significance. This is a law which is at once logical *and* causal. Thus, it claims that the conjunction of an intention state and knowledge that its time object is an indexically singled out 'now' instant, is both a causally sufficient condition *and* logically sufficient condition of the movement of the will. That is, not merely *must* one logically necessarily will if one knows that the time singled out as the time object of the governing intention is the instant 'now', one wills *because* one knows this fact. One *would not will* did one not know that the governing and mutating intention state has at a certain instant as its time-object the instant singled out as 'now'. Whenever we will we intentionally will, and whenever we intentionally will we know that the time of willing is one and the same as the indexically singled out instant of the governing intention. This truth is at once logical and causal.

(2) Certain putative entailments fail to go through. For example: if I intend to perform act Φ' at t', and now it is t', it is not entailed that at t' I try to perform Φ'; for it is not entailed that I know I *now* intend to do Φ'. After all, the intention may slip my mind, I might forget about it, or else I may simply misidentify the time. Again, if at instant t'' I know I now intend to perform Φ'', it is not entailed that at t'' I try to perform Φ''; for 'now' can be a 'fat now', say a whole week, whereas t'' is a mere sliver of an instant. Then what is the position if 'now' is an *instant*? Must one who knows at an instant that he then at that instant intends acting be striving at that instant? Does an entailment hold here? Or does some third possibility lie between a last instant flagging of resolution and the entailment? Does that precious ingredient of the universe, self-determination, lurk in so slight a crevice? I do not think so.

The proper formulation of the entailment-law is as follows. If I know *of* an instant that is currently indexically singled out as 'now' and *at* that instant that it is the intended time of a presently intended action Φ, then necessarily that instant is one in which a striving-to-Φ is occurring. How general is the application of this law? Does it link *all* intentional strivings and knowledge? Or does it merely link those self-conscious strivings that are the product of there-and-then decisions? Here (below) in (3), prior to attempting to demonstrate the entailment-law, I shall consider whether the law is to be understood as restricted in the above manner.

(3) The first thing to note is, that the law as formulated above *re-describes* a psychological state whose essential psychological description is, 'It seemed to me that the present instant was an instant at which I intended Φ-doing', as 'I realised that the present instant was an instant at which I intended Φ-doing.' Therefore it is only under an inessential re-description that the entailment-law holds. Yet this qualification does not seem to blunt its force.

Now we know that actions exist that give expression neither to a there-and-then nor to a prior decision. For example: high-speed actions like jumping out of the way of a bus give expression to no decision. But these actions, being purposive in character, must be intentional actions. Then the law must be understood to apply to them, for it is said to have universal application in the domain of intentional action. Therefore it must govern not merely those acts of which it could be said that 'he decided at that moment to . . .' or 'he had already decided to . . .' or 'he was never in any doubt that . . .', but the entire gamut of acts that are intentional under some description or other. But that in effect is to say that the law must be understood to apply to all actions.

Let us take a closer look at its temporal content. Thus, about absolutely any action I would like to press the following question: *Can an act be intended but its time not?* Now intentional acts can support qualitative predicates that are not intended. For example: I can run intentionally, and intentionally I can be running quickly, and yet simultaneously unintentionally be running comically. Then can the property of occurring *at the instant at which it did occur* be of the latter type? Of course it can be unintended that it occur at, say, 12.00 a.m.; but can its occurring at a time we pick out merely as 'the instant at which it occurred' be unintended? How to find out? Well, what is a test of the unintendedness of a property of an activity? Three factors indicate unintendedness: the lack of an act-desire for the property; the lack of such an intention; and ignorance-of or surprise-on-discovering-that it obtains. Since we are attempting to detect the first two items, the third test must be employed. Thus if I unintentionally run comically, it is clear that I could be ignorant of, and so surprised to discover, that my running was comical, whereas I could hardly relate thus either to my intended running or to its intended speed. Then could I relate in this way to the *time* of intended action? Could I say: 'I did not expect the act at that precise moment'? or: 'I expected it a couple of seconds later'? or: 'I had no precise expectation as to when it should occur'? or: 'I was surprised to discover that it happened at the moment it did'? Surely not, one wishes to say. For how could I be surprised to discover that it happened *when it did* without simultaneously being surprised that it happened *at all*; that is, without in effect deleting the property of being intentional under some description? So, at any rate, one is inclined to say.

But here we must tread a little carefully. Now there can be no doubt that the vast majority of our intentional acts are such that we could not relate to them in this way. Yet this fact is apt to conceal the real issue. For on occasion we do relate so. Thus, I intend making a deeply embarrassing declaration to someone in the next few moments and *find myself embarking on it* a second or so in advance of the chosen time! Then am I not in respect of time as much a spectator of my deed as its recipient? Does not intentional willing leap in ahead of temporal knowing? The interest in this example lies in the fact that, even though choice of time is the norm, here the norm lapses. If I genuinely *found* myself speaking, then I cannot have *selected* that instant for the expression of my intention. However, the act was yet intentional, and therefore must at the time of action have been intended for that time, and therefore at the time of action must have been intended-'now'. Immediately before intending-'now' I intended-'very-soon' and I did not know that I was going to act in that next instant, nor did I know that I was going then to intend-'now'. This means that the intention, which persisted as a state ever since I decided to 'speak my mind', lost one temporal determination and acquired in its place a temporal determination in which that intention was indexically directed to the very 'now' at which that change occurred. Why not? Then *surprise* here reigns over the time of one's intentional action. For one knew in advance of the deed but not of its time. So – immediately prior to the deed – one does not know the temporal determination of the intention that finds expression. *But one does in the very first instant of willing!* And that is what is relevant in the present discussion. For what we are seeking is a case in which action is intended and time not, and what we have been offered instead is a case in which action is intended and chosen, and precise temporal determination intended and not chosen. This is the interest of the example. But it provides no reason for thinking that a 'blur' in time determination in an intention can persist *even into the midst of willing!* It reminds us that it can get to the very gates of willing. But it can get no further. And that is my claim.

Thus, intentional striving must give expression to an intention state whose full description at each instant of its life must involve reference to the segment of the striving phenomenon that is there and then contemporaneous with that segment of the mutating intention state. Therefore provided we bring the seeming-to-one-that-one-intends-at-that-instant-to-act-then state under the description, 'realising-at-that-instant-that-one-intends-to-act-then', the entailment-law looks to have *completely universal* application to the intentional behaviour of self-conscious beings. It is not to be restricted to those cases in which we decide on an instant to initiate action there and then.

(4) Let me express the above in different terms. The claim in question might be expressed in two ways: 'You cannot catch the will by surprise' *and* 'The will cannot surprise you.'

The first claim amounts to the following: that the intention and knowledge of the intention cannot reach the appointed time, be present at the starting line for action, and find the will not there. Alternatively, one cannot so to say tiptoe up to oneself, peer over one's shoulder, and find the will 'dozing' – at the 'starting line'. It is simply not possible that the will should fail to obey such directives as the intention delivers. What is the alternative situation? Might the will simply fail one? Could there be loss of the power to will? But the will is not an act-power, seeing that act-powers are such that willing leads through the use of that power to some desired event, and we do not will to will. While one has the power to will, and can lose that power in certain conditions, the supposition here is that the state obtaining is one in which genuine willing and real intending are open to one.

The second claim amounts to the following. It affirms that the will cannot be acting at a time one does not mean it to be acting. While it can act at a time one *did not think it would* act, which means that it might act at a time one *does not think it will* act, it cannot act at a time one does not intend and believe it to be acting. Thus, it is false to suppose that knowledge of present willing might be caused by present willing but not by present intending-now to will.

A third way of characterising the situation is as follows. Consider the principle propounded by Donald Davidson to the effect that anything that is an action is intentional under some description or other. Then despite the fact that intending and willing are distinct existences, are two and distinct phenomena, the first being cause of the second, this principle is a logically necessary truth. Thus, whenever there is an action, there exists a sort of logical shadow that is inextricably wedded to it, viz. an intention. Then at the time of action what are the temporal properties of this necessarily present intention? Might it be causally active from some earlier time – in a sort of temporal action at a distance? Surely not. Alternatively, might its temporal object lag behind that of the willing it governs? Or be vague? Again, surely not. In short, the intention necessitated by the action must be contemporaneous with the willing, and must take as its temporal object the indexically singled out 'now' that applies to the willing. The mutating intention and the unfolding willing keep strict time with each other.

2. PROVING THE ENTAILMENT-LAW

(1) The reader may protest that I have yet to demonstrate the entailment that I have just now proceeded to generalise, viz. one

linking knowing-of-present-instant-t′-correctly-indexically-singled-out-as-'now'-that-one-intends-acting-at-that-t′ and striving.

Those who resist the entailment must suppose that I can know of an instant that it is an instant in which I intend Φ – without striving to Φ. Then why, according to them, do I *not* strive? Bearing in mind that any reasons for not striving must be reasons for intending not to strive, and that this possibility has been discounted, the most natural answer should be: God alone knows why! Then it follows that God alone must know why I do strive when I do! Thus, when I do (or do not) strive, it is to be presumed that something that is neither intending, nor desiring, nor reasons for acting or intending or striving, must be such as to get the will on the move (or restrain it); for all of these factors obtained when, as this account would have it, I knew of an instant that I intended then acting and yet failed to strive.

Then what can that something be? It is salutary to recall the 'get-out' clauses that may be invoked when, the cards being stacked overwhelmingly in favour of action at some instant, action nonetheless fails to eventuate. The following list seems exhaustive: changing one's mind, forgetting one's intention, being prevented, one's body failing to obey one, fear, terror; as well as the following rather more mysterious 'get-outs': nerve failure, paralysis of the will, anxiety. Now it is apparent that most of these are inapplicable in the case under consideration. For example: those factors which explain why any striving-to-do-Φ failed to realise Φ-*ing* (for the entailment is to strive-Φ and not to Φ); as well as those that are either a form of or else a cause of *lapsing of the intention* (for the entailment is from knowing one intends). Accordingly, the viable set must be some part of the following list: fear, terror, anxiety, nerve failure, paralysis of the will. What else could get between knowingly-intending-this-instant and striving?

The question to be answered is this. Are there any items in the above list which are such that, while not interfering with the case as set up, might yet prevent striving? What about 'failure of nerve'? But 'failure of nerve' must either be an incapacity successfully to act (out of an unnerving factor) or else the actual losing of the intention, and both possibilities are irrelevant to the claim. What of fear or terror? But to be smitten with these emotions on the very eve of action, presumably for reasons of the kind of imminent danger, is to be struck by considerations which, in moving one to fear or terror, tend to destroy resolution: that is, tend to erase the intention. Thus, such strong inhibiting emotions must prevent striving through deleting the main factor on the left hand side of the entailment-law, viz. the intention.

(2) All that remains of the original list is this: paralysis of the will, and anxiety. Now what is 'paralysis of the will'? Is it a condition that can explain, not a loss of one's intention, not a momentary forgetting of the intention, not the failure of one's striving, but an absence of striving when conditions are otherwise optimum? Then we have absolutely no reason for believing in its existence. After all, what would be a *gross example* of such 'paralysis'? What would be a report of that extremity? 'For five minutes I knew that I intended trying to open the front door at each instant of that interval, and my mind was fresh and clear, but for some reason my unshakeably determined resolve had no effect on my will!' No 'blackout', no forgetfulness, no feeling that one 'just cannot go through with it', no loss of determined resolve . . .! I can make neither head nor tail of such a report. Then note: that this unintelligible situation is in all probability no more than a prolonged example of the kind of situation, perhaps enduring for a mere instant, that those who reject the entailment-law must be prepared to endorse. I suggest they are taking advantage of the epistemological 'bad light' that obtains when we attempt to scrutinise the phenomenal contents of an instant!

(3) The last option open to those who deny the entailment-law must be to turn to the final member of the list: that very special phenomenon – anxiety. A word about the phenomenon itself. We know that it is a member of a large and unpleasant familty: anxiety, dread, horror, terror, nausea, fear, disgust . . ., which looks to break up into three irreducible groups: fear (which encompasses terror, horror . . .); anxiety (which, as we shall see, also encompasses sub-varieties of itself); and nausea, disgust . . . Then the varieties of anxiety are the following. It can be object-directed (e.g. about an exam), or object-less ('free-floating'); and object-directed anxiety can be on-account-of-something (e.g. in case the exam paper is very difficult) or not on-account-of-something (e.g. somehow the mere thought of it makes me seize up). Then bearing in mind that this attack of anxiety must wreak its effects, not on the intention, but so to say on the will itself, the only affective condition which seems to stand a chance of meeting the necessary requirements is either object-less free-floating anxiety or object-directed anxiety that is not on-account-of-anything.

What does anxiety do to people? Characteristically, it is an inhibitor. (Though in small doses a spur.) For the basic tendency of anxiety is to make the spirit contract in a kind of frozen cramp. In anxiety we experience a threat to the centre of our self, a threat emanating from the unknown, from the possible, most importantly from the future; and over and above all else, at the sense of helplessness in the face of the need to rely upon nothing but – oneself! when one is thus faced by unknown future demands which may threaten the self at its centre. One, so to say, reaches for a prop and finds – nothing! – but the self that is thus reaching! The affective condition consequent upon this vertiginous experience *is* anxiety. This is its content. Anxiety is, in the final analysis, an affective condition prompted by the awareness that, faced with elemental demands upon the self, there is nothing one can rely upon but oneself. For, despite the resources of character, the sustenance the self can ultimately give to the self is, in a sense, zero. There simply are no props of the kind required. Then as we quail before that unknown, the unknown future in inner and outer reality, anxiety tends to cause abandonment of projects. That is, of *intentions*.

In short, an overwhelming attack of object-less or unrationalised object-directed anxiety, will almost certainly interfere with the case as set up. Such gross anxiety would tend to destroy one's intentions – without the media-tion of *considerations*. This is its especial interest in the present discussion. But I see no reason for supposing that this unusual phenomenon can act directly and without mediation on the will itself! Almost certainly it strikes at the will through striking at desire and thus at intention. I conclude: it cannot meet the impossible demand that those who would deny the entailment-law make of it. Nor, it seems, can anything else.

3. OMNIPOTENT SELF-DETERMINATION

(1) Those who deny the entailment-law must suppose that, when I do not in such optimum circumstances strive, 'God alone knows why' I do not and therefore why I do when I do. Something besides desire, intention, knowledge, reason, must it is assumed goad the will into movement when it moves. What? Since the phenomenon under consideration is the will itself, only one answer seems to be left. Me! That is, this theory must suppose that however much I may have decided to act, it is always in the final analysis up to me yet to make up my mind as I approach the instant of action. In short, I must at that final moment put all my reasons for willing behind me: I must at that point actually transcend them. More precisely still: one *really* acts for *no* reasons; and what we call 'my reasons' can be no more than incentives upon which the will leaps as a diver propels himself from a springboard. Thus, at heart every act turns out to be a Gide-ean

acte gratuit! And so we find ourselves impelled under the influence of this theory to ask misconceived questions like: which was the agency, me *or* my reasons? Whereas the truth of the matter is that the agency was me *and* my reasons. That is, me; that is, my reasons! What is this 'me' otherwise?

(2) Thinking of the contentious entailment-law, the following thought comes to mind. If I tried to perform an intentional action, I must have intended to exercise my will. After all, does not intentional willing necessarily express an intention? Then must not all intentional willing owe its existence in this pellucid manner to a governing intention? So what need of an intermediary agency? What need of 'me' as interloper? Why not an entailment-law?

Immediately, this seems to deflate the law to nothing. And the truth is that the law is both of great importance and also nothing to write home about. It is important in that it disproves what might be termed *the thesis of omnipotence*; and by that I have in mind the pernicious idea that true self-determination must be answerable to *nothing* (as if people were like a Saul Steinberg figure that is engaged in drawing itself)![1] And it is of moment secondly because it intelligibly links present action with the preceding cogitational procedures that culminated in the crystallisation of decision. Yet it is at the same time a triviality in that it is circular.

To repeat: its significance resides in the fact that it holds up the mirror to the processes occurring in a mind that engages in willing. *For this is how action takes place* and how it preserves its crucial link with the past. For with the assistance of the entailment-law, the act emerges translucently from the intention, and characteristically that same intention was at an earlier moment formed through deciding, and persisted until the act. And as we have just noted, there can be no mystery about how the intention leads into the action. For if at some instant t′ there occurs the realisation that that instant is a 'now' at which one intends to begin acting, then inevitably that instant is one in which the will is *beginning to move*. Necessarily, their time is one and the same. (Think how people begin to wheel around *as* they remember they have forgotten something.)

And yet it is natural to think that something more needs to be interposed between intending and trying if the act is to be one's own: something one might term 'a leap of the will'. But that creates a gap that could never be closed. It is a false account of self-determination. Certainly, as the setting for action comes into view, intentions require supplementation by additional

---

[1] A coat of arms for the existentialists!

determinations *cast in the ostensive mode*: for example, as I round the corner the intention to get *an* apple becomes an intention of getting *that* apple in the bowl before me in this very instant. But that is *all* that is needed if the will is to move. And yet it is natural for action thus determined to seem automatic. For it seems to locate the originating forces outside the self and within the intention. Thus, we find ourselves in the ridiculous position of playing off a person and his intentions one against the other! We stand in serious need of a dialectical synthesis: of the self as self-determining, and as determined by reason; and of the self as self-determining in the present, and of self-determining the present in the past. Being people, we are vehicles of reason and of our past reasonings.

Now I suggest that this seeming automatism amounts to no more than this: that in the instant in which actual time and intended-act-time are seen to coincide *there is nothing left for one to do but act.* Small wonder, for their time is one; and the great error is to postulate a temporal gap, as if to allow space for some unmotivated mental mid-air leap. Yet it is a parody of this account to suppose that in that instant of realisation one has lost the power of choice; for that is precisely what one is exercising. We are here running our head up against nothing but – commitment! Therefore we are seriously misled if we take that supposed automatism to signify, if only in the least degree, that the act was taken out of our hands; for example, if we make of the mind an alien force that precipitated us into action. It was self-determination. Therefore in deciding to act (and so forming an intention) and thereafter abiding by that intention, oneself determines (through *mental agreement* but through no further *willing*) what in a knowledge-context entails movement of the will. All one need do to ensure action, provided the world suitably co-operates, is knowingly to abide by one's intention until the chosen instant. Action inevitably ensues.[2]

The process whereby one's intentions acquire further ostensively given determinations can readily come to an end. All that is then required, if the will is to move, is the occurrent knowledge that a certain present instant is the time of intended action. And so the transition from intention to will is entirely pellucid. Indeed, what else but intention could get the intentional will on the move? A self-determination that is modelled on the miracle?

---

[2] In this I find myself in disagreement with none other than Franz Kafka, amongst whose aphorisms occurs the following daunting thought: 'It is conceivable that Alexander the Great, in spite of the martial successes of his early days, in spite of the excellent army that he had trained, in spite of the power he felt within him to change the world, might have remained standing on the bank of the Hellespont and never crossed it; and not out of fear, not out of indecision, not out of infirmity of will, but because of the mere weight of his own body.' 'Reflections on Sin', in *The Great Wall of China and Other Pieces*, aphorism 36, London: Martin Secker, 1933.

That is, intervention as an outsider in the interior mental mechanics of one's own actions, breaking free from one's own desires and values? (From nature itself!) But this would be to conceive of self-determination as akin to the whims of a Deity responsible to nothing. Shakespeare, in depicting the sickness of omnipotence, was presumably thinking of this problem when he had Caesar say (concerning intended action): 'The cause is in my will: I will not come. That is enough to satisfy the senate.'[3] For this fantastically supposes the explanation of intended action to lie in the motion of the will, understood as an explanatory ultimate. But that would banish intelligibility from all action!

4. A DIALECTICALLY ENRICHED ACCOUNT OF SELF-DETERMINATION

(1) As the problem is not, 'Which was the agency: me *or* my reasons?' – the truth being that it was 'me *and* my reasons', i.e. 'me, i.e. my reasons' – so it is with the other misconceived oppositions. Thus: not, 'Which was the agency: me in present *or* me in past?', the truth being that it was 'me in present *and* in past', i.e. 'me, in present *and* in past'. It is clear that we need an enlarged conception of the self: as embodied, to be sure; but also as endowed with reason, as moved by desire, as extending internally into the past, as occupying space . . . For there is a tendency to think of the self as a pure particular, devoid of body, internalised history, reason, desire; all of which are construed as alien items impinging from without upon this isolated and featureless entity.

This is profoundly confused. The life of man stretches from remote past towards projected future, and like a narrative involves intelligible relations across time, through space, between mind and body, from reason to desire . . . Thus, we enlarge our picture of man from a point consciousness in such a manner as to permit a non-alienating causal efficacy within him on the part of his past, reason, body . . . Recognising that an internalised history is of the essence of self-conscious consciousness, we do not *oppose* a man at one time to himself at another time, just as we do not consider that the thoughts and guilts that well up from his past are the thoughts and guilts of another. Man, who is something more than a point consciousness, must put something *behind him*: the fruits of time and nature; and in this sense be able to rely upon achievements, health, knowledge, desire, reason, body – that is, upon *himself*! For if anxiety is the affective consequence of an

---

[3] *Julius Caesar*, Act II, Scene ii.

awareness of the fact that *in extremis* one has nothing to rely upon but a self that cannot function as a prop, this is not to suppose that one has *nothing* to rely upon; that is, that the self upon which one thus insubstantially depends is – *nothing*!

(2) Yet this misconceived account of self-determination is not pure error. For it might, with a little indulgence, be seen as a confused but still insightful way of drawing attention to two particular modes in which the past (and reason, and body, etc.) can scale us down to size. The first mode being pernicious, the second beneficial. Let us take the past as a case in point.

First, there are ways of relating to the past that are 'in bad faith'. Thus, a man can relate to his previous decisions as to the decrees of an authority he dare not question. Thereby he places his present self in subjection, as to a destiny, to a tyrannical past self. This is a loss of freedom – akin to the compulsions of the obsessional – and rationality. For the 'authentic' and rational relation to one's past decisions is, that they are perpetually open to review. Not like the clay that will never set, yet not such that one's past is understood to have constructed iron railroads down which one is destined to travel, but something in between. In short, something between uncertainty and fate, viz. *commitment*. In this respect man's past is perpetually renewed, in an act of loyalty across time, in each instant. Thankfully, something real inhabits the vast terrain separating the omnipotent point consciousness (a God without a kingdom!) from the rigid and impotently fated being (a pawn at the mercy of the World): the first being the manic, the second the depressive, posture. That something is the actual, more or less rational, by and large committed, human animal.

The second insight buried in the distorted omnipotent theory of self-determination is this. When this account characterises reason and the past (etc.) as alienations, it may perhaps with a little charity be said to be to this extent insightful: that it is precisely because of our servitude to these items that we fall short of omnipotence. They are the carriers of our finitude. For it is because we are beings with such determinations as rational, and embodied, and historical, that we are finite. Thus, we saw in chapter 1 that we are not free to choose our beliefs, that rationality of belief entails submission to reality, and therefore to evidence and so also to the past; and we know that a man depends upon his body as he does upon the very ground upon which he walks; etc. Therefore if falling short of infinitude were a form of alienation, then reason, the past, the body, should count as alienating factors. But because no condition of 'authenticity' or rationality is possible in their absence, they do not. Since rationality is a potentiality of our being, but infinitude not, the latter characterisation must be the true one. That is, a falling short of infinitude cannot be a falling short of a potentiality. Infinitude is not an unrealised potential. At best it is an inaccessible ideal.

(3) Let us return to the determination of action. We saw how natural it was to feel that, if knowing one this instant intends Φ-ing entails Φ-striving this instant, then the *will* can have nothing to do with the generation of the surface body phenomenon φ: that whatever the striving may be, it cannot an exercising of the *will*! For it can seem as if the knowing and the intending together take the whole matter *out of one's hands*. That is, if desires, beliefs, intendings, knowings, jointly entail striving; and if the self considered as pure particular – and therefore without the mediation of its reasonings, its desires, its internalised history – contributes nothing towards Φ; does it not seem that *willing* cannot have occurred? For do not we ourselves seem to have been short-circuited out of this picture?

Thus, our fantastic conception of action is of a psychological event, emanating neither from one's reason nor from one's desires nor from one's past, but from the self *simpliciter*! Rather as one may dream of a seeing of objects that is mediated neither by the object's sides nor surface, nor by the light it reflects, nor the sensations it causes in us the viewers: an unimaginably immediate perception: a kind of metaphysical X-ray that cuts through to the object in one blow! So we tend to operate with too narrow a conception, not merely of self-determination in action, but of *action itself* ! We suppose that genuinely to self-determine, even genuinely to act, one must either actively choose the causal antecedents of action *or else* break free of and go beyond those we would normally term 'operative'. We see these as exhaustive alternatives, and opt for the latter. Thus, we imagine that we manipulate ourselves, conceived of as a mental point, into action. This is the mental mid-air leap. The *acte gratuit*. So *all* action is free action, and all free action of the type of the *acte gratuit*! Thus far the theory.

(4) When self-determination occurs the self opts for certain ends. And inasmuch as it is up to the subject at each instant whether to abide by his earlier decisions, those decisions are at each instant perpetually renewed; not in the manner of an omnipotent deity; but in the way that is open to a rational and committed free agent. Then each of these several elements of the actual situation of self-determination finds distorted representation in the extreme and unacceptable theory we have been considering.

5. THE DIALECTICS OF DESIRE

(1) The dialectic that resolves the problem must show that man, like a narrative, internally stretches *in extenso* across time; for after all his 'past self' and 'present self' are one, viz. his self. And it must show that man as such encapsulates *reason*, the power to be swayed by rational relations like evidence; so that man can self-determine when his rational past decisions determine his present deeds. And it must show that his nature, seeing that man is most truly himself when expressing his powers, is a *desiring* nature; so that he self-determines in acting out of desires that derive from his past reasonings. In short, it must show how he is not in his innermost self a thing devoid of reason, history, desire, body: that is, a featureless point consciousness.

Then since it is man as agent that is our specific concern, we must briefly describe the dialectics of desire. Thus, recognising that desire is a mental force that acts on the self, and noting that the self and its desires are *two*, we tend to think of the causal situation as adequately represented in the model: Desire → Self → Act: O → O → O. Accordingly, it is natural to suppose that the self merely *suffers* its desires and the resultant movement of the mind. And yet we know that willing is a something that is such that its happening *in* one is never its happening *to* one. We know that this property reveals the innermost essence of the phenomenon. Hence we come to assume that the peculiarities of *action*, and most especially of freely chosen or *self-determining* action, can be realised only when the self is set in motion, not by something apart from itself like desire, but by nothing but its very self. Omnipotent self-determination, no less!

(2) Thus, desire is understood as a force, acting as it were from behind, compelling one to go in whichever direction it selects, a something before which one yields as a leaf does to the breeze. In short, to desire is to suffer from one's desires!

But the truth is that desire is object-taking, and acts upon one because the thought of that object *attracts*. Therefore while desire is not the self, it springs into being, unlike the wind that scatters the leaves, through appeal to and in concordance with other endowments of the self. Therefore while some desires are alienating, such as a desire for heroin, while some are sense-less compulsions, such as a desire to circumambulate lamp posts, desire characteristically is what Freud called 'ego-syntonic'. Characteristically, what one desires to do appears as in the self's interests. Indeed, this mental force that bears down upon the self characteristically does so *through* seeming in the self's interests; and, unlike the wind that stirs the leaves, does not originate without the precints of that upon which it acts. Were desire to relate to action as gale to scattering leaves, action would indeed be alienating, a phenomenon with which we could in no way identify. Therefore while it is true, it yet misleads, to say of act-desire that it is a force that bears down upon the self and tends to cause action. It is better expressed thus. Desire is a force, whose origins lie in the animal mind, whether in its reason or values or instincts, that tends of its nature to generate an attracted striving towards the making good of a lack of which the self feelingly seems aware; all of this occurring in an entity whose very nature is such that, being of necessity perpetually aware of such hiatuses and incompletenesses, it is in a perpetual condition of being thus attracted towards what feelingly it seems lacking in.

How unlike the *compulsive desire and act*! How infinitely unlike the *compelling wind and scattered leaves*!

The tendency to oppose self-determination and desire-determination comes in this way from misconceiving the desire force on the model of a physical thrust from behind. And it is aided and abetted by the misconceived view of the self as a featureless point consciousness. The true account is reached when, setting out the distinctive peculiarities of the desire force, as well as those of the self object, we see that the self is as such a desiring self and desire characteristically ego-syntonic. This restores the proper perspective.

CHAPTER 19

The antecedents of action (3): from will to action

or

Transcending the mind-body divide

We saw in chapter 18 that a logical relation links an indexical knowledge of some present 'now' that this is the instant in which one intends acting, and an event of striving. Here we have the first element in a bridge-like structure, in which the act-generative mental machinery operative in bodily action leads to a bodily event (ϕ) that is actively 'done'. In the present chapter I hope to demonstrate that this logico-causal link can be supplemented by two further logico-causal elements of comparable strength and transparency, thereby completing the transition from inner world to outer. My aim is to trace a rigorous and wholly rationalised path leading from mind to body, in this way to close the intelligibility gap, and to do so through appeal to the concept of the bodily will. Only through this phenomenon, it seems to me, can we fully understand how the animal mind can be united with its body. Here alone is openly visible the fact that each half of that elemental divide essentially posits the other.

I. THE SECOND LOGICO-CAUSAL LAW: THE LAW LINKING THE WILL WITH ITS BODILY GOAL

(a) The causal situation in the case of affect and sensation

(1) The relation I shall be examining here in section 1 is that between bodily striving and the bodily event ϕ – usually a movement – that is actively 'done'. Clearly this relation is something more than that between a directed psychological event and its object-content. After all, the event of bodily willing is endowed with a causal power which is an essential property, for bodily willing is of necessity the *causal explanation* of any bodily event ϕ that is actively 'done'. Then to better understand the special character of those causal properties, it helps to compare them with those of two other psychological phenomena which like the bodily will stand in close causal relation with the body: affect and the sensation. The causal relations with

the body of these two phenomena differ, both from one another and from those of the bodily will, whether we are speaking of origins or of effects.

The looser of the two relations is that between affective phenomenon and bodily manifestation: say, between embarrassment and blushing. Contingency characterises this relation in several respects. It is not just that embarrassment need never have caused blushing, and that blushing might have any number of causes and none affective; the relation between affect and manifestation can never be more than loosely regular. These phenomena could not relate as do (say) the phenomena described by purely physical law: for example, in the rigorous manner in which the pressure within a gas relates with its volume. This physical relation has in common with the affective psycho-physical causal relation both that it is contingent and discovered empirically, but is of a wholly different order in that it is governed by a tight categorical law which is such that in requisite conditions one event (e.g. contraction) is *necessitated* by the occurrence of some other event (e.g. impressed force). And a comparable necessitation is found when (say) the statistical radioactive laws find application in standard conditions. Moreover, even though physical laws are contingently true, it is an *a priori* necessity that the physical domain is governed by law. By contrast, it is an *a priori* necessity that affective states *cannot* stand in nomic relation with their bodily manifestations. The psycho-physical causal properties of affective phenomena are of a radically different order from those of purely physical nature. Necessarily, they can be no more than loosely regular.

(2) Consider how the sensation causally relates with the body. One might at first suppose that this relation is no closer than that between (say) embarrassment and blushing. And this is (more or less) true if we are thinking of effects (although the relation tends to be tighter). However, it is far from true in the case of origins. Here the situation is significantly different from the affective situation. First on the count of nomicity, second in so far as the mode of discovery of the existence of nomicity is concerned.

I begin with *nomicity*. The science of anaesthetics reminds us that sensations have regular bodily causes, indeed that type-type psycho-physical law governs their occurrence. It seems that we are not prepared for the possibility of (say) a novel sensation cropping up whose bodily cause is completely irregular: we would not rest content with this state of affairs, and would I suggest follow a procedural rule whereby we continued searching for a regular bodily concomitant. Such a procedure would be tantamount to a search for an explanation of this phenomenon. For what else could count as an explanation? And must not this novel sensation have a – purely physical – cause? In short, categorical laws link sensations with their origin. Thus, the relation of the sensation to the body is of a wholly different order from the affective relation.

Meanwhile, so far as the *mode of discovery* of nomicity is concerned, here too there is a significant divergence from the affective situation. Even though it is an empirical question what the cause of a sensation might be, it is an *a priori* necessity that its occurrence is governed by psycho-physical law. By contrast, while it characterises affect generally that it tends to express itself in a distinctive manner in the body, seeing that almost all affect has a distinctive physiognomy, there is no telling in advance – let alone knowing *a priori* – whether or not those manifestative effects will take a relatively regular form; after all, anger and many other emotions tend to express themseves differently in different societies, eras, sexes, age groups, social classes. In sum, whereas the sensation is nomically linked to its bodily origin, and is known *a priori* to be so, neither property holds in the case of affect. In these respects the sensation is much more closely tied to the body than is affect.

(b) The causal situation in the case of the bodily will (A): considerations of nature

(1) We noted earlier that the relation between bodily willing to ϕ-make and the desired bodily event ϕ must be more than that between directed psychological event and its object-content, since bodily willing is endowed with psycho-physical causal power to effect some bodily event that is actively 'done'. This is a requirement of *nature*. Bodily willing could not be itself without this property, and the existence of this power is known *a priori*. As was the case with the sensation, it is not through empirical inquiry that we know that the above relation is nomic in character. But more, uniquely in the case of the bodily will we are apprised *a priori* of the actual power of the event of willing, a power which we know *a priori* to be expressible in categorical law. For it is an *a priori* truth that in certain given conditions bodily willing to ϕ-make must lead to its goal event ϕ. In sum, the difference with sensation is as follows. In the case of the sensation we know *a priori* that it relates according to categorical psycho-physical law with its bodily origin, but know only *a posteriori* what that origin is. But in the case of the bodily will we know both of the existence-of and the specific content-of categorical law linking it with its effects, and in either case do so *a priori*. All that is contingent in the case of the bodily will is the particular motor-path

through which the 'willed' event ϕ comes into existence as a result of the event of willing.

(2) What kind of a necessitation or 'must' are we concerned with here? Plainly, it is a causal 'must', since we here relate one event and some other non-identical event which owes its existence to the first. And yet it is a 'causal must' with a difference. The following considerations make that clear.

The bodily will possesses the power to engender some desired bodily event (ϕ), and this is part of its nature or *essence*. That essence is not discovered in the way (say) the essence of water (viz. H_2O) was discovered. The essence of water was discovered through setting this item in a wider theoretical context, and managing by such means to explain a myriad of causal properties: it was discovered *a posteriori* thanks to the achievements of an entire empirical discipline. But the power of the bodily will to engender a given bodily event (ϕ), which is an essential property of the phenomenon, is part of its *a priori*-given essence. Taken together, these facts imply that this relation is at once causal and logical. And since it is a categorical rather than statistical law, there must exist a statement in which is expressed the fact that in specifiable conditions its causal product is categorically necessitated. Then being a statement of an *a priori*-given essential property, that necessitation must be at once logical and causal.

What are those conditions? There exists in humans a bodily motor-system whereby (say) a decision to now 'do' some ϕ event normally leads via a regularly used pathway to the event ϕ such that we would say of ϕ that it was actively 'done'. It follows that one standing condition of the law linking bodily willing and its goal event must be that the motor-system be intact, a property we could sum up under 'motor-health'. However, this alone does not suffice if we are to arrive at a statement of those conditions, seeing that extra-systemic influences can be brought to bear upon the functioning of the motor-system in such a way as to prevent the system from functioning. Accordingly, we add a clause that rules out interference in function, and I do so under 'liberty to function' or 'liberty'. We arrive at the following rule. In a situation of motor-health and liberty, the event of bodily willing entails the occurrence of the desired event ϕ. Let us call this 'the Entailment-Claim'.

(c) The causal situation in the case of the bodily will (B): act-mechanistic considerations

(1) There is a second, closely related, argument through which we may demonstrate the existence of the logico-causal relation holding between

the psychological event of willing to ϕ-make and the purely bodily event ϕ. This argument seeks through a different avenue to demonstrate the claim that, in situations of motor-health and liberty, striving to ϕ-make (SΦ) both causally explains and entails the occurrence of ϕ.

The argument reiterates the considerations advanced in chapter 12 section 11 (A3) under 'The argument from mechanism contra the sandwich theory of the bodily will'. Since the argument makes free use of the concept of mechanism, a word here about the motor-mechanism of bodily action. This consists in a physical state such that when bodily striving Sϕ occurs, a causally and temporally ordered sequence of bodily events ϕ_1-ϕ_2-ϕ_3- . . . is set in motion which normally culminates in the desired event ϕ. The inherence of the capacity for bodily willing in a subject necessitates the inherence of just such a physical state. While it may be that there can be more than one mechanistic pathway linking SΦ and ϕ, if bodily willing can occur in some being there must exist at least one such set: ϕ_1-ϕ_2-ϕ_3- . . . ϕ. Accordingly, we may assume that when a subject engages in physical action there occurs the phenomenon of mechanistic activation, Ma, which in motor-health and liberty develops causally and temporally as far as the desired event ϕ along a 'non-deviant' path.

(2) Then the second ('mechanist') argument in favour of the Entailment-Claim begins by asserting that, in a situation of liberty, the conjunction of a striving to ϕ-make and the non-occurrence of ϕ is a complex phenomenon whose explanation lies of necessity in a breakdown in the functioning of the motor-mechanism (M) which stems from a flaw in M. This assertion implies that we would not countenance the possibility that SΦ might occur in conjunction with absence of mechanistic activation (Ma). More, it implies that we understand $\sim$ (SΦ & $\sim$ Ma) to be the statement of a law. That is, it is taken to be a law that $\Box$ (SΦ $\rightarrow$ Ma): a condition-free law which is such that SΦ cannot occur without the occurrence of a phenomenon (viz. Ma) which is such that in liberty and motor-health the phenomenon in question instantiates a temporally and causally ordered sequence ϕ_1-ϕ_2-ϕ_3- . . . which culminates in the desired goal event ϕ.

This law might at first be understood to be no more than a causal law, comparable in character to a claim like the assertion that (say) doubling the pressure brought to bear upon a given body of gas in conditions C1 never occurs without the volume of that gas being halved. That is, that given the first event (SΦ), we would no more be prepared for the absence of the second event (Ma) than (say) assuming that we are given the application of a blowtorch to a block of ice, we would be prepared for absence of change of state in the ice.

(3) But then we note a difference – which emerges when we ask the question: on what grounds do we deny the possibility of SΦ and ~Ma? For it seems that one's certainty on this issue runs ahead of any empirical data. And how comes it that this supposed law is free of conditions? Whence its supposed universality? For are not most causal laws conditional upon context? These questions suggest that the law may be something more than merely causal. Even though the occurrence of Ma when SΦ occurs is causally to be explained by the occurrence of that SΦ, it may be that it is governed by a causal law with a difference. In any case, this is what this present argument is seeking to prove.

The argument first of all makes the assumption that when (in liberty) SΦ is encountered in conjunction with ~ φ, it is *standard procedure* to look for a flaw in the motor-mechanism if we are to explain that conjunction. And this is patently true. However, the argument then puts a contentious interpretation upon this procedure – which it distinguishes from a procedure like (say) looking for a hidden energy source when a gas in conditions C1 fails to contract. The suggestion is that the procedure whereby we inspect M in search of a flaw is not based upon empirical discovery, is nonethelesss not unthinking, and is a 'deliverance' of the Understanding. It supposes the procedure to be grounded upon our grasp of the concept of action.

Now the necessity of 'non-deviant' causal pathways, in the case of perception and bodily action, is a generally agreed philosophical truth. It is a truth whose foundation lies in the concepts involved – as the truth (say) that the progression of time is non-processive in character is founded upon what we understand by the terms 'time' and 'process'. (The passing of (say) an hour not being an event or incident – of one hour's duration!) Similarly the concepts of perception and action sustain the claim that 'non-deviancy' of causal determination is a necessary condition of the instantiation of the types involved. The fundamental and indeed essential links with knowledge-determination and intention-expression, demand non-accidental activation of standard causal pathways. This is a philosophical truth, and entitles us *a priori* to speak of perceptual/motor *apparatuses*. The procedure whereby we seek to explain SΦ & ~ φ (in liberty) in a flaw in the motor-mechanism, is thus interpreted, not as the product of empirical knowledge, but as meeting the demands of intelligibility. It is a Regulative Principle.

(4) To continue with the argument. Let us assume that Ma is the activation of a motor-mechanism for the bodily act of φ-making. Then the aforementioned requirement of non-deviancy necessitates, not merely that SΦ → Ma, but that □ (SΦ → Ma), for how could the existence of a reliable

non-deviant link between $S\Phi$ and ϕ be a reality if *sometimes* $S\Phi$ & Ma and *sometimes* $S\Phi$ & $\sim$ Ma? Now the phenomenon of striving ($S\Phi$) to do a basic bodily act Φ of ϕ-making can be a reality only if the phenomenon Φ can be a reality. Meanwhile we know that there can be spurious examples of $S\Phi$: say, the seeming-$S\Phi$s of dreams; and that these are adjudged spurious through failing one of the tests whereby we deem an event a bodily striving – in this latter case through the causal properties of the event. Amongst those tests are to be found the regularities which determine the causal power of a prospective $S\Phi$. And this is what is relevant here. For if *per impossibile* it were the case that *sometimes* $S\Phi$ & Ma and *sometimes* $S\Phi$ & $\sim$ Ma, then Φ would not be a reality, nor therefore would $S\Phi$, nor again would $S\Phi$ & $\sim$ Ma.

Thus, it seems that we do not have *truth-conditions* for $S\Phi$ & $\sim$ Ma. And this is a much stronger claim than the corresponding merely causal claim in which we say that we lack physical causal conditions for $S\Phi$ & $\sim$ Ma. It follows that it must be a logical necessity that $S\Phi \rightarrow$ Ma. (This explains the absence of conditions for the application of the law.) It follows also that in a situation of motor-health and liberty, the occurrence of $S\Phi$ entails the occurrence of ϕ – the Entailment-Claim.

2. THE THIRD LOGICO-CAUSAL LAW: THE LAW LINKING WILL AND ACTION

This third logico-causal law, which I shall call the Identity-Claim, takes the following form. The event of striving to ϕ-make ($S\Phi$) – by which I mean the attempt to perform the act we represent by Φ – is on the occasions of success identical with the striven-for act (Φ). I offer below two sets of arguments in support of this claim: (A) and (B).

(a) The argument from mechanism (A)

(1) The first argument (A) is in effect a continuation of the discussion in section 1 (above). I suggested there an interpretation of the procedure followed when, in a situation of liberty (L), we encounter $S\Phi$ and $\sim\phi$. It is not merely that we do not contemplate the possibility that $S\Phi$ occur in the absence of activation (Ma) of the motor-mechanism. This possibility is discounted, not just as a causal impossibility, but as a possibility for which there are no truth-conditions. I suggested that it is a Regulative Principle that we seek the explanation of the conjunction of $S\Phi$ and $\sim\phi$ (in liberty) in a flaw in the motor-mechanism. The grounds of this claim

being that the requirement of non-deviancy in the determination of the ϕ that occurs when Φ, are inconsistent with an irregular relation between SΦ and Ma.

(2) The present argument (A) for the Identity-Claim sets out from the above. The assumption now being that since there are no truth-conditions for SΦ and $\sim$Ma, since *a priori* we do not allow the possibility of SΦ and $\sim$Ma, SΦ must *entail* Ma. That is, SΦ entails activation of the motor-mechanism. The question then arises: what interpretation are we to give of this entailment? Why should it be that bodily striving, in any conditions whatsoever, whether of motor-health or its absence, of liberty or of constraint, be inconceivable without activation of the mechanism for the occurrence of the peripheral goal-phenomenon ϕ? Why should SΦ be *inconceivable* without mechanism M being activated *some* distance (or other) towards the goal-event? Could it be that we are in the presence here of a logically necessary causal nexus between distinct temporally adjacent events?

It sheds light on this problem to consider the following question. By what criteria do we determine whether some event is part of the mechanistic activation-phenomenon? Now we saw that in normal conditions of Liberty (L) and Health (H) the event SΦ must of necessity be co-present with ϕ_1-ϕ_2-ϕ_3- . . . until ϕ. Then how do we identify a member of this set ϕ_1-ϕ_2-ϕ_3- . . .? What informs us that some event is part of that ordered sequence? Well, we know that Ma must in L and H so develop as to involve the occurrence of the entire sequence. And we know that every event-member of that sequence must in L and H lead to the terminal event ϕ. Accordingly, if an event is invariably co-present with Ma, and if it leads to ϕ in L and H, and if in addition it would not have occurred without Ma, it must be *part of* M-activation. But, now, SΦ itself meets these requirements. For if SΦ never occurs without Ma, indeed if we lack truth-conditions for such a conjunction, SΦ must normally be regularly co-present with the entire motor-sequence ϕ_1-ϕ_2-ϕ_3- . . . ϕ. Then why should not SΦ be one or more of ϕ_1-ϕ_2-ϕ_3- . . . ϕ? It may be replied: because SΦ *causes* Ma. But how do we know it does? To which the following answer may be given: because Ma would not have occurred without SΦ occurring. But Ma would not have occurred without Ma. So why should not SΦ be at least part of the M-activation syndrome?

(3) In short, why distinguish SΦ and at least part of the earlier sector of M-activation? But *which* earlier part? No principle exists whereby we may

single out one particular sector of ϕ_1-ϕ_2-ϕ_3- . . . and bring it under the heading 'SΦ', and exclude the remainder of ϕ_1-ϕ_2-ϕ_3- . . . I conclude that SΦ and ϕ_1-ϕ_2-ϕ_3- . . . must be one and the same phenomenon, and therefore that when Ma leads to the remainder of the normal sequence ϕ_1-ϕ_2-ϕ_3- . . . all the way as far as ϕ, this sequence likewise is identical with SΦ. But what more is needed for the occurrence of an act Φ than that the desired event ϕ should non-deviantly occur as a result of SΦ? Therefore Φ must have occurred on this latter occasion. Then since it is truistic that ϕ is part of Φ – the visibility of Φ being realisable at least through the visibility of ϕ – it seems certain that on normal occasions of success, when Ma proceeds non-deviantly to lead to ϕ, SΦ = Φ = ϕ_1-ϕ_2-ϕ_3- . . . ϕ.

(b) The argument from act-types (B)

(1) There are other routes leading to the conclusion that on occasions of success SΦ = Φ. The route (B) which I now follow turns upon an examination of the varieties of bodily action. I discuss the three act-types: instrumental, constitutive, and basic. This classification is exhaustive.

I begin by considering instrumental actions. Far and away the most convincing account of this phenomenon is that an act is instrumental if it is of the kind it is (e.g. door-opening) because it causes via a reliable 'power-line' a distinct event (e.g. the opening of a door) which confers its name ('door-opening') upon the deed. If giving a kick to a door causes the door to open, and would do so regularly, then an act has occurred which is at once a kicking *and* a door-opening. Usage and its concepts follow this rule in singling out and so characterising this act, and we stipulatively deem the act of door opening an 'instrumental act'.

What is it to try to perform an 'instrumental action'? It is to perform an act out of a desire and belief that it might cause some distinct event ϕ'. For example, if one believes that giving a kick to a door might cause the door to open, and gives the door a kick out of that desire and belief, then one performs an act of trying to open a door. And one does so, whether or not the attempt succeeds. Let us now suppose that this instrumental attempt is successful, that the kick causes the door to open, and an instrumental act of door-opening occurs. In what did the instrumental act consist? Plainly, in the act of giving a kick. Meanwhile the event of trying to open the door is also here identical with the act of kicking, for it is *one's way of trying* to do so. In short, the act of trying and the instrumental deed are here one and the same event. Such an account of the situation holds for all instrumental actions, no matter how simple or complex, no matter whether physical or mental. It follows that in the case of instrumental actions *as such*, the successful attempt is one and the same event as the act one succeeds in doing. Thus, the rule that on occasions of success act and attempt are identical holds at the very least of almost all the actions which interest us.

(2) What am I proposing to call a 'constitutive act'? It is an act of bringing about an event within a motor-sequence ϕ_1-ϕ_2-ϕ_3- . . ., which is accomplished by performing or trying to perform the basic act whose motor-mechanism involves the aforementioned ϕ_1-ϕ_2-ϕ_3- . . . . But why believe there *is* such an action? It is because one can at will immediately bring about (say) the contraction of one's biceps: we can obey an order to effect biceps-contraction, and do so intentionally: we merely move the arm. Then since the contraction is not caused by the act, this act cannot be instrumental. And it cannot be a basic act either, since the event the act is the bringing about of is not the goal-event of the motor-sequence. Let us call this third variety of action 'constitutive'.

One way of *bringing about* muscle-contraction is by moving one's arm. And one way of *trying* to bring about muscle-contraction is by moving one's arm. This coinciding of means towards an end in these two cases is because, if we are concerned with 'basic actions', all that one can choose immediately to do is move the limb, and it is this power which I use when – knowing I will succeed – I try to effect muscle-contraction. For normally I cannot try to move my arm *without* moving my arm: I cannot normally try to Φ *in opposition* to Φ-ing. In short, normally I try to do the constitutive deed of muscle-contracting by Φ-ing. Now let us assume that this attempt is successful, and that the muscle contracts. In what did the act of muscle-contracting consist? Surely in the act of arm-moving. For are we to suppose that more than one act occurs on this occasion? Only one act occurs when I instrumentally act: for example, merely by performing the single act of rapidly moving my leg I perform an act which falls under multiple instrumental act-descriptions (e.g. opening a door / making a noise / moving my shadow / etc.). And surely the same principle holds in the case of constitutives. For are we to suppose that a *whole act* of muscle-contracting lies *buried within* the act of arm-moving? More, are we to believe that a *vast myriad* of non-identical *whole-event actions* lie buried within the action whenever one moves an arm? But surely the will moves but once on such occasions, just as was the case in the instrumental situation. And surely only one act-generative force-system, dedicated to the performing of but one act, determined willing on this occasion.

If that is true, then the successful act of trying to produce muscle-contraction *was* the act of moving the arm. Meanwhile the act of muscle-contracting *was* the act of moving the arm. Accordingly, the successful act of trying to produce muscle-contraction *was* the act of muscle-contracting. And this account holds of all constitutive actions. Thus, the rule that on occasions of success the successful attempt is the succeeded-in-doing deed holds of constitutives as such. This argument is less decisive than the argument for instrumentals – which is plainly demonstrative. The reason is that it depends upon one's refusal to locate multiple whole act-events within basic actions in the way proposed – the justification of which is not demonstrative. And yet is it at all plausible to suppose that when we are moving our limbs a vast number of act-events – of *non-identical* and *non-distinct* active 'doings' – all of which are *autonomous whole events* – are taking place? One will have no awareness of any of these supposed act-individuals. Nor will any trying to do any of them have occurred. Nor desire to do any of them. Etc. Etc.

I merely skate over the difficult case of basic actions, and refer the reader to the arguments marshalled at length in chapter 12. But the fact that the Identity-Claim is demonstrably true of instrumentals, and pretty plainly true of constitutives, is strong evidence that it is true of action as such. It seems likely that *general considerations* determine this Identity-Claim, and the fact that it holds demonstrably of instrumentals is evidence that it is universally true.

3. BRIDGING THE MIND-BODY GAP

I now set out the summary situation. The first logico-causal law was that a logico-causal bond links knowing one 'now' intends to either Φ or try to Φ, and an event of $S\Phi$-ing. The second logico-causal law ('the Entailment-Claim') was that $S\Phi$ in conditions of motor-health (H) and liberty (L) entails and is causally responsible for the occurrence of the desired goal-event ϕ. A third logico-causal entailment ('the Identity Claim') may now be added. Namely, that on occasions of success $S\Phi$ and Φ are the same event, and that both are identical with ϕ_1-ϕ_2-ϕ_3- . . . ϕ. Therefore in the normal conditions of L & H a transparent logico-causal entailment links knowing that one 'now' intends Φ-ing/trying-to-Φ with the bodily act Φ: more, links that initiating interior event and an event which is at once $S\Phi$

and Φ. This bodily act-event which flows with logical-causal transparency from the internal event is given to the acting subject both psychologically-immediately as SΦ *and* perceptually-mediately as Φ – necessarily in the proprioceptive mode (and possibly in other sensory modalities). Then since the bodily act Φ necessarily incorporates the purely physical bodily event φ, the inner life of the mind must in the phenomenon of bodily action flow with logical transparency into the merely outer world of the body.

CHAPTER 20

The 'mental pineal gland'

I. RÉSUMÉ: TWO LAWS

(1) My aim in Part IV of this work is to characterise the psychological antecedents of bodily action in such a way as to solve the causal mind-to-body problem for physical action, and simultaneously to demonstrate the essential interdependence of mind and body. Thus far I have traced the inner-to-outer causal thread: from practical ruminative procedure to crystallisation of factual decision, from factual decision to practical decision and therefore to onset of intention, from onset of intention to intending-to-now-this-instant-act, from intending-to-now-this-instant-act to knowing that one does. Then at this point I encountered an unconditional psycho-psycho law, a law at once causal and logical, linking knowing-one-intends-to-now-this-instant-act with a now-this-instant-striving. And since the time of intentional action can no more be unintended than can the phenomenon we intentionally will, this causal entailment-law must have application in all cases of intentional action. (For intentions are as such *time-sensitive*.)

Thus, we pellucidly linked the (early) chosen procedures of practical cogitation with the (late) phenomenon of striving. What remained if we were to bridge the active mind-to-body gap? We required a transparent account of the connection between striving to do an act of ϕ-making and the ϕ event that is needed if that striving is to count as successful.

(2) When a man raises his arm, two non-identical non-distinct events more or less simultaneously occur: one active and psychological, a striving event, the other a purely physical event of a kind that might instead have been caused by a mere shove, an arm-rise event. How are these two events related? Well, why did the arm rise? No doubt it rose because his motor-system is intact. Yet that merely cites a causally necessary but insufficient *state* condition for an arm-raising act. The *event* explanation of arm rise

598

is that he tried to raise the arm. This event explains the non-identical non-distinct all-but-simultaneous act-neutral event, arm rise. These two overlapping events are linked by an explanatory connection, from try Φ to ϕ: a nomic connection which, like that relating knowing-now-intending with striving, is at once causal and logical.

The law takes this form. Given a human body with a normal motor-system in a context which at that moment permits arm rise and does not interfere with the working of the system, trying to raise an arm is a logically sufficient condition of arm rise. And let us not suppose, because of the odd qualification of 'given a body with a normal motor-system', that these conditions are *outré* and exceptional; on the contrary, that precisely characterises their absence. For without actually being the cause of arm rise – since bodily trying relates *causally developmentally* with the non-distinct willed bodily event – trying in normal physiological circumstances in settings of physical liberty both fully explains and is a logically sufficient condition of arm rise. And all this happens in all cases of arm-raising. In sum: a psychological event, of ontological status $\psi \sim \Psi$, deriving pellucidly and nomically from the properly mental (Ψ) factors of intention and knowledge, is a causally sufficient condition of a simple bodily ($\sim \psi \sim \Psi\phi$) event that might instead have resulted immediately from a mere shove. Thus, three logically necessary conditions of a willed arm rise are: an event of striving, an event of arm rise, and the existence of the relation of being-a-causal-sufficient-condition-of between these events.

We require the occurrence of two non-identical events, one psychological, the other non-psychological, and the relation being-a-causally-sufficient-condition-of between them. No doubt we further require, as emerged in chapter 4, that this causal relation both be dependent upon events occurring within the body and match additional specifications. What these are need not be our present concern, though they must be such that an act-mechanism will have been employed in the genesis of arm rise, and clearly the event of arm rise must find its explanation in the psychological event of trying as *an exemplification of the law*: 'In a person in a free and healthy state (etc.), trying to raise the arm is a sufficient condition of arm rise.' This law-like proposition, expressing a truth which is at once causal and logical, could hold only if there were proper or standard causal paths leading to arm rise, and, therefore, only if there were improper or illicit or (so to say) accidental paths. In sum: the act-desire and intention cause the act-neutral event of arm rise as an exemplification of these laws. Internal phenomena, which are not themselves willed, though for which one has a measure of responsibility, bring about outer or merely bodily willed events along such law-enforced paths. So much for a review of what transpired in the previous chapters 17–19.

2. THE INTERDEPENDENCE OF WILL AND BODY

(a) Tightening the conceptual bonds linking striving and the body

My interests at this point are synthetic rather than analytic. I am interested in connections rather than distinctions. And yet it is not that I hope to *forge* connections. Rather is it that I am concerned to delineate already existent links. I wish to trace already existent *a priori* links between such diverse items as mind, body, will; for this seems the one sure way of healing splits of the kind endorsed by Cartesians and volitionists. Then to assist this enterprise, and in despite of the difficulties created for the word 'relation' by the phenomenon of intentionality, I shall somewhat loosely use 'internal relation' (below) to stand for the essential connection between some one item and a possibly non-existent other; say, of the kind existing between a thought and its object. For I wish above all to delineate relations of essential dependencies.

Schopenhauer said: 'I cannot imagine this will without this body.'[1] If this wonderful remark is right – and we shall see that it is – then the psychological phenomena that occur when one engages in intentional physical action must at the very least depend upon the *supposed reality* of the body. But more: we shall see that the psychological phenomena that occur in physical action, depend in general upon the *actual existence* of the body. And this is the real sense of Schopenhauer's remark. And it expresses a position which I endorse. Then it follows that mine cannot be an interiorist position, even though I believe that trying is a psychological event that causally explains the purely physical willed bodily event in the case of all bodily actions. For what here has come to light is, the essential mutual interdependence of bodily strivings and of the animal body upon each other.

A preliminary word on striving itself. The essential description of trying to raise an arm is, 'trying to raise an arm'. Therefore this psychological event relates internally or essentially to a real or remembered or possibly merely imagined arm-object and to an intended individual rising of that object. Now so far this is nothing special, for the same kind of relation in which external entities are psychologically represented, holds if for example

---

[1] *The World as Will and Representation* 1, Book 2, 18, translated by E. F. J. Payne, New York: Dover, 1969.

I mentally imagine an existent material object. But *three important features* of trying lift it clear of the ruck of other psychological phenomena and put it in a special category of its own. They are as follows. First, while trying relates internally or essentially to the putative act, inasmuch as its essential description cannot but utilise the concept of that act, a correlative internal relation holds between act and trying. Second, while trying relates internally to putative arm-object, inasmuch as its essential description utilises the concept of that arm-object, a correlative and now general internal relation holds between the body and trying. Third – and as we have recently seen – law-like generalities that are at once causal and logical link intending at the time with trying, and trying with the act-neutral event of limb movement; that is, psycho-psycho and psycho-physical laws obtain in this primaeval region of the mind, and we shall see how this tightens the bond between trying in a quite new and radical sense. I will now consider these three claims in turn.

(b) The essential mutual interdependence of trying and act-object

(1) The first peculiarity of trying resides in the fact that the active object of trying itself internally or necessarily depends upon trying. This is in contrast with mental imaging, for the imagined object exists independently of the consciousness that pictures it, so that imagining must be a sheer internalisation of what is distinct and external. But the object of trying necessitates, indeed as we saw in chapter 12 is actually identical with, trying itself. Therefore neither trying nor the act is conceptually or temporally or causally prior to the other. Trying is not an internalisation of what is external, and neither is its putative object an externalisation of trying.

(2) A further consideration shows that the relation between trying and its act-object is even more intimate and egalitarian. Schopenhauer described the body as 'objectified will',[2] and I think we may interpret this as follows. We single out a human body as one object of a certain kind, viz. body of a human, and this animal is such that that object could not be what it is if it did not harbour the somewhere potential for being employed in physical action. An organism that contained *no* potential for action, however deeply buried or inaccessible or even lost, could not be a human being (or a camel or a mosquito, for that matter). This does not guarantee that any organ-part

---

[2] Ibid.

must have the function it has, but ensures that it is part of what is as such a vehicle of the will. 'I cannot really imagine this will without this body' can be supplemented by the equally arresting 'I cannot really imagine this body without this will.'

For what *is* an animal body? It is a material object which provides/provided the matter of a living being capable of supporting psychological phenomena, which logically necessarily include the type consciousness, and in 'Earthlings' naturally necessarily also the type bodily will and perception. Indeed, since various philosophical doctrines – logical behaviourism, functionalism, Wittgensteinian 'criteria' – plausibly posit action as a primary condition of mentality, one might define the body as the provider of the matter of a living being endowed with the potential for bodily will. Indeed, as that before all else! Moreover, although there can be no analytical definition of life[3] – for scientists investigating extra-terrestrial life do not bring strict necessary and sufficient conditions to the task – life involves processes which require fuel, and therefore organs for obtaining it, which in 'Earthlings' take the form of limbs aided by perception. This makes possible a further definition of the body, and once again as an object which is essentially a vehicle of the will – although now in conjunction with those other primordia of animal mind: consciousness and perception; and all with the aim of enabling purposive physical action which furthers the life of individual and species. In this sense, the bodily will proves once more to be the first necessity and ultimate rationale of the animal body.

(3) In sum: trying is neither post nor posterior to action, and is a trying to do what if it succeeds *is* itself. Neither it, nor the attempted act, relates to the other as introjection or projection; and even the physical event one aims at causing is change in what is itself of such a kind as necessarily to harbour the somewhere potential for being the immediate vehicle of the will. This absolute egalitarianism of trying and act, this essential interdependence between what is psychological (ψ) and what is a closely bound and encompassing union of psychological (ψ) and physical non-psychological ($\phi \sim \psi$), takes us far from Cartesianism. It is the externalising and synthesising corrective to the antithesis to logical behaviourism.

---

[3] Whereas our ancestors knew *which* 'what' water was, they did not know *what* 'what'. Do we know either in the case of life? It seems we know *which* 'what', but that this is second-best to nothing, for there can be neither empirical nor philosophical uncovering of the essence of life. The situation in the case of life is strangely disanalogous from that obtaining either with *a posteriori*-given natural kinds like water, or *a priori*-given natural kinds like psychologicality. The explanation must be that life has no essence.

(c) Trying as 'mental pineal gland' (or, the psycho-physical law)

(1) I come to the third unique characteristic of bodily tryings. Thus, this ψ event, though a directed ψ phenomenon and therefore without guarantee of its object in the world, *has no other existence* than as a putative causally sufficient condition, in determinate circumstances, of a determinate bodily event. This characterisation uniquely and exhaustively defines its being. Were the act of trying *otherwise and independently specifiable*, an act like the imaging of a bodily event, then whereas that act would putatively relate to items in the outer world and also putatively be a causally sufficient condition of arm rise, it would retain its identity as a distinctive act of a certain kind. We would then merely *re-describe* the act as 'trying to raise the arm', and its causal efficacy would be a contingent property akin to that of the thought of a steak to cause watering of the mouth. Now that would indeed usher in some version of Cartesianism, and its falsity must be very strongly emphasised. For although trying to raise the arm *is not*: whatever is a causally sufficient condition of arm rise; *it is* and is essentially: an x which in a physically normal human, world permitting (etc.), is a causally sufficient condition of arm rise. This is an essentialist psycho-physical characterisation of bodily trying. Because 'trying to raise the arm' is the essential psychological description of what culminates in arm rise when one raises an arm, we do not *re-describe* any psychological event as 'trying to raise an arm'. Instead, we give the best and closest possible description, indeed its ultimate and essential description; and it is a characterisation that locates causal properties, and causal properties alone, in its essence. For to repeat: were the causal properties of trying an *external property*, like the power of fear to cause pallor, willing would prove to be mythical. Therefore the whole edifice of animal action, and with it animal consciousness itself, must inevitably collapse; for in the animal psyche bodily willing has essential links to the other few primitive originals, viz. perception, sensation, desire, intention; and repercussive links beyond into the mind's depths. Therefore bodily striving, in being essentially a causally sufficient condition of a merely bodily phenomenon *and* a linchpin or centrepiece of the phenomenon of animal consciousness, serves a crucial bridge function between mind and body, not unlike that allotted by Descartes to the pineal gland. It is a key point at which the essential mutual interdependence of mind and body can be openly seen to be part of the scheme of things. It is a psychic promontory that openly juts into the physical world.

In this respect it is to be contrasted with two other closely related primitive inhabitants of the mind: intention and desire. For in their case there exist no psycho-physical laws parallel to: in a body in a normal state, world permitting (etc.), necessarily trying to raise an arm is a causally sufficient condition of arm rise. After all, without fear of the charge of abnormality, one can always rescind an intention or be too anxious to attempt to fulfil a desire when optimum conditions for fulfilment present themselves. This alone obstructs the possibility of a comparable law in the case of desire and intention.

(2) Because trying is a psychological phenomenon, there can be no guarantee of its object; that is, of success. But because it is in essence nothing but a causally sufficient condition in normal circumstances of its physical objective, its causal power cannot be an external property like the power of a thought to cause goose pimples. For we know that the potential for physical action is as primitive a feature of animal consciousness as perception (even as life itself). Are we to seriously envisage a conscious-type organism that nowhere in its psychic depths has ever harboured the most incipient of potentials for actively causing bodily change? In fact, trying to move a limb is a unique psychological event simply in being *standardly* a causally sufficient condition of a physical change; for all other examples of causal power on the part of the mental, like the power of an erotic thought to affect the pulse, are either merely typical or haphazard powers. But even more important is the fact that trying is *in essence* normally a causally sufficient condition of bodily change. For in this we find the material for demonstrating that trying to move a limb is the psychological 'pineal gland'.

Thus, it is a primitive constituent of animal consciousness which yet constitutively or intrinsically cannot in general exist without its bodily phenomenal object. For how could trying be real, and no more than *the* event-causally-sufficient-condition of willed bodily movement, without the guaranteed physical possibility of some actual willed movements? The following should make that clear.

Desire and imagination, while free to range over the unreal, are tied nonetheless in various ways to the world. But the bond between trying to move a limb and the body is tighter. For it is one thing to say: 'I cannot embark upon a trying to move an arm *without supposing there to be* the possibility of arm movement.' It is quite another thing to say: 'I cannot embark upon a trying to move an arm *without there actually existing* the organic based possibility of willed bodily movement.' Yet this we must say. The shift from a purely thought-mediated relation to one that is both that and causal accounts for this dramatic alteration. For how could a causal law have any reality if the world could provide *no* exemplifications of that law? Could it hang in the mid-air of thought? At the very least, this soul must as such be searching for its body?

That the psychologically oriented account that I have offered of physical action has in no way severed mind from body, is evident when we review the features of trying just considered. Thus, a primitive element of consciousness, the trying to perform a physical act, has as object that which both is that act of trying itself *and* change in what necessarily harbours a potential for being the immediate vehicle of such tryings. In short, it is neither post nor prior to that object. Further, because it is essentially normally a causally sufficient condition of bodily phenomena, indeed is nothing but precisely the psychological phenomenon that satisfies that essential characterisation, its reality depends constitutively or intrinsically upon the reality of such bodily phenomenal effects. It seems to me that we have here succeeded in closing the circle, in binding mind and body indissolubly together while recognising their genuine diversity. It is a true synthesis.

3. FROM INNER TO OUTER

(1) A man is attending a political meeting and a snap vote is being taken. He already has the intention of *either* voting in favour of Smith if there are good reasons for so doing, *or* not voting for Smith if there are not. He is as a result actively racking his brains on the issue – everyone has their hands by their sides in abstention – and he has a couple more seconds to make up his mind. Then as an unchosen effect of this active procedure a particular mental event suddenly happens. At exactly three seconds past noon the following unexpected thought flies unbidden into his mind: 'If Smith is elected, it will vex Jones.' That does it. In the identical instant that belief causes in him the quite distinct unchosen belief: there are good reasons for voting for Smith. In the identical instant that belief causes a quite distinct non-cognitive phenomenon: deciding to vote for Smith. That is, in the identical instant he acquires an intention – that he knows to be the intention of voting this very instant for Smith (in the recognised manner, viz. by arm-raising). In the identical instant – and as the exemplification of an unconditional law that is at once causal and logical – a striving to raise an arm commences. In the identical instant – as the exemplification of a conditional law that is at once causal and logical – an arm-raising act commences. A minuscule fraction of a second later – and as an exemplification of that same law – arm rise begins occurring; and this

phenomenon endures for about a second. By four seconds past noon an act of arm-raising has taken place. An act of voting has occurred.

(2) These are the phenomena whose nature and causal and logical relations I have investigated in Part IV of this work; and all in the direction from inner to outer. I believe I have put on open display, by means of the discovery of two laws which are at once causal and logical, the pathways whereby a properly mental (Ψ) item, coming to hold a belief, can in a manner that is both reliable and intelligible and representative of the inner life of the subject issue in a non-mental ($\sim\Psi$) non-psychological ($\sim\psi$) physical (ϕ) event, viz. arm rise. Nothing of this kind holds in the case of any other causal transaction from inner (ψ) to outer ($\sim\psi \sim \Psi\phi$). For example: neither psycho-physical causal laws nor logical laws relate fear to pallor or hunger to salivation or grief to tears; and *a priori* none could. But *a priori* laws of this kind must link the antecedents of physical action with non-psychological merely physical bodily events. Were it not so, *per impossibile*, were it *a priori* true that no Ψ event related via causal-logical law to the merely bodily non-psychological, so that the best we could hope for was a statistically significant but non law-like reaction akin to that linking erotic thoughts with quickening of the pulse, then the owner of this mind could not be an animal as we know it and must relate to his body in some radically different fashion from the way existing animals do. This subject would 'have a body' in a different sense from that which normally applies. 'Having', which normally probably means that its parts are our parts, would then mean no more than standing-in-an-occasionalist-causal-relation-to.

Now in the account which I have offered above, I have provided what are, in effect, two ontological Jacob's ladders – in reverse. For in positing a logico-causal law linking the intention with bodily striving, I provide a completely intelligible route whereby the properly mental (Ψ) systematically causes the psychological non-mental ($\psi \sim \Psi$). Again, in offering a logico-causal law linking bodily striving with the act, and hence with the mere surface bodily event that is willed, I provide a completely intelligible route whereby the psychological non-mental ($\psi \sim \Psi$) causally relates with the non-psychological-non-mental-merely-physical ($\sim \psi \sim \Psi\phi$).

And so we have here two Jacob's ladders in reverse. First, a psycho-psycho law linking intending with trying. It takes the following form: if a man at some instant in time realises of that instant that it is a 'now' in which he intends performing act Φ, then logically necessarily he is trying to do Φ at that moment of realisation. This unconditional law joins the conditional

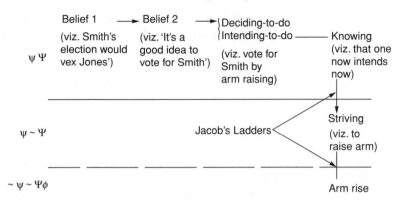

Fig. 17

law uniting trying with bodily phenomena, a psycho-physical law, and together they display, with absolute and pellucid clarity, the transition from some earlier mental event of deciding to the bodily phenomena that are its natural outcome. This is represented schematically in Fig. 17.

(3) Note finally: that a crucial element in this resolution of the Active Mind-to-Body Causal Problem, lies in the fact that we cannot *oppose* the physical to the psychological. And this is something that we can know simply through knowing that those psychological striving events that succeed *openly involve* the non-psychological merely physical surface event ϕ, e.g. arm rise. For this last is a truth of which we can be apprised in advance of reaching a decision on the more far-ranging problem of the truth-value of Physicalism. The aforementioned psycho-physical law linking striving-to-ϕ-make and ϕ permits us, precisely through our knowledge of such a fact, to relate one non-psychological bodily event (ϕ) with a predecessor other ($\phi-1$), and that in turn with another ($\phi-2$), and so on, travelling backwards along the act-mechanism, until at the end-point of this causally bonded process we reach a point at which a psycho-psycho law takes over. This means that we can intelligibly relate the initiating Ψ events with the final $\sim\psi \sim \Psi\phi$ surface event thanks to the existence of a $\psi \sim \Psi$ event that openly involves that $\sim\psi \sim \Psi\phi$ surface event. Were it not for the existence of the domain, the merely psychological $\psi \sim \Psi$, the mind could not intelligibly relate to the body.

Then to repeat: because the $\psi \sim \Psi$ event of physical action *openly involves* the merely bodily event ϕ, so that there is no possibility of this $\psi \sim \Psi$ event's occurring in some *pure $\psi \sim \Psi$ domain* that is such that it relates to the merely physical ϕ domain exactly as does Ψ to $\psi \sim \Psi$, the Ψ can be related in nomic manner to the $\sim\psi \sim \Psi\phi$. Were the relation thus:

$$\frac{\dfrac{\Psi}{\psi \sim \Psi}}{\phi} \quad \text{i.e} \quad \frac{\dfrac{\psi\,\Psi}{\psi \sim \Psi}}{\sim\psi \sim \Psi\phi}; \quad \text{instead of} \quad \frac{\dfrac{\psi\,\Psi}{\text{---}\psi\text{-}\sim\text{-}\Psi\text{---}}}{\sim\psi \sim \Psi\phi};$$

Fig. 18

we would still have the problem of comprehending the transition from $\psi \sim\Psi$ to ϕ. But, in fact, once this $\psi \sim \Psi$ event commences, we are already concerned, not with something that has *crossed* the divide $\psi \sim \Psi$ to ϕ, but with something that *openly dissolves* the opposition of one to the other. Then since it is physical action that is thus uniquely structured, physical action has a proud part to play in this ontological scene. For it emerges that it is *the* favoured agency whereby may be effected an indissoluble wedding of those twin partners that were, had we only known, destined from birth for one another. I mean: mind and body.

Index

Gide, A. 545–6, 578
Gidean '*acte gratuit*' 545–6, 578–9
God 317
Grainger, P. 356
Grice, H. P. 503

handmaiden role of perception in physically
    acting 327, 338–9
Herbst, P. 368
high-speed actions 352–6, 369–70
history, personal, taking possession of one's own
    557
Hume, D. 345–6, 348, 537, 541
'Humean experience' of the self as dispersed
    345–6
hysteria
    as a disturbance in the mental/merely
        psychological relation 497–501
    as a purely mental non-neurological illness
        498
    'blindness', 'pain', 'paralysis', as unreal 497–501
    general schema for 497–500

illusion, argument from for reality of will 386–8
incest, as akin in ways to an observer relation to
    one's own actions 326
incorrigibility in describing one's experience of
    the objects of action 330
individuation
    of properly mental phenomena,
        temporally/a-spatially 482
    of sensations, in body-relative physical space
        479
'inner world', stipulated sense given to the
    expression 363–4
inner world, and traditional volitionism 363–4,
    382–4
instrumental act-desire 324
instrumental action
    Anscombe–Davidson theory of 397, 594–6
    as identical with any successful striving to
        perform such an act 594–6
    defined 594
instrumental striving, physical
    constitution of 398–103
    definition of 398
    interiorist theory of nature of
        arguments against 407–11
        statement of the theory 404–7
    necessarily intentional character of 398
    properties of 398
    psychologicality of 403–11
        a reduced cautious version of this claim
            403–4
        arguments for 404–11

sometimes are physical actions 397–403
    argument for from concept of a way of
        striving 399–402
    argument for from visibility 402
    ways of 399–402
    fallacious objections to concept of 400–1
integration of motor and visual powers 323–5
intelligibility gap between mind and body,
    closing of via bodily will 586–97
intending 549–70 *passim*
    and ambiguity in 'mean' 550
    causally (all but) defining 561–4
    distinguished as explanatory source of action
        from teleological source of some active
        behaviours 559–71
    and explanation of actions 558
    and future 554–7
        as primary temporal orientation of 557
    irreducibility of 550–4
    and 'I shall ' 558
    and omnipotent self-determination 578–81
    and past 555–6
    and predictions 557–8
    and present 557, 565
    as entailing belief in existence of intended
        action 550
    as practical commitment to action 550
    as rationale of action and consciousness
        565–7
    as unanalysable into conjunction of belief and
        desire 553
intentional action, 326–9
    and awareness of act 360
    as ultimate rationale or function of action and
        consciousness 564–5
    limiting cases of 347–8, 360–1
    marks of 351–2
    what makes an action an intentional action
        567–70
    temporal properties of 554–7
intentionality
    agreeing on a workable concept of 481–2
    as not entailed by the property,
        psychologicality 482
    as significant marker of ontological status
        479–7
intentions
    and artefacts 549
    and infinite proximity to will 362
    and lack of immediate power over laughter
        467
    as agency of control over action 362
    as helping to make an act intelligible 547–70
    as source of all meaning outside the mind 549
    as supervisory type cause of action 563–4